HAMAS CONTAINED

Stanford Studies in Middle Eastern and Islamic Societies and Cultures

TAREQ BACONI

HAMAS CONTAINED

THE RISE AND PACIFICATION OF PALESTINIAN RESISTANCE

STANFORD UNIVERSITY PRESS
STANFORD, CALIFORNIA

Stanford University Press
Stanford, California

Printed in the United States of America on acid-free, archival-quality paper

Library of Congress Cataloging-in-Publication Data

Names: Baconi, Tareq, author.
Title: Hamas contained : the rise and pacification of Palestinian resistance
/ Tareq Baconi.
Description: Stanford, California : Stanford University Press, 2018. |
Series: Stanford studies in Middle Eastern and Islamic societies and
cultures | Includes bibliographical references and index.
Identifiers: LCCN 2017050720 (print) | LCCN 2017053020 (ebook) |
ISBN 9781503605817 (e-book) | ISBN 9780804797412 (cloth : alk. paper) |
Subjects: LCSH: Ḥarakat al-Muqāwamah al-Islāmīyah—History. | Palestinian
Arabs—Politics and government. | Palestine—Politics and
government—1948– | Gaza Strip—Politics and government. | Arab-Israeli
conflict.
Classification: LCC DS119.7 (ebook) | LCC DS119.7 .B173 2018 (print) |
DDC 324.25694/2083—dc23
LC record available at https://lccn.loc.gov/2017050720

Cover design: Matt Tanner
Cover photo: Tareq Baconi
Typeset by Bruce Lundquist in 11/16 Baskerville

To Eva

CONTENTS

PREFACE

While finishing this book, I attended a performance of *Les Blancs* (The Whites) in London's National Theatre. This was the last play written by Lorraine Hansberry, the celebrated African American writer and playwright known for her work on identity and race relations in the United States. *Les Blancs* is her only play set in Africa. It recounts the story of an African man who travels from Europe, where he lives with his child and white wife, back to his unnamed birthplace to attend his father's funeral. The anticolonial struggle his father had started there has gained ground, and the nation is on the brink of revolution. Hansberry's protagonist, imbued with European values and the sheen of London civility, is a firm believer in nonviolent protest. He is also a proud and confident man, bristling at the condescension of colonial masters.

Dueling emotions wash over our protagonist as he tries to straddle two worlds and reconcile his dedication to nonviolence with the urgent struggle on the ground. Political discussions in the powerhouse of colonial Europe appear futile and out of touch. Peaceful protest feels wholly inadequate as the protagonist's countrymen and women are slaughtered around him by colonial rifles. Dissonant themes collide, from the incivility and barbarity of armed struggle to the ignorance of the native in refusing European modernity. Questions of identity, violence, race, and nationalism test deeply held convictions, values, and beliefs. Over the course of a few hours, painstakingly crafted worldviews unravel in slow and excruciating ways. Minutes before the curtain falls, the protagonist reaches for his knife, slaughtering his first victim. It is his brother, a priest who had joined a European mission to convert fellow Africans to the Christian faith. With this final act of brutal fratricide, the illusion of peaceful decolonization appears to have been shattered.

Hansberry's eloquent and sophisticated play was unflinching in its depiction of the complex moral ambiguity inherent in the adoption of arms for the pursuit of freedom. I was mesmerized. My companions thought it simplistic and unoriginal. There was nothing innovative, in their view, about contending with the brutality of liberation struggles. A twenty-first-century London audience, it seemed, could grapple with the role of violence in the face of colonial rule. This was understood as a natural and desperate fight for dignity. It was reductionist to conflate anticolonial violence with native barbarism.

Sitting in the darkness of the theater, I thought of Palestine. Lacking the clarity of historical hindsight, the Palestinian struggle for self-determination seems frozen in time, in many ways an interminable anticolonial struggle unfolding in a postcolonial world. It is a world that has confronted the carnage of decolonization. But the battle is still raging in Palestine, with ever-present urgency. The simplistic binaries that frame conversations of Palestinian armed struggle evoke the condescension expressed by colonial overlords toward the resistance of indigenous peoples. "Palestinians have a culture of hate," commentators blast on American TV screens. "They are a people who celebrate death." These familiar accusations, quick to roll off tongues, are both highly effective at framing public discourse and insulting as racist epithets. On the other end of the spectrum, I recalled conversations with Europeans and Palestinians who critiqued my reference to Palestinian armed struggle as "violence." They saw this framing as a form of condemnation, casting armed struggle in a negative light. Support of the rifle, they argued, was not only comprehensible and dignified, but necessary. It was the only way to secure Palestinian rights against a murderous and unrelenting occupation.

As the play ended, I reflected on the history of violence in the Palestinian struggle, the advances it secured and the tragedy it sowed. I considered the fratricide of the play's finale and compared it to the state of the Palestinian territories today, where leaders have turned their guns inward on their people. I thought of Hamas, the movement currently most representative of the notion of armed resistance against Israel. The prevailing inability or unwillingness to talk about Hamas in a nuanced manner is deeply familiar. During the summer of 2014, when global newsrooms were covering Israel's military operation in the Gaza Strip, I watched Palestinian analysts being rudely silenced on the air for failing to condemn Hamas as a terrorist organization outright.[1] This condemnation was demanded as a prerequisite for the right of these analysts to engage in any debate about the events on the ground. There was no other explanation, it seemed, for the loss of life in Gaza and Israel other than pure-and-simple Palestinian hatred and bloodlust, embodied by Hamas. I wondered how many lives, both Palestinian and Israeli, have been lost or marred by this refusal to engage with the drivers of Palestinian resistance, of which Hamas is only one facet. I considered the elision of the broader historical and political context of the Palestinian struggle in most conversations regarding Hamas. Whether condemnation or support, it felt to me, many of the views I faced on Palestinian armed resistance were unburdened by moral angst or ambiguity. There was often a certainty or a conviction about resistance that was too easily forthcoming.

I have struggled to find such certainty in my own study of Hamas, even as I remain unwavering in my condemnation of targeting civilians, on either side. For close to a decade, I have attempted to peel back all the layers that have given rise to the present dynamic of vilifying and isolating Hamas, and with it, of making acceptable the demonization and suffering of millions of Palestinians within the Gaza Strip. The product is this book, which seeks to explore Hamas's world order and present the voice of a marginalized group that remains central to the Palestinian national movement. This book works to advance our knowledge of Hamas by elucidating the manner in which the movement evolved over the course of its three decades in existence, from 1987 onward. Understanding Hamas is key to ending the denial of Palestinians their rights after nearly a century of struggle for self-determination.

It is also a prerequisite to halting the cycles of violence that are intermittently unleashed on the inhabitants of the Gaza Strip. Nearly one year before that evening at the National Theatre, I was talking to a young boy in Gaza. The conversation was during the Islamic month of Ramadan in 2015, and everyone was sluggish from the June heat. I asked him about the school year he had just finished and whether he was happy to be on holiday. He shrugged. "Sixth grade was fine," he said, "a bit odd." He was in Grade A and he used to look forward to playing football against Grade B. That past year, though, the school administration had merged several grades together. The classes were crowded and the football games less enjoyable. I wondered aloud to the boy why the school administration had done that. Annoyed that I was not engaging with the issue at hand, that of football politics, he answered in an exasperated tone. "Half of the Grade A kids had been martyred the summer before," he snapped. The kids who had survived no longer filled an entire classroom.

Gaza's reality can be jarring to any outsider wading in. Tragedy has become routinized, almost mundane, particularly for a younger generation, many of whom know no other life outside this imprisoned land. Initially, one could be forgiven for being lulled into a sense of relative normalcy. During the short time I was allowed to spend there, Gaza bustled with life. Streets were filled with vendors. Cafés teemed with patrons breaking the fast. College campuses heaved with students and faculty attending summer courses. Traffic crept slowly. Night markets and thoroughfares came to life on piers that jutted out over the water from Gaza's sandy beaches. Hotel lobbies were filled with journalists and filmmakers. Yet this illusion of life was shattered far too easily and often. Collapsed buildings sprung into view and humming drones interrupted conversations. Proud flags declaring Hamas's military training sites fluttered as one drove through various cities. Life unfolded against a physical and mental backdrop of destruction. The daily hive of activity that one walked into was little more than a testament to what Gaza could be, in an alternate reality. The quotidian goings-on of Palestinians there spoke of the human spirit of survival and appeared to me, at least, to be a tragic manifestation of endless motion in stillness. Students graduated into unemployment. Vendors sold to cover their costs. Families shopped to survive.

Gaza is held in time, contained from the outside world, nurtured just enough to subsist, never to grow. My time there coincided with the anniversary of Israel's 2014 operation on this narrow coastal enclave. Thousands of Palestinians had been killed. Major swathes of land had been bombed so thoroughly that whole neighborhoods were reduced to mounds of rubble. Infrastructure that was already depleted by years of deprivation under an Israeli-Egyptian blockade was wiped out. Walking through the remnants of neighborhoods, I saw how reconstruction had barely commenced. The landscape of chaos and devastation that had filled news screens a year earlier had given way to a state of controlled collapse. Debris had been swept aside, piled into empty plots of land or dumped in landfills where people hoped it would eventually be used as raw material for rebuilding. Rickety bombed-out houses reverted to homes for families who had nowhere else to go. Vanished walls were replaced with colorful cloths to give the illusion of privacy.

I stood in an open plain in north Gaza and looked over at Sderot, a town in southern Israel. If ever there was a reminder of the political nature of Gaza's tragedy, it was that snapshot. The juxtaposition of Sderot's manicured tree lines and white houses with Gaza's post-apocalyptic landscape elucidated the stark discrepancy in what constituted "life" across the few kilometers that separated those two places. I was one of the privileged handful able to move between those vastly divergent worlds. Standing there, I thought of the little boy whose classmates had been killed in 2014. I recalled speaking with an Israeli woman in a town north of Tel Aviv a few days earlier. As we sat around a dinner table, she bemoaned Israel's militarization and compulsory army service. The woman was heartbroken that her eighteen-year-old son had been forced to participate in Israel's operation that summer. He had returned a changed man, a hardened one, she cried. "Being forced to kill and to see death is a terrible burden on one's conscience," she protested.

"We can forgive the Arabs for killing our children," Golda Meir, Israel's first female prime minister, is rumored to have said. "We cannot forgive them for forcing us to kill their children."[2]

On both sides of the Erez crossing (known to Palestinians as the Beit Hanoun crossing), the main civilian border separating the Gaza Strip from Israel, dehumanization was rampant. I sat in the passenger seat of a speeding and poorly maintained car hurtling across Gaza's traffic lights in an effort to reach my host's home before the mosque's muezzin announced the end of the fast. I was speaking with my driver, a teenager too young to be driving, who was coming up to his last year at school. I asked him what he wanted to do postgraduation—always a fraught topic in a place like Gaza. He said he "was thinking of joining the Izz al-Din al-Qassam Brigades," Hamas's military wing. I had seen posters throughout the city and on mosque walls announcing that registration was open for their summer training camps. A few of his friends had apparently signed up. Why, I asked. He replied that he wanted to "fight the Jews." He'd never seen one in real life, he added, but he had seen the F-16s dropping the bombs.

Almost a decade into the blockade of the Gaza Strip, which had begun in earnest in 2007, "Jew," "Israeli," and "F-16" had become synonymous. A few years prior, this boy's father would have been able to travel into Israel, to work as a day laborer or in menial jobs. While it would have been structurally problematic, that man would have nonetheless interacted with Israeli Jews, even Palestinian citizens of Israel, in a nonmilitarized way. This is no longer the case. One could see in my driver how the foundation was laid for history to repeat itself. Resistance had become sacred, a way of living in which he could take a great deal of pride serving his nation. On the other side of the Erez crossing, he and his schoolmates were deemed terrorists. Gaza was viewed as a backward and enemy-ridden enclave, heavily populated and disintegrating under the weight of its own misery, loathing, and incompetence. An Israeli man reacted with horror when I told him I was going into Gaza. "Where will you stay? They have hotels there?" They do. Beautiful hotels. He shrugged. "They got what was coming to them last summer." Against the backdrop of flares and explosions lighting up Gaza's night skies during Israeli military incursions, some Israelis trek up to raised viewing points, sit on couches, and eat popcorn while watching the "fireworks" over the beleaguered land.[3]

More than two million Palestinians now live in the Gaza Strip. That makes it an urban population larger than most American cities. But the human dimension, so visceral to anyone who walks the streets of any city in the strip, is almost an afterthought, if a thought at all, to many who think of this place. The image of Gaza as a terrorist haven has been all-consuming. As has its image as a war-torn pile of rubble, sterile and devoid of life. The collective punishment of millions has become permissible, comprehensible, and legitimate. Destroying schools and targeting UN shelters, as Israel did in 2014, are military tactics that have been justified as essential for Israel to defend itself against terror. The killing of more than five hundred children during that same operation for many becomes little more than an unfortunate necessity.

Sitting at the heart of this perception, indeed the catalyst that produces it, is Hamas, the party that has ruled over the Gaza Strip since 2007. Given prevalent media discourse, one might be forgiven for thinking that Israel has besieged and bombarded Gaza because it has been faced with a radical terrorist organization in the form of Hamas. But as this book shows, the reality is more complex and is one in which the fates of Gaza and Hamas have been irreversibly intertwined in the Palestinian struggle for liberation from an interminable occupation.

My fixer in Gaza told me a story. There was once a village whose men were all drafted to fight in some faraway battle. While the men were gone, enemy soldiers invaded the village and raped all the women who had been left behind, and went on their way. The women, shell-shocked and bloodied, mourned their fate as they congregated to comfort one another in the village square. One woman was missing. They went looking for her and found her lying under the soldier who had tried to rape her. With her own hands, she had managed to kill him and save herself from the lot of her fellow villagers. Joy at her safety soon soured. The raped women now worried they would be judged by their husbands for not similarly fighting for their honor and fending off their rapists. In no time, this undefiled survivor became a symbol of their shame. Swiftly, they conspired to kill her.

The storyteller turned to me and said, that woman, the survivor, is Gaza. She has refused to submit to Israel's occupation and its rape and pillage of Palestinian land while other Palestinian and Arab leaders have succumbed. She has become a source of pride for Gazans who maintain their armed resistance against Israel. She is now a shameful reminder for those who have accepted their fate. Arabs and Palestinians elsewhere have looked away as she is bombarded, incessantly and mercilessly. Israel has focused all its efforts on shaming and breaking it. For she remains the only proud bit of Palestine that refuses to yield. One only needs to walk the streets of Gaza to feel the pride that people take in "the resistance." In countless conversations, I was reminded that while the Israeli army can drive up to any house in the West Bank and arrest its members—even to the house of the Palestinian president Mahmoud Abbas!—it was unable to step foot in Gaza. At least not without incurring a beating. This strip of land is thought of as undefiled, Palestinian, sterile of Israel's occupation.

Of course, the occupation persists, but it is no longer in people's homes. Palestinians in Gaza celebrate being able to go about their lives without the daily indignities of having Israeli teenagers armed with rifles harass and humiliate them. Close to the buffer zone with Israel, Gazans have paved a road called *shari' al-jakar*, literally translated as "street of spite," as a symbolic claim to sovereignty, spiting their previous overlords by proving they can pave their own roads without Israel's permission. The deep satisfaction derived from such an action is easily understood. Driving around the land where the Israeli settlements in the Gaza Strip had once stood, one can see the wide multilane highways that used to connect the Jewish-only settlement blocks where eight thousand inhabitants lived. Extending alongside them are the dusty, potholed one-lane roads that the 1.8 million Palestinians had been forced to use. Against this blueprint of Israel's colonization of Gaza, Palestinians are now free to build their own infrastructure, wherever they want. And the pleasure felt from this sense of liberty, of quasi sovereignty, is immense. This is so even when everyone understands all too well how truncated such sovereignty is. In matters of life and death, Israel's occupation grinds on relentlessly in the form of an external structure of control on a besieged population. But within this prison cell, Gazans have staked their flag.

Palestinian pride in the resistance has trickled down to the younger generation. I remember interviewing a senior member of Hamas's government at midnight in the sitting room of his private home when his three-year-old son waddled out of his bedroom to embrace his father. He had donned a Qassam bandana and was playing with a plastic gun. The military paraphernalia reminiscent of any army's elsewhere in the world stared back at me. This was an alternate reality, a space where the universe revolved around Palestinians facing Israel's occupation. Gazans lived a life of resistance. This was the first plot of land within the boundaries of what was formerly Mandate Palestine to be governed by a Palestinian party that was unapologetically defiant to Israeli rule. There was dignity and a sense of promise that if "liberation" happened in Gaza, it could be replicated in the rest of the Palestinian territories. Complaining about Hamas's governance of the Gaza Strip, even if in silent whispers, rarely extended to criticizing "the resistance." For many Palestinians, this was the final frontline for guarding against Israeli atrocities.

In the recent past, this notion of armed struggle against Israel has been for the most part monopolized by Hamas, and resistance has become almost synonymous with al-Qassam. There is no doubt that

Hamas carries out terror-inducing activities within Israel and the Palestinian territories. The movement itself, through its various publications, explains how it seeks to create terror to pressure the Israeli government to end its occupation of Palestinian land. Hamas's actions fit into the definition of terrorism used by the U.S. Department of State, which notes that "terrorism is premeditated politically motivated violence perpetrated against non-combatant targets by sub-national groups or clandestine agents."[4] While Hamas itself admits that it has used such tactics, it vehemently rejects being designated a terrorist organization. The logic underpinning this seeming contradiction is the absence of a single definition about what constitutes terrorism.[5] The term is malleable and subjective, and more importantly, it has been used as a tool of war.[6] The definition put forward by the U.S. State Department has consistently and cynically been manipulated to justify illegal and morally reprehensible military measures, in this case by Israel. Furthermore, while the label of "terrorism" under this definition can be applied to Hamas, it fails to account for the terror caused by Israel's relentless military regime over the Palestinians.

It is exceedingly difficult to engage in a discussion on terrorism, which is precisely why it is a powerful device to undermine any legitimacy that organizations such as Hamas may have. Like all definitions of terrorism, the one put forward by the U.S. State Department is highly contested. Why is terrorism limited to subnational groups or clandestine agents if states are the biggest perpetrators of organized violence against civilians?[7] How does one differentiate between indiscriminate violence aimed solely at terrorizing civilians and legitimate armed resistance aimed at securing internationally sanctioned rights that invariably ends up killing civilians? How are civilians defined in a world where the notions of war and peace are increasingly difficult to ascertain, and where the form of warfare has outgrown the very laws that define it?[8]

Classifying Hamas as a terrorist organization has justified sweeping military action against Palestinians, depoliticizing and dehumanizing their struggle. It has also prevented the possibility of viewing Palestinian armed resistance as a form of self-defense within the context of war. The notions of war and peace are subjective for Israel and the Palestinians. For the former, war begins when rockets fall on its territory or when suicide bombers invade its streets. For the latter, war is constant, manifest through a brutal military occupation that has persisted for more than half a century. The transition between war and peace for Palestinians is an imaginary one. Where rocket attacks and suicide bombs trigger claims of self-defense and ostensibly justify Israeli military operations, no similar mechanisms are in place for Palestinians reacting against the act of war inherent in an occupation that is both terror inducing and intentional. While international law has made exceptions for viewing Israeli military operations in Gaza through the lens of a security paradigm, security for Palestinians against consistent Israeli aggression appears to be absent.[9]

In thinking of the morality of Palestinian armed struggle, the knowledge that violence has animated numerous anticolonial liberation trajectories somehow dissipates. The historical context within which Hamas operates, and which has given rise to Hamas as an armed resistance movement in the first place, is overlooked. Palestinians instead are collectively demonized as a people that celebrate death. Their political struggle for self-determination is eclipsed by indictments of their bloodlust. In one of the carnivals in Gaza before the 2014 escalation, Hamas leader Ismail Haniyeh blasted through the loudspeakers to a vast crowd, "We are a people who value death, just like our enemies value life."[10] A few weeks later, as Hamas was boosting the morale of Gazans amid Israel's onslaught, another Hamas leader called on people to face the occupation "with their bare chests," and to embrace death if it came their way.[11] These remarks were used throughout global media channels to signify that Hamas was using civilians as human shields and that Palestinians revere a culture of death where martyrdom is a goal to be rejoiced. While self-sacrifice in the context of national armies and the defense of one's homeland is celebrated the world over, indeed is a foundation of nationalism, Palestinian self-sacrifice is studied as a perplexing anomaly. What compels suicide bombers to don a vest? Why are teenagers eager to join Hamas's military training sites? Why is resistance praised when it has brought catastrophe on Palestinians?

The worldview of Palestinian resistance fighters is that they are engaged in a justified war against a violent and illegal occupation that terrorizes them and their family members. Their adoption of armed struggle, in this particular context, draws on its own legal, political, and theological justifications governing the laws of war and its conduct.[12] Without justifying this resort to violence, one has to see and understand it from a center of gravity that is rooted in the Palestinian territories, not in the West. One has to grapple with the organic thoughts, emotions, and feelings that give rise to a universe that is often at odds with the dominant Western-centric framing of political violence. It is my aim in this book to trace the architecture of this alternate reality from the perspective of Hamas. Stepping away from polemics associated with the use of a deeply charged and ultimately ineffective term such as "terrorism," this book describes violence, military attacks, occupation, suicide bombings, assassinations, rocket fire, and air-raids in their most basic characteristics, while acknowledging and mourning the devastation and human suffering that underpin these acts. The book will have fulfilled its purpose if it presents Hamas's counternarrative on its own terms. Such an undertaking is made with the hope that the movement will emerge and be understood in a wider space where such critical examination has so often been lacking.

In presenting such a counternarrative, the history recounted in this book is by default approached from the perspective of one actor. The book does not claim to offer either a comprehensive history of the three decades between 1987 and 2017 or a review of Israeli policies toward the Palestinian territories. Rather it offers an overview of Hamas's trajectory over the course of this period. This is done while acknowledging that there is no single "Hamas." It is an exercise in futility, as well as fundamentally inaccurate and reductionist, to try to suggest that the movement is some form of monolithic actor. In narrating Hamas's travails, it is important to understand that the movement is a complex and decentralized organization with different facets. Its constituents, like the Palestinians more generally, are fragmented and facing vastly different challenges in their local arenas. A predictable number of contradictions and inconsistencies emerge when studying the movement's different foci. As a multifaceted organization, one that engages in political, social, and military operations, Hamas is an actor with a host of internal tensions that are constantly being balanced.

There is an inherent challenge, therefore, in seeking to offer a high-level reading of Hamas while wishing to remain sensitive to the nuances within the movement. I dealt with this dilemma by expanding the diversity of voices I quoted and the breadth of the archival sources I drew on. But I confess that this is not a study that will manage to render the intricate complexity of Hamas, for instance, by providing a comprehensive review of internal relations between Hamas's inside and outside leadership or between the movement's military and political wings, or the movement's robust social welfare infrastructure. Furthermore, this study has proceeded from the premise that Hamas is at its core a political, not a religious, party. Of course, through its own declaration, Hamas is an Islamic movement by charter and by the faith of its leadership and its member base. While this book has addressed how this belief system impacts Hamas's political outlook, it has not explored the theological underpinnings of the movement's ideology. In other words, this is not a book about Islam, but Islam has a key presence within the book.

To elucidate the arc of Hamas's trajectory since 1987, I relied on an extensive archival source base that was gathered from the Palestinian territories, Lebanon, Jordan, Israel, and the United States. The collected sample comprised thousands of Arabic documents that contain oral, visual, and written discourse published by Hamas between 1987 and 2017.[13] These include the comprehensive collection of *Filastin al-Muslima* (Muslim Palestine), one of the movement's main mouthpieces; the comprehensive collection of Hamas's local mouthpiece in Gaza, *Al-Resalah* (The Letter, or The Message); samples of the publication

Assafir (The Ambassador), which is circulated within the Gaza Strip; *bayanat* (leaflets) issued by Hamas, Islamic Jihad, Fatah, and other factions and their military wings; local, regional, and international news publications that report on Hamas and that include interviews, quotations, or statements made by Hamas members; and electronic publications posted by the movement through its various online channels. Alongside this archival research, I carried out interviews with members of Hamas across all levels of seniority in Lebanon, Jordan, Qatar, the West Bank, and the Gaza Strip, as well as with Israeli and Palestinian politicians, analysts, academics, and activists.

Filastin al-Muslima offered the backbone for this study given its uninterrupted print run.[14] This publication employs writers, researchers, and contributors within the Palestinian territories and abroad who are either openly affiliated as Hamas members, are sympathetic to its cause, or are analysts with significant insight into the movement's operations. It publishes extensive interviews with Hamas's leaders as well as leaflets that are issued by Hamas and distributed to its constituents. It also publishes articles by academics, journalists, and members of other factions to debate issues of importance to Palestinians. I have attempted to highlight where possible when articles were written by members of Hamas or otherwise. Collectively, through the pages of *Filastin al-Muslima*, I was offered a powerful window to understand Hamas's worldview, the manner in which the movement attempts to communicate with its constituents, and the thinking it cultivates.

I systematically reviewed these monthly publications while working to mitigate key concerns that might arise from the use of a publication to gain insight into Hamas's thinking. Acknowledging these publications as the movement's "party line," I couched my analysis of this discourse within the wider reality that Hamas operates in. To do so, I adopted a methodical discourse analysis approach that relied heavily on contextualization, whereby the pieces being reviewed were assessed against a broader reality that drew on secondary literature and alternative media sources.[15] I used news reports as well as studies by think tanks and other organizations operating on the ground to get a sense of the environment in which Hamas's actions were unfolding. Comparing rhetoric with practice offered great insight into the movement's thinking. Therefore, alongside *Filastin al-Muslima*, I systematically reviewed local and regional media outlets that reported on Hamas during this period, as listed in the bibliography. I supplemented this Arabic source base with both international news sources and secondary literature in Arabic and English.

To compile my source base, I relied on the extensive repositories of local and international news articles on Israel-Palestine that are collated in two archives. The first is the Institute for Palestine Studies in Beirut, which collects and saves all news publications on Israel-Palestine in *Al-Watha'iq al-Arabiyeh* (Arabic Documents) Collection. The second is al-Zaytouna Centre in Beirut, which published *Al-Watha'iq al-Filastiniyyah* (Palestinian Documents) for the years 2005–11. These two sources are extensive collections from which even the most obscure reactions to various events can be located. I also benefited greatly from the support and cooperation of *Al-Resalah*'s employees in Gaza City, who were kind enough to share with me the publication's archive, given that these are not housed in other repositories outside of Gaza City to my knowledge.

Using this material, *Hamas Contained* offers an overview of the three decades of Hamas's existence, primarily as narrated from the movement's perspective. In so doing, the book covers the major milestones that Hamas went through as it expanded its notion of resistance from the military arena into the corridors of government. *Hamas Contained* seeks to contextualize these developments within the broader arc of Palestinian nationalism as it explores Hamas's role within the Palestinian struggle for self-determination. In viewing the movement primarily through the lens of its political ideology, the book attempts to elucidate the dynamic that has emerged between Hamas and Israel, as well as Hamas and the Palestinian Authority, over the course of this period.

In the following six chapters, the book covers the movement's trajectory in phases, from the prehistory of its creation in 1987 through its unsuccessful decision to relinquish its government in the Gaza Strip in 2014. The Conclusion opens with the 2014 Israeli operation on the Gaza Strip and brings the story up to the fall of 2017. It then breaks from the narrative approach adopted in the rest of the book to make a number of analytical interventions about Hamas and the current phase of Palestinian nationalism. By eliding the movement's political ideology, as was done to the PLO before it, Israel has maintained policies aimed at depoliticizing Palestinian nationalism, and sustained its approach of conflict management rather than resolution. Through a dual process of containment and pacification, Hamas has been forcefully transformed into little more than an administrative authority in the Gaza Strip, in many ways akin to the Palestinian Authority in the West Bank. At the time of its thirtieth anniversary, the movement appears temporarily—if not conclusively—pacified, and Israel seems to have succeeded in maintaining the permanence of an occupation long deemed unsustainable.

HAMAS CONTAINED

CHAPTER ONE

THE RISE OF ISLAMIC PALESTINIAN NATIONALISM

On the night of December 9, 1987, a group of men crowded into a small house in the Shati refugee camp, named for its location close to the beachfront (*shatt*), in the north of the Gaza Strip. The gathering was hosted by Sheikh Ahmad Yassin, a soft-spoken paraplegic man with a long white beard. Yassin was a refugee from the village of al-Jura, near the town currently known as Ashkelon in Israel, which he had fled in 1948.[1] His visitors were also refugees from towns and villages now within Israel's borders. They had come together that night in haste to discuss the events erupting around them. A day earlier, an Israeli army vehicle had crashed into a line of cars carrying Palestinian day laborers commuting from their jobs in Israel back to their homes in the Gaza Strip. The accident had killed four Palestinian men, three of whom were from the Jabalia refugee camp.[2] Also located in the northern part of the Gaza Strip, the Jabalia camp, known as the "camp of the revolution," is one of the largest refugee camps in the Palestinian territories and one of the most densely populated plots of land in the world. Within hours of the accident, the occupied Palestinian territories of the West Bank, the Gaza Strip, and East Jerusalem, as well as areas within Israel itself, were awash with protests, demonstrations, and acts of civil disobedience. Spreading from the epicenter of the Jabalia camp, the First Palestinian Intifada, or uprising, had begun.[3]

The intifada was a spontaneous and seemingly leaderless mass upheaval. Almost overnight, Palestinians collectively took to the streets to protest Israel's occupying presence within their land. Israel's occupation had begun twenty years prior, in 1967. Although Palestinians had enjoyed periods of relative prosperity during this time, the occupation itself was premised on the economic subjugation of the territories and the denial to Palestinians of their political rights. Over the course of two decades, Israel had expropriated Arab land; expanded an illegal settlement enterprise that fragmented the Palestinian territories; and maintained a repressive military occupation that routinized human rights violations of Palestinians under its rule, including arrests, deportations, home demolitions, indefinite detentions, curfews, and killings. With the intifada, Palestinians rose to shake off the yoke of military rule. They boycotted Israeli goods and refused to comply with the administrative processes underwriting their oppression, including procedures such as the issuance of ID cards and tax collection by the Israeli authorities.

The image of Palestinian youth hurtling stones at Israeli tanks came to denote the spirit of this period. Over the course of four years, the intifada resembled an anticolonial struggle.[4] Protesters clashed with the Israeli army using stones, sticks, and occasionally Molotov cocktails as the Israeli military struggled to quash what was predominantly a civilian uprising. Throughout the territories, decentralized popular committees emerged to organize mass action and shelter the identities of local leaders for fear of reprisals. Demonstrations were soon coordinated clandestinely. Appeals for strikes and instructions for acts of civil disobedience surfaced almost surreptitiously in leaflets left on car windscreens and graffiti sprayed on shop shutters. These memos often carried the imprint of the United National Leadership of the Uprising, a coalition of factions that was created early in the intifada to coordinate activities among the different towns and villages in the occupied territories. The intifada's leaflets articulated the political goals of the uprising: to achieve independence from Israel's occupation and establish a Palestinian state.[5]

Thousands of miles away, the indefatigable Palestinian leader Yasser Arafat watched the spreading protests from his exile in Tunis. Under his guidance, the Palestine Liberation Organization (PLO), the official representative of the Palestinian people and effectively the government-in-exile, scrambled to assume a leadership role over this unexpected mass mobilization. Through its offices in Amman and Tunis, the PLO coordinated with local leaders inside the occupied territories to shape the intifada's trajectory and ensure it remained nonviolent. Simultaneously, and unbeknown to Arafat and the exiled leadership, the men gathered in Sheikh Yassin's home in Gaza also understood the importance of harnessing this outburst of popular sentiment. Less than a week after the Palestinian streets first exploded with pent-up frustration, on December 14, Yassin and his colleagues published and circulated a leaflet that hailed the eruption of the intifada as a rejection of the bloody years of Israel's military rule and a reaffirmation of Palestinian perseverance and steadfastness. "Islam is the solution and the alternative" to the current path the Palestinian struggle had taken, the memo read.[6] Its authors denounced the PLO for failing to end the occupation as they presented an alternative liberation project. The unusual memo did not yet bear the name HAMAS, the Arabic acronym for *Harakat al-Muqawama al-Islamiyya* (Islamic Resistance Movement), also meaning "zeal."[7] Nonetheless, this leaflet marked Hamas's first appearance within the Palestinian territories and, with it, the first formal indication that a new force had emerged to shape this latest phase of the Palestinian struggle for liberation.

ANCESTRAL LEGACIES

Led by Sheikh Ahmad Yassin, Hamas's cofounders viewed the intifada as an opportune time to leverage all the preparation that had been taking place clandestinely for years to create an organization dedicated to "rais[ing] the banner of God over every inch of Palestine."[8] Their leaflets were inconsistently signed at first as the leaders experimented with what to call their nascent organization. Names such as "The Islamic Faction," "Path of Islam," and "Islamic Defense" were tried and tested. In January 1988, a few weeks after the intifada had begun, the name HAMAS was finally chosen. Hamas's creation built on a solid institutional base that had been developed, primarily within the Gaza Strip, over the course of several decades. The new movement was defined as the latest "link in [a long] chain of the Jihad against the Zionist occupation."[9] To bolster Hamas's standing, the founders reached back to the turn of the century and constructed a rich lineage that could be traced to the early days of the Zionist project.

Yassin was instrumental in linking Hamas's founding in 1987 with this legacy of jihad from the 1920s. As a twelve-year-old, Yassin was injured in an athletic accident and developed an acute form of quadriplegia. His deteriorating health prevented him from completing his education in Egypt, where he was enrolled at the prestigious al-Azhar University. Upon his return to Gaza, where his family had settled as refugees, he worked as a teacher and an imam and, in the 1950s, joined the Muslim Brotherhood chapter in Palestine. The Muslim Brotherhood had been founded in 1928 in Egypt by Hassan al-Banna, an Islamic thinker who advocated for the Islamization of society.[10] Throughout the 1930s, al-Banna grew his organization into an Islamic welfare association where groups of young brothers gathered to study and learn Islamic scripture, lead virtuous lives, build their nation, and safeguard it against Western influence and colonialism. Al-Banna's vision was to create a modern Islamic society that assimilated Western progress, such as in the sciences, while remaining true to Islamic virtues.[11]

Although the brotherhood was mainly preoccupied with Egyptian affairs and the British occupation of Egypt, it was also committed to the broader region, with al-Banna viewing Egyptian nationalism as a stepping stone toward pan-Arab and pan-Islamic unity.[12] Underpinning this gradualist approach, from national to Arab to Islamic unity, was the belief that Islamic fraternity superseded loyalty to the nation. Therefore, looking eastward, the brotherhood noted with concern the developments taking place within Palestine, which was conquered by the British from the Ottoman Empire during World War One. In 1922, Palestine was made into a British Mandate under the supervision of the League of Nations, which meant that the British were responsible to guide it toward independence.[13] This charge conflicted with commitments the British had made to the Zionist movement, which had emerged in Europe at the turn of the century and sought to establish a Jewish homeland in Palestine.[14] By the 1920s, Jewish immigration into Palestine was increasing against the backdrop of the Russian Revolution and growing European anti-Semitism. The brotherhood viewed Zionist plans in Palestine and expanding Jewish immigration as one of the most tangible threats facing the Muslim world.[15]

Opposition to Zionism was also gathering pace among the indigenous Arab population of Palestine. Nationalism had slowly begun taking hold in the region as former Ottoman provinces became European colonies. By the time the British Mandate had been instituted, a growing sense of Palestinian nationalism and anti-Zionism had already permeated the elite class of Palestinian urban traders and professionals.[16] These leaders demanded that Britain renounce its commitment to Zionism, stop Jewish immigration, and move Palestine toward independence as an Arab-majority county. Rural Palestinians were also objecting to the economic impact of dispossession from their agricultural land by Jewish newcomers.[17] The powerful religious establishment, headed by the Mufti of Jerusalem, wielded influence in shaping this nascent nationalism.[18] It issued Islamic legal rulings supporting anti-land-sale campaigns to stop Arab landowners from selling their estates to Jewish immigrants, as well as calling for the protection of Islamic holy sites. The Mufti reached out to the international Muslim community as he sought to internationalize the cause of Palestine by hailing the political and religious significance of its Islamic holy places.[19] Despite these efforts, the Palestinian political and religious elite were ineffective in quelling the influx of Jewish settlers. Their subservience toward their British patrons, their conviction that they could lobby the British peacefully, and their bitter factionalism prevented them from successfully promoting Palestinian nationalism.[20]

The failure of the Palestinian leaders facilitated the growth of populist resistance to Zionism within Palestine, led by individuals such as Izz al-Din al-Qassam.[21] A popular speaker, al-Qassam had preached against French colonialism around his birthplace of Latakia, a coastal town in modern-day Syria. Al-Qassam called for jihad, a call to arms, against the domineering European powers.[22] Facing a death sentence for his role in the failed Syrian resistance, al-Qassam fled southward to Haifa, a Mediterranean city in Palestine, where he soon gathered a following by preaching in mosques. Al-Qassam was critical of the Palestinian elite and the religious institutions. He spoke of the need to pursue the modernization of Muslim society, as well as a stricter adherence to Islamic orthodoxy as a framework for progress.[23] From his base in Haifa, al-Qassam resumed the anticolonial struggle that he had commenced in Syria. He roamed throughout northern Palestine, preaching in rural areas to an expanding base of followers composed of predominantly poor and pious peasants. His message centered on the need to support Palestinian nationalism in its struggle against Zionism and colonialism through education, a return to a purer religious life, and jihad.

Al-Qassam presented jihad as a religious responsibility for all Muslims to militarily resist the British Mandate government and Zionism. As one of al-Qassam's followers explained, "All that pertains to such a jihad is dictated in familiar ayat [verses of the Quran]. . . . 'This is jihad, victory or martyrdom,' and such a jihad is one of the religious duties of the Islamic creed."[24] Al-Qassam obtained a decree from the Mufti of Damascus who legitimated the use of violence against the British and the incoming Jewish settlers.[25] By making resistance a core duty of faith, al-Qassam popularized the notion of jihad. The Syrian preacher increased his following and began planning clandestine military operations to counter the Zionist threat and wage a war of liberation against the British.[26] As al-Qassam was laying the groundwork for resistance to Zionism and British rule in Palestine, the Muslim Brotherhood was expanding its own base of operations in Egypt. By the 1930s, it had developed into a sizable welfare association and had begun making connections with the Mufti of Jerusalem.[27]

In October 1935, the threat of the Zionist forces in Palestine was confirmed. The discovery of a secret arms shipment in the Jaffa harbor affirmed to the Palestinians that the Jewish settlers in their midst were arming their militias for an eventual confrontation to take control of Palestine. As the influx of Jewish immigrants had expanded, the possibility of losing their homeland had become a distinct threat for Palestinians. Almost overnight, protests erupted throughout Palestine and swept other major Arab urban centers, including Amman, Cairo, Damascus, and Baghdad.[28] Alongside other groups in Palestine, al-Qassam sprang into action. He took to the hills around Haifa, where he gathered his followers and carried out incursions against British Mandate forces and Jewish settlers. His efforts were sporadic at best, however, and barely took off. Within less than a month, after only a few sabotage attacks, al-Qassam and his group were ambushed by members of the Palestine police force, as the British colonial police were known. In the ensuing battle, al-Qassam was shot and killed.

Al-Qassam's funeral in November 1935 gave voice to the anger and immense frustration felt by the Palestinians at the never-ending swell of Jewish immigration and the unyielding hold of British colonialism. A Syrian preacher who had used Haifa as his base for waging an anticolonial struggle, al-Qassam unexpectedly became one of the most prominent early martyrs in the name of the Palestinian national struggle.[29] His death became a rallying call and, by the spring of 1936, had paved the way for the Arab Revolt, a sweeping protest that set Palestine ablaze in a popular and armed uprising against both Zionism and British colonialism. The revolt involved general strikes as well as significant violence between the Palestinians, the Mandate forces, and the Jewish settlers.[30]

Driven by a groundswell of support that had been expanding for close to two decades, the Arab Revolt made surprising gains in its first two years.[31] Outside Palestine, it was felt heavily within the Muslim Brotherhood's rank and file in Egypt, particularly among those with close connections to Palestine.[32] The organization rallied its leadership behind the cause as it mobilized to contribute to propaganda, pamphleteering, and fundraising in support of the Palestinians.[33] The revolt also provided the impetus (some would say excuse[34]) for the commencement of the brotherhood's militarization, as it prompted an internal decision to establish a military wing called the "Special Section."[35] Initially a clandestine development, the Special Section recruited and trained young brothers in jihad for the defense of Islam, and a number of those brothers participated as volunteers in the revolt. This shift expanded a militant ethos within the organization at the time, with jihad and the attendant glory of martyrdom being elevated into central tenants of the brotherhood through both formal and informal training.[36]

The early success of the revolt in Palestine compelled the British to bolster their military power to quash the uprising. By the end of the second year, with the deployment of one hundred thousand troops, the British military surge began showing signs of success and the rebellion was crushed by 1939, marking a historic milestone in the Palestinian struggle. The force that the British used against the Palestinians effectively decimated their fighting power and ensured their defeat in the confrontation with the Jewish paramilitary units a decade later.[37] After the revolt had subsided, the brotherhood continued to send missions to Palestine to spread the group's message and provide military training to civilians, ostensibly to prepare them for an expected future confrontation.[38] By 1943, it had established a sister organization in Palestine called the Makarem Society, and by 1945 it had inaugurated the first official Muslim Brotherhood branch in Jerusalem. There were about twenty-five branches in Palestine by 1948. These brotherhood posts, which were subject to the control of the Cairo headquarters, entailed a total active membership of between twelve and twenty thousand brothers.[39] With al-Qassam's populist legacy of anticolonial jihad and the expansion of the Muslim Brotherhood into Palestine, the foundation from which Sheikh Yassin would begin building his vision decades later was effectively cemented.

FATAH AND THE PLO

It was only after World War Two that the battle for Palestine resumed. In 1944, the Jewish settlers launched an armed campaign against the British troops, seeking to force their departure and to compel Britain to allow for the expansion of Jewish immigration into Palestine.[40] Broke, frustrated by the Zionist attacks, and unable to align its conflicting commitments to Palestinians and Zionists, Britain turned the issue of Palestine over to the newly formed United Nations. In November 1947, the UN General Assembly issued a "Partition Plan" calling for the partition of Palestine into an Arab state and a Jewish state and setting a deadline for the termination of the British Mandate. The proposed partition allocated 56 percent of Palestine to the Jewish community, which formed about one-third of the population at the time.[41]

The Palestinian leadership rejected the partition of Palestine as well as Zionist aspirations in their land, as they always had, on the grounds that the indigenous Arab majority had the right to self-determination in their own homeland. They sought to prevent the implementation of the United Nations' recommendation.[42] The imminent end of the British Mandate and the international commitment to the creation of a Jewish homeland after the horrors of the Holocaust all coalesced to precipitate violent clashes between Palestinians and Jewish settlers. From the end of 1947, days after the announcement of the partition plan, through May 1948, Palestine was in the throes of a civil war.[43] In March strongly armed and highly motivated Zionist forces began systematically invading Palestinian villages and towns and forcefully expelling their residents. By the spring of 1948, before the British troops had departed, more than three hundred thousand Palestinian refugees had fled or been ousted from their homes. Over the course of these months, the Muslim Brotherhood offices in Palestine mobilized with a call to resistance for the protection of the Islamic holy places.[44] The brotherhood in Egypt also openly recruited volunteers to cross the borders and fight to "save Palestine."[45] Although militarily negligible and numbering around 1,500, these volunteers were reportedly most active around Gaza, Jerusalem, and Bethlehem, as well as against Jewish settlers in the Negev Desert.[46]

On May 14, 1948, the British Mandate officially expired. Upon the withdrawal of the last British troops from Palestine, the Jewish community declared the establishment of the State of Israel. This prompted

Arab countries around Palestine to intervene on the side of the Palestinians, effectively turning the civil war into an interstate conflagration. Israel ultimately emerged victorious, capturing 78 percent of the land of Palestine, significantly more than had been allocated to it under the UN Partition Plan. The 1948 war, known as the "War of Independence" by Israel and "al-Nakba," or the catastrophe, by Palestinians, marked the independence of Israel, a watershed moment when the Zionist project became a political reality. For the Palestinians, this was a point of rupture, an unthinkable catastrophe which marked the disappearance of their homeland. About half the Palestinians from the land that had become Israel lost their homes and property and were scattered through force and violence into the remaining bits of Palestine and throughout the region. The fabric of Palestinian society and economy was entirely decimated.

The scale of the refugee calamity was staggering, as estimates rose to more than seven hundred thousand refugees.[47] Recognizing the extent of the problem, the UN General Assembly adopted Resolution 194 on December 11, 1948, stressing that "refugees wishing to return to their homes and live at peace with their neighbors should be permitted to do so at the earliest practicable date." This resolution firmly established the right of return for Palestinian refugees. Israel, however, promptly closed its borders and prevented any such return. Instead, it seized the lands and homes of the refugees and designated these as property to be used for Jewish-only settlement. Unable to return after the war, hundreds of thousands of Palestinians languished in refugee camps in the remaining 22 percent of Palestine that came under Jordanian and Egyptian control. East Jerusalem and the West Bank were annexed by Jordan, and the Gaza Strip fell under Egyptian administration. Other refugees fled to Jordan, Lebanon, Syria, and farther afield.

By the summer of 1948, therefore, the Muslim Brotherhood branches in Palestine had been divided between Israel, Jordan, and Egypt.[48] In East Jerusalem and the West Bank, under Jordanian rule, the Muslim Brotherhood focused solely on its welfare agenda and Islamization mission.[49] Within Gaza, its experience was more tumultuous. Gaza had been forced to accommodate close to two hundred thousand refugees, more than double its population of eighty thousand inhabitants, in densely populated refugee camps, creating a humanitarian crisis and economic distress. The concentration of refugees and their proximity to their homes, now on the Israeli side of the armistice line, made the Gaza Strip an active spot for incursions into Israel by a range of insurgent movements as well as individuals and families seeking to return to their homes. Alongside social regeneration projects, the brotherhood in this coastal enclave established military training camps to support armed missions aimed at the liberation and return of the Palestinian homeland.[50]

One of the people who passed through these training camps, albeit not as an official member of the Muslim Brotherhood, was Yasser Arafat. Born in Cairo in 1929 to a Gazan father and a Jerusalemite mother, Arafat spent most of his childhood in Egypt.[51] During and after the 1948 war, Arafat engaged in small-scale armed operations against Israel from Gaza in the hope of turning the fortunes of the dispossessed Palestinians. Early after its creation, the Israeli state adopted an aggressive strategy for dealing with Gaza, implementing harsh retaliatory tactics in response to these armed incursions or attempts by refugees to return to their homes. Deterrent actions included operations such as those carried out by Unit 101, under the leadership of a young Israeli officer named Ariel Sharon, which entailed a wide range of operations including invading refugee camps and massacring civilians.[52] Until 1955, Egypt systematically disarmed Gaza's population in a bid to prevent sporadic skirmishes from Gaza into Israel, in the fear that Egypt would be pulled into a confrontation with Israel. This left Gazans defenseless in the face of Israeli aggression. Persistent failure to control the Palestinian operations, however, resulted in more heavy-handed efforts by Israel to reoccupy the Gaza Strip and pacify its population by force through raids, military operations, incursions into refugee camps, and public executions.[53]

By this time, Egyptians—alongside millions of Arabs—were look-ing to a rising Egyptian leader who would have an indelible impact on the political map of the region. President Gamal Abdel Nasser was a staunchly secular and deeply charismatic individual who won over Arab masses. His electric speeches served as a clarion call for unity rooted in Arabness, rather than Islam, and constructed a shared identity for the diverse inhabitants of the region. People throughout the Middle East looked to Nasser as the savior that would unite the Arab world against colonial forces, as well as against the Zionist reality that had taken root within Palestine. Nasser's deep secularism manifested itself domestically in repressive policies that aimed to crush the Muslim Brotherhood in Egypt and Gaza. Against Nasser's iron fist and the rising tide of secu-lar pan-Arabism, the influence of the Muslim Brotherhood dwindled and its support base was depleted.[54] In Gaza, the brotherhood was driven underground, and the few military bases it had established there were effectively dismantled. As the brotherhood's reach diminished, it shifted its focus back to its core, Islamization, in its belief that a righ-teous Islamic society must be nurtured before Western intervention could be successfully confronted. During this time, young members such as Ahmad Yassin, who had returned from Cairo where he was un-able to complete his studies due to his injuries, continued to partake in the brotherhood's clandestine social, religious, and educational services from private homes and mosques.[55]

Yasser Arafat had left Gaza by then and settled in Kuwait, where he worked as an engineer and actively engaged in planning the Palestinian struggle for liberation alongside other students and young profession-als. These emerging young leaders witnessed how Nasser's pan-Arabism was shaping Palestinian nationalism. Throughout the 1950s, Nasser's appeal led to the emergence of organizations that placed the cause of Palestine within the fold of pan-Arabism, as both the catalyst for Arab unity and the litmus test for the success of Arab nationalism.[56] Arafat, however, challenged Nasser's vision as well as that of the Muslim Broth-erhood. He worried about the elision of the Palestinian struggle by regional politics and about making Palestine's liberation contingent on either Arab unity, as Nasser's pan-Arabism advocated, or on the revival of a pan-Islamic virtuous society, as the Muslim Brotherhood did.

Instead, inspired by nationalist movements that had multiplied in the age of decolonization and by contemporary liberation struggles in Algeria, Vietnam, and elsewhere, Arafat advocated a distinctly nationalist vision limited specifically to the liberation of Palestine from Zionism. In 1959, alongside a number of other students, Arafat launched Fatah, the Palestinian National Liberation Movement.[57] Fatah's vision of liberating Palestine effectively entailed waging armed struggle to dismantle what it saw as the colonial state of Israel and reverse the injustices that Palestinians had suffered. This included, primarily, allowing the Palestinian refugees to return to the homes from which they had fled or been expelled. Fatah's creation precipitated an early rift with the Islamic members of the Palestinian national movement, and was regarded bitterly by the Muslim Brothers in Gaza who had enjoyed friendly relations with Arafat prior to his departure to Kuwait. Those members believed that the absence of a distinctly Islamic agenda, what they perceived as a form of "secularism," would prevent Fatah from serving the Palestinian cause or achieving its nationalist goals, as they remained committed to their principles of Islamization.[58]

Fatah's rank and file was composed of *fedayeen*, armed fighters who sacrificed themselves in the name of the Palestinian cause. Inspired by Third World anticolonial movements, Fatah's *fedayeen* waged insurgencies against Israel from Syria, Lebanon, Jordan, and the West Bank.[59] Fatah raids were few in number and had a limited impact on Palestinians. Nonetheless, host countries tried to suppress Fatah and other insurgent groups, as they had a destabilizing effect on the region, often leading to heated skirmishes between Palestinian guerilla fighters and the Israeli army, which carried out punishing reprisals. These scuffles threatened to embroil host countries in direct confrontation with Israel. Nasser in particular sought to avoid such a war until the Arab world was fully prepared. Five years after Fatah was created, Arab leaders convened to discuss ways in which to manage the Palestinian liberation struggle that was unfolding on their territories. In 1964, the Palestine Liberation Organization (PLO) was established, in many ways to act as a tool to control the insurgent factions.[60] The PLO was an umbrella organization that drew into a single framework all the different Palestinian factions that had come into being. Understanding the PLO to be a tool for the Arab regimes to restrain the Palestinian factions and to foil the notion of "independent" Palestinian nationalism, Fatah and other small guerrilla factions refused to join.

Efforts to manage regional instability, however, were ultimately unsuccessful and failed to prevent an escalation that would irreversibly alter the history of the modern Middle East. On June 5, 1967, President Nasser in Egypt mobilized his ground forces in the demilitarized Sinai Peninsula in response to Israeli threats toward Syria, and closed the straits of Sinai to Israeli shipping. Even though Israel understood Egypt's immediate troop deployment to be defensive in nature, it decided to strike first with a surprise attack against Egypt's forces. Catching its neighbor off guard, Israel managed to almost entirely destroy Egypt's air force while it languished on the ground. Jordan and Syria were drawn into the battle, opening up several fronts with Israel. But the Arab forces were unable to reverse Israel's preemptive advantage. Over the course of six days, Israel destroyed and pushed back the Arab forces, vastly expanding the territory under its control and creating another wave of hundreds of thousands of refugees.[61] While in 1948 Israel had seized 78 percent of what had been Palestine, it now conquered the remaining 22 percent. East Jerusalem was formally annexed into Israel, a move that has not been recognized by the international community. The West Bank and the Gaza Strip, as well as the Syrian Golan Heights and the Egyptian Sinai Peninsula, were placed under Israeli military rule, without formal annexation.

By the end of the sixth day, on June 11, 1967, Israel's occupation of the Palestinian territories of the West Bank, including East Jerusalem, and the Gaza Strip, had formally begun. The swift defeat of the Arab forces laid to rest Nasser's vision of Arab unity. The small guerilla factions that had commenced sporadic and ineffective operations against Israel before 1967 suddenly emerged as a powerful alternative to pan-Arabism. Fatah's insurgency imbued the dispossessed and broken Palestinian refugees with agency, pride, and direction. As Fatah's ranks swelled with *fedayeen*, Palestinians celebrated a growing number of military operations and upheld the self-sacrifice of fighters as the highest price to be paid in serving the struggle.[62] Fatah rapidly became a revolutionary symbol, and in 1969 Yasser Arafat wrested the chairmanship of the PLO from the control of the Arab regimes.[63] Under his leadership, Palestinians developed a national political identity and embarked on processes of state-building in exile through a revolution that was aimed at return to the homeland.[64]

The liberation of Palestine through military means, to secure the right to self-determination and the right of return, was central to the Palestinian revolution. "Our correct understanding of the reality of the Zionist occupation confirms to us that regaining the occupied homeland cannot happen except through armed violence as the sole, inevitable, unavoidable, and indispensable means in the battle of liberation."[65] Fatah's statement goes on to describe the necessity of dismantling the "colonial base . . . of the Zionist occupation state" and asserts that its intellectual, social, political, military, and financial elements have to be destroyed before the Palestinian homeland can be liberated.[66] Steadfastness, perseverance, and sacrifice were key for survival in what was seen as being a long-term battle.

From their bases in host countries, factions within the PLO, including Fatah, carried out cross-border attacks into Israel and planned spectacular operations that targeted Israelis around the world. Debates about the killing of Israeli civilians unfolded against the backdrop of a broader global reckoning with the role of violence in anticolonial liberation struggles. The rise of the Global South and the necessity of using force was situated in a context where violence and terror underpinned the control of the colonial masters. Palestinian fighters justified killing Israeli civilians as a necessary response to Israeli aggression against Palestinian civilians and as a much-needed deterrent against future Israeli expansion. Purposeful ambiguity about the civilian nature of Israeli victims was also constructed; given that nearly all Jewish men and women served in the military, how did one distinguish soldiers from civilians?[67]

The PLO's revolution had a liberating effect on the Palestinian psyche. But its practical ability to achieve its stated goals of liberation and the creation of a Palestinian state was less obvious. Given the power disparity with Israel, it became clear even as early as the 1970s that liberation through armed struggle was unlikely. Nonetheless, the PLO's revolution persisted as a means of asserting Palestinian identity, developing political legitimacy, and broadcasting the Palestinian plight globally.[68] For an American administration in the midst of the Cold War, and its view that the Palestinians were allied with the USSR, the PLO's actions were branded as international terrorism and all forms of diplomatic engagement with the group were banned.[69] The PLO's revolutionary tactics also had severe repercussions on the group's relations with its host countries within the Arab world. In 1970, the PLO was expelled from its base in Jordan and moved to Lebanon.[70] In 1982, Israel invaded Lebanon, then in the throes of a civil war, and ousted the PLO, which had become a "state within a state" inside the country.[71] The Palestinian leadership was exiled to Tunis, where its ability to maintain the insurgency against Israel and to lead the Palestinian struggle now had to contend with geographic distance from its homeland.

ISLAMIC NATIONALISM

In the 1970s and 1980s, the PLO underwent a process of recalibration. As the limits of its armed struggle became increasingly obvious, the PLO began pursuing diplomatic and political means to secure Palestinian rights. This evolution coincided with an Islamic revival that gathered pace regionally after the defeat of Nasser's secular pan-Arabism, and eventually, after some time, manifested itself in the West Bank and the Gaza Strip.[72] Fortunes started shifting for the Muslim Brotherhood in the Palestinian territories with an increase in financial remittances from the Palestinian diaspora community as well as from sister Islamic organizations in the Arab Gulf States and in Jordan.[73] Funds were also collected domestically through Islamic almsgiving. As the brotherhood enjoyed this financial upturn, it began investing in civil institutions that could strengthen and expand its mission of social regeneration, including mosques, schools, clinics, and youth clubs.

Having sustained his commitment to the Muslim Brotherhood in Gaza throughout the preceding decades when his work was eclipsed by Arab and Palestinian nationalism, Sheikh Ahmad Yassin was well poised to shape this revival. In 1976, Yassin applied to the Israeli occupation authorities for a license to establish the Islamic Association.[74] This was to be an umbrella organization that would provide legal and administrative cover for the brotherhood's social, religious, educational, and medical services within the Gaza Strip.[75] Ostensibly driven by a policy of noninterference with social Islamic organizations, Israel approved the license and the association was established that same year.[76] Israel had other reasons to support the growth of Islamic movements, particularly in Gaza, as it hoped that cultivating the brotherhood would produce a counterforce that could weaken other Palestinian nationalist movements.[77] The brotherhood's leadership pragmatically enjoyed this tacit arrangement with Israel and viewed it as a means of expanding its reach and confronting what it disapprovingly viewed as the secular influence of nationalist factions. Such competition between the Islamists and nationalists led to bloody and acrimonious exchanges, often in full sight of Israel's occupying forces, which deliberately failed to end these confrontations and continued to enable the brotherhood's growth.[78]

Yassin and his colleagues enlarged their social and charitable infrastructure within the occupied territories, focused as they were on education and religious revival, without revising the brotherhood's belief of the need to postpone confrontation with the occupation to a later date.[79] The brotherhood's focus on gradual Islamization at the expense of immediate resistance created significant resentment.[80] This was not limited to the nationalists who were heeding the call of the PLO's armed struggle. Yassin implemented a strict hierarchical structure within the Islamic Association that created a great deal of frustration from within its own member base, particularly among the younger generation.[81] Largely driven by such frustrations, a splinter organization called Islamic Jihad broke off in 1981.[82] Islamic Jihad emerged as the antithesis of the brotherhood, calling for immediate jihad against the Israeli occupation.[83] Ideologically, Islamic Jihad saw the liberation of Palestine as the path toward the revival of the Islamic nation, effectively reversing the brotherhood's order of priorities. For Islamic Jihad, blind dedication to Islamization compromised the Palestinian struggle. In contrast to the brotherhood's pragmatic engagement with Israel, Islamic Jihad remained categorical in its rejection of dealings with Israel and focused on confronting the occupation rather than on building Islamic institutions to serve the longer-term battle.[84]

Islamic Jihad's early armed operations were relatively minor, yet quite popular within Gaza.[85] The Iranian revolution of 1979, where a Western-friendly regime was overthrown by an Islamic revolution, enhanced the appeal of Islamic revolutionary movements. So did the creation of the Lebanese movement Hezbollah, the Party of God, as a Shia Islamic military organization mobilizing to fight the Israeli occupation of south Lebanon.[86] Islamic Jihad's focus on the liberation of Palestine resembled the PLO's dedication to armed struggle. This accelerated a reckoning that was beginning to take shape within the Muslim Brotherhood regarding the urgency of resisting the occupation as Israel expanded its settlement enterprise within the occupied territories. Israel's accelerated colonization commenced shortly after the West Bank and the Gaza Strip fell under Israeli control in 1967, but began in earnest with the rise to power of the right-wing Likud political party within Israel in 1977.[87] Israeli policies toward the occupied territories signaled to Palestinians the intention of the Israeli government to hold on to the territories it had acquired following the 1967 war.

In the early 1980s, Palestinian brotherhood leaders in Jordan, Kuwait, Saudi Arabia, and elsewhere heatedly debated a shift to armed struggle.

Many of the brothers in the diaspora, particularly in Jordan, as well as those in the West Bank believed that the brotherhood must maintain a longer-term focus on Islamization given the power disparity with Israel. For those within the Gaza Strip, who had weathered the much more brutal repression of the occupation and who were closer to the actions of Islamic Jihad, the urgency of switching to armed struggle was more acute.[88] In meetings between the Palestinian and Jordanian branches of the brotherhood in 1983, it was ultimately decided that Islamization and resistance were not in conflict and did not need to take place sequentially.[89] The discussions between the brotherhood's leaders drew on the early legacies of al-Qassam and the Muslim Brotherhood in Egypt, both of which had instituted a concurrent focus on jihad and Islamization within a pan-Islamic paradigm. Unlike this ancestral ideology, however, the members debated focusing the armed struggle on Palestine rather than a broader regional framework, effectively marking an early sign of the "Palestinianization" of the Muslim Brotherhood in Palestine.[90]

Pursuant to these discussions, Sheikh Yassin and his colleagues began secretly stockpiling weapons in Yassin's home in Gaza in preparation for this anticipated redirection. In late 1985, the brotherhood created the Palestinian Apparatus, an organization set up to manage the international legal, financial, and institutional network of the brotherhood in Palestine. Given that many of the brotherhood's members were scattered across the region, as well as in the United States and United Kingdom, this outfit was designed to facilitate communication and coordination between the internal leadership, those in the West Bank and the Gaza Strip, and those outside. Three figures were central to this work: Khaled Meshal, a young student living in Kuwait; Musa abu Marzouq, another student who was completing his doctorate in the United States; and Ibrahim Gosheh, a refugee from Jerusalem who was living in Jordan.[91] Yassin also oversaw the establishment of institutions that would manage the brotherhood's military operations, including Palestinian Jihad Fighters, a military organization focused on targeting Israeli soldiers and Jewish settlers in the Gaza Strip. For this armed unit,

Yassin chose a close colleague and confidant named Salah Shehadeh, a man born and raised in Gaza, to act as its head. Other organizations included al-Ahdath, the brotherhood's branch for young members, and the Organization for Jihad and Proselytizing, which dealt with Palestinians who collaborated with the occupation and who were consequently accused of treason.[92]

In contrast to the brotherhood's accelerating militarization, the PLO's global revolution was waning. Having been ostracized by the United States throughout the 1960s and 1970s, Yasser Arafat and the leaders of the PLO had begun clandestine efforts to pursue diplomatic channels with the Americans. The PLO's inclusion in diplomacy was made contingent on its complete renunciation of terrorism and its recognition of Israel's "right to exist."[93] This condition meant conceding the goal of liberating the entirety of the land of Palestine and focusing instead on the 22 percent captured in 1967 that now remained under Israel's military occupation. Given the weight of making such a concession, the PLO's process of recalibration unfolded over the course of several years, during which tension between Israel and the Palestinians living under its occupation increased.[94] Intermittent skirmishes proliferated throughout the 1980s and in 1987 bubbled over when the fateful car accident on December 8 sparked the intifada. The unplanned eruption of the First Intifada was a powerful jolt to both the PLO and the brotherhood, each engaged in its respective surreptitious reorientation.

A TURNING POINT

On the night of December 9, Yassin hosted the senior leaders of the institutions that had been created in Gaza over the course of the brotherhood's preparation for its transition to armed struggle.[95] After intense discussions, it was decided that the brotherhood would finally leverage all its preparatory work and spin off a small militarized offshoot that would join the likes of Islamic Jihad in armed confrontation against Israel. The Islamic Resistance Movement, HAMAS, was officially launched in January 1988.[96] Although intended as an offshoot, Hamas rapidly subsumed the parent organization's institutional infrastructure. The Islamic Association, with its powerful footprint of social and charitable institutions in Gaza, almost inevitably became a crucial foundation for Hamas's expansive social wing.[97] Hamas also pulled in the various organizations that had been created over the course of the 1980s and integrated those into distinct political, administrative, and military wings. Hamas's political wing was staffed by Yassin's close associates from the Islamic Association. Its military wing, however, remained limited in size and was composed of disjointed units that were collectively managed by Salah Shehadeh.

A few months after its creation, in August 1988, Hamas issued its charter, "The Charter of Allah: The Platform of the Islamic Resistance Movement (HAMAS)."[98] This document introduced the movement and outlined its mission, values, and goals. It defined Hamas's motto as "God is its goal; The messenger [the Prophet Mohammed] is its Leader; The Quran is its Constitution; Jihad is its methodology; and Death for the Sake of God is its most coveted desire." In this document, Yassin and the other cofounders articulated the chain of jihad that Hamas was presumably building on. The charter celebrated Izz al-Din al-Qassam's jihad and his role in the lead-up to the Arab Revolt in the second half of the 1930s, opportunistically mythologizing him as the forefather of Islamic resistance in Palestine.[99] The charter also hailed the contribution of the brotherhood in the 1948 and 1967 wars against Israel, although such contribution was in reality quite limited.

For all these ancestral models, the liberation of Palestine had been almost incidental, part of the broader mission of Islamic revival as a form of anticolonialism. Nonetheless, Hamas drew on this rich historical narrative to define its nascent ideological platform. The charter positioned Hamas as "a branch of the Muslim Brotherhood chapter in Palestine," while noting that it was a "distinct Palestinian movement." Through its charter, the brotherhood's Palestinianization culminated in Hamas's emergence as both an Islamic and a nationalist party. By defining its nationalism as "part and parcel of its religious ideology," Hamas's leaders demonstrated that Islam was to be the foundation for a political ideology. In so doing, Hamas entered the fold of Islamist parties, or movements that draw on Islam to define a particular political agenda.[100] Rather than the creation of a caliphate or a pan-Islamic entity, many Islamists are driven by "Islamo-nationalism," a means of combining Islamic identity with nationalism.[101] While asserting its nationalism, Hamas's charter also celebrated the transnational Islamism that informed the movement's historical identity and showed that, at least on a philosophical level, the movement remained part of the regional structure of the Muslim Brotherhood.

Hamas's charter offered no explicit indication of the nature of the Islamic Palestinian state or entity it was seeking, in terms of its theological and political structures, neither did it signal that Hamas was looking to break from the modern trappings of a nation-state model.[102] The charter spoke of how such an Islamic polity would allow for Christians and Jews to live in peace and harmony under Muslim rule.[103] Despite this assertion, the rest of the charter shed light on Hamas's understanding of Israel, Judaism, and Zionism at the time it was released.[104] The text was replete with anti-Semitic references that built on age-old stereotypes about the Jewish people, including their alleged accumulation of immense wealth, their treacherous and devious nature, and their ability to influence global media. Hamas attributed Zionism's success in creating Israel to Jewish manipulation of global affairs, including the two world wars and the establishment of the United Nations. The movement drew its insight about Zionism from the *Protocols of the Elders of Zion*, an anti-Semitic text that fabricated a myth about a Jewish plot to dominate the world.[105] Throughout the charter, Hamas used references to Jews and Zionists interchangeably, constantly conflating the two.[106] The charter also described Israeli policies toward Palestinians as the "Nazism of the Jews." It cited the collective punishment and the frequent killing of innocents, including women, children, and the elderly, as the manifestation of Nazi policies in Palestine.

Through its charter, Hamas made clear its refusal to recognize the State of Israel. The document stressed the indivisibility of the land of "Historic Palestine," referring to the land that constituted the British Mandate, located between the Eastern Mediterranean and the River Jordan, over which Israel was established. Hamas defined this territory as "an Islamic land entrusted to the Muslim generations until Judgement Day."[107] This declaration coincided with major developments that were taking place on the track spearheaded by the PLO. In late 1988, a few months after Hamas issued its charter, Yasser Arafat convened the exiled Palestinian leadership in Algiers. The eruption of the intifada had finally compelled the Palestinian leader to officially adopt the policies he had been contemplating for years. Addressing the convened attendees, Arafat gave a speech in which he declared the independence of the State of Palestine and invoked international resolutions that demonstrated the PLO's willingness to accept a state on the West Bank and the Gaza Strip, with East Jerusalem as the capital.[108] Arafat's declaration signaled the PLO's readiness to concede the 78 percent of Palestinian land that had been lost in 1948 and willingness to fulfill the American demand of renouncing terrorism. This signaled to the United States that the PLO was ready to enter into a negotiated settlement with Israel, prompting the administration of President Ronald Reagan to open a dialogue with the PLO in late 1988.[109]

With this long-anticipated about-face, the PLO accepted conditions that the United States had upheld as prerequisites for engagement. Through Arafat's declaration, the PLO transitioned onto a diplomatic track that was focused on achieving statehood on the remaining 22 percent of historic Palestine. The PLO's concessions were anathema for Hamas, whose charter proclaimed that "jihad for the liberation of Palestine is obligatory." No other path for liberation was viable. The movement dismissed diplomatic efforts as contrary to its ideology, primarily because they were premised on the condition of conceding parts of Palestine, but also because Hamas believed they were unlikely to serve Palestinian interests. Hamas lauded the efforts of the PLO in advancing the Palestinian struggle to date but stressed that its "secular ideology is diametrically opposed to religious thought." Now that Arafat had given up on the vision of liberating all of Palestine and dismantling the Zionist state, Hamas rose to articulate an alternative path for liberation. Jihad was defined not as a tactic but rather as a holistic strategy around which the Palestinian community could rally.[110]

Jihad comprised political, economic, social, and cultural facets, or what Hamas often described as an "Islamic renaissance" project.[111] Waging jihad was understood as a way of being, as existing in a state of war or espousing a belligerent relationship with the enemy. Jihad was not limited to armed struggle, although this did comprise a central element of Hamas's mission. Even in the absence of military operations, evoking jihad conjured a sense of identity and purpose that reaffirmed the Palestinian rejection of Israeli control. Hamas began popularizing Islam as a political ideology in much the same way as al-Qassam had half a century earlier in an effort to mobilize the masses against occupying forces.[112]

With Hamas's charter and the PLO's strategic shift, 1988 became a turning point, a moment of transition. In that year, the PLO's resolve to sustain the purity of the Palestinian nationalist struggle—the use of armed force to liberate historic Palestine—appeared to wane. Almost seamlessly, Islamic nationalism rose to carry the mantle forward.[113] Instead of "armed struggle" to regain the "occupied homeland," as the PLO had once expressed its vision, Hamas stated that "there is no solution to the Palestinian problem except through jihad." The movement sought to safeguard the purity of the Palestinian struggle by rejecting the right of Israel to exist and calling for the full liberation of historic Palestine. While the PLO rose at a time of global revolutionary anti-colonialism, Hamas emerged against a regional backdrop of resurgent Islamism. The movement articulated the PLO's original demands in a different ideological framing that was a particular product of its time. As the PLO accepted the loss of cities like Haifa and Nazareth, Hamas promised jihad for their liberation. Like the original PLO before it,

Hamas believed that only through force could Zionism's colonial impact over Palestinian land be confronted.

THE FIRST INTIFADA

Yasser Arafat's speech—and the PLO's implicit acceptance of partitioning the land of historic Palestine into two states—was overshadowed by events on the ground as the intifada gathered pace. Within the occupied territories, Hamas immediately challenged the PLO's redirection of the Palestinian struggle.[114] Rather than joining the local leadership that was coordinating with the PLO to sustain the uprising, Hamas openly competed against it.[115] As leaflets appeared on the streets in the West Bank and Gaza organizing acts of civil disobedience, Hamas proposed alternative strike dates. The movement's intervention was powerful, leading the PLO to accuse it of undermining unity.[116] Given that the intifada had sprung out of Gaza, where Sheikh Yassin had cultivated the brotherhood's institutional reach deep into the local population, Hamas was able to capitalize on a strong following.[117] The leaflets it published were different in language and feel from those officially issued by the intifada's leadership. They introduced a religious element into an uprising that was not thought of by most Palestinians in particularly religious terms.[118] Slogans from Hamas proliferated, its graffiti attacking Jews and Christians as well as secular nationalists. The movement also began printing its own clandestine magazine.[119]

The intifada was for the most part a popular uprising.[120] Palestinians used the means at their disposal to disrupt the occupation. Facing a largely civilian uprising, Israel's response was often brutal. Israeli defense minister Yitzhak Rabin infamously called on the army to "break the bones" of the protestors to deter their actions, sanctioning the use of plastic-covered bullets and live ammunition.[121] The Israeli military imposed crippling curfews and carried out large-scale administrative detention against Palestinians.[122] Hamas and Islamic Jihad did not always abide by the unarmed nature of the protests, as members used stones, knives, Molotov cocktails, and barricades and shot at Israeli military and civilian transportation.[123] Initially, Israel did not alter its policies toward the brotherhood, continuing to view it primarily as an apolitical social institution. This changed when Hamas formalized its nature as a resistance movement with the publication of its charter. As Hamas became a key player in the uprising, its relationship with Israel turned confrontational.[124]

In early 1989, Hamas captured and murdered two Israeli soldiers. Despite the military nature of Hamas's targets, this prompted Israel to declare Hamas a terrorist organization as it moved to arrest three hundred members, including Sheikh Ahmad Yassin, who was sentenced to a lifetime plus fifteen years in prison. Israel also declared dealings with Hamas a punishable offense.[125] This shift in Israel's policy forced Hamas to relocate its decision-making abroad, where legislative and executive branches for the movement were created. Hamas also maintained the presence of a clandestine leadership within the occupied territories. This marked a formal institutionalization of what would come to be known as Hamas's "internal" and "external" leaderships. The internal leadership was divided between the West Bank and the Gaza Strip, with underground members in East Jerusalem and Israel. Given the frequent arrests of Hamas members, the internal leadership also included a sizable constituency within Israel's jails. The external leadership was scattered in the region, where many were active in refugee camps in Jordan, Lebanon, and Syria.[126] A consultative council was created to manage the organization and facilitate decision-making. This was a representative forum that ensured a platform was given to all of Hamas's constituencies, particularly between the internal and the external branches.[127] All major decisions facing Hamas were debated within the council before being outlined in a specific policy or position to the rest of the organization. The vastly different priorities facing various constituencies within Hamas often made the consultative council a site of tension. However, due to its democratic nature, the council remained remarkably resilient and maintained unity within Hamas.

By the fourth year of the Palestinian intifada, in 1991, the uprising in the Palestinian territories had been considerably weakened and fatigue had seeped in.[128] The economy faltered and the social fabric strained as Israel's repressive military tactics divided the West Bank into small, easily manageable units and barred Palestinian workers from coming into Israel for their jobs. From its exile in Tunis, the PLO had worked closely with the local leadership to lead the uprising. Nonetheless, the power dynamic within the territories had shifted, as the PLO's softening coincided with Hamas's rising popularity. This change in fortune was accelerated in 1990 when Hamas made the decision to condemn Saddam Hussein's invasion of Kuwait.[129] In contrast, the PLO sided with Saddam Hussein, who was widely popular among Palestinians given his historic support of the Palestinian cause. Hamas's position was unpopular locally but placed it in a positive light with the Gulf States, which promptly redirected their funds toward the nascent movement, effectively plunging the PLO into a financial crisis. Iraq's invasion of Kuwait forced many of Hamas's leaders who were based there, including Khaled Meshal, to relocate to Jordan, where they benefited from a more developed brotherhood infrastructure. In this period, leaders such as Musa abu Marzouq also relocated from the United States to Jordan, where he was made the head of Hamas's political office. This consolidated the presence of Hamas's external leadership in the Hashemite Kingdom, which agreed to host Hamas on the condition that its activities would be limited to public relations and would involve no military operations.[130]

Throughout 1991 and 1992, Hamas developed its military capabilities within the Palestinian territories. Alongside the changes to the governance structure, Hamas's leadership also transformed its military wing. In 1991, rather than maintaining numerous disjointed and decentralized cells, Hamas institutionalized its military units into a single armed wing. In honor of the person Hamas regarded as its celebrated ancestor, the movement's military wing was called the Izz al-Din al-Qassam Brigades.[131] As leader of Hamas's armed operations, Yassin's close colleague Salah Shehadeh became the first official head of the Qassam Brigades.

Like the PLO before it, Hamas began its military operations by targeting Israeli army posts and settler communities as it detonated car bombs within the Gaza Strip and the West Bank.[132] Leaflets declared that Hamas was attempting to limit civilian casualties, focusing instead on combatants and settlers, whom they viewed as being legitimate targets.[133]

Hamas's campaign prompted Yitzhak Rabin to arrest 413 members of Hamas and Islamic Jihad in December 1992 and deport them to an area called Marj al-Zuhur in south Lebanon.[134] Inadvertently, the deportation placed Hamas in the international spotlight and allowed it to broadcast its message to the world. From their exile, Hamas's internal leaders, typically isolated under occupation, met with their counterparts in the external leadership and initiated communication channels with other organizations, including Hezbollah and, indirectly, Iran. Domestically, exile elevated Hamas's popularity among Palestinians as it demonstrated its leaders' steadfastness in the face of Israeli repression.

By the early 1990s, Hamas had morphed into a powerful player within the territories. The rivalry between the Islamic and nationalist movements that began under the brotherhood in the 1970s and 1980s had evolved into a conflict over the identity and future trajectory of Palestinian nationalism. The lessons that Fatah and the PLO had learned regarding the limitations of armed struggle and their path toward pacification over three decades, from 1959 to 1988, were not seen as relevant or applicable to Hamas. For Hamas, success was thought to be predestined.[135] The movement's leaders believed Hamas's Islamic character would offer a robust ideological framework through which to offset the worldly pressures that had hamstrung the PLO before it. With such firm conviction, Hamas contested the PLO's transition to diplomacy and instead embarked on a strategy of jihad aimed at liberating Palestine.

CHAPTER TWO

MILITARY RESISTANCE
COMES UNDONE

On February 25, 1994, an American Jewish settler named Baruch Goldstein walked into the Ibrahimi Mosque in the West Bank city of Hebron during prayer time. Standing behind the rows of kneeling figures in front of him, Goldstein opened fire. Within minutes, twenty-nine Muslim worshippers had been killed and close to one hundred injured. The atrocity jolted the nascent Israeli-Palestinian bilateral negotiations that had gathered pace in the wake of the First Intifada, prompted by the PLO's strategic redirection in 1988. Less than six months before the Hebron attack, in September 1993, PLO chairman Yasser Arafat and Israeli prime minister Yitzhak Rabin had awkwardly shaken hands in a widely publicized event on the South Lawn of the White House. The leaders had assembled in the American capital to sign the Declaration of Principles on Interim Self-Government Arrangements, popularly known as the Oslo Accords, referring to the capital city where the secretive talks leading to the agreement had taken place.

Following the signing, negotiations between Israel and the PLO in the form of a "peace process" were launched.[1] Goldstein's attack served as a reminder of the bloody challenges this process faced. Forty-one days after the shooting, once the time allotted for Muslim ritual mourning had been respected, a member of Hamas approached a bus stop in Afula, a city in northern Israel. Standing next to fellow passengers, the man detonated a suicide vest, killing seven Israelis. This was on April 6, 1994, a day that marked Hamas's first lethal suicide bombing in Israel. With the

PLO's engagement in diplomacy and Hamas's escalation of armed resistance, the divergent paths of the Palestinian struggle were elucidated.
One week later, another Hamas suicide bomber detonated his explosives
at a bus stop in Hadera, again in northern Israel, killing five Israelis.

These bombs had been assembled by "the Engineer," as their cre-
ator Yehya Ayyash was known. Ayyash, who was Hamas's first bomb-
maker, was born in the West Bank and had shown great talents in
electrical and mechanical work in his childhood. After his studies, he
had joined the Qassam Brigades, Hamas's military wing led by Salah
Shehadeh. Ayyash had a powerful influence on al-Qassam's military
tactics and ultimately became responsible for the movement's adoption
of suicide bombing, what Hamas called its "trademark" or "signature"
operations.[2] As the fighter Izz al-Din al-Qassam had done more than
half a century prior, Hamas extended religious legitimacy to its military
tactics, in this case to suicide bombings, and increased their permis-
sibility among Palestinians. Rather than referring to these attacks as
suicidal, which is sinful in Islam, Hamas called them martyrdom operations and celebrated them as heroic self-sacrifice.[3] Hamas's glorification
of suicide bombing fostered an environment where they were highly
regarded actions, ensuring both the supply of volunteers and the enhanced execution of operations.[4] Before long, they were adopted by
non-Islamic movements, including Fatah, the main party in the PLO,
which had ostensibly "renounced terrorism" in 1988.[5]

COLLAPSE OF THE PEACE PROCESS

The Oslo Accords made history by enshrining mutual recognition between the PLO and Israel.[6] Through the agreement, the PLO's recalibration was completed as the group formally recognized Israel and adopted
diplomatic negotiations as the path toward securing a political settlement.
In return, Israel recognized the PLO as the sole representative of the Palestinians, making no formal indication with regard to Palestinian statehood. The accords launched bilateral negotiations that initiated a phased

approach to the resolution of the conflict. This meant that the parties did not immediately tackle the thorny "final status" issues—refugees, settlements, security arrangements, final borders, and Jerusalem—that would have to be resolved. Rather, it was decided that Israel and the PLO would adopt a staggered strategy that could build confidence and gradually move the parties toward a final "two-state" resolution. A central product of the Oslo Accords was the creation of the Palestinian Authority. This was established in 1994 as a temporary administrative authority that could govern portions of the Palestinian territories for a transitional period of five years, when the conclusive settlement was to be reached.[7] As Israel gradually relinquished control over territory it occupied, responsibility would transition to the Palestinian Authority in the areas of education, culture, health, social welfare, and tourism.

More important was security. A core aspect of Oslo's incrementalism was that the Palestinian Authority would be held accountable for security issues that Israel might face after the redeployment of its occupation forces. The Palestinian Authority's ability to safeguard Israel's security was framed as a litmus test for Palestinian readiness to self-govern and a prerequisite for further Israeli withdrawal.[8] Security coordination mechanisms were put in place between the Palestinian Authority's security forces and the Israeli intelligence and army.[9] These entailed open communication channels aimed at crushing any activity within the occupied territories that was deemed a security threat to Israel, such as resistance operations. The Oslo Accords ultimately segmented the West Bank into distinct zones, only 18 percent of which could ostensibly be administered by the Palestinian Authority with the remaining territory falling under Israeli control. In practice, this meant that Israeli forces could reenter any area within the occupied territories, even those that fell under Palestinian jurisdiction.

Although the Palestinian Authority was restricted to administering the affairs of daily governance while under occupation, responsibility for negotiations in the pursuit of liberation continued to rest with the PLO.[10] Alongside leading the PLO, Yasser Arafat assumed the presidency of the Palestinian Authority as elections for its legislative and executive branches were set for 1996. After signing the Oslo Accords, Arafat and the exiled leadership were allowed to return to the Gaza Strip from Tunis and, for the first time, to lead the Palestinian struggle from within the occupied territories.[11] Palestinians under occupation were hopeful the Oslo Accords would bring statehood.[12] The economy had suffered during the intifada, and Palestinians had watched Israel expand its settlement enterprise on land that was presumably to make up their future state. Israel's settlement expansion persisted even after the right-wing Likud government was replaced by a left-leaning Labor cabinet under Yitzhak Rabin in 1992.

For its part, Hamas condemned the Oslo Accords, as it opposed the recognition of Israel on which they were premised. It joined forces with Marxist and other nationalist groups to form a rejectionist front that called for the continuation of jihad.[13] As peace talks were launched, Hamas maintained military operations against the Israeli army and settlers, even though this put it at odds with public sentiment.[14] But early hope regarding the peace process faded swiftly. Following Goldstein's killing spree, Hamas expanded its attacks to target civilians in Israel with its bombs in Afula and Hadera. Noting this shift, Hamas's leadership pointed to Goldstein's "Hebron massacre" as a turning point.[15] In response to Hamas's bombings, thousands of Hamas members were arrested by the Palestinian Authority and Israel as security coordination mechanisms were initiated throughout the West Bank and Gaza.[16] Israel also pressured host countries, particularly Jordan, to crack down on the political offices of Hamas's external leadership hosted within its borders.[17]

Lethal opposition to the peace process was not limited to Hamas. On November 4, 1995, Prime Minister Rabin was assassinated by a Jewish Israeli ultranationalist at a peace rally in Tel Aviv. The death of a principal architect of the peace process was a serious blow to its prospects. Following Rabin's assassination, Labor foreign minister Shimon Peres was appointed as acting prime minister. One of his first acts in office, in January 1996, was to authorize the assassination of Yehya

Ayyash, the main figure behind Hamas's suicide bombing.[18] Forty days after Ayyash's assassination, Hamas retaliated with another suicide bombing on a bus in Jerusalem, killing twenty-six Israelis.[19]

Ayyash's assassination coincided with the first presidential and legislative elections to take place for the newly formed Palestinian Authority. While sustaining military operations, Hamas contemplated participating in these elections to ensure representation within the political process.[20] After extensive debate, however, the movement's consultative council decided to boycott the ballot box to avoid conferring legitimacy to the Oslo Accords.[21] Expectedly, Yasser Arafat and his party, Fatah, emerged victorious and consolidated their grip on the presidency and the legislature.[22] After the elections, both the PLO and Israel's Labor government indicated a willingness to proceed with the peace process, even though talks were stalling. In response, Hamas strategically persisted in its suicide missions to derail the process, despite continued opposition from the Palestinian public.[23] Hamas's campaign of suicide bombing had a powerful impact on the Israeli electorate, which in 1996 voted to replace the Labor government with a more security-oriented and right-wing Likud government under the leadership of Benjamin Netanyahu.

Netanyahu's cabinet and the PLO paid lip service to peace talks even as it became evident that the five-year deadline for reaching a final settlement, in 1999, would be missed. Aided by Israel, the Palestinian Authority sustained its crackdown on Hamas, causing severe damage to the movement. Hamas was further weakened when the United States designated it a terrorist organization in 1997, thereby limiting its activities internationally, while Netanyahu's government also pursued the movement's regional presence. In 1997, Israel's intelligence agency, the Mossad, attempted to assassinate Khaled Meshal. A Jordanian citizen who was born in the West Bank, Meshal was an early member of the Palestinian Muslim Brotherhood's external leadership and a central figure in the decision to transition the brotherhood into Hamas. During the Gulf War he had fled Kuwait, where he was completing his studies, back to Jordan, where he rose up the ranks of Hamas's political branch in the kingdom.[24]

Israel's assassination operation was badly botched and the Mossad agents were captured by the Jordanians. In a dramatic twist of events, King Hussein of Jordan successfully pressed Netanyahu to release Sheikh Ahmad Yassin, Hamas's imprisoned founder and spiritual leader, in return for the Mossad agents. Yassin's release reinvigorated Hamas, but pressure from Israel and the United States persisted and Jordan was compelled to declare Hamas's presence in the country illegal. Despite being a Jordanian citizen, Meshal was deported to Qatar and the offices of Hamas's political branch that Jordan had hosted were forced to relocate to Doha and Damascus.[25] By the end of 1997, the pressure Hamas was under meant that its suicide operations began to recede as it reverted to focusing on its social infrastructure.[26]

In 1999, the Oslo Accords' five-year deadline expired inconclusively, and that same year Labor candidate Ehud Barak ousted Benjamin Netanyahu in the Israeli general elections. A decorated soldier and former minister of defense, Barak's victory raised hopes that he could resuscitate the faltering peace process.[27] Throughout the peace talks of the 1990s, Israel's settlements had expanded against a backdrop of growing Palestinian frustration, aggravated by Israeli closure and zoning policies that severely undermined the Palestinian economy, weakened its labor markets, and physically separated the Gaza Strip from the West Bank.[28] Hamas was not swept up in the prevailing optimism following Barak's election and maintained that jihad was the only way the Palestinian territories could be liberated.[29]

Abdel Aziz Rantissi was a vocal proponent of this alternative strategy. A pediatrician who had been educated in Egypt, Rantissi had resided in Gaza as a refugee after 1948 and had joined the brotherhood in the 1970s. He had quickly risen to its upper echelons and was one of the handful of men who had sat with Yassin that night when Hamas was created. As PLO negotiators traveled to Egyptian Red Sea resorts to meet with their Israeli counterparts, Rantissi promoted Hamas's "alternative to the [PLO's] path of surrender, and that is the alternative of resistance."[30] Hamas's vision was portrayed as one that would yield "liberation, pride and dignity," while the PLO's policies of negotiations conformed to a "life of humiliation [under] a despicable occupation," witnessed through a Palestinian Authority that remained committed to security coordination with Israel.[31]

Despite this rhetoric, the weakened movement did not carry out any attacks as the diplomatic talks between Barak and Arafat restarted. Noting this unusual calm, leaders explained that while the movement's consultative council decided when to escalate or cease fire, Hamas's military wing followed its own tactical considerations, designing and executing operations autonomously and clandestinely.[32] This separation distinguished the visible leaders of Hamas's political wing from the military arm. In this manner, Hamas's politicians engaged in daily politics without compromising the resistance project.[33] Infrequent operations therefore did not necessarily indicate a shift in strategy. In an interview in Gaza, Rantissi elaborated, stating that "resistance can achieve much [without military operations] by safeguarding its fiery roots, foiling the enemy's stability in Palestine, preparing *al-umma* [the Muslim community] to awaken from its slumber and preventing further concessions" from the PLO.[34]

Hamas's opposition was vindicated in May 2000, when Ehud Barak unexpectedly decided to withdraw Israel's occupying forces from south Lebanon after years of explosive confrontations with Hezbollah.[35] The swiftness of Israel's retreat in the absence of a peace agreement with Lebanon left the impression that it was pressured to let go of the territory because of Hezbollah's armed struggle. Hamas hailed the success of the "Lebanese model" as proof that resistance was the only way to liberate Palestine.[36] It compared this to the PLO, which it described as a weak and frail institution that "jubilantly welcome[s] the resumption of peace talks, despite their conviction that every new chapter is . . . a new temptation for Zionist intransigence."[37]

Given this stance, it was therefore no surprise to Hamas that Arafat agreed to participate in the much touted Camp David Summit, planned for July 11–25, 2000.[38] Camp David was a last-ditch effort by President

Bill Clinton's administration to secure peace between Israelis and Palestinians.[39] Coaxed by Barak's aspiration to move beyond incremental peacemaking toward a comprehensive settlement, Clinton hosted what amounted to a grand gesture to end the conflict. Arafat expressed a great deal of skepticism that this could be achieved. Yet he was cajoled into attending and was promised not to be held responsible in case of failure. As the PLO negotiating team traveled to the wooded presidential retreat north of Washington, D.C., Yassin in Gaza called on the Palestinian delegation "to return to the resistance trench."[40]

Negotiations unfolded under Clinton's personal mediation. Challenging a long-held Israeli policy to maintain Jerusalem as Israel's undivided capital, Barak contemplated its division. His offer, however, dictated that Palestinians would have no sovereignty over the Old City and the site of al-Aqsa Mosque, both located in East Jerusalem where Palestinians were seeking to build their capital. Israel's proposal fell far short of minimum Palestinian demands for sovereignty over East Jerusalem or the right of return for refugees, both issues that lie at the heart of the Palestinian struggle.[41] To the ire of Clinton and the Israelis, Arafat walked away and was instantly lauded a hero in the streets of the West Bank and the Gaza Strip. His rejection of the Camp David proposal had a powerful effect on Israel's political landscape: it weakened the left, strengthened the right, and was perceived as proof that the Palestinians rejected peace. After the talks, Barak infamously declared that Israelis had "no partner" in peace. Following the failure of the summit, and seemingly with it any prospects for maintaining the peace process, Hamas called on the PLO "to join our people, return the Palestinian house to order and unite on a comprehensive jihadist project for our struggle."[42]

THE SECOND INTIFADA

Very soon after the collapse of the Camp David Summit, the leader of the opposition Likud party, Ariel Sharon, decided to visit al-Aqsa Mosque compound in Jerusalem's Old City. Al-Aqsa is the third-holiest mosque in Islam and is housed on the compound referred to by Jews as the Temple Mount, a holy site of great importance in Judaism. Accompanied by more than one thousand security officers on September 28, 2000, Sharon strolled through the grounds of this deeply charged space to assert the inviolability of Israeli sovereignty in the area.[43] Even without his entering the mosque, Sharon's visit to the contested site was sufficiently provocative so as to spark the eruption of the Second Intifada.[44]

After years of Palestinians enduring a stalled peace process, the hope that the Oslo Accords had initially generated among them had given way to deep resentment. Over the course of the Oslo years, Palestinian quality of life and economic development had been severely degraded as a result of Israel's heavy-handed policies and its fragmentation of the Palestinian territories into increasingly isolated silos surrounded by ever-expanding Jewish-only settlements.[45] Furthermore, while Barak's offer at Camp David was being touted by the Israeli and American leadership as generous and far-reaching, it merely demonstrated to Palestinians the width of the gap between their basic demands and what Israel was ready to offer.

In its first few days, the uprising was reminiscent of the First Intifada. Palestinians took to the streets with stones, light arms, and Molotov cocktails to face the Israeli army with its full range of weaponry. Rapidly, however, the Second Intifada (referred to as the al-Aqsa Intifada given its birthplace) militarized. The Israeli army fired between twenty-eight and thirty-three thousand bullets per day against Palestinian stones and light arms throughout October, strategically using disproportionate force to break up protests.[46] Ever the tactician, Arafat moved to harness the bubbling anger on the street. On October 8, he chaired a meeting with PLO factions in Gaza to coordinate activities. In a rare show of unity, for the first time in its history Hamas was represented.[47] Less than a week later, 350 prisoners, including many Hamas and Islamic Jihad members, were released from Palestinian Authority prisons where they had been held under security coordination measures. Israel interpreted this move as Arafat giving the green light for military operations to commence, an abdication of his responsibility to safeguard Israel's security and a reversal of the PLO's commitment to renounce terrorism.[48]

By the end of October, the Second Intifada's first suicide bombing was carried out by Islamic Jihad, resulting in no deaths. Much like the First Intifada, Islamic Jihad, the smaller military offshoot of the brotherhood that had sparked Hamas's formation, was an early instigator in the uprising. In the next three months, two other suicide bombings were executed, neither lethal. These attacks were not claimed by any faction. Aside from Islamic Jihad, the other early instigator from the Palestinian side was Fatah Tanzim, a decentralized movement that had split from Fatah in the mid-1990s.[49] Tanzim's military wing, al-Aqsa Martyrs Brigades, was occasionally aided by operatives from Arafat's presidential guard and the Palestinian security forces, exacerbating suspicions of Arafat's involvement in the armed struggle.[50] By November, Israel had initiated its use of extrajudicial targeted assassinations, carrying out twenty-five before the end of the year, killing ten Fatah and six Hamas members, as well as ten bystanders.[51]

With the intifada expanding, Hamas's publications hailed "the divine intervention" that had derailed the diplomatic process.[52] The movement inundated the streets with daily communiqués, coordinating resistance activities and calling for strikes.[53] Yet for all its impassioned rhetoric, Hamas's militarization lagged behind other factions.[54] Its military wing, al-Qassam Brigades, was allegedly engaged in lighter operations, including stabbings, canister explosives, hand grenades, and ambushes. Those were narrated to full effect in its mouthpieces, where articles reported that Hamas's fighters had "entered the intifada in force and [had already given] the enemy—army and settlers—a taste of death."[55] Publications claimed that attackers were left unidentified for fear of reprisal. Articles often embellished the ferocity of these operations while accusing Israel of underreporting their impact to quell the Israeli public's panic.[56] There was also a constant promise of future escalation. In an interview with Sheikh Yassin, the leader stressed "the intifada will evolve into militarized resistance, and al-Qassam's revenge is only a matter of time."[57] By the end of 2000, al-Qassam released its first leaflet to the people in Gaza glorifying "the martyrs of our righteous people, who have . . . faced with their bare chests and stones the oppression and terror of the sons of pigs and apes."[58]

Despite these claims, Hamas's actions in the first six months of the uprising were relatively minor. During this time, Israel focused its response on Arafat and his party, Fatah. Hamas's slow militarization failed to support its self-representation as the driver of the intifada and threatened its legitimacy as a resistance faction rooted in jihad.[59] By way of explanation, Yassin pointed to the damage the movement had suffered due to security coordination in the 1990s.[60] Alongside such tactical considerations, however, Hamas's leaders alluded to another fear to explain their slow military response. The movement suspected that Arafat would use the intifada to "invest the blood of martyrs" for a better negotiating position with Israel.[61] Hamas's publications speculated about the PLO's desire to eventually "cash in" on the uprising by returning to the negotiating table with a strengthened position.[62]

Consequently, Hamas's leaders debated whether to participate in the uprising or abstain, lest they play into Arafat's hands.[63] For Hamas, the intifada was not simply a means to strengthen the Palestinian negotiating position. Its publications portrayed the uprising as the new phase of Palestinian nationalism, after the PLO's ostensibly defeatist integration into a futile peace process. Hamas's publications presented the intifada as "the sole Palestinian, Arab and Islamic strategy able to end the occupation and stop its expansion into Arab and Islamic regions."[64] Rather than a blip on the diplomatic path, the uprising was seen by Hamas as final proof of the demise of the peace process and of the futility of the PLO's chosen path. Publications proclaimed that "al-Aqsa Intifada crushe[d] with stones the settlement process" and united the Muslim nation behind resistance.[65] As Hamas's spokesman explained, after the Oslo Accords had "interrupted the natural evolution of Hamas's Islamic jihadist program," the Second Intifada marked its resumption.[66]

Hamas's leaders articulated early on what their vision for this new phase of Palestinian nationalism entailed. As Rantissi explained succinctly, "I am not saying that the intifada will lead to the complete liberation of Palestinian land from the river to the sea. Still, this intifada [can . . .] achieve the same accomplishment as Hezbollah in south Lebanon; complete withdrawal from the West Bank, the [Gaza] Strip and Jerusalem without giving up on 80% of Palestine."[67] If that could not be achieved by force, Hamas's leaders reintroduced the prospect of a ceasefire, as they had done previously, noting their willingness for a long-term ceasefire if Israel ended its occupation.[68] Before Hamas had even properly militarized in the intifada, Rantissi issued a leaflet noting that "Hamas and Islamic Jihad may agree to a temporary ceasefire, for a set time period such as ten years, during which the Palestinian people can create their own state within the 1967 borders, with Jerusalem as its capital, without giving up one inch of historic Palestine."[69]

Hamas's statements indicated both that its military operations during the Second Intifada were limited to the goal of liberating the occupied territories, rather than to the destruction of Israel, and that the movement was ready to end violence in return for an end to the occupation. In this way, Hamas accepted the notion of a Palestinian state on the 1967 borders, much as the PLO had done before it, without conceding the goal of liberating historic Palestine by recognizing Israel. Hamas saw itself postponing the full liberation of Palestine to a future battle, the responsibility for which it placed with the wider Arab and Islamic worlds.[70] Like the PLO before it, Hamas regionalized the uprising, addressing the "Arab and Islamic Fronts" in all its leaflets.[71] Placing al-Aqsa at the heart of the intifada, Hamas highlighted the Islamic world's responsibility to safeguard Jerusalem as it called for solidarity protests and the cutting of diplomatic relations between Israel and Arab countries, as well as for financial, military, and diplomatic support.[72] While both Hamas and the PLO limited their immediate goals to the liberation of the occupied territories, Hamas was clear that force was the only way liberation could be unconditional. The movement's publications explained that diplomacy only meant the "return of these lands with truncated sovereignty, subservience to the occupier, distortion of the question of Jerusalem and without the rights of refugees," as the Camp David Summit had clearly shown.[73]

As the intifada got under way, Ehud Barak tendered his resignation and called for general elections. On February 6, 2001, Ariel Sharon was elected Israel's prime minister with a landslide vote in a resounding statement that the Israeli electorate extended a mandate to the government to deal with the Palestinian question militarily. A deeply controversial figure within Israel itself, Sharon was despised by Palestinians as he had built a military and political career rooted in destroying Palestinian nationalism.[74] His ideal outcome for Israel entailed the pacification of the Palestinian territories and their inhabitants, subjugating them to Israeli rule without conferring any collective political rights. His vision for Israel was often interpreted as aiming to secure maximum Palestinian territory with minimal Palestinian inhabitants in an effort to sustain Israel's demographic reality as a Jewish-majority nation.[75] Before his political comeback as prime minister, he had been publicly disgraced for leading the Israelis into the disastrous 1982 invasion of Lebanon. Sharon was often referred to by Hamas and other factions as the "butcher of Sabra and Shatila," in reference to the grisly massacre of at least eight hundred Palestinian refugees in the Lebanese Sabra and Shatila refugee camps during his tenure as defense minister.[76]

Sharon's election had far-reaching consequences. Hamas, as well as Palestinians more broadly, took his victory to mean that the Israeli public was not looking for peace.[77] This dispelled any suspicions Hamas may have harbored regarding the PLO's intentions to resume negotiations. With Sharon's election, the intifada quickly transitioned into a war of attrition. On his first day in office, Sharon launched "Operation Bronze," promising to return security to Israel within one hundred days. Operation Bronze fortified the emergency measures that Barak had taken. The occupied territories were segmented into sixty-four distinct military units where the Israeli army was deployed, home demolitions and bulldozing of Palestinian land was expanded, and targeted assassinations increased.[78] Sharon's actions accelerated the militarization of Palestinian factions that was already underway. Less than a month after he entered office, Hamas carried out its first suicide operation since the beginning of the uprising. On March 4, 2001, a Hamas suicide bomber detonated his explosives in Netanya, Israel, resulting in three deaths and sixty-six injuries.

BALANCE OF TERROR

Hamas rapidly became the central instigator of armed operations against Israel. Al-Qassam adopted what it referred to as a "Balance of Terror" approach: in return for the brutal and indiscriminate killing of the elderly, women, and children, "now, the Zionists also suffer from being killed. . . . Now Israeli buses have no one riding in them and Israeli shopping centers are not what they used to be."[79] Balancing terror was a tool for Hamas to deter Israeli attacks by forcing Israel to anticipate inevitable retaliation.[80] Both fronts locked horns in an increasingly deadly spiral.

Israel maintained its focus on the Palestinian Authority rather than Hamas. In the spring of 2001, Sharon authorized the deployment of F-16s against the Palestinian security infrastructure throughout the West Bank and the Gaza Strip, the first use of such measures since 1967.[81] Bombing Israel's counterpart in security coordination underscored Sharon's dismissal of the Palestinian Authority and his shift toward unilateralism. For Sharon, Arafat was at best inconsequential and at worst an instigator of violence. Against Israel's military arsenal, suicide bombing became a way for Hamas to mitigate the asymmetry of power. On May 18, 2001, less than two months after its first operation, Hamas carried out a second suicide mission in Netanya. Elaborating on the "philosophical premise" underlying the balance of terror, Hamas's magazines wrote that "Zionist invaders are able, with their vast military and their limitless American support, to attack, destroy, decimate. But in return, they cannot protect themselves from being targeted, from providing safety and security to their people, who now live in an un-precedented state of horror, fear, and panic."[82]

Around this time, on May 21, the Mitchell Report was released. Headed by US senator George Mitchell, the report had been commis-sioned to investigate the causes of the uprising and suggest recommenda-tions for preventing escalation and resuming negotiations. The Mitchell Report called for the immediate halting of violence, a comprehensive effort by the Palestinian Authority to prevent terrorism, and an end to settlement activity by Israel. Central to the report's findings was that both parties needed to take measures in parallel to return to diplomatic engagement. Sharon rejected the premise of parallelism. Comforted by an American administration under George W. Bush that was unwilling to step into Israeli-Palestinian diplomacy after Clinton's debacle, Sharon effectively brushed the report aside and maintained his military response to the uprising.[83] Arafat, in contrast, accepted the report. Although the Palestinian Authority's ability to decisively control the violence was by that point questionable, the report nonetheless presented an opportunity for Arafat to reap diplomatic gains from the uprising.

Similar to Sharon, Hamas rejected the notion that both Israel and the Palestinians had to act concurrently through a mutual cessation of fire.[84] It argued that such framing was misleading given that it appeared to arbitrate between two warring parties, not between an occupier and an occupied.[85] In a memo circulated after the report's release, Hamas elaborated that "this crisis is not between two neighboring warriors. . . . In reality it is the aggression of an oppressive occupation on an un-armed population. . . . The occupation itself is the highest form of ter-rorism, violence and aggression."[86] Hamas's publications condemned the implicit "equalization of power" that they inferred from demand-ing that both parties cease violence: that was akin to "compar[ing] the victim to the executioner, the murderer to the murdered."[87] Hamas in-sisted that to end violence, the occupation itself had to be dismantled. Its own attacks were portrayed as self-defense against the inherently vio-lent nature of the occupation.[88]

Hamas's conviction was that suicide bombing could ultimately compel Israel to relinquish its hold on the territories.[89] Ceasefires were only offered in return for such a concession.[90] Hamas's leaders had no interest in reducing violence solely for the possible cessation of settlement activity and a return to the situation prior to September 28, 2000, when the intifada erupted. Until the end of occupation could be achieved, Hamas's publications proclaimed, "martyrs w[ould] create earthquakes underneath Sharon's feet."[91]

True to its word, in the early summer of 2001 Hamas launched its "Ten Bombers" campaign.[92] The movement announced that it had deployed ten bombers who had already infiltrated into Israel. Hamas bred fear by defining the specific number of operations that were to be executed. After every attack there was a known number of remaining operations to follow and those could occur at random, in quick succession or separated by months of horrified expectation. Hamas employed traditional tactics that sensationalized this countdown, including the release of videos of "martyrs" describing their operations and promising others to come. Between May and July 2001, Hamas carried out five suicide bombings, more than all other factions combined. The largest was its attack on a nightclub in Tel Aviv on June 1.[93] The attack killed sixteen Israelis and injured more than eighty. Because of its location, this attack shocked the Israeli public. Hamas celebrated the ensuing chaos and focused on Sharon's inability to maintain the security he had promised.[94]

Hamas's suicide bombings were only one element of its military arsenal, but they were the most important. Despite international and local condemnation, suicide operations were viewed by Hamas as the single most effective weapon to achieve deterrence and derive concessions from Israel.[95] Given the clear impact they had on Israel's social, economic, and political life, they were seen as more powerful than other operations. Hamas's publications stressed their significance and reported that there was an increase in the number of young Palestinians seeking to be "recruited" as they boasted that suicide bombings had been adopted by other groups.[96] Simultaneously, Hamas diversified its resistance techniques. The "ten bombers" mission coincided with the "from martyrs to mortar fire" campaign that Hamas leaders championed.[97] This entailed firing rockets from the occupied territories into Israeli settlements as well as into Israel. The first of these rockets was fired from the Gaza Strip on April 1, 2001. Hamas viewed these operations as relatively ineffective compared to suicide bombing, while noting some benefits, including lower Qassam losses.[98]

Israel took measures to escalate as well. Sharon commissioned his security committee to draft military plans for the full invasion and military reoccupation of the West Bank and the Gaza Strip, including urban centers that the Oslo Accords had ostensibly placed under the Palestinian Authority's control. Even though Hamas's militarization was notable, Israel remained focused on the Palestinian Authority and plans were made for the complete destruction and disarmament of the administrative government and its security forces.[99] Despite this preparation, Israel was compelled to suspend the implementation of its expansive invasion because of a lack of support from the Bush administration, which remained committed to the Mitchell Report.[100] Nonetheless, Sharon demanded that Arafat secure the Palestinian front for six weeks of absolute calm—what he referred to as "not a single act of stone-throwing."[101] Sharon's demand replaced Mitchell's recommendations of a parallel de-escalation with a sequential formula, where the onus was on the Palestinians to control the uprising before Israel was obliged to cease settlement activity or rein in its military operations. Compelled to act, Arafat mobilized to restrain the resistance front, creating tremendous tension among the factions.[102]

In response to Sharon's granting the Palestinian Authority this grace period, the resistance factions matched the offer with one of their own. A joint press release by al-Qassam and al-Aqsa Brigades issued a day later stated that if Sharon could give a window of opportunity before threatening to escalate against the Palestinians, "then we give the Zionist street an opportunity to say its word, to demand from its government to stop terrorism, murder, assassinations . . . and to withdraw from our land. In return, we will stop all martyrdom and armed operations in the occupied land of 1948."[103] Hamas's offer of a ceasefire, as with others before it, reiterated the movement's readiness to end its operations in return for Israel ending the occupation. As its spokesman had previously explained, Hamas strategically targeted both Israel and the occupied territories in its effort to liberate occupied land.[104] In this ceasefire offer, Hamas differentiated between attacks within Israel and those within the occupied territories, further reinforcing its readiness to uphold the 1967 border. While it offered to end the former, Hamas excluded operations within the West Bank and the Gaza Strip from bargaining as they were regarded as a natural response to the occupation.[105]

Hamas's offer of a conditional ceasefire led to reduced operations by the movement in the second half of June 2001. Until absolute calm was reinstated, however, Sharon ensured Israel's military grip would not be loosened, as targeted assassinations persisted.[106] On July 31, 2001, Israel assassinated two Hamas leaders in the West Bank city of Nablus, killing four other Hamas members and two children in the operation.[107] Describing the Nablus attack as a turning point in Israeli policy, whereby targeted assassinations expanded to include political members, Hamas called on Sharon to "assume responsibility" for his actions.[108] A week later, on August 9, 2001, Hamas carried out an enormous suicide operation at the Sbarro Pizzeria in the middle of Jerusalem, killing fifteen and injuring more than ninety. Hamas's decision to break the calm on its military front and launch this attack was strategic. Primarily, it gauged that its constituents favored retaliatory operations at this time given the hardship they were enduring under Sharon's military doctrine.[109] The attack was also timed to derail diplomatic initiatives that were beginning to gather pace after the Mitchell Report.[110] The horrific nature of the Sbarro bombing prompted Sharon to mobilize on the same day. The Israeli army attacked the Palestinian security forces in the West Bank and the Gaza Strip and invaded the northern West Bank city of Jenin. The operation killed five Palestinian officers and injured thirty-one civilians. By the end of the summer, attrition appeared ongoing. Although Arafat had accepted the Mitchell recommendations, both Hamas and Sharon seemed ready to sustain violence until their counterpart yielded ground.

SEPTEMBER 11

The reality on the ground was entirely altered on September 11, 2001, when civilian jetliners that had been hijacked by al-Qaeda crashed into the World Trade Center in New York City, the Pentagon in Washington, D.C., and into an open field in Shanksville, Pennsylvania.[111] The balance that had sustained the war of attrition between Israel and the Palestinians almost immediately shifted in Israel's favor. The 9/11 tragedy paved the way for President Bush's "War on Terror," a key foreign policy doctrine that would have transformative implications for the Middle East. Alongside the nebulous formulation of waging war on an undefined specter of terror, Bush's doctrine included another objective: democratizing the Arab world. Drawing on the rhetoric of a "clash of civilizations," the Bush doctrine divided the world between good and evil, extremists and moderates, as it sought to promote Western liberal and democratic values in countries as varied as Iran, Iraq, and Syria, as well as their regional proxies.[112]

Overnight, the Second Intifada came to be presented as Israel's "War on Terror." Arafat condemned al-Qaeda's actions, as did Hamas, which de-escalated its military front.[113] Nonetheless, evoking the U.S.-Israeli special relationship, Sharon portrayed the Palestinian armed factions as Israel's own al-Qaeda. In a post–9/11 Bush administration, this analogy carried a great deal of weight. Conflating what constituted "Islamic extremism," Hamas's bombs in Jerusalem were described as being one symptom of global "Islamic terrorism."[114] This parity overlooked Hamas's articulation that its military operations were perpetrated solely to end Israel's illegal occupation. It also elided Israel's own lethal operations within the occupied territories, thereby highlighting the violence of only one of the two parties involved in attrition. Israeli media focused on isolated incidents of Palestinians celebrating the 9/11 attacks and on statements by al-Qaeda that linked its crimes to the Palestinian cause.

With the commencement of the War on Terror, attempts to present Palestinian armed struggle as a constituent of global terrorism were formalized. Less than a month after 9/11, the Popular Front for the Liberation of Palestine, a secular Palestinian faction, assassinated Israel's tourism minister Rehavam Ze'evi in retaliation for Israel's assassination of its own leader Abu Ali Mustafa. This attack prompted Israel to launch an "all-out war on the terrorists," a major offensive on October 18 to reoccupy most urban centers in the West Bank. Alongside this operation, Sharon stepped up attempts to get an American green light to remove Arafat from power.[115] This was not immediately forthcoming. Rather, the Bush administration took a decisive move that broke with previous American presidents. Counter to Sharon's aspiration to destroy the prospect of Palestinian statehood, President Bush delivered a speech at the United Nations in November where he recognized the Palestinian right to self-determination in a state of their own. Concurrently, the Bush administration embraced Sharon's rhetoric and asserted Israel's right to defend itself against terror.[116]

Sharon's intensive and violent military surge within the occupied territories triggered another wave of suicide bombing by Hamas and Islamic Jihad. From the beginning of Israel's escalation until December 12, 2001, Hamas carried out eight attacks, including major missions in Jerusalem and Haifa. While some of these were responses to Israel's assassination of Hamas leaders, others were a continuation of the attrition marking relations between the two parties.[117] Nonsuicide attacks also proliferated. Paradoxically, while Israel's offensive targeted the Palestinian Authority's infrastructure, pressure was sustained on the increasingly ineffectual Arafat to rein in the factions.[118] The Palestinian Authority moved to arrest Hamas members and attempted to place both Yassin and Rantissi under house arrest in Gaza, causing violent clashes between Hamas's supporters and Arafat's forces.[119] Hamas condemned the Palestinian Authority's readiness to undermine the armed struggle in accordance with American and Israeli demands, particularly at a time when it was itself under attack.[120] "There is no way the popular resistance of the Palestinian people will be stopped as long as one inch of our land is occupied," Rantissi declared. "Why is there no talk of the crimes of Jewish terrorism, from the murder of children in Khan Yunis [in Gaza] to the assassinations of tens of the purest of our people?"[121]

Hamas's defiance was unsustainable. Attempts to justify its actions as being a response to a lethal occupation, and all its offers of ceasefire, were inconsequential as Sharon launched another "war against terror" in December 2001.[122] This entailed expansive air strikes against the Palestinian security posts in Ramallah and Gaza City as the Israeli army mobilized around the governmental headquarters to place Arafat under confinement. The dangerous escalation on the Palestinian Authority prompted Hamas to draw back its military wing. On December 9, alongside al-Aqsa Brigades and Islamic Jihad, Hamas issued a statement promising "to stop all martyrdom and armed operations within the lands occupied in 1948" for a week.[123] The memo went on to explain that this was "despite the Zionist terroristic and criminal operations against the Palestinian people. [This measure is taken] so as not to give the enemy the chance to undo the Palestinian front."[124]

Hamas's declaration in 2001, a few months after the 9/11 attacks, was its first offer of a unilateral ceasefire, whereby the movement suspended its operations even in the face of Israel's relentless incursions. It was also the first of many occasions that Hamas would be forced to stop its armed struggle to defuse an explosive domestic situation.[125] Hamas's decision was controversial internally given the widespread popularity of armed struggle against Sharon's policies.[126] Al-Qassam made clear that they were unwilling to go one step further in their commitment, stressing that the ceasefire must be seen not as weakness but as a genuine tactic to mitigate domestic unrest.[127] Hamas's leaders in the West Bank reiterated the distinction between Israel and the occupied territories, asserting that resistance within the latter was valid against an occupation that was illegal under international law.[128] Even with this proclamation of legitimacy, other leaders still called for suspending operations within the West Bank and the Gaza Strip while "Hamas monitors the international and Arab situation."[129] Hamas's publications praised the movement as the "guardian of Palestinian unity" and portrayed this step as one that "deflected the spark of civil war" while the Palestinian Authority had allegedly been "driving the street towards conflict."[130]

On January 3, 2002, a few weeks after Hamas's unilateral ceasefire began, Israel seized in the Mediterranean Sea a marine vessel, *Karine A*, which was loaded with weapons ostensibly heading to the Palestinian territories. Despite Arafat's denial of any prior knowledge of the vessel, the ship's capture was seen within Israel as final indictment of his role in promoting terrorism.[131] Sharon declared Arafat a "bitter enemy to Israel," one who had dealings with "terrorist states" such as Iran, from where the weapons allegedly originated.[132] For the Bush administration, *Karine A* was the final straw. Embracing Israel's War on Terror, the United States severed contact with Arafat and extended what amounted to a carte blanche for Israel to sideline the Palestinian president and destroy Hamas itself.[133] With American approval, as Hamas largely held fire Israel launched two major operations in February and March 2002, operations "Rolling Response" and "Colorful Journey." The Israeli army carried out full ground and air invasions against Palestinian villages and towns, and used its military arsenal to make expansive incursions into densely populated refugee camps throughout the West Bank. Close to three hundred Palestinians, thirty-one members of the Israeli army, and nine Jewish settlers were killed. The operations strengthened the siege on Arafat, underscoring suspicions that Sharon had decided to topple the leader.[134]

Unlike previous Israeli operations, these two primarily targeted Hamas, a development that vindicated the movement's aspirations to be the vanguard of resistance and substantiated its claims that its attacks had been particularly painful to Israel.[135] While Hamas's rationale, articulated through its balance-of-terror framework, was that its violence deterred Israeli offensives, these operations suggested otherwise. Hamas's extensive campaign of suicide bombing throughout 2001 had failed to elicit any concessions from Israel.[136] Instead, its actions merely increased the ferocity of Sharon's determination to crush the Palestinian struggle. Asked whether Hamas was still committed to its goals from the intifada, emerging leader Khaled Meshal answered from his base in Doha, "Absolutely. We do not claim that the project of resistance as it currently stands is able to resolve the conflict with the Zionist enemy and liberate all of Palestine."[137] Nonetheless, he went on to say he had full confidence that the resistance "is capable of achieving liberation, step by step . . . through the accumulation of accomplishments, and the draining of the enemy's security, economy, and morale."[138]

This view mirrored the PLO's steadfast dedication to armed struggle in the 1960s and 1970s. Unlike the PLO's early days, however, Hamas had already limited its immediate military goal to the liberation of the occupied territories rather than of the entirety of the land of historic Palestine. Nonetheless, cracks had begun to appear in Hamas's military strategy given Israel's uncompromising response. As Israel's operations unfolded in the first two months of 2002, Hamas did not carry out any suicide bombings, the main marker of its militarization at the time, despite loud threats of retaliation from its military wing.[139] Compared to eight suicide bombings by other factions, including al-Aqsa and the Islamic Jihad, Hamas relied on nonsuicide operations, resulting in nine Israeli deaths.[140] Efforts to reduce its overreliance on suicide bombing were becoming more prominent. By the end of January 2002, the firing of "Qassam 2" rockets into Israel was featuring more frequently in the movement's publications.[141] Hamas presented these activities as "permissible" within its ceasefire framework given Israel's continued offensive.[142] On March 9, at the height of Israel's second operation, Hamas carried out its first suicide bombing since its unilateral ceasefire in December. The Jerusalem attack, which killed eleven and injured fifty, took place at Café Moment, about one hundred meters from the prime minister's residence.

Against the backdrop of Sharon's operations and Hamas's resistance, a post–9/11 reality was starting to take shape. The Bush administration had begun formulating plans to deal with the "axis of evil," which it deemed as countries that supported terrorism, including Iran, Iraq, and North Korea. As part of those plans, the United States pushed for the removal of Iraqi leader Saddam Hussein from power in an effort to advance its democratization agenda in the Middle East. Saudi Arabia, a major American ally, naturally became a key stakeholder in these discussions. As the United States formulated its plans toward Iraq, Saudi Arabia pointed to the volatility that Israel's continued intransigence had on the region. Taking its own measures to end the violence of the Second Intifada, Saudi Arabia offered what became known as the Arab Peace Initiative (API) in March 2002.[143] This was an ambitious and far-reaching proposal for full normalization between Israel and Arab states in return for the former's withdrawal from the occupied territories and the establishment of a Palestinian state in the West Bank and the Gaza Strip, with East Jerusalem as its capital.

The PLO accepted the proposal, which was due to be discussed during the Arab League's summit in Beirut on March 27.[144] With its offer of normalization, the API fell far short of Hamas's conviction that resistance could force Israel to relinquish the occupied territories without additional Palestinian concessions, in the form of recognizing the State of Israel.[145] Despite cracks beginning to appear in its military strategy, Hamas remained committed to armed struggle as a means of defending against further Palestinian concessions. Khaled Meshal would later explain that this commitment was because of a deep-seated conviction that even if Hamas turned to nonviolent resistance or diplomatic engagement, Israel would not ease its attacks.[146] Israel's dismissal of Hamas's unilateral ceasefires merely strengthened these convictions. On the same day that Arab leaders (without Arafat, who remained confined by the Israeli army) convened in Beirut to discuss this proposal, a Hamas suicide bomber detonated explosives at a Passover Seder dinner in Netanya's Park Hotel in Israel, killing sixteen celebrants and injuring ninety.[147] The chosen timing clearly underscored Hamas's strategic use of suicide bombing to derail peace initiatives. The context in which the attack took place, at a holy evening for the Jewish community, horrified the international community.[148] The military plans that Sharon had shelved in the first year of the intifada were pulled out. These became the foundations for "Operation Defensive Shield," which the Israeli army launched the next day.

Defensive Shield was a powerful incursion aimed at "dismantling the terrorist infrastructure." By the time it concluded, Sharon had effectively pulverized the economic, social, and political fabric within the West Bank and the Gaza Strip.[149] In two months, more than three hundred Palestinians and thirty Israeli soldiers were killed. Hundreds of Palestinians were injured, thousands detained, and thousands of homes demolished. Most of the Palestinian Authority's infrastructure as well as Arafat's headquarters in Ramallah were destroyed. As the offensive unfolded, suicide bombings took place almost daily. Hamas's operations were less frequent than those carried out by Islamic Jihad or al-Aqsa Brigades, but they were by far the deadliest. Driven by several factors, the attacks were aimed at derailing the API, retaliating against Israeli operations, and disproving Israel's claims that Defensive Shield was a success.[150] Maintaining its balance-of-terror rhetoric, Hamas's publications reveled in the perception that "resistance shakes the army's base and Sharon's popularity is in the sewers. Al-Quds (Jerusalem), Netanya and Tel Aviv are ghost towns."[151]

Hamas's leaders were fully supportive of escalating the uprising. Rantissi declared, "The continued presence of the occupation means the continued presence of resistance. . . . We either raise the white flag and surrender, or we resist."[152] Justifying Hamas's use of suicide bombings to target civilians, Yassin stressed that "the entire Israeli population is militarized and contributes to the murder of Palestinians."[153] Throughout May, after Defensive Shield ended, suicide bombing persisted from Islamic Jihad and al-Aqsa Brigades. On June 18, Hamas carried out another major attack in Jerusalem, killing nineteen and injuring fifty at the Patt Junction. That same day, Israel launched "Operation Determined Path." Yet again, rather than deterrence, by June 2002 Hamas's actions had caused Israel to escalate its response and avoid any political engagement with the resistance factions or the PLO. Instead of taking measures to end Israel's illegal occupation, the main catalyst for Palestinian armed struggle, Sharon adopted an iron fist to crush the resistance and sustain the occupation. Through Determined Path, Israel reoccupied all the major cities in the West Bank, placing close to seven hundred thousand Palestinians under twenty-four-hour curfew. Sharon's cabinet also began putting together plans for building a wall to separate the Palestinian territories from Israel.

U.S. ROADMAP FOR PEACE

On June 24, 2002, President Bush gave a speech in the Rose Garden of the White House. As his administration was preparing for regime change in Iraq, the president looked farther west than Baghdad. Building on his UN declaration a few months earlier, Bush gave further support to the prospect of Palestinian self-determination. After close to two years of weathering the full might of Israel's army, the Palestinian Authority had been utterly decimated. Out of its remnants, Bush sought to create a democratic Palestinian state. Doing away with the Mitchell Report's recommendations, Bush embraced Sharon's stance and adopted a sequential, rather than a parallel, approach to the conflict.[154] This meant that the ever-elusive goal of Palestinian statehood and Israel's withdrawal were made contingent on reforming the Palestinian Authority to produce leaders who "do not support terrorism."[155] The Rose Garden speech was put forward for ratification by the Quartet, an international organization comprising the United States, the European Union, the United Nations, and Russia, tasked with meditating a resolution to the conflict. While diplomatic wrangling on the final draft of the roadmap would take another year, Bush's speech immediately formalized attempts by the United States for Palestinian regime change.

This important American development prompted the besieged Palestinian leader Yasser Arafat to issue a one-hundred-day reform plan.[156] Fatah, Hamas, and other factions met in Cairo to discuss the reform efforts as well as ceasefire options given the pressure that the Palestinian Authority was under. Hamas's leaders rejected what they called the "Americanized reform."[157] Still, they calmed their military front unilaterally, even though Israeli troops were still deployed, as they engaged in these talks.[158] A few hours before Hamas purportedly agreed to formalize a prospective ceasefire, Israel assassinated al-Qassam's leader Salah Shehadeh on July 22. He was killed alongside thirteen others, including nine children.[159] Palestinians saw what they called the "Gaza massacre" as proof that Israel was intent on undermining the delicate transformation the Palestinian Authority was trying to orchestrate.[160] "It is true that Hamas was preparing to announce a ceasefire in exchange for some conditions," Yassin confirmed, "but after the Gaza massacre and this crime against humanity, there is nothing but jihad."[161]

This chain of events, to be repeated several times in the following months, indicated both Hamas's readiness to suspend its armed struggle while engaging in domestic negotiations as well as Israel's commitment to sustaining a military disposition toward the Palestinians. It is unclear whether a ceasefire would have in reality been implemented successfully. Domestic discussions were fraught as Hamas's leaders, both inside and outside the territories, refused to end suicide bombings within Israel unless Sharon ended his attacks on Palestinian civilians. This created significant tension with Arafat, who was being forced to control the violence.[162] Maintaining his iron fist, Sharon paid no credence to ceasefire calls from Hamas or other factions. In the absence of absolute pacification, Sharon took unilateral measures to strengthen Israel's hold on the territories while forcefully quashing any form of protest.

As Hamas resumed its suicide bombings in the fall of 2002, a few days after Shehadeh's assassination, Israel relaunched extensive operations in the territories aimed at isolating Arafat, initiating demolition operations of his compound and purging cities, towns, and villages of

Palestinian fighters. Sharon's escalation ran counter to America's attempts to calm the conflict ahead of its planned invasion of Iraq in March. Images of Israeli tanks surrounding the Palestinian governmental headquarters rattled America's regional allies. The Bush administration called on Sharon to pull his forces back and allow Palestinians to complete their reform effort.[163] The American push to produce a government that ceased armed struggle heightened tension between the Palestinian Authority and the resistance factions, as well as within Fatah itself as the old guard was being swept aside in favor of American-chosen candidates.[164] Hamas's publications viewed these American policies as indicative of attempts to turn the intifada into "a Palestinian-Palestinian struggle."[165] Violent confrontations on the streets in Gaza between Hamas and the Palestinian forces were perceived by many as the precursors to a civil war.

The volatility of the situation hastily prompted the convening of the Cairo National Dialogues in November 2002, a forum for the various Palestinian factions to negotiate under Egyptian mediation. As Hamas engaged in these talks, for a period of almost five months, it again suspended its suicide bombings.[166] Ideologically, it had every incentive to retaliate, as Israel provocatively carried out twenty-six assassination attempts specifically targeting its members during that time. Instead, its engagement in the dialogues momentarily took precedence. Yassin affirmed from the outset of the talks that "martyrdom operations" had only been temporarily (tactically, not strategically[167]) suspended to allow talks to proceed.[168] Hamas's leaders maintained that "the movement is fully united. . . . [The movement's] position in the inside and outside is to hold onto the strategy of resistance and to refuse [any talk] of ceasefire" as long as the occupation persisted.[169]

The Cairo talks were fraught. Hamas rejected the notion that armed struggle must end as a prerequisite for the withdrawal of Israeli troops. It viewed this formulation as one that legitimized Israel's military action by suggesting it was merely a response to armed struggle rather than a natural extension of the occupation.[170] Hamas's leaders put forward compromises. Rather than cease its armed struggle unilaterally, Hamas maintained that it would stop targeting Israeli civilians in return for mutual guarantees from Israel.[171] The Egyptian mediators overseeing these discussions communicated Hamas's offer to Israel's defense minister, Shaul Mofaz, seeking a commitment for a mutual ceasefire. Hamas's conditions were rejected, however, effectively ending the Cairo talks in January 2003 without an agreement.[172]

In March 2003, a US-led coalition invaded Iraq. Within a spectacularly short amount of time, the coalition completed its mission of removing Saddam Hussein from power. Underscoring the link that the Bush administration had drawn between Iraq and the Palestinians as dual beneficiaries of democratization, major restructuring of the Palestinian Authority was completed that same month. Mahmoud Abbas, a senior PLO leader who was favored by the Americans and Israelis for his explicit condemnation of armed resistance, became the Palestinian prime minister. This post was created specifically to curtail Arafat's presidential power. Abbas was made responsible for peace negotiations, despite Arafat remaining chairman of the PLO. The new cabinet under Abbas was in line with America's vision of leaders "who do not support terrorism." Abbas was a product of the recalibrated PLO, a person committed to the notion that self-determination would have to come through diplomatic negotiations with Israel.

Soon afterward, on April 30, the Quartet finally ratified Bush's Rose Garden speech and released it as a set of parameters entitled the "Roadmap for Peace in the Middle East." Major elements from Bush's speech had been strongly debated behind the scenes. Instead of adopting the sequential approach, whereby the onus fell on Palestinians to de-escalate the conflict, the final version of the roadmap offered a more balanced strategy. While Palestinians were charged with completing their reform effort, preparing for elections and ceasing violence entirely, Israel was obliged to freeze settlement activity and withdraw its troops to the lines they had accommodated prior to the eruption of the intifada. In one of his first moves in office, Abbas adopted the roadmap as a framework for ending the conflict.[173] Sharon's Likud party accepted the document with fourteen reservations that effectively emptied it of any content. Harking back to Bush's Rose Garden speech, Sharon indicated that before resurrecting the diplomatic process, Palestinians must first dismantle "the terrorist organizations."[174]

Sharon's obstructionism meant that the peace process ambled forward, ostensibly under the rubric of the roadmap but in practice through a sequential formula.[175] To meet the Palestinian obligation of ending violence, Abbas reached out to the factions to restart and formalize the ceasefire discussions that had been ongoing since Cairo. Tanzim's al-Aqsa Brigades indicated that they would be willing to accept a unilateral ceasefire if instructed to do so by the newly reformed Palestinian Authority.[176] Hamas resented pressure to end armed struggle while Israel maintained its presence in the territories.[177] To compel the movement to consider his offer, Abbas approached it from the standpoint of political attractiveness: Hamas needed to engage with the Palestinian Authority to play a role in the nascent political framework or risk marginalization in the face of the roadmap.[178] Keeping its finger on the trigger, Hamas begrudgingly acquiesced to ceasefire discussions. It did this with a great deal of disdain. Hamas's publications noted that Abbas made a critical mistake in delegitimizing Palestinian resistance and "equating this proud and brave struggle with 'terrorism.'"[179] Hamas also reminded Abbas that Bush's idea of liberation and democratization led directly to the American invasion of Iraq.[180]

A senior Hamas leader from within the territories, Ismail abu Shanab, played a crucial role in these ceasefire discussions over the summer of 2003.[181] He elicited a willingness from Hamas to "test" a conditional ceasefire for a few weeks, where the onus would be on Israel to release prisoners, stop home demolitions, and end targeted assassinations.[182] This was a clear sign that Hamas's demands had been tempered: instead of seeking the end of occupation in return for the ceasefire, Hamas appeared to debate the prospects of controlling its military operations in return for Israel ending its own targeting of Palestinian civilians. As the ceasefire's architect, Abu Shanab stated that Hamas would not embarrass Abbas if the prime minister was able to get a promise from Sharon to end assassinations and raids.[183] In a summit in June in the Jordanian coastal city of Aqaba, Abbas noted that discussions with Hamas had advanced to serious levels. He stated that although Hamas would not demilitarize, he was twenty days away from reaching an agreement with the movement to commence a ceasefire.[184] Abbas stressed the need for Israeli cooperation before finalizing his agreement with Hamas. He implored Sharon to meet his obligations under the roadmap as he tried to shatter the illusion that violence could be controlled while Israel maintained its aggressive policies and settlement building.

On June 10, just a few days after the Aqaba summit, Israel carried out an assassination attempt on Rantissi in Gaza, once again ensuring that no ceasefire could emerge. Claiming "utmost provocation," al-Qassam called for the mobilization of their cells against all Israeli civilians. "The Israeli message has been received and they should await the response," stressed Yassin, while Rantissi issued a statement in which he declared that "the term 'ceasefire' no longer exists in Hamas's dictionary."[185] Hamas swiftly executed a suicide attack in Jerusalem on June 11, one day following the assassination attempt. The attack, not far from the Mahane Yehuda market, killed seventeen and injured close to sixty. The speed and scale of Hamas's retaliation suggested that the movement had indeed been actively restraining earlier attacks as negotiations with the Palestinian Authority proceeded. They also underscored Sharon's success in provoking responses from the movement, thereby ensuring no progress could be made on the political front.

The assassination attempt failed to derail the domestic discussions entirely. After negotiations with other factions, Hamas announced on June 29 the suspension of all operations against Israel for a period of three months in return for an Israeli cessation of aggression, lifting the siege on Arafat, and releasing prisoners.[186] Hamas's ceasefire took hold unilaterally as Israel continued incursions into Nablus, Jenin, and Hebron and maintained targeted assassinations, despite Abbas's protestations.[187]

Claiming a desire to safeguard domestic unity, Hamas maintained its commitment to this "counter-intuitive" ceasefire, which unlike earlier ones extended to both Israel and the occupied territories.[188] Other factions followed suit.[189] Hamas justified this decision as a "warrior's break," taken at a time when the PLO had adopted the roadmap, and as an effort to prevent a domestic clash.[190] To ensure the ceasefire was not seen as implicit acceptance of the roadmap, Hamas stressed that this initiative was unilateral and extended no legitimacy to Israel.[191]

The ceasefire held for July and August as the Palestinian Authority maintained pressure on Hamas to either disarm or extend the ceasefire by three additional months, which the movement rejected.[192] Concurrently, Abbas accused Israel of failing to address its responsibilities under the roadmap.[193] Israel's continued presence in the territories allowed Hamas to capitalize on "Israeli breaches" to deflect pressure to disarm.[194] Citing more than eight hundred such breaches, Yassin warned that "patience was limited."[195] Hamas's perceived breaches were an exaggeration; in fact Israeli targeted assassinations dropped significantly following Hamas's declaration of a ceasefire. But without progress on the peace front and with no signs that Israel might be willing to relinquish its hold on the territories, talk of disarmament was futile.

On August 15, Israel assassinated a leader of Islamic Jihad.[196] Four days later, in alleged defiance of leaders' commitment to the ceasefire, a renegade Hamas bomber carried out an attack in Jerusalem killing twenty-three people and injuring more than one hundred.[197] Following Hamas's operation, the Israeli army was immediately given instructions to target Hamas's leadership and all its cells in response. A few days later, Israel assassinated Abu Shanab, the force behind Hamas's adherence to the ceasefire.[198]

The unilateral ceasefire had lasted just under two months. Rather than the Jerusalem attack, Hamas viewed Abu Shanab's assassination as the ceasefire's breach, what it called the "grace shot" that ended this initiative.[199] The Palestinian Authority worked to restore calm by calling on all factions to disarm and abide by the ceasefire, to no avail.[200]

Stressing that his credibility had been undermined by Israel's intransigence and America's refusal to pressure Israel to formally implement
the roadmap, Abbas resigned on September 6. Three hours later, Israel
carried out an assassination attempt on Sheikh Yassin. Days later, it
launched another assassination attempt on Mahmoud Zahhar, a senior
Hamas leader based in Gaza, killing his son but failing to kill him. Fatah
decried this escalation and called for international intervention.[201] It
was too late. Hamas retaliated in "self-defense" with two suicide attacks
on September 9, one in Jerusalem's German Colony and the other near
a Rishon Letzion army base.[202]

This rapid escalation demonstrated that both parties had been
standing on alert waiting for the ceasefire to falter. By this point, the
Palestinian political establishment had entirely collapsed and Sharon
had expanded his control over the territories. His actions had weakened
Abbas and the leadership that had been ushered in under Bush's reform
vision. By the end of the intifada's third year, Hamas, like the PLO before it, had come to understand the limitations of its armed struggle in
the face of Israel's military might and noted how its operations failed
to elicit either concessions or deterrence given Sharon's iron fist. Rather
than prompting an end of the occupation through attrition, Hamas instead was repeatedly compelled to cease its armed struggle to safeguard
the domestic front and to ease Israel's military retaliation. All its attempts to negotiate a reciprocal ceasefire that would remove civilians
on both sides from the line of fire were brushed aside by Sharon, forcing Hamas to offer unilateral ceasefires. Yet even with such initiatives
on Hamas's part, Israel obstructed tactics that would move the parties
toward a political settlement, and Abbas failed to elicit any concessions
from Israel.

Hamas's military strategy reflected a fundamental misunderstand-
ing on its part regarding how Israel would react to its operations.[203]
In response to suicide bombing, Israel presented Palestinian resistance
broadly, and Hamas specifically, as a form of international terrorism,
akin to al-Qaeda, bent on its destruction. Any sense that Hamas was

using armed struggle to end Israel's occupation of Palestinian land was circumvented, as Israel positioned its response to the Second Intifada as an existential battle.[204] Hamas's violence allowed Sharon to begin unilaterally reconfiguring the structure of occupation to strengthen Israel's hold on the Palestinian territories in a manner that did not compromise the state's security. Meanwhile, Hamas's deep doubts that Israel would ever willingly let go of the territories were strengthened, as were its suspicions regarding the PLO's ability to secure political gains through negotiations.[205] By the third year of the intifada, Hamas began looking for ways to make its project of jihad both more effective and more sustainable.

CHAPTER THREE

THE POLITICS
OF RESISTANCE

"Like all Israeli citizens, I yearn for peace," Israel's prime minister Ariel Sharon told the crowd gathered at the Fourth Herzliya Conference, in the coastal city north of Tel Aviv, on December 18, 2003.[1] Israel remained committed to the Roadmap for Peace, Sharon asserted, but "the concept behind this plan is that only security will lead to peace—and in that sequence. Without the achievement of full security—within the framework of which terrorist organizations will be dismantled—it will not be possible to achieve genuine peace." In the absence of Palestinian willingness to end terrorism, Sharon announced from his podium, "Israel will initiate the unilateral security step of disengagement from the Palestinians," redeploying its army along new security lines and reducing the number of Israelis settled within Palestinian areas such as the Gaza Strip. Simultaneously, Sharon stated, "Israel will strengthen its control [of other areas] in the Land of Israel which will constitute an inseparable part of the State of Israel."

Sharon's unexpected declaration coincided with Israel's hasty construction of a separation wall that disconnected it from the West Bank. The wall, which Israelis refer to as the "security fence" and Palestinians as the "apartheid wall," is an imposing eight-meter-high, seven-hundred-kilometer concrete structure fitted with electronic fences, barbed wire, and highly sophisticated surveillance equipment.[2] Israel ostensibly built this wall to prevent Palestinian suicide bombers from entering its cities. Rather than building the wall on Israeli land or along the 1967 borders, however, the structure snaked through Palestinian territories, unilaterally seizing more than 10 percent of the West Bank, including whole neighborhoods around East Jerusalem as well as major settlement blocs that were integrated into this de facto border.[3] The structure split whole Palestinian villages in half and had an immediate effect on the freedom of movement for Palestinians within the occupied territories. Jewish settlers living illegally within the same land continued to be linked into Israel through exclusive Jewish-only highways and by-pass roads. On July 20, 2004, the International Court of Justice issued an advisory opinion ruling that the wall was illegal, to no effect.[4] With Israel's planned disengagement from the Gaza Strip and the construction of advanced "security" infrastructure, Sharon was actively restructuring the framework of Israel's occupation.

A MOMENT OF REBIRTH

Sharon's speech in Herzliya left little room for doubt regarding his impetus for disengagement from Gaza. The prime minister stated explicitly his plan to withdraw eight thousand Jewish settlers residing in the Gaza Strip as a precursor to strengthen Israel's grip over areas that "constitute an inseparable part of the State of Israel," namely the West Bank. In the year after Israel withdrew its eight thousand settlers from Gaza and small outposts in the West Bank, twelve thousand Israelis settled elsewhere in the West Bank.[5] The Palestinian West Bank is ideologically more vital for Israel than the Gaza Strip, as it has several Jewish holy sites, including the Tomb of the Patriarchs in Hebron. Israeli politicians, particularly right-wing leaders such as Ariel Sharon who opposed the notion of a Palestinian state, often refer to the West Bank by its biblical name, "Judea and Samaria," reinforcing Israel's religious and nationalistic attachment to these territories.

By the time Sharon made his surprising announcement, close to four hundred thousand Jewish settlers were living illegally in the occupied territories.[6] These settlers were protected by Israel's army and by a powerful military occupation that repressed the indigenous Palestinian residents of those areas. Offering to pull back settlers from Gaza promised to reduce Israel's exposure to Palestinian resistance from the coastal enclave and save significant security expenditure, given that the eight thousand settlers controlled up to 30 percent of the strip.[7] The remaining 70 percent housed 1.8 million Palestinians. More important than security was Sharon's plan to remove these Palestinian inhabitants from Israel's direct jurisdiction. This allowed the state to maintain its control over the territories of the West Bank and East Jerusalem, with their 2.5 million non-Jewish inhabitants. By letting go of Gaza's population of 1.8 million, Israel would no longer fear that the Palestinian population under its control could offset Israel's character as a Jewish-majority nation even as it continued to hold on to the occupied territories.[8]

Sharon's plan was the latest in a long series of measures Israel had taken to separate the Gaza Strip from the West Bank. Although policies of isolation reach back to the 1950s, more contemporary measures began with the "soft quarantining" of Gaza after the signing of the Oslo Accords, including the gradual tightening of border crossings and the construction of barriers to geographically sever the coastal enclave from Israel.[9] Sharon's initiative also reflected a continuation of his use of the pretext of security to unilaterally consolidate Israel's grip on the territories while avoiding any form of political engagement with the Palestinians.[10] This goal was explicitly articulated by Sharon's top aide, Dov Weisglass, in an interview several months later. "The disengagement is actually formaldehyde," Weisglass told the Israeli newspaper *Haaretz*. "It supplies the amount of formaldehyde that is necessary so that there will not be a political process with the Palestinians."[11]

Overlooking these cynical motivations, President George W. Bush's administration lauded Sharon's initiative and portrayed him as an Israeli leader who was willing to make tough concessions, such as withdrawing Israel's illegal settlements from some Palestinian territories, in the pursuit of peace.[12] Hamas understood these calculations and voiced early reservations regarding Israel's disengagement. Analysts writing in its mouthpieces characterized Sharon's plan as a long-term strategy aimed at the annexation of the West Bank, offsetting Gaza's demographic challenge and undermining the chances of a Palestinian state within the 1967 borders.[13] Hamas's leaders stressed that Israel's withdrawal did not mean liberation. Osama Hamdan, Hamas's representative in Beirut, stated, "Withdrawal will not give the Palestinian people their freedom in Gaza. We must not forget that the enemy will continue to surround the Gaza Strip and will be in full control of all its borders."[14]

Concurrently, Sharon's announcement appeared to offer another resounding affirmation of the success of armed struggle, similar to Ehud Barak's withdrawal from south Lebanon three years prior. While acknowledging their reservations, Hamas and other resistance factions were vindicated by the prospective disengagement. Hamas's publications celebrated that Sharon was compelled to let go of Gaza because of the strip's historic legacy of resistance. In their view, armed struggle had forced Israel to regard Gaza's occupation as too costly.[15] Senior leaders such as Abdel Aziz Rantissi noted that so long as the withdrawal did not "come at a price"—by forcing Palestinians to make political or security concessions—then it should be interpreted as a victory for resistance.[16]

Precisely to undermine such claims, Sharon's declaration coincided with powerful operations aimed at ensuring Israel withdrew from a position of strength, without having to coordinate its disengagement with its Palestinian counterpart. In late 2003, Sharon launched "Operation Still Water," an assault on refugee camps in the West Bank aimed at "dismantling the terrorist infrastructure."[17] Hamas similarly resumed its operations. In January 2004, a female suicide bomber carried out a Qassam/Aqsa Brigades joint attack at the Erez border crossing between Israel and Gaza, killing four.[18] Alongside suicide bombing, as the separation wall rose Hamas developed its firepower and launched missiles into Israeli towns and settlements.[19] Rockets were seen as powerful tools in terms of the psychological impact they had on Israelis—by augmenting their awareness of the conflict—and their ability to mitigate the effects of the wall.[20]

Another joint suicide bombing in the southern Israeli city of Ashdod on March 14 provided Sharon with the excuse to ramp up his military operations through "Operation Continuous Story." This was a month-long campaign of raids and assassinations in which the Israeli army was authorized to act without limitation to eliminate "top figures from all terror organizations."[21] Within a week, this full-throttled assault over the skies of the Gaza Strip achieved its declared goal in spectacular fashion. On March 22, Hamas's paraplegic cofounder, Sheikh Ahmad Yassin, was returning from dawn prayers in the mosque near his house. As his companions walked by him down the street, Israeli warplanes flew overhead and dropped bombs on the wheelchair-bound man. The targeted assassination, brutal in its simplicity, killed him, his two bodyguards, and nine bystanders, marking the highest-profile attack on Hamas to date.

Yassin's assassination sent shock waves through the movement. Hamas mourned its founder, whom it regarded as a man of vision, a figure who had worked diligently to counter the Zionist threat to the Palestinian and Islamic way of life by fostering an Islamic cultural and educational renaissance in the brotherhood's early years.[22] Given previous near-misses, Yassin's death was not politically debilitating, as Hamas had taken measures to decentralize decision-making outside the occupied territories as early as the 1990s.[23] The impact of the loss was felt more along the lines of Hamas's internal moral compass. The quiet sheikh was seen as a patriarch, a fatherly figure for many of Hamas's top brass as well as for the rank and file who sought his sermons and guidance. He was also a central figure in Palestinian politics more broadly and had been respected by all factions, as was evident from the mobilization of support following his assassination.[24] His soft power in the region was apparent as condolences from all factions and across the Arab world flooded in.[25] In eulogies, Yassin was described as the "Guardian of National Unity," a "Man of Dialogue," and the "*Umma*'s Martyr."[26]

President Bush supported Israel's preemptive right to defend itself. Reinforcing the analogy with 9/11, Bush said that had he known who the airline hijackers were prior to the attack on the twin towers, he similarly would have moved against them.[27] Others questioned Israel's choice of target, noting that Yassin had been moderate compared to hardliners within Hamas.[28] The distinction between moderate and radical was heavily criticized by the movement, which insisted there was no such classification internally. As it reiterated, even a "moderate" member called for the liberation of the entirety of Palestine, a position seen as radical by the West. Nonetheless, Hamas's leaders acknowledged that Yassin had been a pragmatist. As the first leader to have offered Israel a ceasefire in the 1990s, he had repeatedly issued subsequent offers to Israel, which were brushed aside.[29]

Hamas's publications described Yassin as a vocal advocate of Palestinian unity as well as a supporter of armed struggle.[30] His death had a significant impact, one that appeared to push Hamas toward a greater affinity for the ideas he had embodied.[31] The movement viewed his assassination as an opportunity for factions to coalesce around his vision and form an "Islamic and national front against Israel."[32] In his words of commemoration, Khaled Meshal said that "Sharon did not target the body, for Sheikh Yassin's body was frail. Rather, he targeted the Sheikh's vision, his resistance vision, the one which every fighter believes in."[33] Meshal, now settled in Damascus as a senior leader in Hamas's political bureau, went on to inject a note of hope, remarking that "the assassination of Sheikh Yassin is a moment of rebirth for Hamas, a turn that will move the resistance into a new chapter. This turn will mark the beginning of the collapse of the Zionist entity."[34]

After the bloody summer of 2003, the Palestinian political establishment lay in tatters. President Yasser Arafat remained in confinement and the new government under Mahmoud Abbas's premiership had already collapsed. Yassin's assassination had taken place against the backdrop of vigorous domestic discussions. Factions had gathered again in Cairo as the intifada entered its fourth year to reassemble some semblance of a Palestinian national framework to guide the struggle. Informed by its inability to militarily force Israel into concessions, Hamas sought an alternative strategy to safeguard the fixed principles that it viewed as central to the Palestinian struggle.[35] Like the PLO before it, Hamas defined these as the refusal to concede the land of historic Palestine, a commitment to the right of return of refugees, and the safeguarding of resistance. Through rounds of talks in Cairo, Hamas's leaders made a case for a "joint national program of resistance" to revive the Palestinian struggle. This was described not simply as short-term military gain, what it had focused on during the first three years of the uprising, but rather as a holistic vision that encompassed political and social dimensions.[36]

With Yassin's death, leaders hypothesized that Israel's intention was to provoke and to derail the movement's nascent political ambitions by creating a "stubbornness" and a desire within Hamas to respond to the assassinations of its most valuable leaders.[37] There were, expectedly, promises of retribution. Abdel Aziz Rantissi, a senior leader in Gaza, for instance, aggressively called on all factions to retaliate, assuring Israelis that they should expect a response in the near future.[38] Hamas also capitalized on Yassin's assassination to argue—falsely[39]—that Israel had singled it out as the preeminent resistance faction.[40] Despite this rhetoric, suicide attacks did not follow. Hamas had been battered over the course of the intifada, through both Israeli operations and the crackdown by the Palestinian Authority.[41] It was also struggling with financial constraints as the United States and the European Union had frozen its international fundraising infrastructure through President Bush's War on Terror legislation.[42]

With the loss of their founder, Hamas's leaders reflected on the movement's internal state of affairs as it embraced the "moment of rebirth" that Meshal alluded to. This happened at a paradoxical time, when Hamas was militarily quite weak yet enjoying enhanced popularity, due both to the Palestinian Authority's weakness as well as to the surge of sympathy following a series of assassinations and assassination attempts on its top cadre.[43] The movement had also gained unprecedented access to domestic political discussions through its participation in the negotiations in Cairo, seen as vital given its role in the Second Intifada. Within this new context, intensive sessions within Hamas's consultative council began following Yassin's death. These were rumored to be difficult as a number of prospective candidates vied to replace Yassin.[44] Within a relatively short period of time, Abdel Aziz Rantissi was elected as Hamas's leader within the territories and Khaled Meshal became the head of Hamas's political office abroad. Dismissing rumors of tension, Rantissi embarked on defining Hamas's future path.[45]

There was insufficient time to assess Rantissi's redirection of Hamas. On April 17, less than a month after Yassin's killing, Israeli Apache helicopters flew over Rantissi's car in Gaza City and fired Hellfire missiles, successfully assassinating the newly appointed leader. The air raid also killed his son and the two bodyguards who were in the car with him. Unlike Yassin, Rantissi's tough stance on Israel was reflected in the manner that Hamas's publications eulogized him. Statements declared him "the symbol of resistance," the "Zionist's worst enemy," and "the Lion of Palestine."[46] Al-Qassam along with other military wings called for retaliation against Israelis "anywhere they can be found" and promised a "thunderous" response as they called for the full mobilization of all their cells.[47]

Rather than push Hamas into a military confrontation, however, publications suggested that al-Qassam was at a crossroads "between preserving its base infrastructure and strike force and continuing its strategic choice of jihad and resistance."[48] The scale of these assassinations would have normally elicited devastating attacks from Hamas. Yet if anything, the elimination of one of the most vocal advocates of armed struggle seemed merely to accentuate Hamas's diminishing readiness and ability to execute suicide bombings. Hamas justified its inaction by referring to earlier instances when al-Qassam responded to assassinations of its members only after significant time had passed, as was the case with Yehya Ayyash's assassination in 1996.[49] To be sure, violence spiked between Israelis and Palestinians, but Hamas's retaliatory operations still fell short of its past performance during the Second Intifada.

As the movement reflected on its military strategy, internal discussions proceeded to elect a new leader. Suspicions abounded that Rantissi's replacement in Gaza was Mahmoud Zahhar, a surgeon and one of the founders of the Islamic University in Gaza. Zahhar was one of Hamas's earliest members, and during the deportation of Hamas's members to Lebanon in the early 1990s, he had acted as the deportees' spokesman. In many ways a hardliner, Zahhar had been targeted for assassination numerous times, including in an attack in 2003 that killed his son. Heightened secrecy was accompanied by a sharpened fear that there was a rise in the number of collaborators within the territories, a phenomenon that Hamas worked hard to counter.[50] With these suspicions, Rantissi's immediate successor in Gaza was left unnamed. Meanwhile, given that he resided abroad, Meshal became the visible face of Hamas's leadership.

The blows dealt to Hamas coincided with rising tension in the Palestinian territories. As Israel initially scheduled its disengagement from the Gaza Strip for February 2005, the necessity for Palestinians to resolve domestic issues and discuss prospects for postwithdrawal governance gained urgency. Fatah was dealing with its own internal crises as the nascent leadership that had emerged pursuant to the Bush administration's reforms clashed with older incumbents, precipitating numerous armed confrontations in Gaza. Public frustration with the Palestinian Authority's corrupt leadership was also expanding.[51] These fault lines, along with Israel's imminent withdrawal from Gaza, coalesced to crystallize an opportune moment for Hamas to adopt a more mainstream political role—what analysts in its publications described as the most prominent rise in its history.[52]

NASCENT POLITICAL CONSCIOUSNESS

In the spring of 2004, Palestinian factions began coordinating for the day after Israel's withdrawal from Gaza. From his confinement in the Ramallah headquarters of the Palestinian Authority, President Arafat stressed the importance of integrating the resistance factions into the political process to limit domestic strife.[53] Against the backdrop of increased turmoil in Fatah, a fault line had emerged between the resistance factions and Yasser Arafat on the one hand, and the emerging US-chosen "reformers" such as Mahmoud Abbas on the other.[54] Hamas's leaders concurred with Arafat's sentiment, stressing that factions must negotiate a uniform national agenda ahead of Israel's disengagement.[55] As Musa Abu Marzouq, Meshal's deputy who resided in Cairo, noted, "National unity for us is the highest priority."[56] Talks persisted against the backdrop of Israel's expansive military operations and its insistence on unilateral disengagement.

On May 12, Israel launched "Operation Rainbow," in which it bulldozed whole areas, including civilian homes and refugee camps, between the Gaza Strip and Egypt to widen the buffer zone, killing forty-three Palestinians, wounding hundreds, and displacing thousands.[57] The European Union, the United Nations, and Egypt futilely called on Israel to cease its attacks to allow the Palestinian Authority to secure the Palestinian front ahead of withdrawal.[58] But heavy-handed tactics served Sharon domestically, where he presented his disengagement plan to a skeptical Knesset as the product of military strength.[59] Israel's unilateralism was also aided by international fears of a power vacuum in Gaza postwithdrawal.[60] Such concerns were shared locally. Egypt in particular mediated between the Palestinian factions as it sought a credible postwithdrawal governance framework that would maintain security on its borders and prevent skirmishes with Israel from the Gaza Strip.

Egypt's stance conflicted with Hamas's view that disengagement must not compromise the resistance effort.[61] Nonetheless, the movement participated actively in the talks. Meshal headed a delegation to Cairo where he planned to discuss two issues. The first entailed Hamas's relations with Fatah and the Palestinian Authority, given the latter's commitment to security coordination with Israel. These discussions were part of what was called the "Charter of Honor" between Hamas and Fatah that sought to deflect domestic clashes. The second covered preparations for postwithdrawal plans and focused on a document titled "Document for Governance of Gaza."[62] As Meshal elaborated in Cairo, Hamas viewed Israel's disengagement to be Hamas's entry point into the political establishment. Disengagement from Gaza was "considered an achievement for the path of resistance, not negotiations. Therefore, whoever took part in this path has the right to participate in the outcome."[63]

With this disposition, members of Hamas formulated strategies to regain control of the strip, alongside other factions, within three weeks of Israel's withdrawal by "enhancing security and instituting the rule of law."[64] Hamas adopted the banner of "partners in blood, partners in decision-making" during negotiations, a testament that it believed it had earned the right to become part of the leadership. Meshal was direct in stating that "[governance of Gaza] is our natural right and the right of all our people. We will not allow anyone to unilaterally take over the administration of the Strip."[65] In his view, "The Palestinian people will fill the vacuum quite naturally. We are a free people who can lead ourselves; we do not need an occupation to run our business. We will create a united national and democratic environment of the highest caliber."[66]

Hamas believed that its role in the Second Intifada had boosted its standing considerably and entitled the organization to a role in governance.[67] Through these domestic talks, it looked to leverage this newly developed clout, exhibiting a political consciousness in the process that although present, had not previously been so explicit.[68] Leaders focused on the premise of partnership, stressing their desire to share rather than lead governance in Gaza.[69] Ismail Haniyeh, who had acted as Yassin's assistant and who had gained a more prominent role in Gaza following Yassin's and Rantissi's assassinations, confirmed Hamas's commitment to the formation of a united political program to share governance responsibilities.[70] Hamas asserted the need for a "serious effort to arrange the Palestinian house, buttress participation in political decision-making, and let go of unilateralism," in reference to Fatah's historic dominance of the political establishment.[71]

A significant aspect of the Cairo talks entailed the need for municipal, legislative, and presidential elections to rebuild the Palestinian political body. Affirming Hamas's openness to the democratic process, as was already made clear in 1996, Hamas's leaders reiterated their support of elections. But as Mahmoud al-Zahhar noted from Gaza, elections would be for "the presidency of which system? The legislature of which system? As in, what is the political framework that we will be operating within? There are some who want this to be [the framework defined by] Oslo forever. That's madness."[72] Zahhar's questions touched on the central tension that had always shaped Hamas's engagement with the political system: it disapproved of the premise of the Palestinian Authority and the underlying Oslo Accords that had created it. Rather than being confined to the Palestinian Authority, national discussions needed to tackle the issue of reforming the broader political establishment, namely the PLO.

Hamas advocated that the PLO needed to be more representative by offering proportional representation for the various factions within and outside the occupied territories. This position alluded to a conviction held by Hamas and Islamic Jihad that proportional representation would guarantee them a powerful foothold within the PLO, one that reflected the following they had cultivated over the years. A strong base within the PLO would allow Hamas to revoke—or at least challenge— the concessions the PLO had made in 1988 and its ensuing dedication to the diplomatic process. In effect, Hamas was seeking to circumvent the Palestinian Authority and the American reform efforts that it felt would focus on governance within the territories and institutionalize Palestinian capitulation to the Israeli occupation. Instead, Hamas's leaders advocated for an indigenous reform of the overarching institutions overseeing Palestinian liberation.[73]

While Hamas participated in these talks, it withheld its suicide operations. This gave rise to speculation in the media of weakness and moderation. This was despite the fact that Hamas maintained rocket fire into Israel, which continued its widespread incursions into refugee camps as well as targeted assassinations. Zahhar dismissed these accusations, insisting that it was on the success of its military resistance that

Hamas's entire political platform was being constructed.[74] Highlighting that Hamas was undergoing significant internal change, Zahhar went on to say that "Hamas's program is witnessing an unprecedented revival. The measures of strength and weakness, including the number of new recruits into the movement, opinion polls regarding popular support and social activities carried out by the movement, amongst others, indicate exactly the opposite of what Hamas's enemies wish to portray."[75]

Hamas's focus on the virtues of suicide bombing and armed struggle even as it engaged in discussions aimed at political participation underscored that the two were not incompatible for the movement. Leaders presented Hamas as a party that could "marry" resistance with politics.[76] As if to reinforce this point, on August 31 Hamas carried out two consecutive suicide bombings in the southern Israeli city of Beersheba, killing sixteen and injuring eighty-two. These high-impact operations were allegedly planned in retaliation for Yassin's and Rantissi's assassinations nearly four months earlier. Underscoring Hamas's perception of resistance as a fundamental aspect of its political vision, these attacks bolstered its claims to being a resistance movement as its engagement in the political establishment advanced.[77] The Beersheba operation was the last suicide mission carried out by Hamas during the Second Intifada, as its armed struggle pivoted toward the persistent use of missiles as well as tunnel operations.[78]

Hamas's rockets provided ample justification for Israel's goal of withdrawing from a powerful position by sustaining its military operations against resistance factions.[79] In late September 2004, Israel launched "Operation Days of Penitence," an extensive and lethal ground invasion aimed at compelling Gaza's civilian population to pressure al-Qassam to stop its actions. The operation involved more than two hundred tanks and armored vehicles invading Beit Hanoun and Jabalia in northern Gaza, demolishing 195 Palestinian homes and killing eighty-six Palestinians (about a third of whom were civilians).[80] This operation enabled Sharon to drum up support for the disengagement in the Israeli Knesset. Despite pleas by Egyptian and Palestinian interlocutors for a negotiated withdrawal, Sharon remained committed to unilateral measures, armed with the conviction that there was "no partner" on the Palestinian side.

This self-fulfilling prophecy was rendered all the more acute with the unexpected and sudden death of Palestinian president Yasser Arafat on November 10.[81] The passing of a formidable and controversial figure in Palestinian politics initiated a clash that had long been in gestation between the various factions and figures competing for leadership.[82] For Hamas, it provided yet another major impetus driving its engagement with the political system. Arafat's death in the midst of a highly fragmented and vulnerable political environment cemented the movement's conviction that the Palestinian establishment had collapsed and merited rebuilding, particularly after the battering it had received during the intifada.[83] Hamas looked forward to the emergence of an autonomous leadership, one that could move away from the shadow of Israel and the United States in its formulation of national strategy.[84] Riven by internal divisions, Fatah also looked to fair and representative elections to appoint new leaders, yet disagreements inevitably led to tension regarding the choice of candidates.[85] For its part, Israel insisted that it would not interfere with the choice of emerging leadership as long as it did not "support terrorism."[86]

THE CAIRO DECLARATION

Yasser Arafat's death, after two years in confinement in a compound that had been bombarded by Israel's army, was symbolic of the state of Palestinian politics. After the third burial of a major leader in 2004, factions turned their attention to rebuilding their institutions. Municipal elections were the first point of departure. These were to proceed in four rounds in 2004 and 2005. The first took place in December 2004 and January 2005 in twenty-six districts in the West Bank and ten in the Gaza Strip. Hamas had historically always participated in municipal, student, and union elections as they complemented its extensive social and charitable arm. Through this participation, Hamas buttressed its grassroots credibility, maintaining a strong presence in institutions focused on local administration and municipal services while nurturing the connection to its popular base. Building on its message of reconstituting the incumbent leadership, Hamas ran under the banner of "Change and Reform."[87] Without being overtly political, this message leveraged widespread disapproval with the long-standing and pervasive corruption within the Palestinian Authority, long dominated by Fatah, and offered Palestinians the option of changing their leaders to opt for a new beginning.

On the campaign trail, Hamas exhibited political astuteness and aggressively promoted its candidates, many of whom were highly educated academics and professionals from the movement's political wing and member base.[88] It fought for various municipalities in open and fierce competition with Fatah. In elections in Gaza, for instance, Hamas raised banners stating, "The Choice: Qassam Rocket or a Policeman Protecting Israel," in a clear jibe at the Palestinian Authority's security coordination with Israel.[89] Hamas focused on undermining Fatah's political programs and highlighting their leaders' corruption.[90] Throughout the election cycle, the movement raised objections that its candidates were harassed by Israeli forces who continued to occupy the Palestinian territories. Despite such protestations, Hamas performed relatively well in the first round, winning 36.8 percent of the seats and 50 percent of the votes, relative to 38.9 percent and 32 percent respectively for Fatah.[91] This led the movement's publications to stress Hamas's continued popularity.[92] Clearly demonstrating Hamas's support in Gaza, the movement took control of seven out of ten councils there.[93]

Alongside this round of municipal elections, presidential elections were set to take place in January 2005. Hamas decided to boycott the search for a presidential candidate and kept with its traditional rhetoric that elections for posts within the Palestinian Authority merely legitimated the institution and produced a new cadre of leadership serving Israeli and American interests.[94] This stance conflicted with long debates Hamas was having internally regarding political engagement, which touched on upcoming legislative elections also associated with the Palestinian Authority.[95] Instead, rumors abounded that Hamas had no presidential candidates to field. Seven contestants ran in the elections, which culminated in a victory for Mahmoud Abbas, who gained 62 percent of the vote. Hamas's publications raved that the election was "custom-made" as it speculated on vote rigging and reported on pressure being placed on other viable candidates not to run.[96]

Abbas was the candidate favored to win by the United States, given his support of the Roadmap for Peace and his stance on armed struggle. Expectedly, shortly after the elections, Abbas underscored his conviction that Israel's disengagement from Gaza must proceed within the framework of the roadmap, ensuring Sharon could no longer claim the absence of a committed counterpart. As incoming president, Abbas faced three obstacles: disunity within his party; Sharon's refusal to deal with Palestinians as political counterparts; and Hamas's power.[97] Hamas's strong grassroots support was not lost on the incoming president given his tenuous hold on the political establishment. His commitment to diplomacy and his denunciation of resistance-as-terrorism against the backdrop of Sharon's intransigence were seen as treasonous by Hamas.[98]

In the movement's view, Abbas's responsibility was to reformulate the body politic so that it was inclusive of all factions and rooted in resistance. Hamas's popularity indicated that this sentiment could not easily be swept aside. In his new position, Abbas was indeed proactive in seeking to reform the PLO into a more representative and democratic framework. After his election, he immediately went to Gaza to try to secure a ceasefire from the resistance factions as he began negotiations on several fronts: internal reform, elections, and political participation.[99] Abbas's disposition opened the doors for Hamas to continue its internal debates regarding prospects for political engagement and even to formally consider joining the PLO.[100] Abbas successfully secured a one-month ceasefire from the factions, even as chronic disputes between him and Hamas persisted in light of their divergent views.

Hamas insisted that Arafat had passed away at a time when Palestinians were more besieged than ever, when US bias toward Israel under the Bush administration was undeniable, and when resistance was the only viable strategy. For Hamas, joining the PLO was contingent on "restructuring [it] so that it provides the people with a defined charter that serves the national cause."[101] Aware of Hamas's stance, Abbas sought Israeli confidence-building measures to demonstrate the virtues of negotiations. After the election, Abbas and Sharon resumed negotiations in the Red Sea resort of Sharm al-Sheikh, Egypt, to conclusively end the violence of the Second Intifada. During the talks, Sharon promised the eventual release of hundreds of Palestinian prisoners and the halting of targeted assassinations and home demolitions.[102] In return, Abbas expressed confidence that he could secure a commitment to stop military operations as he persisted in bilateral talks in Cairo with thirteen factions, including Hamas and Islamic Jihad, to formalize a longer-term ceasefire and agree on a framework for domestic power-sharing and an agenda for legislative elections.

Abbas's confidence initially appeared misplaced as Hamas and Fatah's al-Aqsa Brigades declared his verbal assurances to Sharon "not binding."[103] Given Abbas's commitment to the roadmap, it was understood that any move to stop armed struggle existed within the broader framework of disarming the resistance factions. Abbas and his supporters had also begun speaking of the monopolization of arms under the Palestinian Authority as the single governing entity in the territories.[104] Hamas was adamantly opposed to disarming or integrating its military wing into the Palestinian security forces unless the institution was reformed in a manner that did not undermine Hamas's capacity to wage armed struggle. This of course ran counter to the Palestinian Authority's commitment under the Oslo Accords to safeguard Israel's security. While being open to ceasefires, Hamas's fundamental belief in the righteousness of armed struggle against the military occupation remained unshakeable.[105] This conviction was strengthened by what Hamas interpreted as popular support for its tactics, particularly following the municipal victories in areas that had been heavily hit by Israeli firepower retaliating against Hamas's resistance.[106]

But despite Hamas's rhetorical opposition, a flimsy ceasefire took effect in February 2005. The movement's investment in domestic power-sharing discussions was evident by its decision to suspend rocket fire as negotiations unfolded. Providing insight into Hamas's negotiating position, Meshal asserted that "we will move as close to the Palestinian Authority in our political vision and domestic discussions as it moves towards Palestinian rights."[107] When asked whether slogans advocating participation in governance and elections undermined its role as a resistance movement, Meshal answered, "There is no conflict between this and that."[108] To end the occupation, Meshal said, Hamas would take all measures, including reforming the political establishment, participating in decision-making, and partaking in municipal elections. As he explained, "[These] are steps aimed at serving our main strategic goal, which is to rid ourselves of the occupation and to help the Palestinian people live a life which is aligned with resistance; a life which equips them for steadfastness and for the continuation of their long struggle till the occupation is removed from our lands."[109]

For Hamas, resistance naturally encompassed a political element, and the political arena was an extension of military policies, particularly after the failure of armed struggle to achieve its goals. Publications explained that Hamas was seeking to ensure the longevity of the intifada by moving beyond the battlefield. This came through efforts to gain constitutional legitimacy and work with other factions in policymaking and governance to institutionalize resistance as a national policy.[110] Musa Abu Marzouq had previously summed up Hamas's aspirations as "preserving the program of resistance. Despite [armed struggle] being in an ebb and flow, the political framework should be the continuation of resistance, the refusal to undermine it, to remove its arms, or to shackle it with unfair security arrangements."[111] While the PLO's past entry into politics had been premised on concessions, Hamas tethered its engagement in politics to the failure of negotiations and underscored the need to reject any further concessions from the Palestinian side, including any commitment to disarm the resistance factions or to halt fire.[112]

Such a role would provide political backing to Hamas's vision, as the movement would finally have a voice in crafting policy or blocking legislation it deemed harmful.[113] In essence, the movement continued to prioritize the fundamentals of the Palestinian struggle and to refuse what it perceived as the pacification inherent within the Palestinian Authority, with its focus on governance under the framework of the occupation in the elusive hope of statehood. Emotions ran high throughout the talks. Hamas warily eyed Abbas's deployment of security forces on the Israeli-Gaza border as the Palestinian Authority took measures to prepare for Israel's withdrawal. Hamas's publications noted this development with trepidation, asking, "The deployment of the security forces in Gaza, is the repetition of a bitter episode [of security coordination] or the beginning of a new chapter of reconciliation?"[114]

Naturally, Hamas suspected the former.[115] Its publications nonetheless declared that the talks were Hamas's opportunity to align the new leadership with its resistance-based program, given that Fatah was at its weakest point politically and that an administrative vacuum was in the making in Gaza.[116] Maintaining its refusal to commit to a full ceasefire without reciprocity from Israel, Hamas addressed the military calm it had initiated for the duration of the presidential elections and subsequent dialogues.[117] Meshal explained, "Our fingers are still on the trigger. . . . We have a right to defend our people and retaliate against the ongoing aggression. This [calm] is a Palestinian initiative aimed at serving a number of interests and dispelling some dangers, most paramount of which is Sharon's desire to push Palestinians into in-fighting."[118]

With the military calm in place, Sharon managed to secure Knesset approval for the disengagement plan and set a target of August 2005 as preparations continued between the Quartet and the Palestinian Authority to coordinate economic and civil postengagement issues. Around the same time, after three months of domestic talks, the Palestinian factions finally agreed on sustaining a ceasefire until the end of 2005 as they issued their closing statement in March. The "Cairo Declaration," as it came to be called, was a significant milestone and a declaration that quickly became the cornerstone of Hamas's engagement in the political realm. The declaration affirmed "the right of the Palestinian people to resistance in order to end the occupation, establish a Palestinian state with full sovereignty with Jerusalem as its capital, and the guaranteeing of the right of return of refugees to their homes and property."[119]

The Cairo Declaration formalized what Hamas's military disposition throughout the Second Intifada had alluded to: that the movement's immediate political goals were informed by the desire to create a Palestinian state on the 1967 borders. Without the ideological concession of recognizing Israel, Hamas had followed in the footsteps of the PLO decades earlier by accepting the notion of Palestinian statehood on a portion of historic Palestine. Perhaps more importantly in the context of domestic discussions, the Cairo Declaration formalized Hamas's entry into the political arena. The document explicitly stated agreement to "develop the PLO on bases that will be settled upon in order to include all the Palestinian powers and factions, as the organization is the sole legitimate representative of the Palestinian people."[120] Political representation within it was to be based on greater transparency, democratic principles, and pluralism. Agreement on reforming the PLO was a major milestone in Hamas's vision of moving beyond the Palestinian Authority's remit on governance to revive the broader national liberation struggle. The reformed PLO was to be an institution that represented the Palestinian people in their entirety and was committed to their basic national rights to achieve liberation.[121] A cross-factional committee to reform the PLO was created with the understanding that it would work toward the eventual integration of both Hamas and Islamic Jihad.[122]

Having secured a commitment from Abbas and the other factions to reformulate the PLO, Hamas's leadership completed its debates on whether or not it should participate in the upcoming legislative elections for the Palestinian Authority, initially set to take place in July 2005. As the wider national dialogues were ongoing, Hamas's various constituencies had been debating internally the prospect of participating in the legislative elections. Talks were lengthy and time-consuming since input from the leadership abroad, the representatives in the West Bank and Gaza, as well as the prisoners was required. Despite significant debate to address fears of legitimating the Palestinian Authority, members made a case for a greater political role in shaping the national agenda.[123] The movement's strong showing in the municipal elections had an impact on Hamas's leaders, particularly in Gaza, who came out strongly in favor of participation. Leaders abroad and in the West Bank gave more lukewarm reactions (and in cases like Hebron, actively objected), while the prisoners had mixed feelings.[124]

Hamas declared that the perceived demise of the peace process meant that its political participation could not be seen in the context of conferring legitimacy onto the Oslo Accords. In 1996, Hamas had boycotted the legislative elections for fear of legitimating the accords.[125] By the end of the Second Intifada, however, Hamas argued the Oslo Accords had failed. Resistance had also propelled the movement into becoming a more powerful political actor. Along with the prospects of reforming the PLO, it appeared that the entire political establishment was on the cusp of change.[126] At the end of these deliberations, Hamas's consultative council gave the go-ahead to take part in the legislative elections.[127]

Hamas's publications noted that this "represents political astuteness, as seen by the correct timing chosen to participate in Palestinian political life through elections and the ballot."[128] The movement's publications went on to say that elections are "the right [means of participation] to ensure proper reform and to fix the frail Palestinian establishment, turning it into a strong and secure presence to face a brute racist occupation."[129] In essence, the movement defined political participation as a "responsibility" to stop the Palestinian Authority remaining Fatah's "hostage" and to ensure that the establishment could be better equipped to resist the occupation rather than remain subservient to it. Hamas viewed its strong performance in the municipal elections as a platform from which it could launch dialogue with Fatah as an equal rather than a replacement. This approach was described as being true to Yassin's legacy, whereby Hamas sought to foster dialogue and rework the political model into a national framework that was accountable to all Palestinians. This would include the Palestinian refugees in the diaspora as well as Palestinians within the occupied territories.[130]

By mid-2005, Hamas had come to view its political success as validation of its resistance.[131] It rationalized that it would use the Palestinian Authority's legislature to steer Palestinian nationalism away from concessions and back toward the protection of basic rights.[132] Hamas's vision was to revive the legislature, which it believed had become increasingly ineffective and marginalized under Fatah's rule, and bring it back into a mainstream political role.[133] In so doing, the movement hoped to use it as a platform from which to defend the right of resistance, fight corruption, have fair elections, and ensure that comprehensive reform of the PLO would indeed be carried out.[134] In an interview with Mahmoud Zahhar, Hamas's leader asserted that "some of the challenges Hamas faces can be solved through elections. Hamas needs constitutional legitimacy to prove to those accusing it of terrorism that this is not so, and that the Palestinian people stand with it. The movement wants to participate to prove that its program is the optimal one."[135]

Political participation was seen as a natural progression of Hamas's growth and not as something that would jeopardize either its resistance or its Islamic faith. As Meshal explained, "Resistance is a comprehensive and integrated life," one that encompasses politics as well as the military.[136] Meshal rejected phrases such as "transformation into politics," insisting that as an opposition party Hamas had never been far from politics.[137] For Hamas, this endeavor was simply the political manifestation of its resistance strategy.[138] To effectively demonstrate the advantage of this position, Hamas's publications focused on the anxiety its decision was causing within Israel.[139]

The Israeli government as well as Abbas were indeed worried about Hamas's strong municipal performance. Shortly after the Cairo Declaration and Hamas's decision to participate in the legislative elections, the second round of municipal elections took place in May in seventy-eight districts in the West Bank and five in Gaza. Hamas won 35.4 percent of the seats and 33.7 percent of the votes, compared to 35 percent and 40.2 percent for Fatah, respectively.[140] Hamas's strong performance was even more impressive as it won fifteen out of eighteen municipal seats in the West Bank, taking over Fatah strongholds such as Qalqilya.[141] Rather than the presidential elections, Hamas saw these contests as the real measure of popular support.[142] Although the movement had performed well in previous such elections, at this point Hamas appeared to be at the height of its efforts to engage with the political establishment and these successes had a significant impact in concretizing its political aspirations.[143] With Hamas's strong showing in the second round of municipal elections, Sharon communicated his worries about Hamas's participation in the upcoming legislative elections to the Bush administration in the hope that Hamas would be prevented from participating. For his part, despite his concern about a Hamas victory, Abbas was committed to allowing the movement to run as a means of ensuring the legitimacy of the elections.[144] Rooted in the conviction that Hamas was unlikely to win, both Abbas and the Bush administration pushed for Hamas's inclusion in the democratic process as a way of taming the movement.[145]

GAZA DISENGAGEMENT

The ceasefire that Abbas had secured with Israel for the remainder of 2005 was a delicate one. Tensions simmered within the Palestinian territories as well and threatened to bubble over with Abbas's decision in June to postpone the elections.[146] Hamas protested this move and described the unexpected delay as a blow to democracy and an action that cast doubt on the credibility of the Cairo Declaration, in which the factions had unanimously agreed to the timing of the elections.[147] Hamas chastised Abbas for his unilateral decision, which it characterized as serving Fatah's interests rather than those of the Palestinian people. It insisted that by unilaterally postponing the legislative elections, Abbas was bowing to international pressure to curb Hamas's political ambitions.[148]

Abbas's decision was indeed shaped to a large extent by fears of a Hamas victory. With American approval, the elections were delayed to buy Fatah more time to prepare. This measure demonstrated the Palestinian Authority's predicament as an entity stuck in two different negotiation tracks that were ultimately at odds with each other. On the one hand, as the newly elected and Western-approved leader, Abbas was engaged in diplomatic negotiations with the United States and Israel to move beyond the Arafat era and lay the groundwork for future Israeli-Palestinian peacemaking. Central to this trajectory were efforts to disarm the resistance factions and integrate their forces into the Palestinian Authority to ensure its monopoly on the use of force ahead of Israel's disengagement.[149] Doing so was made difficult by the unilateral nature of Israel's imminent withdrawal and by the fact that the Palestinian security forces had been severely weakened by Sharon's bombardment during the Second Intifada. On the other hand, the Palestinian Authority was engaged in discussions with resistance factions to reform the PLO and give Hamas and Islamic Jihad a stronger say in the national agenda.

This balancing act began to falter as Israel launched a campaign against Hamas and Islamic Jihad in the summer of 2005, eliciting rocket fire from both factions in Gaza. Hamas noted that the Cairo Declaration called for a bilateral cessation of violence and made room for self-defense.[150] It insisted that the movement had not offered a "free ceasefire" and pointed to the Palestinian Authority's failure to derive any concessions from Israel during the calm.[151] Israel mobilized to retaliate; it recaptured the West Bank city of Tulkarem and threatened to expand its targeted assassinations.[152] Concurrently, acting on previously issued orders from Abbas to maintain calm on the Palestinian front, the weakly armed Palestinian security forces that had been deployed around Gaza mobilized against resistance factions, precipitating what was to become the first of many domestic clashes following Abbas's election.[153]

Hamas regarded the Palestinian Authority's mobilization as a sign of Abbas-Sharon collusion to limit its political participation.[154] Expressing distrust of Abbas and his security forces, an editorial in Hamas's publications stated that "the Palestinian Authority . . . has revealed its true nature, and has announced war on Hamas, with banners and slogans such as . . . 'No Weapons Other Than the Weapons of the Legitimate Authority.' It has as such ended the 'honeymoon' that Abbas has been enjoying with the resistance parties whom he had courted."[155] Hamas believed that Abbas and Sharon both felt that the movement had become too powerful and they were working to undermine it ahead of the Gaza withdrawal.[156] The crackdown, so soon after Hamas's emergence as a promising political player, marked an important turning point in domestic relations, one that eroded the performance of fraternity that had for some time shaped engagement between factions. Hamas perceived Abbas's policies as representative of an institutionalized refusal to allow it into the political process and marking his continued dedication to the diplomatic process.[157] It interpreted his postponement of the elections as a step to solidify Fatah's political hold and to undermine Hamas's ability to capitalize on its newfound clout or play a role in the governance of Gaza.[158]

These suspicions brought into question Hamas's commitment to its "red lines" of avoiding Palestinian infighting, as al-Qassam issued a statement justifying its readiness to attack any force aimed at undermining resistance.[159] "The Qassam continue on their path of jihad and resistance, hitting the enemy settlements . . . [and] occupation's deputies, those who try to distract us from the Zionist enemy and who undertake his role in hitting the Islamic guerilla fighters."[160] In carrying out "Zionist orders" to stop resistance, al-Qassam insisted that the Palestinian security forces had effectively become part of the occupation and were thus legitimate targets of resistance.[161] Adopting such a position, Hamas set the groundwork for associating the Palestinian Authority with Israel in a manner that would facilitate future conflicts between the two, in effect undermining its oft-reiterated dedication to preserving unity.

Nonetheless, the imminent power vacuum in the Gaza Strip pushed Palestinians to reassert calm.[162] By July 19, both Hamas and Fatah issued appeals for unity and initiated a truce between the fighting factions without effectively finding means to coexist. As the deadline for Israel's withdrawal approached, Abbas's security forces redeployed around Gaza in August to ensure a smooth process. These were a fragmented group, answering to different command structures and poorly armed.[163] Under Abbas's orders, they were prevented from carrying out preemptive attacks on Hamas and other factions, essentially making the truce contingent on the absence of disarmament initiatives. While Israel persisted in demanding that Abbas dismantle the "terrorist infrastructure," it offered no incentives given its persistent failure to cease settlement expansion, release prisoners, or end targeted assassinations as had been agreed at Sharm al-Sheikh. Despite Abbas's restraint, Hamas continued to view the security forces as a threat since their raison d'être (even if yet to be fulfilled) was the demilitarization of resistance.

Domestic tension was not limited to the Palestinian territories. Sharon's withdrawal plans exacerbated major political and social fault lines within Israel. As the first leader to pull back the expansion of settlements within the Palestinian occupied territories, Sharon faced immense internal backlash. Antidisengagement protests proliferated as settlers worried about a precedent being set for further pullbacks from the West Bank. While acknowledging that disengagement was a pretext for strengthening Israel's hold over the West Bank, Hamas's leaders celebrated this imminent "victory" as a development that both undermined the Palestinian Authority's call for negotiations and shattered the image of the Israeli army's indestructibility.[164] To Hamas's leaders, the withdrawal signaled that the Zionist enterprise had begun reversing its expansionist ideology.[165] The unilateral nature of the disengagement underscored that it was not taking place as a result of diplomatic engagement, further weakening the position of the Palestinian Authority and leaders such as Abbas.[166]

A few days ahead of the disengagement, Hamas's leaders hosted a press conference in Gaza City on August 13 and declared that "this accomplishment is the first step towards the liberation of our land and the retrieval of our Jerusalem and our rights. This is not, as Sharon wishes, the first and last step. . . . We will refuse for Gaza to turn into a prison for our people."[167] Hamas reiterated its readiness to engage in postwithdrawal issues including development, reconstruction, and reform.[168] It proposed to form a committee to oversee both the disengagement and ensuing tasks. Cognizant of the Palestinian Authority's anxieties about its role, Hamas stressed that it was not acting as a "state within a state," as it sought to assuage fears that it was seeking to supplant the Palestinian Authority or undermine its sovereignty. Rather, Hamas claimed to present its proposal as a means of enhancing partnership and transparency and ending unilateralism as a precursor to the reformulation of the PLO.[169]

Israel's withdrawal plans entailed the relocation of eight thousand Israeli settlers from twenty-one settlements within Gaza and four settlements in the West Bank. A forty-eight-hour voluntary evacuation commenced on August 16 to allow settlers to move out on their own accord. After this period ended, thousands of Israeli army soldiers were sent in to forcibly remove hundreds of families who refused to leave. The evacuations entailed long hours where settlers barricaded themselves and faced off with the army. After the settlers were relocated, the Israeli army destroyed all the settlements left behind, leaving synagogues intact. By September 2005, Israel had successfully removed its illegal settlements from the Gaza Strip and scenes of Palestinians celebrating over the remnants of their former oppressors' homes dominated the news.

Israel's disengagement from Gaza instantly began shaping the Israeli public's opinion regarding the removal of settlements. The withdrawal came to be seen as a litmus test: if Palestinians were able to build a developed city-state in Gaza, akin to a Singapore on the Mediterranean, then that would allegedly pave the way for further withdrawals elsewhere, leading to renewed efforts at Israeli-Palestinian peacemaking.[170] Significant plans had been drawn up by the Quartet behind the scenes to consider economic initiatives or development prospects that could underpin Gaza's growth. Yet despite much promise and hope, these blueprints remained stillborn.[171] Citing security concerns, Israel almost immediately began imposing a suffocating system of closures that severely restricted the movement of goods and persons between the Gaza Strip and Israel or the West Bank. After having razed thousands of Palestinian homes between Gaza and Egypt, on the Rafah border, Israel built a seven-meter-high wall that caged Palestinians in.[172] Despite the signing of the "Rafah Border Agreement," which coordinated the Palestinian Authority's administration of Gaza's borders with Israel, in practice Israel maintained full authority over access into the coastal enclave.[173] Given that the Israeli and West Bank markets were central to Gaza's economy, the closure policies nipped in the bud any prospects for growth or development within the Gaza Strip. By the end of Israel's withdrawal, rather than promoting Gaza's economic development, Israel had reconfigured its occupation to take the form of a stifling, externally imposed structure of control.[174]

Sharon's unilateral disengagement—and the sheer fact that he was willing to withdraw from illegal settlements—provided the Israeli leader with sufficient clout internationally to pressure Abbas to confront the resistance factions. Having agreed to the postponement of the elections once, the Bush administration refused further delays. It insisted that Abbas move to disarm Hamas, as the United States rejected the idea of an armed militia participating in the democratic process.[175] Concerns regarding Hamas's participation were not assuaged as members of the movement openly discussed how resistance could be sustained or even exported to the West Bank from Gaza after Israel's withdrawal.[176] The importance of armed resistance was apparent in Hamas's rejection of disarmament and its view that Gaza's liberation was incomplete since borders were still controlled by Israel.[177] Addressing the issue of disarmament, Meshal agreed with the need to form a single command structure for Palestinian armed forces, but he viewed a pluralistic political framework as the only way such a structure could come to pass.[178]

Calls for disarmament precipitated domestic clashes again throughout the fall months following Israel's disengagement. Hamas held firm in calling for the legitimization of resistance weapons and implored the Palestinian Authority not to allow "the enemy's" constant calls for disarmament to cause civil war.[179] Hamas's refusal was further supported by continued Israeli incursions and military operations within the Gaza Strip throughout the postdisengagement period. Rising tension coincided with the third round of municipal elections, where Hamas performed somewhat poorly given that it focused on 104 districts in the West Bank and none in Gaza. Hamas won 26 percent of the seats and 36 percent of the votes relative to Fatah's 57.3 percent in both. By the end of the fourth round, however, Hamas had gained 30 percent of the seats and 50.1 percent of the vote, relative to Fatah's 32.9 and 30 percent, respectively.[180]

Hamas's strong performance heightened Abbas's worries ahead of the delayed legislative elections, rescheduled for January 25, 2006. Bitter spats between the parties surfaced intermittently, from violence on the streets in Gaza to campaigns of arrest and acts of vandalism in the West Bank, as well as verbal attacks in media outlets. Hamas claimed it put "no trust" in the Palestinian Authority, which it alleged had gone back on all agreements made between the parties after Arafat's death.[181] However, while stressing the right to armed struggle and self-defense, Hamas maintained the military calm it had committed to.[182] The movement also appeared invested in portraying a softer image ahead of the elections to assuage doubts about its participation. Mahmoud Zahhar, for instance, granted an interview to the Israeli newspaper *Haaretz* in which he discussed the possible revision of the Hamas charter.[183] Hamas's spokesperson in Gaza was also quoted stating that Hamas's "charter is not the Qur'an," indicating Hamas's alleged willingness to recognize Israel.[184]

As the new year dawned, heated debates erupted among representatives of the factions gathered in Cairo. Hamas's persistent refusal to officially extend the ceasefire beyond the end of 2005, as had been initially agreed, merely strengthened its position ahead of the legislative elections.[185] By leveraging its refusal to disarm against the Palestinian Authority's appeals to do so, and by emphasizing Israeli anxiety about its participation in elections, Hamas portrayed itself as a party that prioritized Palestinian rights over foreign interests.[186] The movement highlighted this approach as being in stark contrast to Fatah, whose image among Palestinians at the time was of a corrupt party that was subservient to Israel.[187] Leveraging what it saw as its just cause and strong popular support, Hamas aimed to get 25 percent of the vote, as that would give it a voice in shaping policy without compromising its politics.[188] On the eve of the movement's eighteenth anniversary, Meshal praised "this new energy in our political life," asserting that "we feel our way, we practice our democracy, we elect our leaders, we build our institutions. . . . This political movement will be victorious for our people the same way our resistance was victorious on the battlefield, God willing."[189]

ELECTION VICTORY

Hamas ran for the 2006 legislative elections on the same platform of "Change and Reform," a far-reaching agenda that presented its strategic trajectory for the liberation struggle alongside promises to tackle daily administrative challenges within the territories. This juxtaposition between mundane hardships and the lofty aspirations of self-determination spoke to the breadth of Hamas's political vision. Leveraging its clean track record of municipal governance, in sharp contrast to the governmental institutions under Fatah, Hamas portrayed itself as a party that could address the failures of the incumbent and reconfigure the political system in accordance with its values. Its electoral manifesto spoke of resuscitating the core principles of the struggle, including the indivisibility of the land of historic Palestine; the unity and eventual return of the fragmented Palestinian people; and the right to resist the occupation in the quest to form an independent state.[190] Candidates stressed that these principles had been raised by liberation factions prior to the emergence of Hamas, including the PLO. Hamas believed, however, that its faith and Islamic principles would empower it to resist veering off course like the PLO had. While these principles were held as long-term goals to be achieved as the "Zionist project" weakened, Hamas accepted transitional stages in the shape of a state on the 1967 borders, with Jerusalem as its capital, to which the refugees could return. Consonant with its roots, and like the PLO before it, Hamas positioned the Palestinian cause within the broader fold of Arab and Islamic politics.[191]

In service of this vision, Hamas's agenda listed items dedicated to the release of prisoners detained in Israeli jails, as well as the criminalization of security coordination with the occupation.[192] These measures demonstrated the movement's desire to politicize the Palestinian Authority away from its focus on governance. Hamas addressed the urgent need for constitutional amendments in the political establishment; fighting corruption; restructuring the security forces and judicial systems; and reforming social, educational, and economic initiatives consistently with its Islamic values.[193] Hamas's schemes were premised on the fundamental belief that the daily reality, as well as the liberation struggle itself, merited a holistic shake-up to break the incumbent's monopoly. Such a restructuring, Hamas thought, would realign political institutions for the people within and outside the occupied territories, provide them with the legitimacy that was sorely lacking, and prepare them to achieve their freedom.[194] The presence of an organization that explicitly refused to recognize Israel or to abide by previous peace agreements was seen as a powerful way to reconfigure the relationship between Palestinians and their occupier.

Precisely because of these motivations, a great deal of anxiety overshadowed preparations for the elections. Both the Bush administration and Abbas felt that Hamas's participation was imperative to give the elections a veneer of legitimacy. Since Abbas had delayed the elections once to give Fatah more time to prepare, further delays were not possible. Given the dangerous escalation that attempts at disarmament had caused, Abbas also did not pursue this option, despite American pressure.[195] Hamas dismissed American hypocrisy in pushing for disarmament as a prerequisite for participation in democratic elections, citing the Irish Republican Army as a historic precedent, as well as the more recent elections promoted by the United States in Afghanistan and Iraq, where armed factions ran against each other.[196] Closer to home, Fatah itself had armed militias.[197] Hamas called on Palestinians not to fall for attempts to preempt the elections, stressing that the Americans promoted democracy only when it suited their purposes.[198] Having pushed for Hamas's involvement, Abbas insisted that elections were taking place within the framework of the Oslo Accords. This conflicted sharply with Hamas's premise that al-Aqsa Intifada had rendered Oslo "dead and gone" and that elections constituted a new political environment rooted in the Cairo Declaration.[199] Without directly addressing these diverging views, elections got under way at the end of 2005, with Israel begrudgingly acquiescing to Hamas's participation, albeit with obstructions in East Jerusalem.

From the outset, Hamas's strength in electioneering and crowd mobilization was distinguishable from the factionalism within Fatah, which had split its candidates into two separate lists.[200] Hamas leveraged its role as the opposition party, capitalizing on the public's frustrations with Fatah and its leader in areas such corruption, lawlessness, and poor social services.[201] It differentiated itself as a united movement with a strong social infrastructure that had been developed over the course of several decades and had a reputation for honesty, with highly educated candidates who were able to tackle chronic deficiencies.[202] Furthermore, Hamas portrayed Fatah as being subservient to Israeli and American demands, even when those came at the expense of local needs.[203] Assessing Abbas's tenure, Hamas insisted that he had failed to achieve any of his promises, despite talk of reform and democracy. Lawlessness in

Gaza, often by Fatah's own forces, was—for Hamas—proof of Abbas's inability to control the security establishment.[204] His failure to derive the concessions that Israel had outlined in Sharm al-Sheikh, despite the resistance factions adhering to their ceasefire, showed that Abbas remained too weak to influence Israel. Moreover, Hamas claimed he had undermined "Palestinian successes" such as Israel's withdrawal from the Gaza Strip by acquiescing to Israel's control and movement of goods and people into the strip.[205]

On Election Day, Hamas launched its campaign from Sheikh Yassin's house, affirming its rootedness in the spiritual leader's vision and the movement's commitment to its Islamic principles and program of resistance.[206] The elections proceeded without serious incident with a 77 percent voter turnout. They were deemed a model of democracy in the region by foreign observers, including former US president Jimmy Carter. Through its campaign, Hamas looked toward a post-Oslo reality where it could work with other factions to "build the Palestinian national project on a solid foundation that can withstand pressure."[207] With the aim of breaking Fatah's unilateralism and deflecting worries about its Islamic nature, Hamas offered a "civilizational renaissance project" that was open to "all those who suffered under Zionist brutality to come in as partners in the liberation struggle."[208] It extended its arms to Christians and reaffirmed its commitment to the role of women.[209] In contrast to Hamas's aspirations for the domestic reconfiguration and structural re-orientation of the struggle, Fatah remained committed to the notion of a strategic peace in line with past agreements, while affirming the right of resistance in self-defense, as stipulated by international law.[210]

In a historic watershed that marked the culmination of its politici-zation, Hamas won 76 of the 132 seats of the legislative council rela-tive to Fatah's 43. Proclamations of "Tsunami! Earthquake! Coup!" peppered the movement's publications, given the unexpected scale of the victory.[211] Hamas immediately dismissed the notion that this out-come was simply a protest vote against Fatah's corruption. As a senior leader in Beirut stated, "This is a peaceful coup on the present decrepit

political reality, which was born out of defeat, corruption and acquiescence to rotten political solutions. . . . These results are an excellent
political renewal, as if the Palestinian people are reborn, and it's a new
birth for the project of resistance, for the development of a society of
resistance, for a shaking-off of all the institutions."[212] Reaffirming this
renewal, Abu Marzouq said, "We will not be in the politics of free concessions. What was before January 25, 2006, will be different from what
comes after, in terms of the mechanisms for engaging with the Zionist
enemy. Because that old manner of dealing with the enemy did not
produce any gains on the ground. It produced castles in the clouds."[213]

Hamas looked toward a different form of politics. Instead of "settlement and negotiations" came a program of "change, reform and resistance."[214] Through its election, Hamas had found a way to transition
the goals that had animated its armed struggle during the Second Intifada into the political arena. An inadvertent revolution had propelled
the movement into a leading position within the Palestinian struggle
for liberation. By early 2006, Hamas had built a solid foundation from
which to intervene in the broader quest for national self-determination
and bring its uncompromising vision of Islamic Palestinian nationalism
into the heart of Palestinian political institutions.

CHAPTER FOUR

STRANGLING HAMAS

Hamas's 2006 electoral victory caused utter confusion within the administration of George W. Bush, given its focus on democracy promotion in Palestine, and in Iraq, as a test case for the region. The most immediate reaction was trepidation regarding the place of a designated terrorist organization in public office. As Elliot Abrams, a senior member of the Bush administration, had noted in anticipation of a Hamas victory, "Legally, we had to treat Hamas as we treated al Qaeda."[1] In high-level meetings within the White House shortly after Hamas's victory was confirmed, it was quickly decided that the optimal response was to adopt a strategy that could isolate Hamas and reassert Fatah's dominance.[2] The dual-pronged plan was to be implemented on several levels: military, financial, and diplomatic.[3]

The American approach was rooted in the belief that Palestinians had voted for change, seeking a less corrupt government than Fatah's, but that they still desired a negotiated peace settlement in the form of a two-state solution, unlike Hamas.[4] In reality, Palestinians had voted Hamas in for a number of reasons, including frustration with Fatah's corruption, resentment at the failed and endless peace talks, Hamas's reliability in providing welfare services, and indeed its defiant rhetoric against the occupation. Support of armed struggle or Hamas's Islamic ideology did not feature prominently in its electoral platform or constitute the majority of its votes.[5] Nonetheless, Hamas's leaders interpreted the movement's victory as a resounding endorsement of its worldview, not simply an affirmation of its clean governance and its strong social and charitable institutions.

President Mahmoud Abbas and the European members of the Quartet initially viewed Hamas's inclusion in the political system as a development that could offer diplomatic opportunities or moderate the movement.[6] In contrast, convinced it could reverse the election results, the Bush administration decided to focus on its support of President Abbas and began a secretive "train and equip" program aimed at bolstering Fatah's arms and capabilities.[7] This initiative raised worries within some corners of the American establishment that weapons might ultimately fall into the wrong hands and be used against Israel. But the administration pushed forward. To circumvent congressional obstacles against arming Palestinians, the United States leveraged networks in Saudi Arabia and the United Arab Emirates to fund the arms that were then delivered to Fatah through Egypt and Jordan.[8]

A financial blockade was also instituted against the Palestinian government. Prime Minister Ehud Olmert, who stepped in as acting prime minister after Ariel Sharon was incapacitated by a stroke, announced that Israel would withhold tax and custom duty revenues collected on behalf of the Palestinian Authority, worth about $55 million monthly. The United States similarly stopped any financial aid and began actively pressuring other nations to do the same.[9] Secretary of State Condoleezza Rice traveled to Arab Gulf countries to press them to end their financial support. Most countries, including Saudi Arabia and Egypt, rejected her calls. Given that the Palestinian Authority relied heavily on aid to support 140,000 civil servants and 58,000 security personnel, it was feared such financial restrictions would be debilitating.[10] Israel adopted other measures to cripple Hamas's rise to power. It hindered the travel of Hamas's parliamentarians in all Israeli-controlled areas, effectively rendering politicians residing in the Gaza Strip unable to travel to the West Bank. Israeli military officials also debated severing the Gaza Strip conclusively from the rest of the territories and making its border with Israel an international crossing.[11]

After congratulating the Palestinians on their successful democratic election, and following intensive discussions and pressure from Secretary Rice, the Quartet issued a statement noting "that it was inevitable that future assistance to any new government would be reviewed by donors against that government's commitment to the principles of nonviolence, recognition of Israel, and acceptance of previous agreements and obligations, including the Roadmap."[12] These conditions mirrored the prerequisites the PLO had to fulfill for diplomatic engagement almost two decades prior. Even though the PLO's acceptance of these conditions and extensive peace talks in the interim years had still not compelled Israel to relinquish its hold over the territories, the same demands were now put to Hamas. Until these demands were met, the United States and Israel launched what Hamas's publications referred to as an "iron-wall" strategy aimed at suffocating its government.[13] Once Palestinians felt this burden, the two allies hoped, they would force Hamas to either accept the Quartet's conditions or prompt Abbas to call for new elections.[14]

THE REVOLUTIONARY GOVERNMENT

In the first days after its victory, in early 2006, Hamas appeared unperturbed in the face of this international mobilization.[15] It stressed that the people's choice had to be respected if an Algerian-style revolution was to be avoided.[16] Publications declared that the international community had to respect the will of the Palestinian people given its habit of preaching the virtues of democracy.[17] Anxiety that a "terrorist organization" had been democratically elected was seen by Hamas as proof that the prevalent paradigm through which the Palestinian struggle was perceived in the West was flawed. For Hamas and its supporters, their actions constituted armed resistance against a terroristic occupation.[18] Certain that the movement could circumvent the blockade, Hamas's leader Khaled Meshal remarked, "If the door to the West is shut, then the doors to the Arab and Islamic East must remain open."[19]

Leaders believed that the righteousness of their cause would mitigate the American-led isolation. Alongside confidence that Arab and
Islamic communities would come through, Hamas expected other
heavyweight countries such as Russia to support its vision and counter "Western" reactions. Hamas also hoped the European Union and
the Quartet would be less "subservient to Israeli conditions" than the
United States.[20] Certainly there were signs that such prospects existed.
As America mobilized its diplomatic power around marginalizing
Hamas, Russian president Vladimir Putin insisted that Russia, one of
the four Quartet members, had never designated Hamas a terrorist organization. Similarly, to counter the movement's financial isolation, Iran
said it would support Hamas's government.[21]

Domestic concerns were initially more acute as a number of unprecedented constitutional challenges arose. Over more than a decade,
Fatah's hegemony over the political establishment and American reforms had undermined the liberation agenda of the PLO. This was
effectively subsumed into the governance agenda of the Palestinian
Authority, which adopted—symbolically—an oversized role as government. Hamas's election halted this institutional assimilation and
delivered challenges on two fronts. The first related to the division of
manifestos within the Palestinian Authority itself. Hamas's majority in
the legislature meant that it could nominate the incoming prime minister and cabinet. This executive team, the "Hamas government," had
to coordinate activities with the office of the president under Abbas.
While this bipartisan division between the presidency and the cabinet is
not unheard-of in presidential-parliamentary systems, it had significant
complications in this case due to the vastly conflicting ideologies of both
parties.[22] More worryingly, on the second front, was Hamas's continued
exclusion from the PLO. The reforms outlined in the 2005 Cairo Declaration seeking to incorporate Hamas and Islamic Jihad into the PLO
remained outstanding. Until those were completed, the PLO failed to
represent a significant constituency, which now included the acting government, creating a debilitating crisis of legitimacy.

These complications surfaced shortly after Hamas's victory was confirmed. Signaling an initial impetus to address these issues pluralistically, Hamas extended a formal request to Fatah to form a coalition government.[23] Having long criticized Fatah's monopolistic hold on power, Hamas hoped to avoid defaulting on past rhetoric. The prospect of a coalition government promised to mitigate Hamas's political inexperience and preempt donor concerns regarding key ministerial postings, such as finance, interior, and foreign affairs.[24] But early signs were not encouraging. Fatah had been dealt a serious blow and many of its members advocated remaining in opposition while reflecting on the internal status of their party.[25] Others refused to legitimate Hamas's program, which they felt would isolate Palestinians.[26]

One of the most vocal opponents of unity was Mahmoud Dahlan. A refugee from Gaza, Dahlan had risen through the ranks of the Palestinian security forces to become America's strongman in the territories and the lynchpin of security coordination with Israel. He was much despised by Hamas for his role in cracking down on the resistance factions under the rubric of security coordination throughout the 1990s.[27] Reflecting wider sentiment, Dahlan told a rally that it would be "shameful" for Fatah to even consider entering a coalition government with Hamas.[28] Hamas's leaders viewed such threats as reflecting not only a desire to avoid sharing a government with Hamas, but a broader strategy aimed at undermining the movement.[29]

Fatah's monopolization of the political establishment meant that Hamas faced enormous institutional inertia. This was exacerbated by the international community's overt and clandestine support of the incumbent. As discussions among factions progressed, the Palestinian Authority's leadership initiated measures to mitigate Hamas's entry into politics. In an extraordinary session, the outgoing legislature proposed and passed bills to expand the remit of President Abbas's office at the expense of the incoming cabinet in areas such as security and the judiciary. These measures effectively reversed the recent American-led reforms that had curbed the authority of President Arafat, recentralizing political power within the hands of the president.[30] Hamas's publications viewed these activities as part of an "international conspiracy" and called the extraordinary session "unconstitutional."[31] Articles condemned Abbas's authoritarian hold on power as leaders remarked that "when [the Bush administration and Israel] pushed reforms on President Arafat, the goal was to pass the authority to the prime minister, particularly over the security forces. Is now the time for this authority to be returned to the president, now that Hamas has come into government? That is illogical and unacceptable."[32]

Political wrangling among factions persisted for close to three weeks as Hamas drafted an agenda for a unity government that could satisfy other parties. It focused on areas of potential overlap: a Palestinian state on 1967 land, with Jerusalem as its capital; the legitimacy of resistance against the occupation; the right of return; and the need to resuscitate and reform the PLO.[33] Despite room for agreement, Hamas's efforts fell short of Abbas's minimum requirements. In his letter of designation inviting Hamas's incoming prime minister Ismail Haniyeh to form his cabinet, Abbas effectively reiterated the Quartet's conditions.[34] Given that the Palestinian Authority was a product of the PLO's commitment to the Oslo Accords, Abbas insisted that the incoming cabinet would need to explicitly recognize the PLO's manifesto—including recognition of Israel, renunciation of violence, and commitment to all past agreements signed with Israel—in order to safeguard international legitimacy.[35]

Addressing Hamas's refusal to recognize Israel, leaders within Fatah insisted that administration of the territories necessarily meant daily interaction with Israel in issues related to movement, water, electricity, and trade. Furthermore, Abbas highlighted that constitutionally the PLO negotiating committee spoke on behalf of the speaker of the legislature, the prime minister, as well as the foreign and finance ministers. Even if those politicians refused to attend negotiations, agreements were effectively made in their name.[36] As a senior Fatah leader said, "If new parties come into power in Spain or Italy, they would still recognize their membership in NATO. Recognition does not have to come from the party—but the government would have to respect past agreements."[37]

Fatah's leadership was working from the premise of continuity, on the basis that the PLO was an authoritative body, akin to a sovereign state, recognized through its adherence to past agreements. Hamas dismissed these "delusions." Citing the absence of sovereignty, repeated American and Israeli intervention, and the vacuous nature of past agreements given Israeli intransigence and its expanding settlement of the West Bank, Hamas questioned the basis of international recognition. It insisted that the Cairo Declaration had made clear the PLO's illegitimacy given that movements such as Hamas and Islamic Jihad had been absent from decision-making when past agreements were signed.[38] Before past agreements could be upheld, Hamas insisted that the PLO would have to be reformed so that all political parties could have a say in reconstituting its manifesto. The widely understood but unspoken implication was Hamas's desire to reverse the trajectory that the PLO had taken and the concessions it had made under Fatah's tenure, given the failure of the diplomatic path in securing Palestinian rights.[39]

Abbas's conditions, Hamas argued, meant that it was being asked to govern as Fatah would.[40] Instead of conceding, Hamas unilaterally formed its own cabinet, explicitly underscoring the refusal of other factions to join it in a coalition government.[41] The proposed cabinet was given a vote of confidence as the tenth Palestinian government on March 28, 2006.[42] Ismail Haniyeh was appointed prime minister, Mahmoud al-Zahhar foreign minister, and Said Sayyam minister of interior. The fact that figures such as Zahhar and Haniyeh were senior members of the movement's political bureau as well as politicians in its government was an early indication regarding the absence of any real differentiation between Hamas-as-movement and Hamas-as-government.[43] In a resounding speech delivered to the legislature after the confidence vote, Haniyeh outlined the cabinet's three areas of focus: security on the ground, PLO reform and anticorruption, and economic growth.[44]

Hamas's agenda called for "the formation of an independent and fully sovereign Palestinian state, with Jerusalem as its capital," and stated its legitimate right to resistance for the removal of the occupation beyond the 1967 borders.[45] In a pragmatic nod, the agenda stated that "the government will deal with [past] signed agreements with a high-level of responsibility, in a manner that protects the interests of our people, preserves their rights and does not harm their fixed principles."[46] This was a clear statement that Hamas accepted the parameters of statehood as defined by mediators seeking a two-state solution. But the movement rejected that the new government would explicitly meet the Quartet's conditions or embrace the concessions that the PLO had historically made. Haniyeh insisted that once the PLO was reformed into a fair, representative body, past agreements would be reassessed to determine what benefit they held.[47]

In a letter directed to the prime minister, Abbas stressed that elections "do not constitute severing or overturning the principles, responsibility and legal and political commitments of the Palestinian Authority, with its terms of reference as embodied in the PLO manifesto."[48] He warned against taking any measures that might turn international legitimacy against the Palestinians and cause their isolation.[49] "The only way in front of us is the path of peace: calm, economic growth and the resumption of negotiations with Israelis on two paths. The first concerns the outstanding daily modes of interaction. . . . The second is on the final status issues outlined in the Roadmap and the Oslo Accords."[50] Granting Hamas's cabinet a grace period despite his skepticism, Abbas hoped that Hamas would quickly learn what he believed was the inevitability of his outlined path.

But for Hamas, the formation of its cabinet was the first step in wholly reconstituting the structures of the political system, not institutionally, but strategically. As Meshal explained in a press conference from Cairo, "The world will see how Hamas can encompass resistance and politics, resistance and government. Government is not our goal, it is a tool. . . . Democracy is not a substitute for resistance. Democracy is our internal choice to reform our house, whereas resistance is our choice in facing the enemy. There is no conflict between the two."[51] Meshal emphasized that opposition to the Quartet's conditions and perseverance in the face of the blockade constituted forms of resistance. He promised that Hamas would never contradict its ideals; it would not cease military operations, condemn resistance factions, or arrest resistance fighters.[52] Much to the discomfort of those vested in the peace process, Hamas's politics of resistance reassessed how Palestinians dealt with their occupation.[53] In so doing, Hamas attempted to break from the trappings of self-governance, to repoliticize the Palestinian Authority away from its administrative focus and dedication to endless peace talks, and to rupture the continuity that President Abbas and the incumbent leadership hoped to secure. In essence, Hamas sought to reverse the institutional inertia that had pacified the Palestinian leadership, and to resuscitate the calls for liberation that had marked the PLO's early history.

The core of Hamas's aspiration rested on institutionalizing the notion of "resistance" into the very philosophy of the order it envisioned. Musa abu Marzouq explained, "We are in government, yes, but the government is not whole. We are a government under occupation. We cannot assume that we have a government similar to others in the world. Or as the Americans demand, that we act only as a government. Hamas's program in government is one which is aligned, which is compatible, with its program of resistance."[54] Whether discussing economic measures or regional relations, corruption reforms or the security establishment, decisions were to draw on a mantra of resistance. Reform, for instance, entailed rebuilding institutions to serve Palestinians rather than Israelis, to be tools for liberation rather than occupation.[55] The oft-repeated example was that of the security forces, which would cease to operate on the premise of ensuring Israel's security and would become an army of resistance to protect Palestinians against the brutalities of the occupation.[56] The fragile, aid-dependent economy would be cleaned up to reduce vulnerability to foreign agents, enhance accountability, and tackle corruption.[57] Ministers spoke of a resistance economy, one that encouraged local production and promoted self-reliance, much in the same way as during the First Intifada.[58] This notion of quotidian resistance permeated all sectors, including health care and industry.[59] In terms of the judicial system, ministers spoke of an independent legal framework, one immune to prolific interference.[60]

In essence, Hamas's vision was to build a society of resistance.[61] Even though this aspiration collided with domestic inertia and international marginalization, Hamas defiantly presented its cabinet as the international blockade began to take its toll in March 2006. Unemployment had soared, poverty levels expanded, and public hospitals and schools were compromised throughout the territories. The blockade was particularly harsh in Gaza, where Israel shuttered all access into or from the strip for 60 percent of the time from the moment Hamas was elected. This was criticized as a form of collective punishment against civilians to penalize them for their democratic choice.[62] Worried about the prospects of an economic collapse, President Bush declared that the United States would begin bolstering supplies to the Palestinians through international agencies such as the United Nations and the US Agency for International Development. This served the dual purpose of averting a humanitarian crisis and competing with Hamas's social and charitable infrastructure.[63] The Europeans also began exploring means of putting together a transaction system that could deliver aid while bypassing Hamas's government. Prime Minister Olmert continued to withhold the Palestinian Authority's revenue, stressing his intention to boycott the government while maintaining relations with President Abbas. Olmert's aide, Dov Weisglass, explained that Israel's approach was "to put the Palestinians on a diet, but not to make them die of hunger."[64]

Hamas interpreted Israel's actions as a "declaration of war," an effort to aggravate divisions between the presidency and the cabinet.[65] Rather than being drawn into battle, Hamas's parliamentarians presented their case to the international community.[66] One of the first actions taken by Zahhar as foreign minister was to reach out to UN secretary general Kofi Annan in a letter outlining Hamas's commitment to the rights of the Palestinian people. He called on the United Nations to press the international community to revise its "rash boycott," adding that the United Nations should take action to end Israel's continued violation of international law.[67] Hamas's publications reported that the greatest challenge facing the movement was to secure financial backing to cover the government's monthly budget of $170 million.[68] Refusing to link financial aid to the Quartet's conditions, Hamas's leaders appeared strong-willed. "If the Palestinian people rejected these conditions, and the flow of money stopped, what is the result—that the Palestinian Authority collapses? Is [the donor community] willing to deal with that option?"[69]

Shortly after the cabinet was formed, Meshal and other leaders embarked on a tour throughout the Middle East and Russia to cultivate alliances, communicate Hamas's political program, and raise funds for the government.[70] As customs and tax revenues were withheld by Israel and aid was frozen by the international community, Hamas's government faced an immediate budget deficit. This became the movement's foremost priority.[71] The fact that Hamas's delegation was composed of members from the movement's political bureau rather than elected governmental officials emphasized the movement's role in seeking to end the financial blockade of Hamas's elected government. While countries such as Egypt and Turkey welcomed Hamas's leaders, signaling the potential for warm relations, others such as Jordan severed ties.[72] Through the regional tour, Hamas's leaders defended the government's stance. Addressing calls for more flexibility in dealing with the Quartet's conditions, Meshal stated, "We have shown enough flexibility. We cannot say more than the official Arab and Palestinian position, which is to call for a Palestinian state on the land occupied in 1967. The problem is not with us. It is not with Hamas, as in the past it was also not with the official Palestinian and Arab positions. The problem has always been with Israel."[73]

In Moscow, Meshal was asked whether Hamas would ever alter its charter so that it would end the call for Israel's destruction. He asserted that if Israel abided by certain conditions, comprising "withdrawal from Palestinian land beyond 1967, including Jerusalem, implementing the right of return, releasing prisoners, destroying the wall and removing settlements," then Hamas "would be prepared to take steps that could produce a real peace in the region."[74] Meshal insisted that the movement had explicitly stated its desire to work with the international community to achieve a state based on the 1967 borders.[75] He stressed that the constant offering of ceasefires on land occupied in 1967 was another indication that Hamas implicitly recognized Israel.[76] Meshal's views were mirrored by others; Hamas's finance minister in Gaza stated that "a long-term ceasefire as understood by Hamas and a two-state settlement are the same. It's just a question of vocabulary."[77]

Hamas's stance made clear that explicit ideological revisions would not be forthcoming before ironclad assurances that its demands would be met. Hamas leaders noted in private that they were willing to put these offers forward in full confidence knowing that Israel would never accept a Palestinian state on 1967.[78] Hamas's gamble paid off in the sense that its bluff was never called. The movement's repeated invocations of its willingness to accept the 1967 borders for a future Palestinian state, with East Jerusalem as its capital, were consistently ignored by Israel.[79] They also fell far short of expectations within the Bush administration of what Palestinian concessions needed to be. American officials involved in the peace process believed behind closed doors that in pursuit of the two-state solution Israel would retain its major settlement blocs and the right of return will not be implemented.[80] In the accepted wisdom of the peace process, this was viewed as the starting point for negotiations rather than the mutual Israeli-Palestinian recognition of the 1967 borders as a basis for negotiating land swaps. While accepting the 1967 line was a major concession for Hamas, the Israeli government had itself not shown interest in preserving the 1967 line, but had rather deliberately blurred the border by continuing massive settlement expansion to ensure the irrelevance of the Green Line in any future negotiation.[81] This underscored Hamas's sense that the PLO's blind and subservient dedication to negotiations had ensured that the demands Palestinians needed to meet kept shifting, while Israel sustained its colonization of Palestinian land.

Instead, Meshal and other Hamas leaders developed a defiant negotiating position. "Why do we self-flagellate?" he went on to say during his tour. "Why do we take on the responsibility of a situation or a reality, when everyone is convinced that what has brought us here is Zionist intransigence, American bias and the inability of the world to push back on Israel and obligate it with the rights of Palestinians?"[82] Hamas's thinking was grounded in a revolutionary's mind-set, questioning why past policies enacted by the PLO had to persist in light of the most recent democratic election. Perhaps more importantly, leaders argued that the agreements were redundant given Israel's chronic failure to meet its own responsibility.[83] Meshal responded to persistent calls from Abbas to accept past agreements: "There is proof that Israel does not care for the Palestinian people, does not recognize their rights and does not abide by any agreement signed with them. Moreover, it does not even consider Mahmoud Abbas nor Yasser Arafat as Palestinian partners. . . . Where is the benefit for the people to tie themselves in agreements that time has annulled?"[84]

A DESPERATE AND BOLD MOVE

Hamas's political overtures went unheeded and unchallenged. American positions hardened when Hamas refused to condemn a suicide bombing by Islamic Jihad in Tel Aviv, on April 17, 2006, killing eleven. While Abbas and the international community condemned this as a deplorable act of terrorism, Hamas's leaders concurred with Islamic Jihad that it was legitimate self-defense against Israel's aggressive occupation policies.[85] This response increased tension with Abbas. As an architect of the system Hamas was challenging, Abbas opposed the movement's agenda and was supported in this opposition by the United States, which regarded the Palestinian president as a bulwark against Hamas's "radical Islamic ideology." While groups within Fatah were being secretly armed under the US "train and equip" mission, insistence remained on Hamas to disarm and integrate its fighters into the Palestinian security forces. Analysts in Hamas's publications viewed America's stance as indicative of emerging regional dynamics where the United States and Israel aligned themselves with moderate states against "radical Islam."[86]

Less than a month into its first government, Hamas's isolation became evident as early hopes that it could circumvent the blockade began to falter.[87] Seeking to secure funds for the running of the government, given that all other forms of public revenue had been frozen, Hamas's leaders sought donations from various countries in the Middle East. During their regional tour, Hamas's leaders met with resistance factions and Iranian officials in Syria and secured a commitment from Iran to underwrite portions of the government's financial responsibilities.[88] Concurrently, Hamas officials expressed disappointment that Arab leaders had succumbed to American pressure or their own internal fears of Islamic parties rising to power.[89] Rather than pledging financial support to offset the loss of international aid, as Hamas had hoped, Arab countries merely promised to maintain their previous level of funding at the Arab Summit that followed Hamas's victory.[90]

In Gaza, as the blockade's impact began to be felt, many turned to illicit smuggling from Egypt through the Rafah border. After Hamas's election victory, underground tunnels between Egypt and the Sinai Peninsula gradually increased in number. This took place as the Rafah border remained shut and Israel continued to severely restrict movement of goods or persons into or out of the coastal enclave. Smaller, near-surface tunnels allowed for food and consumer items to be brought into Gaza, while Hamas began building more sophisticated and deeper tunnels to smuggle in weaponry and arms.[91] Hamas's efforts to arm itself in Gaza exacerbated tensions between Hamas's cabinet and Abbas's office in the spring of 2006. Relations were already quite negative as efforts to isolate Hamas manifested themselves domestically. These became evident as Abbas resuscitated the offices of the PLO, reversing the institutional integration between the Palestinian Authority and the PLO that had proceeded under his tenure.

For instance, rather than relying on the Palestinian Authority's foreign minister, Abbas reinvigorated the dormant role of the PLO representative for international affairs. Given that the Palestinian Authority technically answered to the PLO, this allowed Abbas to consolidate his authority.[92] For Hamas's leaders, the timing of these actions and their unilateral implementation betrayed the intention of using the PLO to circumvent the movement's cabinet.[93] Hamas argued these provocations were destructive since they transferred power to unelected, unaccountable, and opaque institutions.[94] Hamas's leaders decried widespread "piracy" and "kidnapping" of governmental institutions across the board, in foreign and diplomatic missions; in media and broadcasting; in border crossing and security; and in governance of Islamic endowments.[95] Hamas's publications insisted that Fatah's refusal to hand over the government forced Hamas's cabinet into crisis management rather than strategic governance, curtailing its ability to fight corruption and enact laws.[96]

In April, Meshal articulated Hamas's frustration in an emotional speech in Damascus as the blockade took its toll.[97] "Some members of our flesh and blood are conspiring against us. They are executing a premeditated plan to ensure we fail. . . . Not for their personal gain, but to serve the interests of the enemy, they starve their people and encourage chaos."[98] Meshal addressed the recentralization of governmental power in Abbas's hands after Hamas's victory. "What is happening on our Palestinian land is not the result of a shadow government. . . . This is a parallel government, no, it is a replacement government, looking to steal our jurisdiction and the rights of our people. . . . Opposition is natural; let them oppose and contradict us, as we did them in the past. But there is a difference between opposition and conspiracy. What is happening today is conspiracy."[99] Hamas's publications argued that Fatah's

move to create a parallel government amounted to a coup.[100] With domestic turf wars, hostilities rose. Lawlessness and violence spilled into
the streets, particularly in Gaza, as political tension translated into rivalry among and within factional armed forces.

The delineation of jurisdiction over the security personnel between
the president and the cabinet rapidly became a major fault line.[101] The
official Palestinian security establishment had traditionally been staffed
by Fatah, raising suspicions within Hamas regarding the allegiance of
the sixty thousand troops that answered to Dahlan and ultimately the
president. Hamas's minister of interior Sayyam claimed that he attempted to mobilize the security forces to rein in the chaos on the street,
to no effect. Meanwhile, he noted, private armed forces and provoca-
teurs had been unleashed to cause disturbances and embarrass the government. Although Dahlan and Abbas both denied that Sayyam lacked
influence over the security forces, it was apparent that the Palestinian
Authority's institutions were partisan and were easily removed from
Hamas's jurisdiction, officially or otherwise.

Allegedly to defuse the lawlessness and circumvent this internal opposition, Sayyam called for the formation of a three-thousand-person
Executive Force, a lightly armed militia comprising several factions
and reporting directly to the minister of interior.[102] Hamas's leaders re-
alized this move would escalate tension, particularly with other armed
factions. But they regarded this initiative as being both "a desperate
and a bold" move to assert Hamas's authority as a government able to
offer security to the people.[103] Hamas's cabinet backed Sayyam's decision. It asserted that he was constitutionally authorized to create such
a group, given that the ministry of interior was responsible for civil
order and that he needed to reassert calm. Haniyeh assured President
Abbas that the multifactional Executive Force would eventually be integrated into the official Palestinian security body.[104]

Expectedly, the Executive Force's creation marked an escalation
in the arms race within the territories as acrimonious exchanges between the two rival factions ensued, each backed by its own exter-

nal funders: the United States for Fatah, and Iran for Hamas. Fatah viewed the Executive Force's establishment as an unconstitutional move to create a Hamas-affiliated force. Hamas dismissed such claims and retorted by noting precedents such as "Death Squads" and the "People's Army" militias that had previously been formed by Dahlan, ostensibly without presidential decree.[105] The deepening pains of the blockade exacerbated the tension. The dire financial situation became increasingly visible as the Palestinian Authority's offices began shutting down in Gaza. In the first two weeks of May, armed men stormed Hamas's ministries, instigating clashes.[106] While these were portrayed in the media as Hamas-Fatah skirmishes instigated by the Executive Force, many on the ground believed that the clashes were provoked by members of Fatah's security forces to raise the heat on Hamas.[107]

By the end of May, the Quartet admitted that its policies were impacting the entire population of Palestinians, particularly in Gaza, and recognized that this could cause a humanitarian disaster.[108] Even the disappointing Arab pledges were failing to reach Hamas's government as the Arab League avoided banks that could be persecuted under American antiterrorism laws.[109] Hamas grew increasingly resentful of the "Zionist offensive" carried out with American support and Arab complicity.[110] In an interview with Meshal, Hamas's leader sullenly called the blockade "political blackmail" and insisted that if Arab nations had the political will to break it they would have found a way to transfer their pledges.[111] Hamas's leaders were explicitly bitter that even after Hamas's having made significant concessions in accepting the formation of a Palestinian state on the 1967 borders, members of the international community still strived to isolate the movement and defeat its political ambitions. Hamas's leaders were also particularly resentful about what they perceived as support for the blockade from Fatah.[112] While the movement claimed it had raised a total of $500 million worth of pledges from its tours, which would cover it for three months, wire transfers were impossible.[113] Hamas's leaders attempted to circumvent this by carrying briefcases of money across the Rafah border between

Egypt and Gaza, prompting Abbas to call for legal action against smugglers. Hamas's publications portrayed the president as working with the United States and Israel to starve the people into submission, while Hamas was "smuggling" money in to feed them by standing firm against American diktats.[114]

THE JAWS OF RESISTANCE

Several efforts were ongoing to end the internal strife and address the economic and political impasse. Most notable were discussions taking place in locked prison cells where incarcerated members from various factions were negotiating a possible structure for unity. These discussions led to the publication of what came to be known as the "Prisoners' Document," an unexpected intervention produced by prisoners from Fatah, Hamas, Islamic Jihad, and other factions. The proposed framework for unity enshrined many issues that had already been settled, including statehood on the 1967 borders; UN Resolution 194 for the right of return; and the right to resist within the occupied territories. The document was released as Hamas ministers convened in Cairo with Abbas in the hope of achieving three urgent goals: reducing tension; developing a united political vision between the president and the cabinet; and enhancing security.[115] Upending the course of these discussions, the prisoners' document offered a way for Abbas to circumvent the prospects of lengthy negotiations. Seizing on the document, the Palestinian president issued a surprising ultimatum and called for a public referendum to be carried out within ten days on the content of the prisoners' document.[116]

Hamas had formally conceded to the items outlined in the prisoners' note through the Cairo Declaration in 2005 and its own governmental agenda. The document went one step further, however, as the imprisoned signatories committed to unity on the basis of international legitimacy. This carried severe implications for Hamas's leadership, given its conviction that past agreements were illegitimate. The fact that prisoners are a revered constituency within the Palestinian public meant that there was little room to dismiss their proposal.[117] Hamas's leadership reacted sharply, opposing the referendum.[118] As Meshal stated, "The Oslo Accords took place, as did many other agreements before and since, and no one had thought about a public referendum. Why go back to the street today?"[119] Leaders worried that Palestinians might support this document in their desire to end the sanctions. A poll produced by Birzeit University in the West Bank at the time confirmed Hamas's fears, showing that 77 percent of Palestinians favored recognition of Israel, less than five months after voting Hamas into the legislature.[120]

Under Haniyeh's leadership, Hamas's cabinet sought to limit the fallout as it worked with president Abbas's office to reach a compromise.[121] Haniyeh's pragmatic efforts faced significant obstruction as both Israel and Palestinian factions, as well as internal Hamas forces, sought to prevent a rapprochement from emerging.[122] In early June 2006, Prime Minister Olmert leaked information that Israel had approved three presidential trucks with approximately three thousand arms to be delivered to Fatah across the Allenby Bridge from Jordan, further inflaming tension among factions.[123] From the Gaza Strip, rocket fire increased. This raised suspicions that Hamas's external leadership, along with leaders within Gaza who were committed to Hamas's project, were encouraging al-Qassam to prevent Haniyeh from adopting a moderate position in discussions with Abbas.[124] On June 9, Israel carried out an air strike that killed a family of seven in Beit Lahiya, Gaza, who were picnicking on the beach. Officially breaking the ceasefire that had lasted since the Cairo Declaration the previous summer, al-Qassam promised "earthquakes."[125]

Discussions persisted directly between Abbas and Haniyeh. Introducing some reservations, the prisoners' document was amended to declare a

> commitment to establish an independent and sovereign Palestinian state on all the land that was occupied in 1967. . . . We are supported in this by our nation's historic right to the lands of our fathers and forefathers, by UN conventions and by the body of international law.

... [We continue to uphold] the right of the Palestinian people to maintain resistance ... in all forms. Resistance will be focused on land occupied in 1967. [This is alongside] political efforts, negotiations and diplomatic initiatives.[126]

Circumventing the need to explicitly recognize past resolutions, the cabinet intimated the role of international legitimacy and made room for political and diplomatic initiatives.[127] All factions apart from Islamic Jihad signed this revised document on June 27.

This agreement was in essence a key text that offered a platform for unity between Hamas and Fatah within internationally defined principles animating the Palestinian struggle. But the breakthrough was almost immediately sidelined by escalation on the military front. On June 25, al-Qassam, accompanied by the Popular Resistance Committees and the Army of Islam, two armed factions in Gaza, went into Israel through an underground tunnel. Emerging on the other side, the fighters ambushed an Israeli army post and captured a young Israeli soldier, Corporal Gilad Shalit, dragging him back into the Gaza Strip through the tunnel.[128] Hamas's publications declared Shalit a prisoner of war, taken to negotiate the future release of Palestinian prisoners.[129]

The abduction was upheld as proof to skeptics that Hamas was still active on the resistance front.[130] It was also an indication of divisions within Hamas, whereby hardliners were resisting efforts by figures such as Haniyeh to "domesticate" the movement.[131] Israel's response was swift and expansive. Deploying its army into Gaza for the first time since its disengagement, shortly after the unity deal was announced, Israel launched "Operation Summer Rains." This entailed both bombardment and ground incursions in an effort to stop rocket fire into Israel. Simultaneously, Israel mobilized to arrest sixty-four members of Hamas, including a third of the cabinet.[132] The situation intensified a week later. Citing solidarity with Palestinians in Gaza and expanding on low-level skirmishes with Israel, Hezbollah opened a front against Israel's border with Lebanon.[133] Following a barrage of rockets into

Israel's northern towns, Hezbollah infiltrated Israel and captured two soldiers, killing eight in the raid.

With these dual offensives, Hamas celebrated Israel being trapped between the "jaws of resistance."[134] Israel retaliated against Hezbollah by carrying out expansive air raids throughout Lebanon.[135] Over the next few weeks, Israel maintained heavy bombardment against its northern neighbor, expanding its military offensive beyond Hezbollah to hit Lebanon's strategic infrastructure and to launch air raids on heavily populated districts. Israel's military approach in Lebanon produced what came to be known as the "Dahyieh doctrine," a strategy that entailed the use of disproportionate force and heavy bombardment against civilian areas to maintain military deterrence.[136] This policy referred to al-Dahyieh, a densely populated neighborhood in south Beirut where members of Hezbollah reside. Through extensive aerial shelling, Israel flattened whole swathes of south Beirut, resulting in devastating human and economic losses. By the end of the war, the Lebanese government reported more than 1,100 Lebanese citizens had been killed, thousands injured, and close to a million civilians internally displaced.

Yet Hezbollah was able to stand firm against Israel's onslaught and, by sheer survival, emerged as the most powerful nonstate actor in the region. Despite Israel's staggering military mobilization, the war was widely seen as a strategic loss for Israel and for the Bush administration, which had supported Israel's actions by providing precision-guided bombs, ostensibly to limit civilian casualties.[137] Alongside this war on its northern front, Israel maintained its operation on its southern border with Gaza. Hamas's publications perceived Israel's massive "overreaction" as an indication of the significant psychological damage the movement had inflicted on the state.[138] Condemning the arrest of Hamas's political members, its publications said that "the Zionist occupation does not know how to get rid of Hamas and how to finish with the Palestinians. The last invention is the arrest of ministers and deputies. If the occupation could, it would arrest the world's ten million Palestinians so it could live in peace."[139]

Protests peaked with Israel's arrest of Hamas's chairman of the leg-islature on August 5, an act that Haniyeh referred to as "piracy and state terrorism."[140] It was seen as dismissing the internationally sanctioned immunity of politicians and undermining the "constitutional foundation of the legislature."[141] Israel's actions confirmed Hamas's suspicions that it was seeking to undermine the movement's government, and bolstered Hamas's dismissal of the Palestinian Authority as a sovereign or author-itative body. This strengthened Hamas's message to Abbas that there was no value in holding on to past agreements given that Israel vio-lated them at will.[142] The imprisonment of the majority of its legislature undermined Hamas's dominance and compelled Haniyeh to consider alternatives: accepting a unity government with a minority presence for Hamas; forming a technocratic cabinet; or dissolving the Palestinian Authority to demonstrate irrefutably the absence of sovereignty.[143]

While the cabinet was dealing with this crisis, al-Qassam maintained rocket fire, which it boasted reached as far as the city of Ashkelon in southern Israel, and promised more "Shalit operations."[144] By its tenth week, Israel's attack on Gaza had left 230 Palestinians dead and the strip's only power generation plant destroyed, leading to fears of a hu-manitarian catastrophe. Under the bombardment, Egyptian mediation that had been initiated to secure Shalit's release quickly dissipated.[145] Despite its offensive, Israel failed to retrieve the captured soldier or to stop rocket fire, paving the way for Hamas to claim it had also emerged victorious. Alongside Hezbollah, the parties boasted that resistance had destroyed fears of Israel's airborne strength and broken its ability to present itself as impregnable.[146] Inevitably, a groundswell of support for the resistance, and in turn for Hamas, was seen as the movement won in local elections in bodies such as the Union of Engineers and the Union of Nurses.[147] Hamas used this popularity to fight against accusations that it had been weakened by the blockade.[148] But this rosy picture met with harsh reality on the ground. Aside from the devastation wrought by Israel's attack, the economic blockade had taken a toll. While sup-porting Hamas's resistance, much anger was directed at Hamas's government as workers carried out strikes to demand their unpaid salaries and institutions struggled to operate. Tension between factions persisted, reaching dangerous levels as Hamas's leaders warned that weapons were being smuggled into Gaza to precipitate domestic confrontations.[149]

CONSPIRACY OR PARANOIA?

As the war with Israel subsided, discussions between Haniyeh and Abbas resumed in Gaza City. Given the advanced state of negotiations before the war broke out, a National Reconciliation Document was quickly agreed upon. Enshrining earlier discussions, the document went one step further and called for "respect" of all past agreements signed by the PLO that "safeguard the interests of our people."[150] As the basis of a unity government, this agreement—with its acceptance of 1967 and UN Resolution 194—reflected a concerted effort on Hamas's part to lift the blockade, engage with the international community, and enter into a unity government with Fatah.[151] Hamas's position had shifted toward accepting international parameters and had found a pragmatic formula to manage internal dissent while allowing the unity government to remain committed to its international agreements. This failed to assuage American and Israeli opposition, even as the Israeli government itself refused to commit to the 1967 border as the basis for a future Palestinian state, as evident by its relentless settlement expansion.

Even after the unity agreement, the Bush administration remained committed to isolating Hamas until it meets the Quartet's conditions and outlawing any engagement with a Palestinian government that includes Hamas until then.[152] Likewise, Israel's foreign minister stated that if Abbas "joins a terrorist government led by the Hamas, I am afraid that there will be problems ahead. I think that [Abbas] and the new government that he is about to establish will have to clarify this [situation], not only to Israel, but to the international community as well."[153] Clarification was decisively offered in Abbas's speech at the UN General Assembly in September 2006, shortly after the agreement was finalized. The president affirmed the mutual recognition between the PLO and Israel as the basis of any future Palestinian government and reiterated the desire to explicitly abide by the Quartet's conditions.[154]

Leaving no room for flexibility around Hamas's position, Abbas effectively annulled the domestic unity agreement less than a week after it was produced, undoing the formula that the parties had painstakingly constructed to allow for domestic partnership. Facing American and Israeli demands to draw explicit concessions from Hamas, as well as pressure from within his party to undermine Hamas's cabinet, Abbas felt there was no space for maneuver.[155] The president stated that discussions "had returned to zero" and that Hamas's inability to abide by past PLO agreements, particularly the recognition of Israel, was "undemocratic."[156] Condemnation was swift. Hamas denounced Abbas's holding of domestic politics hostage to the "Americans and Zionist representatives" the president had met in New York.[157] "The main problem now on the Palestinian arena . . . is recognition of Israel!" its publications bemoaned. "The makers of the Oslo project . . . are so fully convinced [in their efforts] that they are ready to take Palestine, its people and its struggle into the abyss to serve two goals: recognize Israel and maintain past agreements with it!"[158]

Hamas's leaders looked to Israel and stressed that many political parties in the Knesset, including the mainstream Likud party, refused to recognize that Palestinians even existed as a people or to recognize the prospect of a Palestinian state.[159] The anticlimax of having reached a unity agreement only to have it undermined, along with the ongoing blockade and Israeli incursions, combined to precipitate Gaza's disintegration. In the fall of 2006, around seventy thousand civil servants took to the streets to protest their lack of pay.[160] By the end of the demonstrations, clashes between security men, reportedly part of the Palestinian security forces, and Hamas's Executive Force had left twelve dead, more than 130 injured, and public buildings vandalized. The airwaves were filled with provocation; while Fatah pointed to Hamas's "militias" cracking down on protestors, Hamas accused the president's security forces of fomenting protests to embarrass the government.[161] With this instability and the absence of prospects for unity, Hamas's leaders from Gaza embarked on a regional tour to break the blockade.[162]

After three months in the region, in December, Haniyeh's delegation was on its way back into Gaza through the Rafah crossing with Egypt. As the prime minister waved at crowds that had gathered to welcome him home, shots were fired in his direction, killing his bodyguard.[163] Hamas's leaders were incensed at this assassination attempt and pointed to Dahlan as the figure responsible. Dahlan provocatively retorted that "assassinating Haniyeh is an honor I cannot claim," as violence escalated.[164] Qatar began mediation efforts to secure a new unity agreement around the Quartet's conditions.[165] Egypt also resumed attempts to secure Shalit's release as it worked with Hamas to define the parameters of a prisoner swap.[166] On December 19, a gathering took place in Gaza between Abbas, Haniyeh, and Minister of Interior Sayyam, along with representatives from the security forces and the Egyptian security delegation. The meeting produced a ceasefire agreement between Hamas and Fatah and reiterated the authority of Hamas's minister of interior over the security forces.[167] Yet slanderous accusations and suspicion persisted as the gap between the political leaders and their armed militias appeared unbridgeable.

Despite reinvigorated diplomacy, Abbas cited vanishing hope for unity. Backed by the United States, he took the decisive step in early 2007 to call for new presidential and legislative elections, expressing his frustration with Hamas's political games and dismissing its fearmongering that there was a conspiracy aimed at collapsing its government. In a provocative speech, Abbas talked about the foolishness of rocket fire and of Shalit's abduction. Rather than the occupation, he blamed Hamas for the deaths of hundreds of Palestinians in Israel's attacks and for the persistent blockade. He bemoaned the movement's naiveté and its willingness to undermine the political establishment in pursuit of fantasies of resistance.[168] Abbas's words starkly illuminated the divergence between his commitment to international legitimacy and Hamas's rootedness in resistance. While Abbas blamed Palestinian deaths under Israeli firepower on Palestinian resistance, Hamas viewed Israel's occupation as the culprit.

Hamas's publications decried Abbas's call for early elections as a "flagrant violation of the constitution and a coup over democracy."[169] Haniyeh rejected Abbas's accusations of Hamas's intransigence and insisted that there had been an "unannounced decision," led by the United States, to bring down Hamas's government. "From the very beginning, we have lived through the withdrawal of powers from this government for the benefit of the presidency. We have inherited a government with no information, no finances, no crossings, and no embassies."[170] Hamas was given no chance to succeed, Haniyeh insisted.[171] Abbas's attempts to call for new elections were widely condemned, not just from Hamas.[172] They also injected more uncertainty into an explosive situation.[173]

For Hamas's leaders, the events at the end of 2006 signaled irrefutably that a conspiracy had been planned by "rogue elements" within Fatah. They stressed that opposition from Fatah was not party-wide but limited to a coterie of individuals who had been handpicked by the Bush administration to carry out this conspiracy. Headed by Dahlan and including members of the security establishment, these men were referred to by Hamas as the "revolutionary current."[174] Unbeknown to Hamas, a clandestine security committee had indeed been established, which brought together Israelis, members of the Palestinian security forces, and American advisors to deal with the security challenge presented by Hamas.[175] Without directly referring to this group, Hamas accused Fatah individuals of obstructing the Palestinian democratic transition and using American and Israeli support to leverage the deep state that had been created under Fatah's tenure.[176] Hamas's publications described the ensuing violence as a sign that reconciliation was impossible and that the imminent battle would be existential: the clash was not limited to control of the Palestinian Authority but encompassed the core principles of the Palestinian struggle.[177]

Hamas's rhetoric indicated that the movement believed Abbas was conceding, inadvertently or otherwise, on core tenets of Palestinian nationalism by remaining committed to the Oslo project.[178] Skirmishes erupted again in early 2007 in north Gaza and began expanding into the West Bank, as Hamas reported on attacks against its politicians and offices in Ramallah.[179] Accusations from Fatah and the PLO reiterated the instability caused by the Executive Force, noting specifically its tactic of carrying out extrajudicial executions of opponents in Gaza.[180] Hamas refuted these accusations as it decried the attacks by "hired hands" within Fatah, describing their attempts to export unrest to the West Bank on the assumption that Hamas was weaker there.[181] Claiming to be facing a campaign against "anything Islamic," the movement "advise[d] those who are riven with blindness and hate not to misinterpret Hamas's patience and the restraint of its followers."[182]

Drawing on Israeli and international media, Hamas hypothesized about the alleged US-led planned coup. The movement's publications discussed a series of initiatives it believed were underway: strengthening Abbas and Fatah; fomenting a clash; and forming a subservient Palestinian state that recognized Israel.[183] Having imposed a financial blockade aimed at weakening Hamas's government while strengthening Abbas's authority, the "revolutionary current," Hamas guessed, was now mobilizing to engineer the cabinet's collapse.[184] Publications surmised that Secretary Rice had secretly agreed with Abbas to scuttle the latest unity agreement to prevent any legitimacy being conferred on to the movement.[185] The chaos on the streets and Abbas's ultimatum around the Prisoners' Document were both seen as US-hatched initiatives.[186] Rice's tour of the Middle East, during which she had called on foreign ministers to desist from supporting Hamas, further strengthened these suspicions, as did news of American financial assistance delivered to Abbas. Hamas viewed these American efforts as attempts to reframe the region around the so-called moderate–radical axis.[187] Hamas suspected that portions of the tax revenues withheld by Israel and owed to Palestinians would also be transferred to the president's office.[188] It latched on to Israeli news articles and academic debates about collusion with Fatah, both financially and through security coordination, including reports quoting the former director of Israel's Internal Security Agency affirming that Abbas had appointed Dahlan in charge of forming a military unit to counter Hamas.[189]

Hamas believed Abbas was being groomed to emerge victorious from a future confrontation, actively precipitated or otherwise.[190] These suspicions were not unfounded. The United States was indeed actively implementing its "train and equip" program, providing arms and training for Fatah's security forces to prepare them for a clash with Hamas. As Secretary Rice later explained, the administration believed that Hamas was getting arms and training from Iran, and therefore the administration was doing what it could to prepare "the good guys" to emerge victorious.[191] Through this program, the United States effectively provided Dahlan with carte blanche to deal with Hamas.[192] America's security coordinator on the ground, Lieutenant-General Keith Dayton, openly called on the Quartet to support Abbas "by whatever means necessary" to take on Hamas, despite Quartet members voicing reservations about taking sides in a civil war.[193] Under the pretense of "security reform," the United States began financing a training camp for the presidential forces outside Jericho in the West Bank. These guards were to be bolstered by two thousand troops from the Badr Brigade, a division of the Palestinian Liberation Army in Jordan.[194] Hamas saw this move as the first step in expanding Abbas's security forces of 3,700–4,700 to "the tens of thousands."[195] In contrast to flagrant American support for Abbas's forces, Hamas's Executive Force was coming under a concerted campaign of arrests in the West Bank.[196]

As infighting expanded, Hamas reported on a "Zionified current" targeting its officials, particularly in Ramallah and Nablus.[197] Faced with such antagonism, Hamas's spokesman said the conflict was not "between the two Palestinian organizations [Hamas and Fatah], but rather it is between Hamas and its political agenda . . . and the followers of a revolutionary current with foreign agendas."[198] He continued to assert the movement's position. "We are eager to maintain the unity of the Palestinian people, avoid its bloodshed and undermine civil discord. But from the point of self-defense, we do not allow anyone to assault our leadership, or the Palestinian cause."[199] Hamas viewed this "revolution-ary current" as threatening to destroy the Palestinian social fabric at the bidding of the "Zionist entity."[200] Urgency and anxiety regarding a possible war permeated Hamas's leadership. It predicted a battle aimed at Hamas's elimination, stressing that it was being "forced" to act in self-defense and to "put an end to the chaos."[201]

Sporadic efforts to hold off such an outcome recurred, as Hamas's leaders tried to demonstrate flexibility and Abbas sought to avoid being seen as explicitly siding with the United States and Israel.[202] Haniyeh issued appeals to walk back from the abyss by calling for an end to media and military incitement and a restart of domestic discussions.[203] Hamas's leaders reiterated their readiness for a political solution. In an interview in early January 2007, Meshal said:

> As a Palestinian, I speak of an Arab and a Palestinian demand, to have a state on the 67 borders. True, by inference, this will mean there is an entity or a state called Israel on the rest of the Palestinian lands. That is a reality, and I will not deal with this reality by recognizing it or vali-dating it. It is just a reality based on historic circumstance. Today, we speak of a Palestinian and Arab preparedness to accept a Palestinian state on the 67 borders. . . . The question is, is there an Israeli, Ameri-can or international readiness to recognize this?[204]

But Hamas's efforts to negotiate around the Quartet's conditions met with unrelenting pressure to explicitly recognize Israel, a stance that Hamas openly admitted was merely strengthening its desire to fight for the Palestinian right to dissent.[205]

THE MECCA AGREEMENT

Hamas's leaders were not the only ones targeted for assassination. In early 2007, President Abbas's forces reported that they had detected explosives that had been planted for him. The lethal volatility of the situation compelled Abbas and Meshal to meet face-to-face in Damascus, the first such meeting since Hamas's rise to power, and agree to the formation of a unity government that could mitigate infighting.[206] Before the ink had even dried on the Damascus Agreement, as it came to be known, clashes erupted once more in Gaza. Hamas's leaders remarked that "there is no longer a shadow of a doubt that a decision had been taken in the darkened corridors" of Fatah's revolutionary current to spark a civil war.[207] At the end of a bloody January, Saudi Arabia's King Abdullah reached out to the Palestinian leaders and invited them to Mecca, promising an opportunity for discussions away from the glare of media attention and international pressure.[208]

The ideological chasm between Hamas and Fatah was evident from the opening speeches.[209] Abbas lamented the "black days" as he reaffirmed his commitment to the formation of a unity government that would be internationally recognized.[210] In contrast, Meshal wanted "a real partnership . . . I believe that the international community cannot but respect our wishes if it finds us united."[211] Hamas's leader spoke of focusing first internally, on PLO reform and on Arab and Palestinian legitimacy, and *then* on reaching out to the international community. "The Palestinian people are not asking for the impossible, my brother Abu Mazen [Abbas], [they] are asking for their legitimate rights, and the international community must respect that wish."[212] Privacy from media intrusion gave room for optimism, and an agreement was reached within two days.[213] Despite previous failed breakthroughs, Hamas's publications lauded the Mecca Agreement as an exceptional success due to the credibility conferred by Saudi sponsorship.[214] Hamas celebrated its "political victory," underscored by its ability to withstand American or Israeli diktats.[215] The movement portrayed itself as a pioneering example of an indigenous popular Arab political party, "a moderate Islamic one," rising to power and engaging in pluralistic democratic governance.[216]

The Mecca Agreement outlined broad areas of consensus and paved the way for the division of cabinet posts in a unity government. Without making ideological concessions, Hamas acquiesced to relinquishing domestic power in order to lift the blockade and end lawlessness.[217] The movement gave up six of its nineteen ministries to Fatah and another four to independents, including the key positions of interior, finance, and foreign ministries.[218] In so doing, Hamas conceded positions of influence within its government to assuage international concerns. The movement may have seen this as a political victory that left its ideological principles intact, but leaders also stated they felt Hamas had made significant practical concessions to find common ground with Abbas.[219] The extent of Hamas's relinquishment of power betrayed a desire to offload its governance responsibilities, given its failure to circumvent the blockade, while maintaining its ideological platform.

Moreover, the Mecca Agreement demonstrated Hamas's willingness to put some distance between the positions the government might take and its own ideology as a movement and a political party within that government. Hamas's gesture in Mecca was met with a great deal of criticism internally as it undermined the movement's initial rationale for engaging with the political process. For instance, Islamic Jihad's leader stated that the Mecca Agreement produced not the "resistance government" Hamas had promised but merely one embroiled in administrative and political duties.[220]

The Mecca Agreement suggested a possibly different outcome to previous reconciliation efforts. Saudi Arabia offered the Palestinians an incentive of one billion dollars in aid to implement the deal as members of the international community, including France and the European Union, voiced cautious optimism. Within Europe, some member states saw the unity government's political agenda as the first step in Hamas's moderation. Having seen the failure of the Quartet's conditions and the blockade, and noting Hamas's diplomatic gestures, they suggested initiating engagement with the movement and allowing it to fulfill the Quartet's conditions de facto through governance.[221] This offered hope to Hamas that the Quartet's position would be weakened, as it criticized the absence of any initiatives from the Arab world to lift the blockade.[222]

The United Nations and members of the Quartet also welcomed this deal as a first step toward moderating Hamas.[223]

The Bush administration, however, stated that it could not deal with a Palestinian Authority that included Hamas. Even if the government itself accepted the Quartet demands, the onus would be maintained on Hamas as a political party to fulfill those same requirements. Cutting through this optimism, it made it a priority to dissolve the national unity government.[224] Despite this opposition, Hamas and Fatah moved toward implementation. On March 17, they put forward the political agenda of the new cabinet, which called for "respecting" past agreements made by the PLO; the right of return based on UN Resolution 194; and the right of resistance as defined by international law, meaning that civilians would not be targeted in armed operations. The movement placed the onus of responsibility on the PLO to manage negotiations with Israel in the understanding that all agreements would be presented to the PLO for a vote. It also called for maintaining calm on the military front and seeking Shalit's release.[225] Furthermore, despite calling for the right to resist, the unity government adopted a decision to implement a ceasefire, which factions such as Islamic Jihad refused to do.

The Mecca Agreement indicated Hamas's willingness to abide, on a practical level, with the demands of the international community. Rather than acknowledging these concessions, Israel condemned the incoming cabinet.[226] In particular, it denounced its commitment to the right of return through UN Resolution 194, a key demand for the Palestinians writ large—not just Hamas. This underscored Israel's unwillingness to deal with certain political aspects that form the core of Palestinian nationalism, not of Hamas's political agenda. Israel also condemned the agreement's emphasis on putting future peace resolutions to a vote, a condition it insisted would provide terrorist organizations with a political voice. It stated that it would continue withholding funds owed to Palestinians and would consider options to downgrade its relations with Abbas.[227]

Hamas prepared to support Abbas's marketing of the agreement to end the Palestinians' isolation as Meshal embarked on a regional tour to convince countries to lift the blockade.[228] Abbas, for his part, toured European countries, asserting that the Mecca Agreement kept all past PLO decisions intact.[229] Bilateral discussions continued in Damascus and Cairo to build on the momentum and tackle wider issues related to PLO reform. The greatest challenges arose around security issues aimed at ending the proliferation of arms and delineating the role, if any, of the resistance weapons.[230] The newly appointed minister of interior, an independent, was tasked with the monumental job of streamlining the security forces to stop the violent domestic clashes and to deal with the private militias, particularly in Gaza.[231] He produced a one-hundred-day plan to carry out this task and called for the backing of the presidency and the cabinet.[232] Within three days, the minister had resigned, citing fears that he would be held accountable for an impossible task, given what he perceived as the absence of any jurisdiction for the ministry over the security forces and the institutionalized opposition from establishment figures within the national security services.[233] His remarks validated Hamas's early objections regarding jurisdiction.

Fatah's institutional entrenchment across all levels of government, from municipalities to foreign consulates, appeared to undermine claims that the government was indeed one of unity. Other challenges abounded. Abbas appointed Dahlan as a security advisor, further aggravating matters. So did ongoing American financial and military support to the presidential guards and the ensuing militarized lawlessness of various gangs and militias.[234] Within weeks, the security situation unraveled once more. Kidnappings and skirmishes resulted in the death of more than twenty-nine Palestinians in March 2007 alone.[235] By mid-May, brutal clashes and acrimonious exchanges dominated the streets. Blaming the presidential guards, Hamas condemned the "dogs" for carrying out extrajudicial assassinations of its members, for torturing Hamas supporters, and for attacking its institutions.[236] A full-blown armed conflagration between the parties was underway.

The conflict lasted one week and caused the death of close to fifty Palestinians. Feeling besieged by the "conspiracy," Hamas stated that Israel had graduated from its subversive plots with Fatah's security forces into explicit collusion with "revolutionaries and renegade Fatah gangs."[237] In all its accusations, perhaps out of goodwill or to control tensions, Hamas distinguished between the "rogue elements" within Fatah, which it accused of working outside the rule of law, and what it regarded as "official" Fatah. Nevertheless, it blamed Fatah's leadership for providing these "perpetrators" with institutional cover. As events in Gaza turned ever more violent, Hamas stressed that the patience and silence it was allegedly abiding by could not be sustained indefinitely. The movement warned it would mobilize its forces to deal with conspirators as it would collaborators, and that it was no longer going to sit idly by as its supporters were executed in cold blood.[238]

By the end of May, it was clear that both leaderships were unable to control their forces. Narratives and counternarratives dominated the airwaves. Fatah claimed Hamas was "shooting and weeping," blaming the movement for kidnapping and torturing its followers, shooting them in the legs, and setting up random checkpoints to terrorize people in Gaza.[239] Hamas in turn pointed the finger at Fatah, stating it had carried out cold-blooded executions in front of the security forces. The murder of two imams, pulled out of their mosques in early June, was seen by Hamas as a point of no return. "The executions . . . will not pass unpunished. That is a vow we have taken, there is no turning back."[240] According to General Dayton, the American advisor to the Palestinian security forces on the ground, Gaza had disintegrated into a plethora of armed groups that called themselves armies working outside the authority of any one faction. Dayton accused Hamas of carrying out aggressive attacks against Gazans and Fatah's security forces, claiming these actions cost it popular support while insisting Fatah's forces were holding firm.[241] Hamas, on the other hand, insisted that it was upholding a unilateral truce in the face of aggression from "rogue elements" within Fatah.[242] It condemned Abbas's continued silence and

threatened that its calm demeanor would only be a precursor to a mas-
sively destructive storm if the offensive were to continue.[243]

By the beginning of June, Gaza fell into an exhausted calm almost
as spontaneously as the initial violence had erupted. This barely lasted
a few days. Violence resumed as Hamas preemptively mobilized all
its forces and moved to take full control over the Gaza Strip. Hamas
achieved its goals in spectacular speed as it carried out brutal acts of
violence against its political opponents, killing Fatah leaders and Palestinian security forces and forcing many of them to flee the coastal
enclave.[244] Within four days, al-Qassam had captured all the major public institutions within the Gaza Strip and had consolidated its control.
Hamas reported on troves of American weapons it had found stored
in preparation for the coup Hamas had anticipated.[245] This vindicated
voices within the Bush administration who had opposed the American "train and equip" program for fear that weapons would fall into
Hamas's hands. Dayton's assertions about the efficacy of Fatah's armed
forces and Dahlan's boastful confidence suddenly rang hollow.[246]

By the end of June, Hamas had taken full control of the Gaza Strip.
Less than two years after Israel pulled out of its illegal settlements in the
strip, a decision often portrayed as a painful step and a litmus test for further Israeli withdrawals, Gaza came under Hamas's rule.[247] Hamas assumed the ultimate responsibility for its decision to mobilize al-Qassam
as forcefully as it did. Accounts from the ground reveal both that Hamas
had indeed worked to strengthen its forces in the months leading to its
military push, and that its leaders openly admitted its forces made many
mistakes and used brutal tactics to overwhelm Fatah's troops.[248] Equally,
the Israeli and American actions that precipitated this crucial development remain overlooked and underreported. American officials continued to stress that Hamas had imagined the conspiracy it was facing. But
the evidence that has emerged since the rupture underscores the role
of the Bush administration and of Israel in fomenting this clash alongside their Palestinian strongmen.[249] A damning report released a short
while after Hamas's takeover from an investigative committee in Fatah's

military office also raised serious and troubling questions regarding the extent of Dahlan's role in creating the war.[250]

In the eighteen months following Hamas's election victory, more than six hundred Palestinians had been killed. A brief episode in Palestinian democracy had ended in fratricide.[251] Like the PLO before it, Hamas's political vision, and with it the internationally sanctioned right of self-determination, right of return, and right to resist—demands that form the core of Palestinian nationalism—had effectively been neutralized by foreign intervention. Instead of the United States (and members of the international community) engaging with the concessions Hamas had made or applying pressure on Israel for its own failure to meet the same demands that were being placed on Hamas, funds and arms poured into the territories to quash the prospect of any form of viable or unified Palestinian resistance to Israel's ongoing occupation. On the eve of Hamas's takeover of Gaza, a leaked report noted that Abbas had asked for Israeli intervention to assist Fatah's forces in combating Hamas's offensive. A senior member of Israel's security establishment was quoted as being "happy" at the prospect of Hamas taking over the Gaza Strip, as that would then allow Israel to declare the coastal enclave a "hostile territory."[252] This development, the culmination of policies aimed at severing Gaza from the territories that had officially begun with Sharon's disengagement two years prior, was now imminent.

CHAPTER FIVE

INSTITUTIONALIZING
THE DIVISION

Hamas's takeover of the Gaza Strip in June 2007 ruptured the Palestinian territories, politically and institutionally.[1] Within hours of Hamas securing its grip over the coastal enclave, President Mahmoud Abbas declared a state of emergency and dismissed the unity government that had been negotiated in Mecca a few weeks earlier. Out of his base in Ramallah, in the West Bank, he formed an emergency cabinet under Prime Minister Salam Fayyad. Previously a finance minister, Fayyad was a technocrat favored by the West because of his American education and tenure as a World Bank economist as well as his vocal denunciation of armed struggle.[2] In the Gaza Strip, Hamas became the sole governing authority. With this separation, a Palestinian Authority in the West Bank came to coexist with a Hamas government in the Gaza Strip.

Hamas's decisive victory over Fatah's security forces was instantly classified as a "coup" by President Abbas and by regional and international actors. After the gunfire subsided, Abbas delivered a bitter speech accusing Hamas of undermining the unity government and separating Gaza from the West Bank to create an Islamic emirate.[3] In light of the rapid efficacy with which Hamas had taken control, Abbas suspected premeditation.[4] He insisted that the coup was the culmination of months of planning and that past unity agreements had been mere manipulations as Hamas strategized to take over the Palestinian Authority. He criticized the movement's heavy-handedness during the fighting and scorned its hypocritical veneer of religiosity. Abbas demonstrated significant bitterness regarding assassination attempts allegedly by Hamas that he had escaped during the previous eighteen months.[5]

Hamas's leaders rejected this narrative. Khaled Meshal explained the takeover as a "security situation that had been forced onto Hamas."[6] He wondered how the movement could carry out a coup against a government it had been democratically elected to lead.[7] In press conferences and declarations, the movement's leaders explained that Hamas had been forced to act preemptively for self-preservation, having witnessed with much trepidation American training and financing of the Palestinian security forces.[8] The leaders denounced charges that drew on Hamas's Islamic character to suggest it had orchestrated a coup to establish an Islamic emirate. Hamas noted that it had barely accepted a Palestinian state within the 1967 borders because it was committed to the territorial integrity of Palestine.[9] Ismail Haniyeh, who remained prime minister in Gaza, insisted that there was no way Hamas would divide the West Bank from the Gaza Strip, establish a stand-alone emirate or any form of separate ministate.[10]

From his base in Cairo, Musa Abu Marzouq expanded on this, saying, "Gaza is not the state of Hamas, nor the West Bank the state of Fatah. It is not even that the West Bank and Gaza are Palestine. We believe that Palestine is within its known historic borders, and we believe that the West Bank and the [Gaza] Strip cannot be separated."[11] Hamas's leaders stood their ground and called for an impartial investigation to review the backdrop to the takeover.[12] They reached out to Fatah and Arab officials seeking mediation and stressing that division served only the occupation.[13] Amid impassioned accusations on both sides, Hamas issued conditions for reconciliation with Fatah, the first of which was the removal from power of figures within the Palestinian security services that Hamas held accountable for the carnage.[14] It produced detailed reports outlining the actions that were taken against the movement in the days leading to its mobilization, in both Gaza and the West Bank.[15] Abbas's efforts to "reclaim Palestinian legitimacy" through an emergency government staffed with "moderates" and his continued silence toward the atrocities carried out by Dahlan's forces were not viewed by Hamas as harbingers of positive relations.[16]

With this institutional rupture between the Gaza Strip and the West Bank, the international financial blockade that had been put in place against the Palestinian Authority following Hamas's election victory morphed, as it became far simpler to geographically delineate Hamas's jurisdiction. Israel and the United States promptly redirected the withheld tax revenue and other financial support to Abbas's government in the West Bank, and the blockade was reconstituted to focus exclusively on the Gaza Strip.[17] All five crossings leading into the territory from Israel were shut as was the Rafah border with Egypt, hermetically sealing the strip. Israel and the Palestinian Authority in the West Bank also withheld revenue that would have normally been redirected to the government's branches in Gaza.[18] Israel cut fuel shipments by half and reduced imports into Gaza to the minimum amounts of food and medical supplies required for survival without sinking Gaza into a humanitarian catastrophe.[19]

Aside from the long-term economic and social impact of stifling Palestinians in this manner, the Gaza blockade that was instituted in 2007 had a more immediate effect. Food shortage and health-care crises were felt almost instantly as poverty rates and unemployment soared. Rapid economic deterioration was compounded by the fact that Gaza had suffered decades of de-development, whereby its economy had contracted and its infrastructure regressed as a result of Israel's isolationist policies toward the strip, which began officially following the Oslo Accords.[20] Freedom of movement into and out of the Gaza Strip ground to a halt, effectively severing Gaza from the West Bank and the rest of the world.[21] The blockade's philosophy took on a geographic dimension: while the West Bank under Abbas's leadership could be embraced and empowered, Gaza under Hamas's control was to be ring-fenced. The reasoning was presumably simple: once Gazans suffered and their lives were badly hit relative to West Bankers, they would revolt against Hamas's authority. This would pave the way for Hamas's collapse and the return of the Palestinian Authority, under Mahmoud Abbas's leadership, back into the Gaza Strip, thereby reunifying the Palestinian territories under a single leadership committed to negotiations with Israel.

CONSOLIDATION IN GAZA

As a result of the rupture, the Gaza Strip became the first portion of Palestinian land to be entirely "liberated." Although direct Israeli presence in the form of illegal Jewish settlements had ended a few years prior, in 2005 with Sharon's disengagement, the occupation had persisted through systems of enclosure, military operations, and security coordination with the Palestinian Authority.[22] With Hamas's takeover, the slim territory by the Mediterranean came under absolute internal Palestinian control, as Hamas's government rejected any official engagement with the Israeli state. Imposed curfews, home demolitions, and midnight raids by Israel's occupying forces, or by Palestinian security following Israeli orders, were no longer a daily occurrence as they were in the West Bank. Yet "liberation" was of course a matter of rhetoric rather than reality. While Gaza became a territory where a defiant Palestinian government emerged, the occupation apparatus had been reconfigured into a structure that contained and isolated the enclave militarily, diplomatically, and economically.[23]

Rather than being liberated, the Gaza Strip turned into the world's largest open-air prison, incarcerating and collectively punishing close to two million inhabitants following a democratic election. With the Gaza Strip blockaded, fortunes turned for the West Bank as financial largesse was redirected to Abbas's emergency cabinet. Constitutionally, this cabinet had a limited validity of thirty days, following which new elections had to be completed. After the interim period passed, however, the cabinet's mandate was extended by executive order, with the full backing of Israel and the United States and fierce opposition from Hamas.[24] Abbas took other executive measures. At risk of prosecution, he prevented any civil servant from reporting to Hamas's ministries in

Gaza. He reassured all employees that they would continue to receive compensation from the Palestinian Authority in Ramallah despite boycotting their workplace.[25] Hamas's ministries suddenly faced a debilitating vacuum of civil servants.

Shortly after the separation, President Abbas met with Israeli prime minister Ehud Olmert in Sharm al-Sheikh, where he renewed his commitment to the Arab Peace Initiative (API), including its provision to dismantle the terrorist infrastructure.[26] The emergency government sought to nationalize the resistance factions in the West Bank and gain a monopoly on the use of force. Moving to pursue disarmament, Fayyad's cabinet issued decrees against armed factions, outlawing all weapons including those carried by Fatah's al-Aqsa Brigades. It also declared Hamas's Executive Force and al-Qassam to be "illegal militias" and commenced a widespread campaign against Hamas's forces and institutions.[27] Resistance factions decried Abbas's efforts to strip their fighters of weapons at a time when the "occupation continues to carry out massacres."[28] They issued leaflets of condemnation against "the announcement that resistance is no longer a policy within this government, as if the occupation has been removed from our territory. . . . [We] call on our people to oppose this contemptible position . . . and to respond to it by escalating resistance against the Zionist occupation."[29] Hamas's publications described as "bizarre" Abbas's description of resistance factions as "illegal militias," given their role in the struggle.[30]

Abbas's actions accelerated diplomatic overtures with the United States that sought to isolate Hamas and strengthen its counterpart.[31] In the final year of the Bush presidency, Secretary Rice reinitiated prospects for a peace conference to concretize Bush's vision for the creation of a democratic and peaceful Palestinian state.[32] The juxtaposition of the blockade on Gaza with openness in the West Bank created a great deal of resentment within Hamas's government. Abbas was viewed as a coconspirator with the Americans and Israelis in plans to isolate Gaza. "What is happening to the Palestinian people these days is tragic. It is the result of the obvious confusion of Fayyad's illegitimate government and the policies of President Mahmoud Abbas. These have harmed the Palestinian people and deprived tens of Palestinian children their sustenance. These are inhuman and irresponsible policies."[33] Publications described Abbas as a "self-appointed . . . security agent to the occupation."[34] Hamas reported on the Palestinian Authority's "sterilization campaigns" in the West Bank throughout the summer.[35] As Abu Marzouq stated, "What took place in Gaza over the past few years is repeating itself in the West Bank today; raiding and burning institutions, arresting people and torturing them, targeting and liquidating individuals."[36]

The divergence between the two governments became increasingly visible as Hamas swiftly consolidated its own power within the Gaza Strip.[37] Hamas asserted its rule by removing Arafat's portraits, distributing its own green banners, and deploying its security guards at major junctions and government buildings.[38] After its crushing victory over Dahlan's forces, Hamas developed an aura of invincibility and mobilized to violently and firmly crush any opposition to its rule within the coastal enclave.[39] Hamas alleged that it did not target opposition factions in its quest to achieve security, claiming that it implemented a general amnesty as soon as the takeover ended.[40] It contrasted its policy of allowing Fatah flags to hang out of buildings in central Gaza with Fayyad's government, which it accused of taking draconian measures against Hamas in the West Bank.[41] Hamas's assertions of positive plurality were strongly contested, most scathingly in a report issued by the Palestinian Centre for Human Rights in Gaza, which accused the Executive Force and al-Qassam of a wide range of human rights abuses, including attacks on journalists, policing of public spaces, illegitimate arrests, torture and inhuman treatment of prisoners, and intimidation of civil servants.[42]

The movement's security forces clamped down on lawlessness by forbidding the public use of "non-resistance firearms"—including during weddings and celebrations, as was custom—and instituting regulations governing ski masks and other forms of provocation. Hamas cracked down on gangs, drug traffickers, and money launderers and began "policing indecent behavior."[43] Domestic policing and law enforcement were carried out by Hamas's Executive Force, which had integrated members of al-Qassam.[44] Hamas reined in powerful families who had previously acted above the law and contributed to the violence that had ravaged the strip.[45]

The government also worked to control radical Salafi jihadists, such as smaller offshoots of al-Qaeda and other transnational terror movements that resided in Gaza. The movement's leaders reiterated that there was no major institutional presence of Salafi jihadists but rather a number of individuals who were susceptible to such ideologies.[46] Hamas adopted a consultative approach coupled with an iron fist when dealing with these groups, hosting sessions aimed at discussing and debunking the Salafi interpretation of Islam as a way to reverse their ideological conviction through diplomacy.[47] The success of this approach was made evident early on through Hamas's role in negotiating the release of Alan Johnson, a BBC reporter held hostage by Jaysh al-Islam (Islamic Army), a Salafist movement in Gaza.[48] Hamas's opposition to any form of transnational terroristic ideologies was concretized by its decision not to implement *shari'a* law in Gaza after its takeover, choosing instead to uphold conservative social values and the slow, organic Islamization of the strip.[49]

Hamas leaders called on journalists to come and report on Gaza's transformation.[50] Citing a drop in crime rates, publications conducted interviews with families who now presumably felt safe to go to beaches and remain outdoors late into the night, and whose little children were able to fall asleep without the sound of gunfire in the streets. Hamas's magazines reported on the popularity of songs such as "Hamsawi [a Hamas supporter] fears not death" and "Executive Forces, may God be with them." Even traffic was ostensibly more organized, with volunteers going out on to the street to restore order.[51]

As quiet indeed returned to Gaza, a new dynamic emerged for Hamas, whereby Hamas-as-movement, led by the political bureau and armed by al-Qassam, defined the overall trajectory of the movement.

Under this umbrella, Hamas's government became the body responsible for administering the civil and social affairs of the Palestinian inhabitants within the Gaza Strip. In essence, Hamas's government became a de facto administrative authority operating under the guidance of the movement, which did not get involved in the daily affairs of governance.[52] Therefore, while reining in domestic instability and enforcing the rule of law, Hamas nurtured an environment that was supportive of armed struggle against Israel, where "resistance weapons" from all factions were permitted as long as they were confined to designated areas such as the borders of the Gaza Strip.[53] Hamas's aspirations to safeguard resistance were evident. From mid-July, a month after its takeover, rocket fire from the Gaza Strip into Israel increased. This was mostly carried out by Islamic Jihad with acquiescence from Hamas's government. Israeli military operations into Gaza also escalated and took the form of air strikes and ground incursions.

By mid-September 2007, Israel had declared Gaza "hostile territory," a milestone that in many ways marked the culmination of the initiative set in motion by Prime Minister Sharon's disengagement.[54] Israel sustained its tight grip on the borders, maintaining a "drip of welfare support" to the strip; this was described by a border agent as "no development, no prosperity, only humanitarian dependency."[55] By this point, Hamas's government in Gaza was scrambling to address internal concerns and was shaping a governance agenda that could serve Hamas's liberation project. In shaping its government, Hamas maintained the institutional integrity that had been developed under the Palestinian Authority. Its leaders admitted inexperience in governance, and initially at least, there was to be significant continuity in the administration of policies in areas such as health, education, and justice.[56] The key early challenge was the need to replace segments of the civil service given the orders Abbas had issued for boycotting Hamas's ministries. In both developing governing experience and reaching out to a body of replacement employees, Hamas was aided by its decades of experience running a welfare system.[57]

Soon after its takeover, Hamas's government declared that the cabinet was addressing three priorities: security reform, economic development, and national unity.[58] In terms of security reform, Mahmoud Zahhar, who remained as foreign minister of Hamas's government, outlined plans to implement Hamas's "Change and Reform" agenda to base the security forces on merit rather than affiliation, to root out corruption, and to remove collaborators.[59] He stressed that the forces would be built on "a national basis," which meant that they would include members from key factions. "[Hamas] will never allow the situation in Gaza to go back to the way it was last June . . . to return to the previous murderous whirlpool. If dialogue resumed between Hamas and Fatah, there will be points added onto the agenda; the most important of which will be that the security forces will not be handed over to those traitors and criminals."[60]

As for economic development, Hamas's government was intent on pursuing options that would circumvent the crippling blockade and make the strip self-sustaining.[61] Measures were taken in the fields of low-tech and small-scale manufacturing, and agriculture, to build Gaza's internal capacity to meet the needs of the population. Leaders spoke of leveraging Gaza's young and educated workforce to plug the need for employees in the public sector and to keep Gaza's local economy running.[62] Gazans reportedly volunteered as health-care professionals, lawyers, teachers, and social workers as the strip adapted to its isolation.[63] However, apart from health and education, most of the bureaucracy of the Palestinian Authority ceased functioning in the early days after the takeover.[64] Hamas's government therefore relied heavily on international organizations working within Gaza, including the UN Relief and Welfare Agency (UNRWA) that assumed a significant portion of the social burden through its local infrastructure. Alongside these survivalist adaptations, Hamas's minister of economy hinted that the government was pursuing indirect talks with Israel through regional and foreign mediators to reach an agreement on opening the borders, which was essential for the survival of a manufacturing sector.[65]

Despite this focus on internal sustenance, household income dropped sharply and dependence on food aid expanded.[66] The desperate situation led to—and was ultimately mitigated by—a rapid shift toward a tunnel-based economy.[67] Tunnels between the Sinai Peninsula in Egypt and the Gaza Strip, passing underneath the Rafah border, had historically been used for smuggling contraband and resistance weapons, particularly during the Second Intifada. After Israel's disengagement from Gaza and as policies aimed at isolating Hamas gathered force, the economic value of the tunnels increased even before the movement's electoral victory. With the blockade and the absence of any official trade channels, tunnels became Gaza's economic lifeline. From twenty tunnels in mid-2007, the number began expanding soon after Hamas's takeover as all basic supplies and goods, as well as weapons, were transported into the Gaza Strip via tunnels. As Hamas oversaw a concerted drive to expand the tunnel infrastructure in Egypt, it began creating a shadow subterranean economy that benefited Hamas's ruling class rather than the traditional mercantile sector within Gaza.[68]

The third priority for Hamas's government was reconciliation with Fatah, despite Hamas's efforts to consolidate power. Hamas reported that work in this vein was severely compromised by the Palestinian Authority's repressive disarmament policies in the West Bank.[69] It alleged that much of the intimidation that Hamas's members felt was religiously motivated, as individuals were mocked, berated, and cursed for their faith and arrests were made on mere suspicion of affiliation to Hamas by noting a long beard or a woman's veil.[70] Hamas condemned actions by Fayyad's government to institutionally purge the movement and its members from government agencies, public bodies, and NGOs.[71] Attacks on Hamas's West Bank parliamentarians were seen as a vile transgression of political immunity and a dangerous precedent by the Palestinian security forces.[72] Hamas denounced these "political arrests" and rejected claims that there were similar arrests of Fatah members in Gaza.[73] This was untrue. Hamas's shift toward the enforcement of law and ending security chaos produced a totalitarian order under its rule in Gaza where, like the

Palestinian Authority, Hamas carried out widespread campaigns against opposition factions and their institutional presence.[74]

This mutual crackdown on opposition factions was an important factor undermining prospects for reconciliation. But it was not the only one. In the fall of 2007, the United States invited Israel and the Palestinian leadership to an international peace conference to be held in Annapolis, Maryland. In the run-up to the November conference, Abbas attended monthly meetings with Olmert and American diplomats to prepare for the negotiations, much to Hamas's chagrin. The movement viewed the Annapolis conference with skepticism, as little more than a photo opportunity to demonstrate support for Abbas and boost Olmert's domestic ratings.[75] Since planning for the conference was taking place against the backdrop of the blockade, Hamas understood that diplomatic progress was contingent on its isolation.[76] For the movement, Abbas's acquiescence to Gaza's isolation was evident in the stringent demands he placed for the resumption of domestic unity discussions with Hamas. The Palestinian leader felt personally betrayed by Hamas's actions and bitter at alleged evidence he had seen that Hamas had planned to assassinate him earlier in the year. Abbas demanded a formal apology and Hamas's relinquishment of power in Gaza as preconditions for unity talks.[77] Negotiating with Hamas from its position of power, with its de facto government, was seen by Abbas as rewarding the "coup." Hamas interpreted Abbas's stance as a desire to entrench the division, in contrast to its efforts, which allegedly included "knocking on all doors" to resume discussions without preconditions.[78]

On November 27, Abbas's negotiating team within the PLO participated in the Annapolis Peace Conference. During the summit, Bush reverted to the principles that had been highlighted in the Roadmap for Peace as he called for a negotiated agreement, stressing that Israel would be required to dismantle the settlements and allow for the creation of two independent and democratic states.[79] With conciliatory remarks from both Abbas and Olmert, the conference ended with a memorandum of understanding that called on Palestinians and Israelis to launch bilateral negotiations to tackle final-status issues at the end of 2008 and move toward the formation of a Palestinian state.[80] Hamas's publications criticized the PLO's readiness to engage in negotiations while Gaza remained besieged and while the Palestinian Authority was waging a "war of eradication" against resistance fighters in the West Bank.[81]

Less than a month after the conference, the Israeli army increased its military activity in the Gaza Strip to end rocket fire into Israel.[82] Rocket fire from Gaza had intensified after Hamas's takeover, with an average of three rockets per day in 2007.[83] Although missiles had been fired mostly by Islamic Jihad, Hamas responded to Israel's escalation with its own rockets on Sderot in south Israel.[84] This exacerbated tensions as Israel threatened military action and imposed a "total blockade."[85] Fuel shortages plunged Gaza into darkness as some Gazans abandoned cars and began relying on donkeys for transport.[86] In early 2008, international concern heightened around the extreme depletion of food and health-care resources. Hamas decried the blockade and accelerated its focus toward expanding the tunnel infrastructure as a lifeline. Given the Palestinian Authority's acquiescence, Hamas condemned Abbas's "policies of starvation" as publications reported on the crippled economy; severed industrial and commercial contracts with regional and foreign firms; a severe shortage of medicines and health-care services, causing sharp rises in mortality; and general hunger due to loss of income and increased poverty.[87]

While Israel was held as primarily responsible for this rapidly deteriorating situation, the movement's magazines also directed their anger at Egypt, which was seen to have adopted a hardened attitude toward Hamas to limit its influence on the Egyptian Muslim Brotherhood.[88] Hamas's condemnation of Egypt related to the latter's decision to keep the Rafah border shut. Hamas nonetheless benefited from the blind eye that President Hosni Mubarak's regime turned to the tunnel industry between Gaza and the Sinai.[89] Tunnel trade, however, was insufficient to meet Gaza's needs, at least not by early 2008. As international pressure mounted, with Gaza teetering on the brink, Israel allowed the entry of one week's worth of cooking gas, fuel, food, and medicine on January 22, 2008.[90] On the same day, Hamas destroyed the seven-mile Egyptian-Gazan border at Rafah by blowing it open in seventeen places. More than seven hundred thousand Palestinians from Gaza spilled out into Egypt in search of food, fuel, and medical supplies. Hamas's "orchestrated" initiative boosted its image and presented it as the "savior" compared to Abbas.[91]

In under two weeks, Mubarak's forces had driven the Gazans back into the strip and bolstered their security on the Rafah border.[92] Nonetheless, riding this popularity wave, Hamas's external leadership headed a summit in Damascus for those who "expressed a desire to hold onto the fixed principles [of the Palestinian struggle]," on January 23–25. The conference, which Hamas estimated was attended by about 1,200 participants, was held under the banner of resistance as a strategic choice to "liberate Palestine from the river to the sea."[93] Attendees included figures from diverse professional and personal backgrounds who shared the belief that Palestinians had the right to Palestine, to refuse recognition of Israel, and to continue resistance "to achieve historic and national goals, most important of which are the rights of liberation and return."[94]

In his speech at the conference, Meshal called on Arab leaders and Islamic delegations to share this vision and to reconsider their commitment to negotiations after the "lean years." The power imbalance with Israel and the absence of any negotiating cards made talks futile. Meshal decried as crimes the prosecution of fighters, the dismantlement of the military wings in the West Bank, and the acquiescence to disunity as demanded by Israeli and American powers. "Stop the negotiations. Arab brothers, brothers in the authority, show the world that you have the courage to say no," Meshal implored. "Show the world that you have been angered, that you can suspend the negotiations. Do something. It is unbelievable that the Palestinian people are being slaughtered . . . and we continue with these absurd talks," Meshal concluded.[95]

For Hamas, before talk of statehood and governance came talk of unity and liberation.[96] As Abbas reaffirmed his commitment to the peace process through the latest conference at Annapolis, Meshal stressed the sanctity of the resistance weapon in Damascus.[97] International diplomatic engagement with the former and isolation and starvation of the latter communicated quite clearly what concessions Palestinian political parties needed to abide by to gain entry into the international community. As Hamas's political overtures had been ignored during its years in office, the movement saw through its geographic "liberated" base in Gaza an opportunity to implement its own defiant government of resistance that would safeguard what it viewed as the purest principles of the Palestinian struggle. While Palestinians would suffer in the short term under the difficulties of the blockade, Hamas's leaders reiterated that these were normal challenges on the long path toward liberation, and they felt vindicated in steadfastly holding on to their ideological convictions.

FIRST HAMAS-ISRAEL CEASEFIRE

In early 2008, Hamas's publications began reporting on Israeli war plans.[98] Hypotheses surfaced that Israel was nervous about providing Hamas with too much time to develop its military capabilities given Israel's experience in Lebanon in 2006, whereby Hezbollah exhibited surprising firepower capacity six years after Israel's withdrawal from south Lebanon. Hamas boasted that it was a far deadlier foe than Hezbollah considering geographic proximity to high-density Israeli towns and army bases around Gaza's periphery.[99] Ever since Hamas's takeover of the strip, publications reveled in the perception that Hamas presented a security threat to Israel.[100] Reports latched on to Israeli worries about the movement's strength and fears regarding the potential to replicate Hamas's takeover in the West Bank. While interpreting these as "exaggerations" by Zionist media to justify future Israeli attacks, Hamas nonetheless used the reports to project strength, nurture its resistance legacy, and consolidate power.[101]

Hamas's leaders expected Israel to mobilize to end rocket fire from Gaza, which had persisted unabated; secure the release of the captured

Israeli soldier Gilad Shalit; reduce Hamas's capacity to launch missiles; end weapons smuggling from Egypt; and weaken Hamas politically and militarily in an effort to force the collapse of its government.[102] Reporting on Israeli media and political debates, Hamas's publications concluded that agreements had been made between Abbas and his Israeli counterparts to defeat Hamas so that Abbas could "return to Gaza on the backs of an Israeli tank."[103] Osama Hamdan, Hamas's representative in Beirut, noted that an attack on Gaza would merely fulfill secret objectives shared by Abbas and Fayyad.[104] For Hamas, escalation promised a return to the natural mode of engagement between occupier and occupied. The movement reiterated that the blockade constituted an act of aggression in its own right, thereby underscoring the need for armed struggle, rather than diplomacy, to bring it to an end. Sharon's disengagement from Gaza had heightened Hamas's conviction in the capacity of violence to achieve concessions.[105]

Hamas and other factions had consistently used rockets to protest the blockade, which they viewed as an act of war. Furthermore, like Israel, Hamas sought to increase its deterrence and, in its case, to prevent Israel from reinvading by air or land.[106] From its base in Gaza, al-Qassam was reportedly working on two levels: strengthening its offensive capabilities by advancing its rocket technology and investing in strong defensive infrastructure, primarily in the form of tunnels throughout Gaza.[107] Al-Qassam also relied heavily on tunnels to facilitate the establishment of a relatively robust weapons manufacturing sector within Gaza.[108] Such local industry contributed to an arsenal that Hamas claimed was quite developed. Furthermore, al-Qassam's spokesman discussed the cache of modern weapons that had fallen into Hamas's hands after routing the Palestinian security forces. He noted that these weapons had been provided by the United States and Israel to prepare the Palestinian security forces to fight Hamas; they were also weapons the Palestinian Authority had previously confiscated from Hamas in 1996.[109]

After the escalation of hostilities in January and in the context of this persistent chokehold, Hamas sent a suicide bomber into Israel on

February 4. It was the first suicide mission since 2004, killing a seventy-three-year-old woman in the southern town of Dimona.[110] Rocket fire also continued, resulting in the death of the first Israeli in nine months on February 27.[111] This prompted Israel to unleash "Operation Hot Winter," an expansive air and ground attack on Gaza that killed 110 Palestinians in five days.[112] The European Union denounced Israel's "disproportionate" response and policies of "collective punishment," while analysts interpreted this operation to be a dry run for a future invasion.[113] Hamas emerged relatively unscathed, boasting of victory as it maintained rocket fire.[114] "Palestinians have emerged victorious from the five-day war waged by the Zionist occupation on the Gaza Strip. If anyone wanted to protest the word 'victory,' then we could say that Palestinians succeeded in frustrating all the Zionist goals, both those pronounced and left unpronounced, including the stopping of rocket fire, creating a schism amongst the Palestinian people and the resistance, and collapsing Hamas's government."[115]

Steadfastness against Israel's superior military arsenal was portrayed as a victory. Hamas combed through Israeli and international media for reports describing Gazan "resilience" and used those stories as positive reinforcement for the population.[116] It tried to mitigate resentment from people in Gaza by paying for homes destroyed in bombings, while paradoxically maintaining attacks that were used by Israel to justify its reprisals.[117] Hamas viewed its policies in Gaza as an existential mission to safeguard the broader Palestinian struggle. As its publications exclaimed, "The suffering of people in Gaza is extremely difficult, but we have said from the beginning, this battle is not the battle of the people of Gaza on their own. It is the battle of all Palestinians. Collapse [in Gaza] will lead to a Palestinian collapse. Victory will lead to a Palestinian victory."[118]

Given the volatility, indirect ceasefire discussions between Hamas and Israel began in Cairo in the spring of 2008. By their sheer occurrence, these talks had the immediate effect of validating Hamas as Israel's counterpart in Gaza. Sharon had for years refused to negotiate with Hamas during its resistance campaign in the Second Intifada. Now that the movement had effectively been ostracized from the political establishment, Israel opened indirect channels with the movement instead of going through the traditional PLO channels. Intentionally or otherwise, this normalized Hamas's rule, vindicated the movement, and inevitably entrenched division with the West Bank. Other diplomatic coups that recognized, even implicitly, Hamas's rule over Gaza had the same effect. For instance, Hamas viewed former American president Jimmy Carter's openness to meet with its leaders as the "most important political event on the Palestinian arena since the 2006 legislative elections."[119]

In Cairo, indirect ceasefire talks with Israel proceeded slowly. Hamas insisted on extending any prospective ceasefire to both the Gaza Strip and the West Bank.[120] More importantly, it resolved to link any ceasefire with eased border crossings into Gaza. For its part, Israel attempted to expand talks to include a prisoner exchange deal involving Shalit's release and to prevent weapon smuggling.[121] Both parties bargained hard, underscoring how military escalations on the battlefield made room for backdoor diplomacy aimed at altering the status quo between them. Israel announced that rather than restricting its security policies to retaliation, it would start carrying out preemptive attacks at will. Hamas promised to expand its use of the newer Hezbollah-type Katyusha rockets that it had only used sparingly until that point.[122]

Hamas held firm. Refusing to succumb to military threats and weathering the economic stranglehold were celebrated as successful acts of resistance.[123] This wherewithal and Hamas's negotiating stance stood in stark contrast to the Palestinian Authority's performance and strengthened Hamas's calls for an alternative national strategy. After the Annapolis conference, expectations were significantly scaled back from the promise made to tackle final-status issues by the end of 2008.[124] Nonetheless, monthly meetings between Abbas and Olmert persisted. Hamas's publications denounced Abbas "gifting [Israeli leaders] boxes of Syrian baklava as Gaza was being slaughtered," stressing instead that there was still time for resistance to be adopted: "Enough stubbornness, your project has failed."[125]

On the Israeli side, political support for peace talks was challenged by instability on the Gaza border. Israelis complained that their goodwill gesture of withdrawal from Gaza had been rewarded by a terrorist takeover.[126] This was done with little reckoning of Israel's role in creating the dynamic of isolation that had emerged in Gaza or the impact of Israel's failure to take concerted action on the peace front. As the peace process stalled, it became clear that the American-Israeli effort to bolster the West Bank at Gaza's expense was failing. A poll by the Palestinian Centre for Policy and Survey Research showed that only 42 percent of Palestinians supported Fatah compared to Hamas, which received 35 percent support—a narrower gap than immediately following Hamas's takeover of Gaza. Another poll by the same center showed that Ismail Haniyeh would beat Abbas in presidential elections.[127]

By June 19, 2008, almost a year after Hamas took power in Gaza, Cairo successfully got Israel and Hamas to agree "in principle" to a phased six-month ceasefire. Indirect negotiations had lasted three months. This was the first official ceasefire to be negotiated, albeit indirectly, between Israel and Hamas rather than between Israel and the PLO. The ceasefires that Hamas had agreed to during the Second Intifada had either been unilateral or been negotiated under the auspices of the PLO. In effect, this agreement represented the bifurcation of the Palestinian political establishment. The culmination of efforts to isolate Hamas had resulted in a de facto Israeli divide-and-rule approach for engagement with the Palestinians: Hamas for Gaza, the Palestinian Authority for the West Bank.

Through the agreement, Israel relented to gradually relax some of the crossings into Gaza to allow for the passage of basic goods, without removing the blockade, in return for an end to rocket fire. Hamas acquiesced for the ceasefire to commence in Gaza, without extending it to the West Bank. The movement refused to link ceasefire discussions with a prisoner exchange deal, which it insisted should be negotiated separately.[128] The parties agreed that the ceasefire would commence following a test period, after which Israel would proceed to reduce the economic blockade if Hamas managed to maintain quiet on the border. Subsequent talks would then address the prisoner exchange, extension of the ceasefire to the West Bank, and the cessation of arms smuggling.[129] Hamas's biggest challenge was curbing the resistance activities of other factions, including Islamic Jihad, as well as defectors to other extremist groups or rebellious members of al-Qassam.[130]

This ceasefire marked an important development whereby through Hamas's validation as the effective ruler of Gaza the movement became the entity responsible for pacifying the resistance front. By default, Hamas developed a monopoly over "resistance," becoming the party that oversaw the coordination of military operations by all factions to ensure they collectively agreed to and abided by decisions to escalate or cease fire.[131] Hamas had no illusion that Israel viewed this break as an indefinite one. The movement understood the calm as a precursor to an invasion aimed at securing Shalit's release and ostensibly toppling its government. It expected Israel to claim some form of ceasefire violation to excuse retaliation.[132] For Hamas, the ceasefire was a time to catch its breath, to build its internal political and military capabilities, and to allow Gazans some respite.[133] As analysts in its publications stressed, the ceasefire is "nothing more than a compulsory twist on the bloody road between Hamas and Israel. Consequently, there is no escape from a powerful military [Israeli] assault on Hamas in Gaza, given political, military and security concerns. . . . This calm came as a warrior's break for both sides. . . . Fighters trenches' not negotiators' hotels are what [will] resolve the conflict."[134]

OPERATION CAST LEAD

Rocket fire from Gaza receded throughout the summer of 2008. Israeli restrictions on basic supplies into Gaza were also eased, but marginally. The persistent blockade allowed for increased food, water, and medical supplies to enter, yet permissible quantities barely met the needs of Gaza's population.[135] Israeli politicians admitted in closed rooms to a policy of keeping Gaza's economy "on the brink of collapse," just above what would qualify as a humanitarian catastrophe.[136] Understanding the temporary nature of this ceasefire, Hamas leveraged the calm to prepare for the anticipated attack by strengthening its defensive infrastructure.[137] It also turned its attention to domestic governance and reconciliation talks. Shortly before the ceasefire was signed, Hamas reported that Abbas had softened his preconditions for negotiations and accepted an invitation from Cairo to begin a dialogue.[138] Faltering peace talks under American mediation coupled with Hamas's success in forcing Israel into discussions had concretized the movement's role in Palestinian politics and weakened the case for sustaining negotiations with Israel.[139]

Hamas eyed Abbas's reversal suspiciously.[140] It continued to condemn the Palestinian Authority's "terroristic procedures" against its members, as well as Islamic Jihad's, in the West Bank.[141] Hamas publications such as *Filastin al-Muslima* and *Al-Resalah* were reportedly prevented from distribution; Islamic institutions were shut down; and mosques were desecrated during the holy month of Ramadan in what Hamas referred to as the "War on the Mosques."[142] Alongside suspicions of the Palestinian Authority, Hamas viewed Egypt's mediation wearily. Egypt's decision to maintain the closure of the Rafah border caused Hamas to suspect it was seeking to sustain the blockade and reassert Palestinian Authority rule in Gaza.[143] Publications reported on efforts by Hamas's leadership to transfer the reconciliation file to Syria, a move that the Egyptian authorities allegedly opposed.[144] Given these worries, Hamas was defensive and anticipated it would be pressured by Egypt into concessions in both the prisoner swap negotiations with Israel, as part of the ceasefire agreement, and domestic reconciliation talks.[145]

Between August 15 and October 10, Cairo hosted the factions for reconciliation talks. Negotiations focused on five areas: government, elections, security, the PLO, and internal reconciliation. After marathon discussions, Cairo produced a framework for reconciliation—effectively a roadmap that could unite the factions around a single Palestinian vision. The Cairo Initiative sought the creation of an interim (possibly technocratic) government that would allow the blockade to be lifted and prepare for new presidential and legislative elections; agree to a national strategy under the PLO's leadership for ending the occupation beyond 1967; and reform the security apparatus.[146] These parameters were broadly in line with what Hamas had previously accepted as part of the unity government before its takeover of Gaza. Yet the movement now voiced reservations.[147]

Hamas's objections were to a degree shaped by perceptions of Abbas's collusion with Egyptian mediators. After its experience in the run-up to the split between Gaza and the West Bank, Hamas dealt with Abbas's maneuverings as tactical moves aimed at usurping power within the political establishment to ensure Fatah's hegemony.[148] The movement's intransigence underscored that Hamas had become less incentivized to accept what it had previously acquiesced to. Policies of marginalization meant that Hamas's political concessions had gone unheeded, creating a situation where the movement could implement its vision without being challenged. Hamas focused on consolidating its grip in Gaza and eventually pulled out of the talks, citing Abbas's policies against it in the West Bank.[149] During the Mecca Agreement, when Hamas had been riddled with unmet responsibilities as a result of the financial blockade, the movement had been compelled to compromise. By mid-2008, it felt less of a need to show flexibility in the pursuit of reconciliation. For the time being, consolidation of power appeared to precede reconciliation.[150]

The reason for Hamas's ability to mitigate the blockade was primarily the tunnel economy. Gradual expansion since Israel's disengagement accelerated significantly after Hamas took over the strip, such that by the summer of 2008 there were more than five hundred tunnels snaking beneath the Rafah border, bringing in a monthly revenue of about $36 million to Hamas.[151] The tunnel business became a sprawling enterprise of operators and merchants that was "legalized" by Hamas's government, which established an authority in the southern Gazan municipality of Rafah to regulate the tunnel trade. The Rafah municipality

also allowed Hamas to control the entry of weapons into the strip.[152]
Hamas's self-assurance belied a level of diplomatic hardening as well
as confidence in its military capacity. Discussing an anticipated Israeli
attack, a senior leader in Hamas's external branch noted that the movement was ready, as "Gaza 2008 was not Gaza 2005."[153]

Such posturing, however, rang hollow, as Hamas maintained a firm
grip on rockets from Gaza, indicating a desire to avoid any conflagration
with Israel. Despite the near absence of rocket fire, Israel maintained a
tight ban on entry or export of goods from Gaza and a total ban on the
movement of people.[154] As domestic Palestinian talks faltered in late
2008, so did the ceasefire agreement with Israel. On November 4, in a
dramatic escalation, Israel broke the ceasefire by raiding the Gaza Strip,
citing preemptive self-defense against an attack tunnel that Hamas was
allegedly building to capture Israeli soldiers.[155] Hamas denied these accusations, noting that its tunnels were being built for defensive or economic purposes. It responded with a barrage of rockets over the border.
This skirmish, although brief, demonstrated Israel's desire to end the
ceasefire, as Hamas had anticipated. For its part, the movement sought
the opportunity to renegotiate the terms of the agreement. Israel had
not only failed to sufficiently relax the blockade, a key condition of the
truce, but had evidently continued its incursions into Gaza. This was
even though Hamas had been remarkably effective, as Israeli security
officials openly admitted, in enforcing the truce from the Gazan front.[156]

On December 18, Hamas's leaders announced their refusal to extend the six-month ceasefire, given Israel's unwillingness to abide by
its side of the bargain. This decision was opposed by Abbas and the
Egyptian mediators.[157] Hamas's decision was portrayed as the trigger
for Israel's military offensive against Gaza. Privately, however, before
the truce had ended, Khaled Meshal had conveyed through indirect
channels Hamas's willingness to renew the ceasefire, despite Israeli
violations. In a letter addressed privately to international mediators,
Meshal wrote that should a "new [ceasefire] proposal be submitted to
the movement by any party, the movement would be willing, together

with the other Palestinian resistance movements, to consider it seriously and responsibly provided it entailed bringing a complete end to the siege on Gaza, opening all the crossings including the Rafah crossing and applying the [ceasefire] equally to the West Bank." International mediators confirmed this message was hand delivered to senior members at Israel's Ministry of Defense, a claim that is denied.[158]

Alongside Meshal's backchannel negotiations, on December 23 Mahmoud Zahhar declared from Gaza Hamas's willingness to renew the truce if Israel lifted the blockade.[159] The timing of Zahhar's message, after Hamas had launched missiles into Israel, demonstrated the movement's intention of using force as a bargaining tool and underscored its refusal to secure calm while subject to a blockade. Much as it had done throughout the Second Intifada, however, Israel brushed aside Hamas's efforts to deescalate. Israel showed no desire to engage with Hamas beyond the initial ceasefire discussions, whereby it had defined expectations for the emerging dynamic with Hamas: managing the blockade to sustain life in Gaza in return for an end to rocket fire. For Israel, this offensive had been in gestation and preplanned since the ceasefire was first set in place. In fact, Israeli news articles reported that Israel had negotiated the June 2008 truce with Hamas precisely to give its army enough time to prepare for the invasion.[160]

In a press conference following a meeting with Egyptian president Hosni Mubarak in Cairo, Tzipi Livni, Israel's foreign minister, stated in reference to Hamas's rocket fire, "Enough is enough. The situation is going to change."[161] Less than five days after Zahhar's renewed ceasefire offer, on December 27, Israel launched the first phase of "Operation Cast Lead," an extensive aerial bombing campaign. The operation coincided with the American presidential transition, as President Barack Obama was set to assume office in January 2009, and also preceded Israeli elections. On the opening day of the operation, Israeli fighter planes flew over the Gaza Strip and dropped bombs on a graduation ceremony that Hamas was hosting for its civil police force, killing ninety-nine celebrants and graduates.[162]

Despite anticipating the attack, Hamas was caught off guard by the timing and scale of Israel's offensive. Israel's aerial assault was followed by a ground-air phase that lasted three weeks until January 18, 2009. During this time, Israel carried out extensive bombing campaigns with hundreds of air strikes throughout the Gaza Strip. Flying over the most densely populated centers of Gaza City, Khan Yunis, and Rafah, Israel targeted buildings, mosques, hospitals, and houses. Using the full range of its weaponry, Israel's planes even dropped white phosphorus bombs, a chemical that causes severe burning and is outlawed by international law for use among civilian populations.[163] From the ground, Hamas and other resistance factions maintained rocket fire into towns in southern Israel, launching around thirty missiles per day.[164]

The sheer scale and ferocity of Israel's offensive against Hamas's relatively weak rockets led to heavy civilian casualties within Gaza quite early on.[165] It was unclear what the end point of the incursion would be, as Israel maintained ambiguity about the goals it sought from Cast Lead. At its most basic level, the operation was an effort to end rocket fire that had created panic and protest within Israel, and it also aimed to stop weapon smuggling into Gaza. More importantly, Israel hoped to inflict significant pain to rebuild the military deterrence that had been shattered following its failed excursion into Lebanon two years prior, a defeat that hung over its performance during this attack.[166] More specific goals included attempts to gain clarity on (or even release) Gilad Shalit and to pressure Gaza's civilian population to rebel against Hamas. A more ambitious aim yet was a desire to forcefully pacify Hamas or even topple the movement.[167]

The one clear aspect of the operation was Israel's intention to weaken or decapitate Hamas without directly reoccupying the strip.[168] This kept with a strategy that had been initiated by Sharon's disengagement from the Gaza Strip in 2005: to externally control the coastal enclave without assuming any direct governing responsibility for the territory or its inhabitants. Through military power, Israel sought to force acquiescence and to pressure Hamas into pacification. From the year 2000 until Operation Cast Lead broke out, Israel had killed more than 3,000 Palestinians in Gaza, including 634 children.[169] Seen in this context, Cast Lead was a continuation of Israel's use of sheer force to break Hamas, and in the process to circumvent all the political gestures that the movement had offered Israel. This was despite warnings from senior figures such as the previous head of the Mossad, Efraim Halevy, who insisted that Hamas had already indicated a willingness to compromise to achieve a two-state solution and was open to negotiations.[170] In so doing, Israel was using military might to turn Gaza into little more than a humanitarian problem.[171] Israel also initiated a concerted media drive to justify its ferocious bombing campaign—entirely disproportionate compared to rocket fire emanating from Gaza—by asserting its right to defend itself against what it characterized as fanatical terrorists hoping to destroy the state.[172]

Given America's preoccupation with the presidential transition, European countries clamored for an immediate ceasefire.[173] Within the Arab world, the fissures that had come to dominate the region after two successive terms of the Bush administration became apparent. Hamas, a democratically elected and armed Islamic government, sat at the epicenter of these divisions. As Israel's offensive got under way, countries in the camp Bush had designated as "moderate," including Saudi Arabia and Egypt, led the effort in the Arab League to condemn the attack while urging both parties to end violence. Similar to the PLO, these actors decried Israel's escalation while blaming Hamas for rocket fire. They pursued a formula where the end of hostilities entailed calm on both the Israeli and the Gazan fronts.[174]

Hamas rejected this equalization and dismissed statements that assigned responsibility for the invasion to its rockets. The movement protested that it had offered a ceasefire in return for ending the blockade. For Hamas, such statements from Arab countries failed to account for the violence inherent in maintaining Gaza under such a state of duress.[175] The movement criticized the "deep slumber" of "moderate" Arab leaders and their implicit endorsement of Israeli actions.[176] It also condemned Egyptian president Mubarak's decision to keep the Rafah border shut throughout the operation.[177] The optics of having Israel's foreign minister and chief architect of Cast Lead advocate war against Gaza from an Arab capital on the eve of the operation was not lost on the Arab world. It reinforced the sense that Israel and the moderate Arab countries, as well as Palestinian leaders such as Abbas and Fayyad, were now allies in the fight against the resistance effort.[178]

On the other side of the Arab divide was the so-called radical camp composed of countries such as Qatar, Iran, and Syria. As the Arab League issued its condemnation, Qatar hosted an emergency "Defiance Summit" to consider ways to end the aggression. Egypt and Saudi Arabia boycotted the gathering, as did Abbas.[179] Iran and Turkey came out in strong support of Gaza and began diplomatic proceedings to impose a ceasefire. In Turkey's case, relations with Israel reached an unprecedented level of tension over the course of the attack.[180] For the "radical camp," the return to a ceasefire necessitated ending the blockade. Rather than a formula rooted in "calm for calm," these countries mirrored Hamas's rejection of ceasefire calls that did not demand lifting the blockade as a prerequisite to ending rocket fire.

The fighting took a significant toll. Palestinian sources estimated that by its twelfth day, 770 Palestinians had been killed and 2,500 wounded. Doctors and medical institutions in Gaza estimated that 40 percent of those killed were women and children and that deaths included entire families of noncombatants. On the Israeli side, four deaths were reported.[181] Talks were launched behind the scenes between Foreign Minister Livni and her counterpart Secretary Rice in the United States. Against the backdrop of a rising Palestinian death toll, discussions produced a memorandum of agreement that stipulated the United States would assist Israel in bolstering its security against Hamas and in putting an end to weapon smuggling.[182] American guarantees meant that Israel's concerns about rocket fire would be addressed without having to end the stranglehold on Gaza.

Three weeks after Cast Lead began, Israel declared a unilateral ceasefire on January 16. An estimated 1,400 Palestinians, the majority of whom were civilians including an estimated 300 children, had been killed. Thirteen Israelis, four of whom were civilians, were also killed. Israel's military strategy and the ensuing unilateral ceasefire under-scored its policy of isolating Gaza through the blockade and using sheer force to instill deterrence.[183] Having acquiesced to Hamas's rule, as seen by the first ceasefire, Israel now approached the Gaza Strip exclusively through the prism of security, without engaging with Hamas's politi-cal demands. Israel had long sustained a diplomatic process with the Palestinian Authority in the West Bank in order to manage, rather than resolve, the conflict.[184] With the division of the Palestinian leadership, a similar framework was being instituted in the Gaza Strip. Through Cast Lead, it became clear that rather than managing the conflict through diplomatic means, this process was unfolding militarily through a dia-logue of violence, given Hamas's uncompromising rhetoric.

Despite the significant human and economic devastation wrought on Gaza, it was unclear initially whether Israel had successfully instilled lasting deterrence. Predictably, even though it had been entirely over-whelmed by the attack, Hamas hailed it a victory. Israel had failed to achieve its goal of dismantling the organization or stopping the mis-siles, which remained relatively consistent until the final day. Israel had also been unable to release Shalit.[185] As soon as the operation sub-sided, Hamas issued a leaflet affirming its victory in remaining steadfast against the onslaught.[186] Compared to the inability of Palestinians to hold up against Israel's invading army during operations such as De-fensive Shield in 2002, Hamas's ability to hold firm and even inflict damage on the Israelis in 2008 was seen as a sign of military progress and growth.[187] The movement rationalized the horrible human loss as the product of hysterical helplessness on Israel's part. "As the invading Zionists failed to face our fighters . . . and their efforts were frustrated in breaking Hamas . . . they began to feel hysterical. So revenge was poured on our institutions, mosques, hospitals and places of worship."[188]

Hamas's publications described this war as a "strategic transfor-mation in favor of the Palestinian cause and the project of steadfastness and resistance."[189] While noting that it was merely one milestone ahead of the next confrontation, articles reported that the sheer force of the offensive had entirely altered the political landscape of the Arab world.[190] There were elements of truth in this assessment. Cast Lead strengthened Arab mobilization around Palestine and embarrassed states such as Saudi Arabia and Egypt that had moved closer to Israel, given that states such as Turkey had rallied around the Palestinians.[191] It also brought to the surface divisions within the Arab world and revealed the stark gap that existed between the leadership and their populations in 2008 and 2009. During the three-week period of the attack, the Arab street rose en masse to protest Israel's continued subjugation of Palestinians.[192] Criticizing official Arab policies, Hamas expressed gratitude for this solidarity, regionally and internationally.[193] It cited protests in Arab capitals in which mock-up Qassam rockets were displayed. Hamas claimed these had become the symbol of resistance and had achieved what the Arab armies had failed to.[194]

Hamas also reported on polls that showed a rise in support for the movement and for launching rockets into Israel.[195] While Hamas's popularity had been weakened as a result of the blockade, mobilization in support of the resistance boosted it temporarily.[196] Hamas saw this endorsement as an invaluable gain that intensified the opposition front within the Arab world to "American and Zionist plans" for the region. Gaza, for Hamas, became a bellwether against which official regimes would be judged.[197] The movement predicted fewer obstacles would stand in the way of its resistance goals now that the "true face" of the occupation had been revealed. It hoped that the justifications for settlement and negotiations had dissipated entirely.[198] Hamas called on the incoming American administration to recalculate its policies toward the movement and the legitimate resistance of the Palestinian people. It went on to say, "We promise you that we will not rest, and our eyes will not shut, until we see the generals of war and destruction . . . being led like the war criminals they are to the international courts."[199]

Even as the upsurge in sympathy dwindled once the extent of the destruction sank in, Hamas still managed to capitalize on the ground-swell of support. Just like Hezbollah in 2006, Hamas's legacy as a movement that stood firm against Israel's unrelenting military power was confirmed. Rather than further isolation, Hamas reported on increased contact with the European Union and the United States.[200] On the other hand, Hamas's publications described the Palestinian Authority under Abbas's leadership as "the biggest loser of the war."[201] For Hamas, this had been the Palestinian Authority's opportunity to realign itself with the people. The movement noted that while it blamed the Americans and the Israelis for the "Zionist massacres," Abbas had foolishly blamed Hamas for the offensive and failed to demonstrate any solidarity as the Palestinian Authority cracked down on all forms of protest in the West Bank.[202] Hamas's position elevated the movement's standing in the eyes of Palestinians while painting Abbas in a shameful light.[203] The Gaza war, Hamas believed, demonstrated most starkly that the Palestinian Authority had outlived its purpose as the Palestinian struggle reverted to its true principles under Hamas's "government of resistance."[204]

PARALLEL PALESTINIAN NATIONALISMS

In January 2009, Barack Obama became the forty-fourth president of the United States and raised hopes that America would revise its policies in the region. In Israel, Operation Cast Lead had failed to boost Olmert's ratings and the right-wing Likud leader Benjamin Netanyahu was elected prime minister. Noting this shift, Hamas's publications stressed "the score between the Zionist occupation and the Gaza Strip has not been settled. The forces that will come to power within the Zionist entity, and those surrounding Netanyahu, consider themselves in a constant confrontation with the Gaza Strip. The war is simply taking a rest. It has not stopped."[205] As hostilities ended, Cairo led efforts to formalize the ceasefire and commence reconstruction in Gaza. Given soured relations between Hamas and Egypt, the movement attempted to shift mediation to Turkey or Syria, without success.[206]

Negotiations proceeded on several tracks: reconciliation, reconstruction, and ceasefire. In terms of the ceasefire, Israel persisted in its refusal to lift the blockade and attempted to link the truce with a prisoner
exchange agreement that would release Shalit.[207] Hamas maintained its
insistence on tackling these two files separately, despite the overwhelming force that had been used against it and the threat of its resumption.
"We are not in a hurry and are not panting after a ceasefire," declared
one leader. "The Israeli occupation needs this calm as much as our people do, for the enemy has failed to get security for their settlements, and
has failed to break the will of the resistance."[208]

Hamas also showed a solid stance in discussions related to reconstruction and reconciliation. Shortly after the military operation
ended, a reconstruction conference was hosted in Sharm al-Sheikh
that brought together more than seventy countries and sixteen international organizations committed to rebuilding the Gaza Strip. Donors
attempted to channel reconstruction funds and oversight through the
Palestinian Authority in the West Bank, which had no access to the
Gaza Strip, in an effort to sideline Hamas.[209] The movement objected
to its marginalization. As Hamdan noted, if the leadership of the Palestinian Authority "failed to return to Gaza on the back of an Israeli
tank [during Cast Lead], it will not return on the back of a cement
mixer."[210] Mired in these complications, reconstruction efforts stalled.
Reconciliation talks stalled as well. Initially, Hamas appeared to soften
its stance and accepted an agreement that was similar to the one it had
turned down a year earlier.[211] This indicated Hamas's recognition that
stakes were higher after Cast Lead, as Egypt emphasized the importance of reconciliation to ensure the delivery of aid into Gaza and to
begin the reconstruction there. For all its tough rhetoric, Hamas also
accepted that the Gaza Reconstruction Committee would be headed by
Abbas.[212] Yet policies that obstructed unity persisted.

The Obama administration made clear that the United States would
only deal with an interim government that accepted the Quartet's conditions and assigned Salam Fayyad as prime minister. Hamas rejected

this intervention, which it viewed as an attempt to scupper talks and delay reconciliation until the official end of Hamas's four-year term in January 2010.[213] During this time, Hamas's publications surmised, the United States hoped that Gazans would blame the movement for slow reconstruction.[214] This delay indeed diminished Hamas's popularity. Israel maintained almost impermeable control over the borders, allowing only the most vital food and medicine to get in. By the summer of 2009, six months after Cast Lead had ended, many in the strip began resenting Hamas for their misery.[215] Polls gave Fatah a rating of 35 percent compared to Hamas's 19 percent.[216]

This popular disparity was made more acute by the economic support that the Palestinian Authority was enjoying. Under Fayyad's leadership, the Palestinian Authority had adopted an expansive economic policy focused on growth and development.[217] The establishment of strong and transparent institutions, Fayyad hoped, would pave the way for the emergence of a de facto Palestinian state and pressure Israel to withdraw to the 1967 borders. As calm was reinstated on the streets in the West Bank and the quality of life enhanced, particularly relative to Gaza, the Palestinian Authority's crackdown on the resistance factions persisted. This pattern led Hamas to condemn the government in Ramallah as a violent police state.[218] Ironically, Hamas's low level of popularity in Gaza also had to do with its own repression, particularly against rival factions. Despite its talk of plurality, Hamas undermined Gaza's civil society through strict limitations on participation in political life and increased constraints against NGOs.[219] Seeking to ensure security, Hamas also adopted a tough stance by clamping down violently on Salafi jihadist movements within Gaza.[220]

Against the backdrop of the Palestinian reconciliation talks, President Obama traveled to the Middle East and delivered a historic speech at Cairo University. Addressing the region's chronic conflict, he described "a world where Israelis and Palestinians are each secure in a state of their own."[221] His secretary of state Hillary Clinton followed up with an unusually tough line by calling on Israel to halt settlement expansion as a precondition for bilateral negotiations. Despite protestations from Israeli politicians, Israel initially appeared to acquiesce to Obama's redirection. In a speech at Bar Ilan University in Israel a few days after Obama's Cairo address, Netanyahu spoke openly of a "demilitarized Palestinian state side by side with the Jewish state."[222] Members within his party were more intransigent, however, and possibly more representative of the Likud party's vision, which cohered with the rightward stance of other ministers. Avigdor Lieberman, Israel's foreign minister and deputy prime minister, publicly rejected Palestinian statehood and the agreement that had been made at Annapolis.[223] His position effectively mimicked Hamas's own refusal to accept past agreements made by the PLO. Hamas pounced on this similarity, arguing that the movement's own implicit acceptance of the two-state solution was more aligned with Obama's vision than was Netanyahu's.[224]

The Obama administration's hopeful push toward the resumption of the peace process meant that domestic reconciliation talks stalled. Abbas was less likely to jeopardize American sympathies by entering a unity deal with Hamas. By the end of August, Hamas issued a pessimistic release bemoaning the lack of agreement after a litany of unproductive discussions. The movement predictably attributed the failure entirely to Fatah's unilateralism and Abbas's inability to compromise.[225] Hamas insisted that talks were failing because of Fatah's continued arrests of Hamas's political activists in the West Bank, completely overlooking its own clampdown in Gaza.[226] After endless hours of discussion, it was evident that both parties engaged in the charade of reconciliation with little political will to make the required concessions or compromises.

The irreconcilable tracks of Hamas's government in Gaza and the Palestinian Authority in the West Bank became increasingly evident toward the end of 2009. In the fall, the investigation launched by the UN Human Rights Council to look into the activities of Hamas and Israel during Operation Cast Lead was published, despite Israel's adamant refusal to cooperate with the investigation. The findings were released in a report widely known as the Goldstone Report. It was named after the lead author, South African judge Richard Goldstone, an instrumental figure in undermining the apartheid regime in South Africa from the inside. The Goldstone Report found that Israel was guilty of war crimes during the Gaza offensive, including the deliberate targeting of civilians and institutions such as hospitals with lethal force. Hamas was also accused of war crimes for the indiscriminate firing of rockets into Israel. Most revealingly, the report found no evidence that Hamas had deliberately fired rockets from civilian homes or stored weapons in mosques, claims that Israel had stridently upheld as the reason it invaded civilian areas so aggressively. Rather, the report identified instances where Israeli army officials used Palestinians as human shields during their ground invasion as they entered into urban spaces.[227]

The Obama administration feared that escalating the report to a vote at the UN Security Council would deal a fatal blow to the peace process that it was hoping to resume. Seeking not to undermine Obama's support, Abbas decided not to endorse the report's findings and unsurprisingly came under vicious criticism from Palestinian factions, including Fatah. The public outcry prompted Abbas to attempt a reversal, eliciting accusations that he was "spineless."[228] Seizing the moment, Hamas withdrew from the reconciliation talks and distanced itself from the Palestinian Authority. Hamas's spokesman stated, "It has never happened in history that an occupied people try to prove the innocence of their occupier. This is a scandal. It has shown that the Palestinian Authority is hostage to the occupation, if not a tool to implement its decisions. This is not a passing mistake. It is a systematic attempt to prove the innocence of the occupier."[229]

Despite Abbas's compromises and Fayyad's successful economic policies, the peace process still failed to engender any progress. Having called for a complete cessation of settlement building before peace talks could commence, Secretary Clinton loosened her tough stance in November and praised Netanyahu for reducing settlement activity to a "slower rate."[230] Facing pressure from the Israeli government, Judge Goldstone retracted the findings of his report in an op-ed in the *Washington Post*, writing that Israel did not intentionally target civilians.[231] This retraction was seen as a bewildering example of backtracking under international pressure, underscoring what Hamas viewed as international bias.[232] These factors played into Hamas's hands. Against the backdrop of the Palestinian Authority's humiliation, Meshal declared Hamas's intention to launch a new political initiative from Damascus. He invited all factions to attend and to formally move away from the diplomatic path.[233]

A few weeks after the Goldstone incident, Hamas celebrated another coup for the resistance front. It exchanged a one-minute video of Shalit, which showed proof that the soldier was being kept alive, for twenty Palestinian prisoners. "The Israeli occupation has been forced to submit to the will of the resistance," editorials declared. "This step has paved the way for a larger operation, a larger exchange."[234] Hamas's ability to secure concessions from Israel underscored the power of the movement's strategy, particularly when compared to the constant failure of its counterpart in the West Bank. A year after Cast Lead, coincidentally Hamas's twenty-second anniversary, the movement appeared more confident than ever in its rule over the Gaza Strip.

Addressing a well-attended anniversary festival on December 14, Haniyeh turned to the initiative that Meshal had alluded to from Damascus. The prime minister called for a comprehensive conference that would bring together Islamic and national factions to agree on a common agenda to salvage the struggle. Hamas's initiative capitalized on the Palestinian Authority's low popularity by calling for the resuscitation of Palestinian institutions in a manner that sustained resistance. Haniyeh stated that such a political program needed to be based on a commitment to the recovery of Palestine, the right of return, and the indivisibility of Jerusalem.[235] Reinforcing its ideological foundation, Hamas reiterated that giving up on any one of these principles was akin to defaulting on a central pillar of Islam.[236]

It was from such a position that Hamas governed Gaza, as a ruling party whose mission was to safeguard these principles against all odds by integrating the political and civil infrastructure into a broader liberation project. The realities of governance, the blockade, and the fierce military confrontations with Israel had, Hamas's publications conceded, "forced calm on Hamas's government."[237] Ceasefires had become an official political framework through which the broader movement could balance its strategy for national liberation with the demands of governance. But the movement had built a de facto administration authority and sustained a foothold in the Gaza Strip from which it could launch its project. With that accomplishment, Hamas's position as a leader of the Palestinian struggle in its own right had unquestionably been validated.[238]

This confidence was manifesting itself on the ground. Egypt's commitments as part of the ceasefire following Cast Lead to crack down on Hamas's tunnel infrastructure proved ineffective. In 2009, Hamas began a major initiative to expand its tunnel infrastructure such that by mid-2010 investments began paying off. Shortages of food and consumer goods became more manageable and small reconstruction projects were initiated.[239] Hamas also began increasing tax and customs duties on trade within Gaza as a means of diversifying revenue.[240] Leaders in Hamas's government spoke of turning inward and focusing on state building and sustainability. For Hamas, Gaza became the model space for the Palestinian struggle. This was compared to the West Bank, which Hamas's leaders viewed with disdain given its subservience to the occupation forces. The movement's leaders openly admitted to shortfalls and mistakes in their governance, which they attributed to inexperience. But they maintained that these were minor shortcomings compared to what they viewed as authoritarianism in the West Bank.[241]

These characterizations of minor shortcomings were in fact a significant misrepresentation given Hamas's repressive policies within Gaza. Despite Hamas's tunnels, the levels of suffering in Gaza as a result of the blockade's collective punishment of the population could not be denied, and this gave rise to international solidarity efforts. On May 31, an international flotilla comprising six civilian ships, referred to popularly as the *Mavi Marmara* flotilla, attempted to break the blockade on Gaza by sailing to the ports of the coastal enclave to deliver aid. The flotilla was intercepted and boarded by armed Israeli soldiers in international waters, resulting in a violent confrontation that caused the death of nine Turkish nationals on board. Hamas declared those killed by Israel as "martyrs" and described Israel's attack as an act of "piracy."[242]

In the West Bank, where the Abbas government had failed to compel Israel to cease settlement building, the Palestinian leadership acquiesced to indirect negotiations as pressure persisted by the United States for direct talks to be launched. Hamas was skeptical of such discussions. Claiming that there was a robust and more representative coalescing around an alternative national project that was rooted in resistance, Hamas hosted what Meshal described as a "historic meeting" in Damascus.[243] This brought together thirteen opposition factions that strongly rejected any form of negotiations, indirect or otherwise, with Israel. In effect, as PLO-Israeli negotiations proceeded on one track, Hamas launched its own coalition of factions, ostensibly to mitigate the PLO's failure, as Hamas noted it was preparing for the next stage following the collapse of the Abbas-Fayyad government.[244]

After four months of fruitless diplomacy, Abbas succumbed even further in August 2010 and accepted the resumption of direct negotiations with Israel without a prior cessation of settlement expansion. As talks were about to be launched, al-Qassam carried out "Operation Torrent of Fire," on August 31 in the West Bank. Hamas fighters opened fire on settler cars in Hebron, killing four settlers from Kiryat Arba. Al-Qassam adopted this attack as one of many to be carried out in response to crimes of the occupation. The second operation came less than twenty-four hours later, in Ramallah, injuring two settlers.[245] Entirely shattering the Palestinian Authority's assurances that it had successfully dismantled the resistance infrastructure, the attack deeply embarrassed Abbas. The Palestinian Authority's reaction came in the form of a swift and comprehensive clampdown on all resistance activities in the West Bank, magnifying an already brutal campaign against Hamas. For the movement, this "hysterical reaction" showed that Israel had successfully "turned the Abbas-Fayyad Authority into a tool in the occupier's hand."[246] Addressing the "ferocious campaign," one article proclaimed, "Could anyone have imagined the reactions of these forces following the murder of four Zionists, when they did not lift a finger at the murder of 1,300 Palestinian at the hands of the occupation in Gaza?"[247]

Hamas's publications reported that al-Qassam's attacks were widely praised, as they showed the movement's ability to maintain its resistance capacity despite the clampdown on its forces.[248] Attacks from the West Bank in particular were viewed as powerful on a strategic level. The timing of these attacks, aimed to shock onlookers out of their belief that Hamas had been pacified in the West Bank, coincided with the resumption of Israeli-Palestinian peace talks. The hysteria that ensued was understandable given that the Abbas-led negotiating team was about to land in Washington, where they were to claim that the Palestinian Authority had successfully eradicated armed resistance. Responding to Fatah's accusations that Hamas had undermined the Palestinian struggle by weakening the position of negotiators and giving Israel the excuse to retaliate in the West Bank, Hamas noted that the negotiators had no place being in Washington in the first place.[249] "Mahmoud Abbas has forgotten that the Palestinian principles—the land, Jerusalem, return, ending the occupation—are not his. . . . He has not been delegated to speak on behalf of the Palestinian people, which has not elected him."[250]

With such acrimony, it was no surprise that reconciliation remained inconclusive.[251] Negotiations were most complicated when it came to the issue of the security file. Egyptian mediators communicated to Abbas that there were "red lines" that the American and Israeli administrations prohibited Abbas from stepping over. These included conditions that Hamas had to disarm and that ultimate security control must remain with Abbas.[252] These demands were easy for Hamas to refuse, as it called for a "real reconciliation," or none at all.[253] In effect, two national strategies had come into being and the two competed for legitimacy. In Gaza, Israel's attempts at instilling lasting deterrence failed as a new dynamic developed between Israel and Hamas, one rooted in defiance and violence. While Hamas sustained its role in the Gaza Strip, at significant cost to Palestinians there, quality of life was enhanced in the West Bank through economic development. Both these strategies, force and diplomacy, failed to elicit any political concessions from Israel, which continued to control all aspects of life in both the West Bank and the Gaza Strip. Under the weight of an unyielding occupation, these dual and competing national liberation strategies exacerbated domestic fragmentation, ensuring that the Palestinian division between the Gaza Strip and the West Bank was institutionalized. In the absence of reconciliation, Hamas and Fatah appeared to be involved in a zero-sum game where the popularity of one necessarily meant the undermining of the other. This was a game that was astutely and effectively played by Israel, which sustained negotiating tracks, direct and indirect, with both parties separately while obstructing any unity between the two.[254] In light of this dynamic, the possibility of political gain and concessions from Israel were tethered to a clear rivalry, reshaping the makeup of Palestinian politics and validating Hamas as a prime interlocutor where it had once been a marginal player.

CHAPTER SIX

REGIONAL
MISFORTUNES

On December 17, 2010, a street vendor named Tarek Mohamed Bouazizi set himself on fire in a Tunisian market. Bouazizi had suffered under the dictatorship of President Zine el-Abidine Ben Ali, which had been in place for twenty-three years. His self-immolation painfully captured the desperate frustration that many young Arabs felt, from North Africa to the Persian Gulf. Like wildfire, this spark spread through the Middle East as an exasperated populace rose to bring down corrupt and dictatorial overlords. The young women and men taking to the streets had grown accustomed to the mantra of Arab exceptionalism to democracy: the notion that stability was the product of imposing patriarchs ruling with an iron fist. Chants calling for dignity, pride, accountability, jobs, and political engagement shook this belief to the core.[1] On January 14, two weeks after the protests began in Tunisia, President Ben Ali stepped down. The power of the masses in removing an Arab dictator shattered the image of regime permanence that autocrats had carefully cultivated through years of brutal repression at the hands of securitized deep states. Unlike the much detested American invasion and occupation of Iraq in 2003, Arabs celebrated that Ben Ali was cast aside by popular demand.[2]

Ten days later, on January 25, Egyptian streets overflowed with protestors calling for the downfall of President Hosni Mubarak's regime. The contagion was spreading. Hamas celebrated these revolutions as a sign of the reawakening of the Arab people after decades of stagnation under unjust rulers.[3] The movement perceived itself to be a popular force, one that was closely connected to the masses, and therefore saw its place as being alongside the protestors.[4] It saluted the "Tunisian intifada," calling it "a prominent milestone in the contemporary history of our Arab nation and an affirmation of its aspiration for freedom and dignity."[5] From his base in Damascus, Hamas's leader Khaled Meshal lauded the Egyptian revolution. "Blessed are the hands of the Egyptian people, Muslims and Christians. . . . The Muslim nation has missed the Egypt that knows its bearings, its loyalty, its allies, duties and enemies. . . . May the Egyptian people be blessed and may Gaza and Palestine be also."[6]

Hamas viewed the Arab upheaval as the culmination of years of change, marked by increased religiosity and the success of the resistance in Lebanon, Palestine, and Iraq. Magazines described the uprisings as an extension of the rejectionist front that Hamas and Hezbollah embodied. For Hamas, the protests reflected a broader denunciation of "Zionism and American imperialism" and of US-backed dictators that served American interests at the expense of their own people. Hamas declared a turning point had been reached. Having seen the Israeli army "defeated" by Lebanese resistance in 2006 and bearing witness to Gaza's steadfastness during Operation Cast Lead, the masses now viewed resistance to foreign agendas as feasible.

For Hamas, Palestine was central to the Arab revolutions—even if the peoples' demands revolved around domestic politics and issues related to freedom, political participation, and social justice. "The Arabs have slept for a long time, but they have now awakened. And Palestine is in their hearts, Jerusalem in their culture. Resistance moves them, Gaza is present in their humanity, liberation in their political speech, as they proclaimed 'Palestine is our destination.'"[7] The movement saw Palestine as the litmus test that would determine whether Arab rulers were ultimately responding to grassroots demands or maintaining their subservience to the United States and Israel.

A STATEHOOD BID AND A PRISONER SWAP

Less than a week after Egyptians took to Cairo's Tahrir Square in early 2011, a coordinated armed operation against several prison compounds in Egypt led to the escape of more than twenty thousand prisoners, including members of the Muslim Brotherhood, Hamas, and Hezbollah. Blame and conspiracy theories filled the airwaves. Was this an attack by Islamist movements seeking to overturn the government, or by the government releasing thugs to undermine protests? A day later, Mubarak's military was deployed throughout the increasingly restless Sinai Peninsula, a zone that had been demilitarized since 1967.[8] Even with this military surge, Mubarak failed to quell the protests against his regime, and on February 11, the Egyptian president was the second Arab leader to be toppled. He announced he would step down and was replaced by military generals. Given that Hamas blamed Mubarak's regime for bias in the Palestinian reconciliation talks, for maintaining the blockade on Gaza, and for repressing Hamas's fighters, Mubarak's removal was celebrated.[9] Hamas also predicted Mubarak's removal would have dire consequences on the Palestinian government in the West Bank, given that it viewed his regime as the Palestinian Authority's "unbreakable backbone."[10]

More broadly, Hamas saw Mubarak's fall as an event that would herald the weakening of the so-called regional axis of moderation, including Jordan, Saudi Arabia, and the United Arab Emirates, all of whom Hamas believed had allied themselves with the Americans and Israelis.[11] Hamas's rhetoric was challenged as protests began expanding into Syria against President Bashar al-Assad's dictatorship. Syria had hosted Hamas's political leaders since they were expelled from Jordan in the early 2000s. Assad's regime was seen as part of the so-called radical axis given, among other things, its support of Palestinian resistance. With the spread of the Arab uprisings, Hamas's argument that protests were rooted in resistance and directed primarily at moderate Arab leaders who were aligned with the United States began to crumble. For the first few months of the Syrian uprising, Hamas maintained a low public profile on this issue and focused instead on linking the Palestinian Authority with other regimes that were feeling the brunt of the popular anger on the street.[12]

Compared to Hamas's seeming good fortunes on the Egyptian front, the Palestinian Authority was contending with an untimely scandal. In early 2011, the Qatari media and broadcasting channel al-Jazeera published *The Palestine Papers*, a sprawling repository of leaked documents that al-Jazeera had sifted through to investigate "the truth behind the Arab-Israeli peace process."[13] The papers included notes, documents, and memoranda that covered PLO actions between 1999 and 2010. The timing of the papers' release was catastrophic as their revelations underscored the assertions of regional protestors regarding the futility, collusion, and corruption of their leaders. *The Palestine Papers* elucidated the extent to which PLO negotiators had conceded on behalf of Palestinians in negotiations with Israel. The leaked records demonstrated that the PLO, and in rarer cases Israeli negotiators, had gone far beyond declared red lines and had been willing to give up significantly more than publicly acknowledged. The revelations were an indictment of both the Palestinian negotiators and the Israeli government. They demonstrated how PLO negotiators had failed to safeguard Palestinian rights, and even raised speculation that the Palestinian leadership had been aware of Israeli military plans in Gaza.[14]

In Israel's case, the papers underscored the government's unwillingness to secure a resolution even after significant concessions had been made by the Palestinians.[15] *The Palestine Papers* vindicated Hamas's assertions of both the Palestinian leadership's subservience to the United States and Israel as well as the futility of negotiations. Blowback was instantaneous as the PLO's chief negotiators resigned. Condemnation of the "Ramallah government" came from Fatah as well as Hamas. As a Hamas parliamentarian stated, "The people who revolted in Egypt and Tunisia will revolt in the face of those who have squandered their rights."[16] Hamas's publications asserted that the Palestinian Authority lost all credibility, with undeniable proof that it could not be trusted to protect Palestinian rights.[17] Possibly as a way to deflect from this scandal, and after Obama's failure to revive the peace process, Abbas pressed forward with a strategy aimed at internationalizing the Palestinian struggle.

Early in the year, Abbas had announced his intention to pursue a statehood bid, whereby he would rally UN member states to recognize the State of Palestine at the UN General Assembly in September. Hamas viewed the pursuit of symbolic gestures such as declarations of statehood as yet another distraction from the required political work of uniting the factions around a national project aimed at confronting the occupation. It interpreted Abbas's move as merely the continuation of efforts to perform sovereignty under occupation, much like the creation of the Palestinian Authority itself.[18] Abbas's mission coincided with continued crackdown against dissent in the West Bank.[19] Hamas pounced, with bitterness, on Abbas's dual strategy of suppressing resistance and advancing the statehood bid. "Of what Palestine are they talking, of what independence, of what sovereignty? Will the country which they are pursuing be built on the corpses of Islamic guerilla fighters? Are independence and sovereignty built in this manner? What the Abbas-Fayyad Authority is doing is to dig its own grave."[20]

Hamas painted a picture of itself as being aligned with the Arab masses against authoritarian regimes such as the Palestinian Authority. Yet a Palestinian uprising was not forthcoming. Instead, in March, semblances of unrest were felt as protestors began calling for an end to the division between the West Bank and the Gaza Strip.[21] Fearing escalation to popular demands for regime change, both the Palestinian Authority and Hamas's government immediately announced reforms. The former called for municipal elections to take place in July 2011 and reshuffled the cabinet under Prime Minister Salam Fayyad. Municipal elections in the West Bank were seen by Hamas as a sign that Abbas was looking to institutionalize the division.[22] More importantly, the Palestinian Authority issued an invitation to Hamas to hold presidential and legislative elections by September as a way to end the division. Tellingly, Hamas rejected Abbas's call, stressing that a unity deal needed to be reached before elections could be carried out in order to address the effects of the split.[23]

Hamas took its own measures in Gaza as its government announced the creation of additional ministerial posts to enhance overall performance, increase transparency, and expand skills and expertise within Prime Minister Ismail Haniyeh's cabinet.[24] The new positions focused on refugees, prisoners, and Jerusalem affairs.[25] Hamas's government denied that changes were a reaction to popular mobilization and suggested that they had commenced a year earlier as Hamas sought to enhance its governance over Gazans.[26] The reforms demonstrated a notable shift in the movement's effort to extend its governmental focus to areas that were not specifically limited to Gaza but rather to the Palestinian cause more broadly. In addition to serving as a response to the Arab revolutions, these changes signaled an important milestone in Hamas's effort to settle into Gaza and consolidate its grip on the Palestinian cause. The movement described these reforms as steps taken to transition its government from crisis management in the years following the territorial division to effective governance and growth. These moves signaled Hamas's belief that reconciliation was unlikely and, indeed, given the regional climate, perhaps undesirable.[27]

Measures by both the Palestinian Authority and Hamas's government failed to contend with the real source of discontent on the street. To address demands for an end to factional division, Abbas pushed for reconciliation by offering to go to Gaza to agree on the formation of a technocratic government and schedule new elections. Abbas's timing betrayed his intention of seeking unity prior to his statehood bid, given fears about the absence of a single Palestinian government that was acceptable to the international community. Hamas dismissed Abbas's initiative as purely cosmetic, particularly given continued security coordination with Israel.[28] Hamas reiterated its call for a "real reconciliation" or none at all. It defined this as a holistic agreement on a united national agenda rather than negotiations over the formation of an interim government and timing of elections—what it viewed as temporary solutions.[29]

After five years of governance, Hamas regarded reconciliation as a process of working alongside the West Bank government to reconstitute and resuscitate the PLO, and to reconcile the two conflicting liberation strategies (negotiations or resistance), rather than seeking unity within the structures of the Palestinian Authority.[30] This stance proved that despite the hardships of the blockade, and given the tunnel economy in Gaza, Hamas was not sufficiently pressured into submission.[31] Hamas's stance undermined the political rationale of the blockade and underscored that its only impact was the collective punishment of ordinary Palestinians living in Gaza. Prospects for reconciliation remained slim as neither party exhibited a willingness to compromise on what each viewed as the optimal national trajectory or to make the concessions for sustainable unity. Meshal reported that reconciliation was "further off than ever before."[32] Yet neither faction could be publicly seen as obstructing reconciliation given fears of a popular backlash. Further, unofficial mediation by civil society and the private sector was prevalent. But these initiatives were not promising. According to one of Hamas's representatives present at the meetings, "[Abbas] has, unfortunately, demeaned the issue of Palestinian reconciliation . . . [to the] formation of a technocratic government, and the setting of a date for the presidential and legislative elections. As if nothing happened. As if there is no political and institutional conflict within the Palestinian arena."[33]

Offering insight into the altered dynamics and Hamas's power, one of Hamas's leaders noted, "We said in all honesty that there is a government with power and control in Gaza, one which does not accept pre-conditions."[34] Hamas's confidence was supported by a construction boom taking place within Gaza in 2011. International donors had pledged millions of dollars in investment to reconstruct the strip after Israel's destructive assault.[35] However, having failed to pressure Israel to lift the blockade, these pledges for the most part did not materialize.

Instead, with Egypt and Israel's unwillingness to ease border crossings, tunnel trade into Gaza mushroomed and advanced to a level whereby Hamas's newly built sophisticated tunnels could transport in heavy building material.[36]

By mid-2011, Gaza's economy was thriving at a level whereby estimates for the time it would take to reconstruct the strip dropped from eighty years (based on the international reconstruction framework) to five (based on tunnel trade).[37] This unofficial growth held disproportionate benefit to Hamas rather than the traditional mercantile class. These operations allowed Hamas's government to enjoy financial autonomy, reducing the impact of the blockade and both the government's and al-Qassam's reliance on the movement's external leadership for fundraising. With the Palestinian Authority continuing to pay the salaries of workers who had been ordered to boycott Hamas's ministries, Gaza's economy had consistent liquidity. However, this subterranean economy was unsustainable. Given the blockade, Gaza was unable to export any of its goods or develop lasting industry or a manufacturing base. Kept as an isolated strip of land, Gaza was on its way to becoming a saturated market, one that would suffer a deep supply glut.[38] While allowing Hamas to consolidate its grip, tunnel revenue also began raising questions regarding the transparency and cleanliness of Hamas's government, a key factor that had propelled the movement to victory against the Palestinian Authority in 2006.[39]

Other signs that Hamas's confidence may have been premature were abundant. In the spring of 2011, Vittorio Arigoni, an Italian peace activist who resided in the Gaza Strip, was murdered by Salafi jihadists. This underscored the security concerns that Hamas faced in Gaza as unrest spread throughout the Sinai Peninsula. Since taking over in 2007, Hamas had worked hard to instill security and to clamp down on manifestations of international terrorist groups within the Gaza Strip. But its ability to control the coastal enclave worsened after Egypt's postrevolution military regime adopted a policy of releasing jailed Islamists, including those who had been convicted of terrorist attacks.[40] Hamas had viewed with trepidation the ensuing proliferation of Salafi presence and worried that the kidnappings and lawlessness that had rocked Gaza in 2007 might resume. This was particularly the case given the relative ease of movement through the tunnels between the Gaza Strip and the Sinai Peninsula. Hamas's security forces swiftly mobilized to capture Arigoni's three murderers as the government boasted it had clamped down on destabilizing elements to prevent them from "terrorizing" Gaza.[41] The responsible men, whom Hamas described as belonging to a "mentally deviant" group, were killed by clashes with Hamas's security forces.[42]

Domestic threats coexisted with fears of border instability as skirmishes became more frequent between Israel and Gaza in the spring, threatening to undermine the ceasefire that held in place since Cast Lead in January 2009. Israel increased its incursions into Gaza and its targeting of Hamas in an effort to stop rockets launched from other groups, particularly Islamic Jihad and Salafi jihadists.[43] While noting its right to fire rockets in self-defense, in reality Hamas again mobilized to contain the factions and prevent the escalation spilling over into a broader conflict.[44] Hamas's attempts to maintain calm highlighted the movement's precarious position of having to pacify the resistance front to mitigate Israeli reprisals while maintaining the legitimacy of its resistance government. After Cast Lead, Hamas's role as a de facto government responsible for policing resistance had become more evident than ever, highlighting the manner in which governing responsibilities weighed down the broader movement's ability to sustain armed struggle.

Influenced by the threat of instability, and more so by popular pressure to end the division, behind-the-scenes discussions between Hamas and Fatah resumed under Egyptian mediation. The impact of protests and Abbas's statehood bid aligned and made way for a breakthrough. On April 27, a month after Abbas's initial call for elections, a surprise announcement was made that an agreement had been reached between Hamas and Fatah in Cairo. The Cairo Agreement, as it came to be known, called for the reactivation of the PLO through the creation of an interim leadership committee that would oversee preparation for presidential and legislative elections. Addressing Hamas's insistence that there be a national framework for the struggle, the committee was charged with reforming the PLO as a precursor to the unification of the political institutions and the security forces of the Gaza Strip and the West Bank as well as the reconstruction of Gaza.[45] In the interim, the agreement called for the formation of a unity government of independents, security and election committees, and the reactivation of the legislature.[46]

The unexpected announcement was met with jubilation among Palestinians, and Hamas's publications reported on feelings of euphoria flooding the streets of Gaza in May 2011.[47] The agreement was held as proof that the protestors had been heard, and Hamas lauded post-revolution Egypt's ability to break away from "previous bias" in mediating between factions.[48] From Meshal's base in Damascus, where he was also talking to the Syrian regime about the reconciliation file, Hamas's leader announced that the negotiating factions would immediately implement the provisions of the unity deal.[49] Meetings in Cairo began immediately to lay the groundwork as the Arab League, alongside Egypt, agreed to oversee implementation. Hamas reported that one of the most sensitive challenges of reintegration was the issue of its political prisoners in the West Bank. Senior Hamas leaders declared that they had provided President Abbas with a list of 150 names of prisoners to be released, a request they were monitoring with Egypt.[50]

Forming a unity government was daunting, as it entailed reunifying all the institutional divisions that had occurred over the course of the past five years, including the revision and reassessment of laws and legislation that had been passed by the two separate governments.[51] Other challenges included institutional and administrative tasks such as reconciling the salaries and positions of civil servants in both governments. This was particularly difficult in Gaza, where out of necessity Hamas's government had hired an alternative body of civil servants after the Palestinian Authority's boycott order. Merging the governments promised to entail significant job losses as both Hamas and Fatah vied to safeguard the interests of their own employees. It quickly became evident that the task of realizing the reconciliation, institutionally and politically, was immense.[52] Within weeks, public bickering increased, specifically around the prisoners.[53] The other point of contention was the choice of prime minister, as both parties provided lists with their suggested candidates. Abbas held firm to Salam Fayyad, a choice that Hamas stridently refused.[54]

Both Hamas and the Palestinian Authority appeared intent on pushing forward with their own agendas while paying lip service to the notion of unity. Hamas's leaders believed that if Abbas had the will to push reconciliation through, he would not let issues as minor as employee salaries get in the way, particularly after Hamas had offered to give up its ministerial positions.[55] As Abbas's statehood bid approached, Hamas reported on the president's procrastination. At the end of August, Hamas alleged that Abbas had sent a delegation to Gaza with a message to Ismail Haniyeh that the Palestinian Authority would be unable to complete the implementation of the reconciliation agreement until after the September vote in the United Nations on the Palestinian statehood bid. In the meantime, Abbas would be open to enhancing cooperation "between the two governments in Ramallah and Gaza."[56]

Hamas was also responsible for failing to truly pursue reconciliation.[57] The movement's readiness to give up on its ministerial seats was accompanied by the demand for a role in reshaping the Palestinian struggle, a mission its leaders appeared to be fulfilling unilaterally. Against the backdrop of unity talks, Meshal traveled throughout the region, including to Egypt and Qatar, to discuss Palestinian internal affairs. His diplomatic mission reflected Hamas's intention to capitalize on the regional flux to strengthen bilateral relations with neighboring states.[58] The movement was rooted in the belief that regional fluctuations would isolate Israel and promote Hamas's role as the leader of the Palestinian struggle.[59] With instability in the Sinai, Hamas reported on Israeli worries that its southern border was now less secure. On August 18, militants from the Sinai Peninsula carried out an attack in Israel close to the southern city of Eilat, on the Red Sea coast. Although

the attack was not executed or claimed by Hamas, Israeli officials indicated that they believed the attackers had originated from the Gaza
Strip. Israel mobilized rapidly and carried out targeted assassinations
throughout Gaza, killing fifteen Palestinians.[60]

Hamas claimed that Netanyahu was using the "boogeyman" of
Gaza to deflect from the social protests that had begun in Israel a few
weeks prior.[61] Its publications hypothesized that Israel was considering
an attack on Gaza, effectively to end the truce and to release Shalit,
but was worried that "Egypt after the revolution is not Egypt before."[62]
This betrayed a hope held by Hamas that postrevolutionary Egypt
would stand in solidarity with Gaza in the face of Israeli offensives.[63]
Publications hypothesized that Israel was facing an existential threat,
its neighbors turning against it: first Turkey following the *Mavi Marmara*
attack, and then Egypt.[64] Hamas saw the change in the region as part of
an "Islamic renaissance" that rejected Israel politically and diplomatically. As Hamas's publications argued:

> The Zionist entity had tamed the Arab mentality. It had bought re-
> gimes, subjugated others, and weakened peoples. [Arab] regimes coop-
> erated in terrorizing and oppressing their own people . . . and reached
> a stage of even making alliances with [the Zionist entity]. That was a
> past—painful and bitter—phase, where Arabs lost a lot of their power
> cards. Now the Arab renaissance has returned to normal. Two coun-
> tries, one Arab (Egypt) and one Islamic (Turkey), one with its people
> (Egypt) and one with its government (Turkey) raising their voice loudly
> against the Zionist entity.[65]

While Hamas focused on its regional positioning, Abbas faced the
international community as he submitted his application for statehood
to the United Nations on September 23, 2011.[66] Although popular on
the ground, particularly in the West Bank, Abbas's bid was largely symbolic. For Hamas, Abbas's drive to achieve statehood had become an
obsession in the PLO's political thinking.[67] As the movement's spokes-

man remarked, "Hamas supports whatever effort or popular mobilization in any arena or international platform that results in prosecuting
and isolating the Zionist enemy."[68] Concurrently, however, leaders
noted that these efforts needed to fit within a defined national strategy
and that symbolic achievements should not be pursued at the expense
of other, real aspects of the liberation strategy, such as resistance. For
Hamas, the central question was not whether Abbas would be able to
push through the UN vote, but whether the Palestinian Authority would
be able to stand its ground against international opposition to achieve
the rights that Palestinians were fighting for. Until Abbas could put forward a strategy to safeguard those rights, Hamas believed, the UN vote
was little more than a media bubble.[69]

Despite immense pressure, particularly from the Obama administration and Israel, who both opposed such "unilateral actions," Abbas
submitted his statehood application. As the president celebrated his
grand gesture, Hamas announced its own major success in Gaza. On
October 18, a month after Abbas's bid, Hamas completed a prisoner
exchange deal with Israel under Egyptian mediation. The agreement,
which Hamas called "Operation Loyalty of the Free," entailed the
release of Israeli soldier Gilad Shalit, who had been held in captivity
for close to five years, in exchange for 1,027 Palestinian prisoners.[70] A
hugely disproportionate agreement that underscored the power discrepancy between Israel and the Palestinians, Hamas nonetheless lauded
this exchange as a historic success. Having refused to link negotiations
for Shalit's release with ceasefire talks, at a staggering cost to Gaza,
Hamas was ultimately vindicated. Its ability to hold on to Shalit despite
Israel's attempts to free him and despite the known network of collaborators within Gaza was described as legendary.[71] With this diplomatic
coup, Hamas rejoiced in its role as a powerful counterpart to Israel and
as a Palestinian government that was able to effect real change on the
ground. As Meshal noted, "We are now experts in the Israeli mentality,
because God has shown us who they are," while he suggested that other
Palestinian negotiators take note.[72]

Capitalizing on its success, Hamas paradoxically upheld the Shalit deal as a true sign of its desire to maintain domestic unity and portrayed the exchange as being a Palestinian, not a factional, achievement. The movement's publications noted that the prisoners to be released were from different Palestinian factions. Although this was likely the product of the negotiations, Hamas presented the diverse release as emblematic of the absence of favoritism toward its own people.[73] Prisoners were to be released to Rafah and Ramallah in batches, where politicians from Fatah and Hamas could welcome them side-by-side. As Meshal said, the deal "is non-sectarian or tribal. We are one blood, even if we differ in politics. The prisoner exchange creates a favorable atmosphere to achieve reconciliation."[74] The geographic breadth and the political diversity of the prisoners reaffirmed "what Hamas has always called for, that the Palestine it seeks is Historic Palestine, from Rafah [in the south] to Ras al-Naqoura [in the north]."[75]

Israel's act of undermining Abbas by opposing his statehood bid while rewarding Hamas sent another resounding message regarding the potential of resistance. While both factions failed to pursue reconciliation with any degree of commitment, the prisoner deal's timing also underscored Israel's role in catalyzing the division between the two factions and playing the two off each other. As Hamas's prisoner exchange overshadowed the Palestinian Authority's internationalization strategy, Hamas portrayed itself as the leader of Palestinians, not of Gaza or the resistance. In publications celebrating this deal, an ode to al-Qassam, the perpetrators of Shalit's capture, read, "Al-Qassam Brigades are no longer a military wing that belongs to Hamas only. Al-Qassam Brigades have become Palestine's army, the protector of our homes, and the first line of defense for Jerusalem, the first squad in the liberation project."[76] Hamas's vision of al-Qassam as a national army underscored its view of the Gaza Strip as a launch pad for the Palestinian struggle and its role as the leader of the Palestinian national movement after the PLO's failed project of negotiations. Hamas's publications viewed al-Qassam as having become a strategic player in the region.[77] Prisoners who were released talked of how Hamas's governance now provided a climate conducive to resistance, as al-Qassam began preparing for what it described as the full liberation of historic Palestine.[78]

THE DOHA DECLARATION
AND OPERATION PILLAR OF DEFENSE

From this position of strength, Hamas maintained overtures to reconciliation. On the day of the prisoner exchange, Meshal stood in front of the first batch of released prisoners in Cairo and extended an invitation for a meeting with Abbas.[79] This politically savvy gesture, at a time when Hamas was riding a popularity wave, called for factions to meet again to finalize outstanding issues.[80] Throughout the winter of 2011, talks continued in Gaza, Amman, and Ramallah.[81] These proceeded alongside pressure from the United States and Israel, following Abbas's application to the United Nations, to return to peace negotiations as the only viable way to end the conflict. Much to Hamas's consternation, Abbas agreed to participate in "low-level" talks at the Israeli embassy in Amman.[82] The resumption of negotiations, after almost sixteen months of silence between Israel and the Palestinians, expectedly worsened the mood in the domestic discussions.

Hamas's broader reality also began shifting. What had begun as a cry for pride and dignity on the Arab street had, by the first anniversary of the uprisings, been replaced by regional proxy battles waged by ideologues.[83] The Arab uprisings had quickly expanded beyond a confrontation between citizens and governments to encompass three other dimensions: the cold war between Iran and Saudi Arabia for regional dominance; the struggle among Sunni states, namely Saudi Arabia, the United Arab Emirates, Qatar, and Turkey, for regional influence; and competition between Islamist parties such as the Muslim Brotherhood and transnational Salafi jihadist networks like the nascent so-called Islamic State.[84] Seeking to safeguard their regimes, states poured money, arms, and resources into the proxy wars that were breaking out in Libya,

Yemen, Syria, and Egypt. Rather than an opportunity for democratization, Arab and Islamic rulers viewed the uprisings as existential threats as well as an opportunity to consolidate regional influence.

Like other actors, Hamas tried to manage this fast-shifting network of alliances as its leaders persisted in efforts to develop strong bilateral regional relations.[85] In late 2011, Ismail Haniyeh left the Gaza Strip for his second regional tour as Meshal continued on his diplomatic efforts, visiting Qatar, Syria, and Turkey and attending a conference in Tehran where Iran's leaders reiterated the centrality of the Palestinian cause to the Islamic nation.[86] Although Meshal was hosted at this conference, the movement's close relationship with Iran was coming under significant strain as President Assad's regime brutally militarized against Syrian protestors. Iran and Hezbollah, Hamas's traditional allies, came out in support of Assad's regime, while the Sunni Gulf States, weary of expanding Iranian influence, called for Assad's removal.[87] In late December 2011, Hamas took the bold step of distancing itself from the Syrian republic in a move that firmly positioned it in the Sunni bloc and on the side of the protesters. Khaled Meshal and the rest of Hamas's external leadership relocated their base from Damascus to Doha.

Hamas's decision almost instantly severed the financial support the movement received from Iran as funding was promptly redirected to Islamic Jihad in Gaza, leading to some tension between the factions.[88] Among the Arab Gulf States, in contrast to both Saudi Arabia and the Emirates, Qatar supported the regional Islamic parties and used its immense wealth and soft power (chiefly the broadcasting channel al-Jazeera) to expand its influence. Hamas decisively aligned itself with Qatar as the Muslim Brotherhood began exhibiting strength in post-Mubarak Egypt, boosting Hamas's confidence that the Arab uprisings were unfolding in its favor.[89] While the movement's regional fundraising under the external bureau was suffering, Hamas's government and its internal leadership were buoyed by the tunnels in Gaza.[90]

It was therefore quite an unexpected surprise when, in February 2012, the Doha Declaration was announced.[91] This was an agreement signed surreptitiously at the top level directly between Meshal and Abbas, a development notable in its own right for the absence of the prime minister of Hamas's government, Ismail Haniyeh, as a signatory. This document illustrated quite unabashedly the shifting centers of power in the region as Qatar, rather than Egypt, assumed the role of factional mediator. It also demonstrated Hamas's strength relative to the Palestinian Authority given its ability to shift the negotiations to its patron. The declaration called for the formation of an interim technocratic government headed by Abbas and charged with supervising general elections and commencing Gaza's reconstruction. Circumventing the nitty-gritty details being hammered out by the negotiating committees in Amman, the Doha Declaration was portrayed as a pragmatic step to undo the domestic stalemate and provide a comprehensive high-level framework for unity. Significantly, the declaration allowed the factions to sidestep the key issue of contention, the appointment of prime minister, by allowing Abbas (unconstitutionally) to hold both the presidency and the premiership.

The government was defined, according to Hamas, as an apolitical cabinet whose mission was to support reconciliation and elections.[92] The declaration came at a time when the exploratory talks between the Palestinian Authority and Israel had expectedly reached a dead end. Caught off guard, Prime Minister Netanyahu stated, "I have said many times in the past that the Palestinian Authority must choose between an alliance with Hamas and peace with Israel. Hamas and peace don't go together."[93] It was not only Israel, however, that had been unprepared. Meshal's acceptance of the Doha Declaration came as a surprise to many Palestinians, including Hamas members, not least because of Qatar's role as mediator.[94] The fact that Hamas's top political leader had agreed to this deal, at a time when the movement's negotiators held firm in their demand for PLO reform prior to the formation of an interim administrative government, elucidated the divergent priorities within Hamas's constituencies. Meshal's move was interpreted by many as an internal power play to reassert the dominance of the movement's external political bureau over Hamas's government and military wing in Gaza. This suspicion was strengthened by the fact that Hamas had begun its internal elections in the spring of 2012.

Meshal's decision created significant tension within Hamas, particularly between the external leadership under his lead and senior leaders within Gaza such as Mahmoud al-Zahhar.[95] Yet with Meshal's residing outside the Gaza Strip, where he was more attuned to broader developments, it was also understood that he was attempting to manage Hamas's regional relations.[96] Specifically, the agreement underscored Meshal's attempt to capitalize on recent fortunes and Qatar's backing to secure Hamas's role in shaping a united national agenda alongside the Palestinian Authority. Nonetheless, Meshal's decision demonstrated significant willingness to make concessions. Even according to Hamas's spokesman, the movement showed great flexibility in this declaration. It acquiesced to postponing the release of political prisoners until after reconciliation. It allowed for Abbas to head the government, albeit as an independent.[97] Furthermore, Meshal explicitly underscored the role of popular unarmed resistance in the struggle against occupation, a position that was received with surprise.[98]

But one particular aspect of the Doha Declaration carried significant import: Hamas's acquiescence not to hold on to the post of prime minister or lead any of the key ministries. This concession amounted to an effort by Hamas to relinquish responsibility for the financial and administrative burdens of government within the Gaza Strip. Meshal's readiness to do so was driven by the financial constraints Hamas was facing following the depletion of Iranian funding. Furthermore, despite the buoyant tunnel trade, the economy in Gaza was predictably unsustainable and uncertain and left the majority of Gazans suffering the impact of the blockade. This became evident as an energy crisis gripped the strip in early 2012, leaving Hamas exposed to accusations of corruption that it was benefiting from the tunnel trade at the expense of average people.[99]

The deal underscored Meshal's prescient understanding of the detriment Hamas as a movement faced as a result of its governing responsibility within the Gaza Strip, where it was held accountable by the people for the impact of the blockade and where it was placed in the situation of having to police resistance from other armed factions. For Meshal, shedding this institutional weight was not to come at the expense of Hamas's participation in the leadership of the Palestinian liberation struggle as inherent in the PLO, or a similar framework of liberation. In effect, Meshal was attempting to capitalize on Hamas's popularity, flexing local power through its foothold in Gaza and regional power through its bilateral relations to maintain the movement's involvement in setting the agenda of the national struggle. He pursued this while hoping the agreement would allow Hamas to break free of the administrative constraints of the Palestinian Authority and the movement's role as a de facto government in Gaza.

Less than three weeks after the agreement was declared, Israel launched "Operation Returning Echo," on March 9, 2012, allegedly to preempt a major attack that was being planned from the Gaza Strip. This assault was the most violent since Cast Lead and lasted for close to a week, killing twenty-seven Palestinians, effectively ending the ceasefire that had been negotiated in 2009.[100] Israel had reportedly been worried about weapon smuggling through the Sinai tunnels into the Gaza Strip and was seeking to reassert its dominance.[101] But the timing of the attack raised suspicions that Israel was seeking to undermine the high-level decision taken by Abbas and Meshal to end the division. For the duration of 2011, rocket fire had been effectively controlled and Israel had not incurred casualties, compared to twenty-three civilians that had been killed in Gaza by Israeli incursions.[102] Meshal, who was being hosted by President Erdogan in Turkey at the time, noted that this was Israel's attempt to drag the Palestinians into another war and undermine the unity agreement.[103]

Israel's escalation marked the continuation of its double-pronged strategy of isolating Hamas within the Gaza Strip alongside the pursuit of military deterrence through disproportionate force, even when Hamas proved effective in policing resistance. Hamas's publications also suggested these incursions allowed Israel to investigate Hamas's military capacity and willingness to retaliate.[104] The answer was not immediately forthcoming. Led by Islamic Jihad, resistance factions retaliated heavily with close to three hundred rockets into Ashdod, Beersheba, and southern Israeli cities. The scale of the response was justified as self-defense aimed at breaking Israel's unilateral escalations, a sign that Palestinians also sought deterrence.[105] Hamas's efforts to pacify the resistance front that had held largely in place since 2009 could not stand in opposition to an escalation of this scale. As Hamas's spokesman said, "Palestinian resistance broke the occupation's formula by insisting to confront its crimes with full power and determination."[106] Similarly, Islamic Jihad's leader noted, Israel wanted free rein to carry out targeted assassinations, then to compel Egyptian mediators to reinstate the ceasefire. By retaliating powerfully, resistance factions were forcing the occupation to submit to reciprocity.[107]

While Hamas's publications declared that the resistance factions created a powerful united military front, al-Qassam Brigades were in reality largely absent.[108] Addressing this, an Islamic Jihad leader noted that Hamas's government was active in providing the right environment to protect the resistance effort. "The resistance is complementary not competitive," and the roles change depending on needs and requirements.[109] In this case, it allegedly meant a behind-the-scenes role for al-Qassam. Other factions noted that al-Qassam's participation would have led to an Israeli invasion, which was undesirable.[110] This dynamic was indicative of a reality that had emerged in Gaza after years of Hamas's rule, whereby the movement's government created an environment that was conducive to, and indeed supportive of, an active resistance front. Even when al-Qassam was physically missing from the battlefield, resistance existed under Hamas's umbrella, given that it provided the legal and political cover for every fighter on the field.[111] In effect, Hamas had institutionalized resistance within the Gaza Strip and developed a monopoly over the military front.

This skirmish proved that through Operation Cast Lead, Israel had failed to instill lasting deterrence. Rather, a delicate equilibrium between calm and violence had been instituted, one that often tipped in favor of violence following provocations by Israel. Despite the assault, the Palestinian unity deal held. On May 21, a few weeks after the Doha Declaration, a roadmap for reconciliation was agreed on.[112] Administrative delays ensued and persistent worries about the intentions of both parties were prevalent.[113] But with regional changes redrawing priorities for the Palestinian parties, Hamas had guardedly optimistic hopes that reconciliation could pass in a manner that was acceptable to it.[114] During this time, the Muslim Brotherhood's Freedom and Justice party in Egypt was sweeping into power in the wake of postrevolution elections. This boosted Hamas's sense that regional developments were working in its favor. "The transformations in the Arab World intersect with Hamas's resistance project," publications proclaimed. "Hamas has won twice: once with the fall of the regimes, and once with the arrival of the Islamists to positions of power."[115]

On June 28, 2012, the Muslim Brotherhood's Mohamed Morsi became Egypt's first democratically elected president. The brotherhood's rise to the leadership of the region's most populous nation was a watershed moment in Middle East politics, as the spotlight turned on the brotherhood to determine how it would govern after years of weathering repression. For Hamas, Morsi's election heralded a new era that would offer a lifeline to the Gaza Strip. The movement celebrated this success as brotherhood flags and Morsi's presidential portraits proliferated in public spaces throughout Gaza.[116] Leaders capitalized on this favorable regional shift as Meshal embarked on a tour to Cairo, Morocco, and Tunisia, where he met with leaders of the reinvigorated North African Islamic parties.[117]

But Hamas's intense performance of solidarity with its parent organization exposed both Hamas and the Muslim Brotherhood to stinging accusations. Palestinian media portrayed Hamas as a party whose allegiance was pan-Islamic rather than national. Across the Rafah border, antibrotherhood Egyptian media vilified Morsi for his association with Hamas, which was untruthfully portrayed as the cause of unrest in the Sinai Peninsula. Media wars were amplified as the Sinai became increasingly unstable.[118] Worried about attacks emanating from the peninsula, Israel warned Egyptian authorities that weapons were coming in from Libya and other conflict zones. Israeli security officials claimed that al-Qaeda had begun providing arms to their forces in the Gaza Strip from the peninsula.[119]

As Meshal toured the region, on August 5 a brutal attack by unknown assailants on the Rafah border killed sixteen Egyptian soldiers. Although the assailants were widely assumed to be Salafi jihadists, Hamas and the Gaza Strip inevitably got caught in the crossfire. Hamas condemned this "crime" in strong terms. Yet almost immediately, Egyptian media pointed to Gaza as the location from which the perpetrators had originated, despite Hamas's strong denunciation of such "rumors."[120] Reacting to the mass uproar in Egypt, Morsi promptly sealed the Rafah borders and closed the tunnels, sharply overturning Hamas's hopes for greater openness between Egypt and Gaza under his presidency.[121] Hamas's government deployed heavy military around the tunnels from the Gazan side to prevent anyone entering.[122] The government also reached out to the factions in Gaza and declared that it saw no proof of involvement from anyone in the strip. Clearly alluding to Salafi jihadists, both Hamas and Islamic Jihad stressed that the resistance factions refused to serve as a protective cloak for movements that were "ideologically deviant."[123]

The Rafah operation created a significant rift in Hamas-Egyptian relations at a time when this alliance was anticipated to move in a more positive direction. Hamas's government stated that the attack was meant to embarrass Morsi domestically and noted that it had received assurances from Morsi's cabinet that there was no proof the attackers had come from Gaza.[124] Yet placed in a difficult position, Morsi was nonetheless pressured to focus on domestic issues and distance himself from the Gaza Strip. Tarnished relations between Gaza and Egypt undermined the prospects of relaxing the Rafah border and heightened surveillance of the tunnel trade as Egyptian public opinion swiftly turned against

Hamas.[125] Meshal confirmed that Hamas would work with Egyptian intelligence to return security to the Sinai, dismissing all media claims that the movement was working to take over the Sinai as "Zionist propaganda."[126] As Mahmoud Zahhar said, "Why would Hamas break the strategy underpinning its resistance and for the first time in its history carry out an attack outside the occupied territories?"[127]

The Rafah incident was a stark reminder of the rapidly evolving landscape in which Hamas was operating. The tightening around the tunnel trade threatened to cut off the strip from any trade with the outside world given that the blockade remained impermeable. When this was coupled with the drop in Iranian funding, Hamas was in a precarious position. Not unrelated, Gaza's borders with Israel were also becoming volatile as skirmishes became more frequent following Israel's last operation. Throughout the fall of 2012, Hamas's publications reported that Israel was actively targeting its safe houses and training centers and expanding its assassinations.[128] Rocket fire also persisted from Gaza in protest of the blockade and as an affirmation of the right to self-defense.

On November 14, Israel mobilized and escalated to a surprising level given the relative calm of the preceding years. Citing its intention to destroy Hamas's rocket-launching capabilities, Prime Minister Netanyahu claimed that the attacks "made normal life impossible."[129] Without prior warning, Israel assassinated Ahmad Jabari, al-Qassam's second-in-command, marking the beginning of what Israel called "Operation Pillar of Defense." This attack conclusively ended the 2009 ceasefire and elevated the sporadic skirmishes of the summer into a full-blown military offensive. The reasons for Israel's escalation are disputed and include arguments relating to a show of strength given Netanyahu's call for elections in January 2013 and a desire to opportunistically weaken Hamas while it was struggling. Israel's choice to assassinate Jabari was heavily questioned and gave rise to accusations that Israel was seeking to undermine the viability of ceasefires, given that he had been an active player in enforcing the calm from Gaza's side since Cast Lead.[130]

Regardless of the specifics of this particular escalation, Pillar of Defense kept with Israel's strategy of isolation and deterrence toward Gaza.[131] Israel pushed forward and targeted key sites that were thought to be of military importance to Hamas, including training camps and government buildings. Israel also fired at apartment blocks and residential areas, claiming they were used for the storage of weapons. Alongside other resistance factions, Hamas retaliated with hundreds of rockets into southern Israeli towns, demonstrating a higher military capacity than it had done to date. Unlike Cast Lead, this military assault came after years of Hamas consolidating its grip on the Gaza Strip, expanding its tunnel operations, and boasting that al-Qassam had become a national army. For Hamas, this escalation was a strategic moment, a time when its resistance forces gained further experience in fighting, developed their strategy, and committed to strengthening their capabilities.[132]

According to Hamas's publications, al-Qassam had studied the 2006 war between Israel and Lebanon and had developed plans and operational manuals based on that model. During Cast Lead, al-Qassam had primarily focused on its defensive strategies and stood firm in steadfastness to limit Israel's ability to invade, allegedly using a mere 5 to 10 percent of its military power.[133] By November 2012, however, Hamas claimed it was able to go on the offensive as it coordinated with Islamic Jihad to an unprecedented level.[134] From Hamas's perspective, the scale of such tactical coordination on the field was a new and positive development, as the merging of the two most powerful resistance factions. Enhanced military performance, compared to Cast Lead, became a precursor to a joint offensive strategy that Hamas felt could put the resistance forward on the path toward liberation, rather than relying on haphazard firing of missiles.[135] Seizing on these signs of military progress, Hamas's leaders confirmed that they felt their liberation project was moving in the right direction, particularly when viewed in the larger arc of the movement's history.[136]

President Morsi began immediate efforts to mediate a ceasefire, with support from Secretary of State Hillary Clinton, weeks before President Obama was sworn into office for his second term. Negotiations proceeded indirectly between Israel and Hamas rather than through the PLO, further validating the movement as Israel's counterpart in the Gaza Strip. On November 22, ten days after the war began and following the death of 174 Palestinians and six Israelis, a ceasefire was agreed. Both parties claimed victory. Israel stated that Hamas's rocket capabilities had been heavily destroyed. Hamas believed it had emerged victorious as the ceasefire committed Israel to facilitating access and movement from the Gaza Strip.[137]

The reality was more complex. Israel again failed to instill lasting deterrence. Even though on a practical level Hamas was effective in policing borders, ideologically it remained committed to resistance to end the occupation and was often unable or unwilling to control the activities of other resistance factions. Israel also worried about Hamas's strengthened military capacity given the relatively permeable tunnel trade. Operation Pillar of Defense was an effort to weaken Hamas's military arsenal and initiate another period of calm. Instead of engaging with Hamas's political agenda in pursuit of a more durable settlement, Israel continued to view Hamas through a security prism, reinforcing a belligerent equilibrium held in place through violence. In turn, Israel's approach boosted Hamas's resistance legacy.[138] Moreover, given that Israel remained opposed to reoccupying Gaza and given Hamas's effectiveness in controlling the enclave, Israel appeared to have acquiesced to its rule. Having hit Hamas's military infrastructure, the ceasefire compelled Israel to ease the blockade, essentially lifting Hamas's financial burden at a time when the tunnel trade was uncertain.

In return for the stabilization of its rule, Hamas succumbed to an explicit demand to end hostilities from the Gaza Strip, in fear of further Israeli reprisals. In favor of stability and access, and in service of a longer-term vision of liberation, Hamas accepted the need to pacify the resistance front in the short term. Such pacification was seen as an opportunistic and pragmatic short-term concession that allowed Hamas to survive without ideological default and to continue strengthening its longer-term vision of growth and militarization.[139] Nonetheless, Abbas accused Hamas of agreeing to what effectively amounted to security coordination with Israel while vilifying the Palestinian Authority for doing the same in the West Bank.[140] Abbas's accusations were accurate, but the movement benefited from the fact that it remained ideologically defiant. This allowed Hamas to sustain its resistance legacy even when, in practice, it did police armed struggle. It also leveraged its perceived success to develop its diplomatic and political reach more broadly as it celebrated the shifting regional climate.[141]

In December 2008, during Cast Lead, Israel's foreign minister Tzipi Livni had declared from Cairo how Israel was intent on destroying Hamas's weapons. In November 2012, during Pillar of Defense, Meshal and the head of Islamic Jihad stood in the same Arab city and spoke of Gaza's victory. In the aftermath of the war, Egypt refused to maintain the blockade. President Morsi traveled to Gaza and made a political appearance with Haniyeh, paving the way for other political breakthroughs, including visits by a Tunisian ministerial delegation, Arab foreign ministers, and the Turkish foreign minister. After Israel's operation, intentionally or otherwise, Hamas's political isolation was shattered.[142]

A few weeks later, a group of Hamas officials and supporters traveled to Gaza from Lebanon to show solidarity. On their way in, one of Hamas's senior leaders in Beirut wrote:

> We entered Gaza with our heads held high, through the gates of resistance. Our passports were stamped 'Rafah crossing,' where we were greeted by men of resistance. This was a crossing run by a government whose leader is a resistance fighter, and its program is a resistance program. [A government] whose main concerns are protecting the resistance, supporting it politically, facilitating its movement, and building a society of resistance. We did not enter Gaza from the gates of security coordination. We did not enter Palestine from the gates of recognition and negotiations.[143]

On December 7, Meshal returned to Gaza after an absence of forty-five years, where he attended Hamas's twenty-fifth anniversary carnival. His ability to travel to Gaza without being subject to an Israeli targeted assassination confirmed suspicions that in the ceasefire agreement Israel had agreed to safeguard Hamas's rule in Gaza, as long as its military front was tightly controlled.

During his stay, Meshal spoke of unity and of how "Palestine is too big for one faction to be responsible for," a reference to Hamas's alleged desire to enter into a unity government.[144] His trip coincided with Fatah delegations visiting Gaza as well, as both the Palestinian Authority and Hamas gave a nod to reconciliation once again.[145] By the end of Israel's operation, Hamas's legitimacy as a resistance movement had been strengthened, an agreement for an easing of the blockade had been instituted, and Hamas's rule in Gaza temporarily stabilized and empowered. The Doha Declaration invariably remained inoperable as each party pursued its own national agenda. While Hamas celebrated its victory in Gaza, Abbas received news that the United Nations had approved his statehood bid and granted Palestine nonobserver member status. As one of Hamas's ministers noted, "There is no political will from either side to move closer [toward reconciliation] at this point. . . . Until that political will is present to deal with the highest national interests, unless there is the preparedness to pay the price of reconciliation, until there is a sovereign decision towards the importance of conceding and offering what is needed . . . I do not expect any imminent breakthrough."[146]

AN EGYPTIAN COUP AND THE SHATI AGREEMENT

In January 2013, Qatari reconstruction projects in the Gaza Strip commenced after significant support and facilitation from the Egyptian side.[147] The Qatari grant, reported to be around $400 million, focused on completing highway infrastructure, housing for prisoners released after the Shalit deal, rehabilitation centers, prosthetic limbs, and hospital and various industrial and agricultural facilities.[148] By April, Hamas's internal elections were complete, close to a year after they had started. The unusual length of the cumbersome election cycle was due to both Hamas's expanded geographic reach and the difficulty of carrying them out in the West Bank, a key area, given intensified security coordination between Israel and the Palestinian Authority.[149] Khaled Meshal was reelected as the head of Hamas's political bureau and Ismail Haniyeh as his deputy. Haniyeh remained acting prime minister of Hamas's government in Gaza.

Meshal's reelection demonstrated his lasting influence within the movement despite the significant controversy of the Doha Declaration. Given the movement's funding needs and the regional turmoil, Meshal had emerged as the powerhouse behind Hamas's diplomatic relations and its regional realignment.[150] His reelection heightened rumors that Hamas was moderating, given his recent activities and his diplomatic focus alongside occasional rumors that he was advocating nonviolent resistance. Hamas distanced itself from such speculation.[151] It reiterated that it rejected the "moderate-radical" binary: the only axis it belonged to was Palestine and resistance. Hamas stressed that its relationship with any one country did not come at the expense of its relationship with any other.[152] Walking a fine line, Hamas's leaders attempted to mitigate the sensitivities that had emerged with Egypt as its government took measures to tighten internal security.[153]

Shortly after President Obama's reelection, John Kerry, who replaced Hillary Clinton as secretary of state, was dispatched to the region to resuscitate the Israeli-Palestinian peace process. The Kerry Initiative, as it came to be known, constituted familiar elements, including an economic package to strengthen the Palestinian Authority in the West Bank.[154] Hamas objected to the initiative and accused Abbas of having delayed reconciliation so as to give the peace process another chance.[155] As Kerry's initiative got under way, Hamas's government released a communiqué calling on the government in Ramallah to stop "holding onto American illusions and running after the clouds of peace."[156] Both parties pursued their own diplomatic measures while blaming their counterpart for institutionalizing the division.

This diplomatic tug-of-war came to an abrupt end on June 30, as massive protests against President Morsi rocked Egyptian streets. The turmoil came after months of clashes between the Egyptian military and the elected leaders of the Muslim Brotherhood.[157] Instability in the Sinai, Morsi's increasingly authoritarian executive orders, and the agitation of the military leaders seeking to maintain their vested interests all served to undermine Egypt's democratic transition as protestors called for early presidential elections. Within three days, Defense Minister Abdel Fattah al-Sisi had carried out a military coup against President Morsi.[158] Although Egypt did not disintegrate into violence like Syria, the coup was far from bloodless as clashes erupted between Morsi supporters and military personnel in the weeks following Morsi's removal. Terrorist activities from Salafi jihadists persisted throughout the Sinai Peninsula. The early hopes that Egyptians had harbored regarding a more hopeful future paved the way for the reinstitution of a more autocratic and brutal regime than the one that had been ousted under Mubarak. In Egypt, the region's proxy wars aimed at maintaining the incumbent regional order against change appeared to have triumphed.[159]

The Egyptian coup irreversibly overturned Hamas's regional calculus.[160] Hamas had aligned itself with both the spirit of the revolution and rising Islamic democratization in the Middle East. With Morsi's removal, Hamas witnessed an early indication that the tide had swiftly shifted the other way. The backlash against both Hamas and the Muslim Brotherhood was instantaneous. Hamas condemned the coup and Morsi's removal as overturning the people's democratic choice.[161] Its rhetorical support of the brotherhood exacerbated its vulnerability as it lay in the crossfire rocking Egypt. Anti-Morsi demonstrators resurfaced accusations that Hamas was responsible for the prison break that had taken place in the early days of the Egyptian uprising. That attack had released thousands of prisoners, mainly Islamists, including President Morsi himself. Hamas had long refuted these accusations and protested that it was being scapegoated for domestic purposes. The movement noted that there was not a single shred of proof that Hamas had been involved in Egyptian affairs.[162]

Egyptian military authorities nonetheless began procedures to block the Rafah tunnels and all access into Gaza. Fatah also came out strongly against Hamas. Shortly after Morsi's ouster, it called on Hamas to stop interfering in the domestic affairs of neighboring countries, particularly Syria and Egypt.[163] Fatah leaders denounced the coverage of al-Aqsa and al-Quds, Hamas's main broadcasting channels, as blatantly supportive of the brotherhood in Cairo.[164] Further, the Palestinian ambassador to Egypt stated that Hamas's military—often on display in Gaza—and its explicit support of the Muslim Brotherhood in Egypt were forms of intervention in Egyptian domestic affairs.[165] By the summer, exchanges between Hamas and Fatah had turned acrimonious. Fatah stressed that Hamas was taking the people of Gaza hostage to their regional politics and their attempts to build a global Muslim Brotherhood movement.[166] Hamas denied all these charges, reaffirming its age-old policy of not interfering in other countries' domestic affairs.[167] Hamas's spokesman blamed Fatah members and those loyal to the Mubarak regime for waging a media war of incitement and provocation, as he insisted that Hamas had remained neutral toward Egyptian affairs.[168] In July, Hamas issued orders to close Fatah's news outlets Ma'an and al-Arabiya in Gaza for allegedly failing to maintain professional reporting standards and for inciting against Hamas. Ma'an had reported a few days prior that Hamas had welcomed and hid Muslim Brotherhood members escaping from Egypt, resulting in heightened security around the Rafah border.[169]

The Egyptian ambassador to the Palestinian territories stressed that any extraordinary measures taken on the Rafah borders were to maintain Egypt's national security and should not be seen as an attack on Gaza. He underscored that these measures would be revised as soon as the turmoil in Egypt declined.[170] Despite these assurances, matters worsened. In August, Egypt's military launched an expansive attack on pro-Morsi demonstrators who were calling for his reinstatement, killing close to two thousand Egyptians. A second terrorist attack on the Rafah border a few days later left twenty-five Egyptian soldiers dead. Almost overnight, rhetoric was prevalent that the Muslim Brotherhood were terrorists. Osama Hamdan, who had been elected as Hamas's head of international affairs in Beirut, noted that linking resistance with terrorism was not new, except that now it was being done by Arab countries that were also involved in the Palestinian cause.[171] These debates spilled into wider narratives that were shaping increasingly toxic regional alliances.

Hamas's leaders worked to put out fires elsewhere. Relations with Syria remained sour as President Assad stressed that Hamas must choose between being on the resistance front and aligning with Syria, or on the Muslim Brotherhood front and aligning against Syria, given that Syria considered the Muslim Brotherhood a terrorist organization.[172] With Iran, Hamdan noted that Hamas had begun to repair the relationship and that there was total agreement as far as the Palestinian cause was concerned, despite disagreement on Syria.[173] Iranian funding had, however, not resumed toward Hamas. Similarly, while Hamas and Hezbollah may have disagreed on Syria, both parties claimed they were still joined in a commitment to maintain resistance against Israel.[174] Rumors abounded that Hamas's relationship with Qatar had also taken a hit, although Hamas denied those claims as well, given Qatar's generous grants in Gaza.[175]

But it was in its relationship with Egypt where Hamas was dealt the most powerful blow. Financially, the closure of the tunnels, cutting off the strip from any trade with the outside world, meant that Gaza's economy swiftly collapsed. Given that Israel's border crossings remained tightly managed and—even with loosened access following the ceasefire agreement—engineered to sustain Gaza just above a humanitarian catastrophe, internal desperation increased. As this was coupled with the loss of Iranian funding, Hamas's financial health had become precipitous overnight, making the movement more sensitive to the burdens of government in the Gaza Strip.[176] The equilibrium that had been established with Fatah in reconciliation discussions was subsequently disrupted.

Gaining the upper hand, Abbas issued an ultimatum that unless an interim government was formed by August, he would unilaterally propose dates for presidential and legislative elections. Hamas's leaders accused the Palestinian president of capitalizing on its ill fortunes.[177] The Palestinian Authority also persisted in highlighting Hamas's links to the Muslim Brotherhood in Egypt. This had the dual effect of heightening suspicions regarding Hamas's involvement in Egyptian affairs and bringing the movement's loyalty to Palestinian nationalism into question. Hamas's leaders were clear in their regrets that what happened in Egypt was a coup against democracy. Given the regional climate, this position was easily distorted into one where Hamas was actively supportive of Islamic dominance in Egyptian politics.[178]

Hamas in turn accused Fatah of creating unrest to get Gazans to rise against the movement. Suspicions gathered as Tamarod, the protest movement that had called for Morsi's removal in Egypt, began promising protests to bring down Hamas's rule in the Gaza Strip.[179] Hamas decried rhetoric from Fatah's leaders about tightening the noose around Gaza and referring to it as a "rebellious strip." It described this as incitement to recreate the Egyptian experience (of overthrowing the Muslim Brotherhood) in Gaza.[180] Hamas mitigated these threats by cracking down on opponents, many of whom were Fatah members, raising significant objections from the West Bank.[181] Hamas viewed Fatah's attempt to push it into a corner as little more than "cheap opportunism" to take advantage of the blow dealt to political Islam in the region. In attempting to have Hamas wrangle its way out of being portrayed as the obstacle to reconciliation, Haniyeh offered to open up Hamas's government in Gaza to all factions. Yet rather than appearing conciliatory, this merely underscored Hamas's effort to off-load the burden of governing the enclave as its financial bankruptcy became increasingly perceptible.[182]

Hamas's entrapment in Gaza became more evident by the day as the campaign against it continued unabated. Egyptian forces carried out large operations in the Sinai, destroying all the tunnels into Rafah in September 2013.[183] The impact of the blockade sharpened as remaining tunnels operated for only about four hours a day. Electricity generation within the strip dropped as fuel shortages sharply increased.[184] Fatah's spokesman argued that Hamas's political choices, ideological and organizational links with the Muslim Brotherhood, and determination to continue its revolt against Palestinian legitimacy were all reasons behind the suffering in Gaza.[185] Fatah's accusation was notable in that it shifted blame for the blockade from Israel's occupation and the Egyptian regime to Hamas and its policies regarding the Palestinian struggle.

Hamas leaders did not express—at least not publicly—any regrets regarding their strategic choices. In a speech marking the second anniversary of the Shalit prisoner exchange, Haniyeh struck a defiant tone. He noted Hamas's pride in Morsi was natural given their shared Islamic roots and aspirations for the Muslim nation, but that in no way brought into question Hamas's allegiance to Palestinian nationalism.[186] Yet even with Hamas's apparent resolve, increased desperation was tangible as Hamdan threatened from Beirut that if the blockade was not lifted, Hamas would do what "no one has imagined it could do" to get it removed.[187] Movement leaders blamed the Palestinian Authority for withholding fuel shipments to Gaza, noting that this demonstrated its complicity in the blockade. By the winter of 2013, the energy crisis was having a real impact and all construction activity that had been facilitated by the tunnels had stopped.[188] Rainwater caused significant flooding as sewage began to run down streets.[189] Haniyeh reached out to the emir of Qatar to talk about electricity shortages.[190] In early December, Meshal and members of Fatah met in Doha at Meshal's request to air out differences and recriminations that had been exchanged over the previous months. The two parties agreed to maintain open lines of communication, as Meshal raised humanitarian concerns regarding the situation in Gaza.[191]

Hamas's responsibility as a de facto government over two million Palestinians had clearly overwhelmed the movement's priorities as Gaza's isolation truly began to take its toll. The blockade was not the only threat to Hamas's stability. On December 24, Israel carried out an attack on Gaza, again breaking the ceasefire that had been in place since November 2012.[192] A few weeks later, on January 16, Israel launched further air raids against four targets in retaliation for rocket fire into Ashkelon. The missiles were fired by Islamic Jihad, but Israeli leaders placed full responsibility with Hamas, given that it had acquiesced to policing resistance from Gaza. Islamic Jihad stated that continued Israeli violations of the ceasefire, including failure to lift the blockade, risked its collapse.[193]

To avoid an escalation at a time of heightened difficulties, Hamas called on Islamic Jihad to retreat. Islamic Jihad acquiesced, noting that Israel wanted a truce where it could continue its attacks on Gaza as it saw fit.[194] This skirmish, seemingly typical in the relations between Israel and the Gaza Strip, marked a further development in Hamas's short-term pacification as the movement's priorities shifted toward averting a humanitarian catastrophe. With the closure of the tunnels, the blockade was fulfilling its original purpose of isolating and weakening Hamas's practical ability to wage armed resistance. This was noted by Fatah as well, which accused Hamas of policing resistance to safeguard Israel's security despite the movement's rhetoric.[195]

In January 2014, the Egyptian Ministry of Interior revealed new details regarding the "terroristic operations" of the Muslim Brotherhood. Suspects had "confessed" to planning attacks alongside Palestinian brotherhood members, noting that they had received weapons training in Gaza. The suspects claimed that since January 25, 2011, and specifically under President Morsi, the brotherhood had expanded its base by reaching out to other extremist groups in the region. This included Hamas, which ostensibly provided brotherhood members with logistical support, hosted them in Gaza, and gave them training in al-Qassam's camps.[196] Suspects "confessed" that it was after a series of meetings in Gaza that two of the Salafi groups based in Sinai, Ansar Beit al-Maqdis and Kata'eb al-Furqan, were established.[197] Hamas denied these accusations.[198] Since 2013, Hamas had allegedly begun dealing with Salafis in Gaza with an uncompromising iron fist.[199] Nonetheless, Fatah's spokesman continued to call on Hamas to sever its ties with the Muslim Brotherhood as Egypt's judiciary considered classifying the parent movement a terrorist organization. Failure to do so would place the responsibility on Hamas for Gaza's blockade and for the millions of Palestinians who would be impacted by Egypt's decision.[200]

Hamas fought these allegations even as Egypt began considering Hamas's classification as a terrorist organization.[201] The movement condemned Egypt's conflation of its national liberation project with terrorism, noting that it was unprecedented for an Arab state to use such a "Zionist classification."[202] Without shirking from asserting its identity as an offshoot of the Muslim Brotherhood, and noting its ideological connection with the movement, Hamas's leaders reiterated that Hamas was a national resistance movement committed to the Palestinian cause.[203] Hamas also maintained efforts to salvage its regional relations. Mahmoud Zahhar reached out to Iran as well as to Syria and Hezbollah. While Hamas's leaders noted that the dynamic with Iran could return to normal, given the centrality of the Palestinian cause, Syria and Hezbollah were "more complicated."[204]

By early 2014, therefore, the tides had shifted. Haniyeh started the year by confirming that Hamas was not seeking a new war with Israel.[205] In a press conference in Gaza City on January 16, Haniyeh also appeared more compliant to the Palestinian Authority as he stated that Hamas would permit all those who escaped Gaza following the clashes with Fatah in 2007 to return, with full immunity, to reunite with their families. He announced that Fatah prisoners held for political reasons would be released, and declared 2014 to be the year of reconciliation, as it became clear that the power dynamic was clearly in Fatah's favor.[206] In a meeting with Fatah officials on February 7, Haniyeh committed Hamas's government to reconciliation as a strategic choice.[207] Despite the expected dissenting voices, Hamas's leaders claimed they were ready for Fatah "to take the chairs" as long as it "gave them the country"—an indication that they did not want to rule through the government but wanted rather to protect the resistance project through the movement.[208]

By April 2014, it became increasingly evident that the tireless efforts of Secretary of State John Kerry would fail to produce a political settlement between Israel and the Palestinians. In a leaked recording of a closed-door meeting, Secretary Kerry warned that Israel risked becoming an "apartheid state" if the US-sponsored peace process failed to produce a two-state reality.[209] Addressing the faltering negotiations, the PLO issued conditions that any future resumption of talks with Israel must be based on the 1967 borders and include the full cessation of settlement building activity, including in East Jerusalem.[210] Until then, and with confirmation regarding the failure of Kerry's initiative, Fatah's delegation made its way to Gaza to discuss reconciliation under Egyptian mediation.[211]

With remarkable speed, on April 23 an agreement was signed between Hamas, Fatah, and other PLO factions. This came to be known as the Shati Agreement, named after the refugee camp where it was negotiated. Israel immediately stated it would refuse any negotiations with a Palestinian government that included Hamas, as Netanyahu again stated that Abbas "needs to choose between peace with Israel and peace with Hamas."[212] For his part, Obama asked Kerry to stop his diplomatic efforts, stating that the leaders in Israel and Palestine lacked the will to make the concessions for peace. He noted that the reconciliation agreement was "unhelpful."[213] Praise for the unity deal was forthcoming from Russia, China, the European Union, and the United Nations.

For Hamas's leadership, American and Israeli exceptionalism to this reaction clarified the political blackmail that Hamas had been facing.[214] Hamas declared that the Shati Agreement, like others before it, produced an apolitical interim government charged with preparing for elections, uniting the institutions within the West Bank and Gaza, and facilitating reconstruction.[215] This was an explicit indication on Hamas's part that the purpose of this agreement was solely administrative, an indication that was necessary given the significant resentment within

Hamas to the deal.[216] In other words, this was a decision by Hamas to give up governmental control to alleviate the suffering of people in Gaza. Once a new government was formed, the legislature would be reactivated and a new leadership voted in to study all the laws that had been passed separately between Gaza and the West Bank. A new election law would then be produced, allowing for elections within six months.[217] It was agreed that this interim government would be formed within five weeks, after which the PLO committee would meet to oversee reconciliation and the path forward.[218]

Hamas's government in Gaza prepared to step aside to make way for the incoming cabinet. The movement circumvented calls to recognize Israel, stressing that the negotiations were the purview of the PLO and that the incoming cabinet had nothing to do with recognizing Israel or other political affairs.[219] To affirm that stance, Abu Marzouq stressed that Hamas had no objections regarding the choice of prime minister.[220] In addressing the administrative issues, Abu Marzouq explained that any institutional merger between the two governments would look after employees on both sides. As for al-Qassam, Abu Marzouq stressed that the military wing was not part of the reconciliation deal and was a separate "national resistance weapon."[221] This underscored Hamas's desire to limit talk of reconciliation to institutional matters that did not address the movement's role in the broader liberation struggle or compel Hamas to give up its effective control of the Gaza Strip through disarming.[222]

Discussions around the formation of the Government of National Consensus, as it came to be known, began in early May. Despite a few instances of public bickering, Fatah noted that talks progressed calmly and would end within the allocated five-week timeframe. On May 27, a joint press conference declared the independent Rami Hamdallah as the prime minister of the incoming government and stated that the rest of the ministerial names would be announced by Abbas. This was viewed as "the end of the division, and the opening of a new page for history and the nation."[223] Israel announced that as soon as the new government was formed, it would immediately be blocked by the state. This was despite Abbas's assertions that the government would be composed of technocrats who had nothing to do with Hamas and who would take the position put forward by Abbas, which was to recognize Israel and stop terrorism. Abbas reiterated his openness to return to the negotiating table if Israel focused on the 1967 borders and ended settlement expansion.[224]

On June 2, the new government was finally announced and Israel began enacting security and financial measures against it. Hamas noted Israel's "hysterical reaction" as a continuation of Sharon's policies of ensuring Palestinian division. In contrast, it welcomed the American and European announcements that they would consider engaging with the technocratic government—itself a notable shift.[225] Abbas immediately assigned the elections committee to begin preparing for presidential and legislative elections within six months.[226] The spokesman for the unity government discussed the huge task inherent in ending division within the Palestinian arena as he called for support from all stakeholders.[227]

With the Shati Agreement, Hamas appeared to have successfully off-loaded its role as a de facto administrative body within the Gaza Strip while maintaining, for the most part, effective control within the coastal enclave. Aside from giving up on all ministerial posts, including the post of prime minister, Hamas had conceded that the Rafah borders into Gaza would be overseen by the Palestinian Authority, thereby theoretically forfeiting a significant lever of control. Nonetheless, al-Qassam Brigades were explicitly outside the remit of the incoming cabinet, and Hamas made clear it would not disarm and the Gaza Strip would not demilitarize. The focus of the reconciled government was limited to the institutional reintegration of the governing authorities of the West Bank and the Gaza Strip. For Hamas, making this concession on the administrative level was in the hope that the subsequent step would be the broader merger between the two national movements.[228] That could only be taken on the level of PLO reform after the administrative rift had been healed. Given Hamas's weakness and the Palestinian

Authority's cynicism about the peace process, the Shati Agreement was promising in its timing. Yet expectedly, as had consistently been the case with previous such deals, the absence of political will and the ease with which Israel turned to obstructionist military policies ensured a repetition of earlier patterns. A lethal chain of events would soon unfold to envelop the Gaza Strip in yet another wave of destruction.

CONTAINMENT
AND PACIFICATION

In 2015, the United Nations issued a report asserting that by the year 2020 the Gaza Strip would be uninhabitable if the situation that had prevailed since the blockade was instituted in 2007 persisted.[1] With strong population growth, tightly controlled access of people and goods, and intermittent large-scale and immensely destructive and lethal military incursions by Israel, the Gaza Strip was deemed to be approaching the point of collapse. The report failed to compel members of the international community to take concerted measures to address this reality. In early 2017, Gaza suffered another humanitarian crisis, precipitated directly by the blockade, which remained administered by both Israel and Egypt. The strip's two million inhabitants were receiving two to three hours of electricity per day, down from about four hours which they had been receiving since 2014. Hospitals were operating on emergency generators, the risk being that life-saving equipment could falter; sewage was being pumped into the Mediterranean as treatment plants were no longer operational; and drinking water and medical supplies were facing a severe shortage. International organizations declared Gaza on the brink of "total collapse."[2] The estimates first put forward by the UN report were revised, and they noted that the Gaza Strip could reach the point of being unfit for human life sooner than the initial estimate of 2020.[3] It was the onset of an expansive military assault, weeks after the Shati Agreement had been signed in the summer of 2014, that had accelerated Gaza's swift deterioration.

OPERATION PROTECTIVE EDGE

In the first half of June 2014, after the Shati Agreement had been signed, Palestinian factions were hammering out the details of the Palestinian Authority's administrative return to the Gaza Strip. Hamas was seeking to off-load its governing responsibilities, such as the salaries of its forty-thousand-strong civil service, as a result of the financial constraints it was facing. The blockade had finally achieved its alleged purpose of weakening Hamas's government and making room for the Palestinian Authority to return to Gaza. Yet the Ramallah leadership was driving a tough bargain, as it was unwilling to assume responsibility for a greatly dilapidated and battered Gaza Strip, particularly without effective control of the enclave, given Hamas's refusal to disarm.[4] This was met with a great deal of resentment inside Gaza, where people believed President Abbas was using the issue of employee salaries as a scapegoat to pressure Hamas and avoid reconciliation.[5] For his part, Abbas was dealing with the implications of Israel's strident refusal to allow the passage of the unity government, which were likely to take the form of measures to isolate the Palestinian Authority and withhold tax and customs revenue collected on its behalf.

The delicate balance being managed between Hamas and the Palestinian Authority against Israeli obstructionism was upended on June 12. That evening, three Israeli teenagers who were returning from their religious schools in illegal settlements in the West Bank back into Israel were kidnapped. As pictures of the students blasted on TV screens around the world, Israel launched an expansive search and rescue operation called "Brother's Keeper" throughout the West Bank, including in areas that fell under the control of the Palestinian Authority. President Mahmoud Abbas condemned the kidnapping and promised to work with the Israeli forces to locate the teenagers and arrest the perpetrators.[6] Behind the scenes, Netanyahu received intelligence that the teenagers had most likely been killed and that the operation had been carried out by rogue members of Hamas, most likely without the leadership's consent.[7] Withholding this information from the public,

Netanyahu pursued an aggressive invasion of the West Bank, ostensibly to locate the teenagers, carrying out arrests, home raids, and curfews; confiscating property; and increasing military checkpoints.[8]

Within days, around 350 Palestinians—many of them Hamas members who had been released in the Shalit deal—were reincarcerated; five Palestinians were killed and hundreds of sites were ransacked and destroyed.[9] The Palestinian Authority called on the international community to restrain Israel's actions and requested that the United Nations offer protection to the Palestinian people.[10] On June 30, the bodies of the murdered Israelis were discovered. On July 2, a day after their burial, Jewish Israelis kidnapped and burnt alive a Palestinian student in East Jerusalem. The Palestinian Foreign Ministry asked for international support and condemned this murder as "Jewish terrorism."[11] Increasing suspicions that Israel was using the pretext of this kidnapping to drive a wedge between the newly united Palestinian factions, Netanyahu pressed the international community to force Abbas to end the Palestinian Authority's partnership with Hamas, which he described as "the kidnapper of children."[12]

Israel's heavy-handed tactics in the West Bank, predictably, increased rocket fire from the Gaza Strip. The majority of the rockets were not initially fired by Hamas. The movement had explicitly indicated at the beginning of the year its desire to avoid another conflagration with Israel in order to give Gazans a respite. But in light of its precarious financial situation and the pressure to respond to Israel's lethal incursions into the West Bank, Hamas was compelled to act.[13] Its leaders assumed responsibility for the missiles and stressed they were retaliatory strikes against Israeli aggression. As a senior member of al-Qassam stated, "Al-Qassam will not stand idly by, and will not allow the enemy to isolate the West Bank and Gaza. Palestine is one, its people are one, its resistance is one."[14]

Hamas's leadership blamed Israel's mobilization for breaking a ceasefire that had prevailed since November 2012.[15] Since Operation Pillar of Defense, Hamas had been very effective at limiting rocket fire into Israel, even establishing a police force to restrain armed operations, despite Hamas's increasingly desperate situation after the closure of the Rafah tunnels. Rather than easing access into the strip, as had been agreed upon in that ceasefire, Israel had maintained its chokehold and failed to commence procedures to ease the blockade beyond a marginal level.[16] Alongside the reduction in Iranian funding and the closure of the tunnels, Israel's blockade had driven Hamas to concede—in desperation and amid much internal dissent—its governing power in Gaza to the Palestinian Authority. Although this development fulfilled what was ostensibly Israel's core rationale for the blockade—to weaken Hamas's government—Israeli policies persisted unabated.

With rocket fire expanding, Netanyahu claimed the need to once again use force to weaken Hamas's military capacity. Netanyahu pointed to security concerns that had arisen after the discovery of tunnels from Gaza into Israel earlier that year and announced plans for a major offensive that he promised would reinstate the calm Israel had enjoyed over the previous two years.[17] "Operation Protective Edge," as it came to be known, entailed an aerial bombardment campaign followed by a ground invasion aimed at destroying Hamas's network of tunnels, what Israel referred to as "terror tunnels."[18] Israel's stated goal was to degrade the "terror organizations' military infrastructure, and [. . . neutralize] their network of cross-border assault tunnels."[19] What followed was an expanded and more devastating repeat of what had taken place intermittently since 2006: a disproportionate and highly lethal military campaign aimed at forcing Hamas into another period of calm. As with past escalations, the assault was portrayed as necessary self-defense against Hamas's consistent aggression, overlooking the movement's effectiveness at restraining rocket fire from Gaza and the violence inherent in the act of the blockade itself.

The assault lasted fifty-one days. The Israeli army attacked the densely populated coastal enclave with the full force of its military might, including F-16s, drones, Apache helicopters, and one-ton bombs. Through air raids, Israel bombed residential apartment blocks, family homes, hospitals, ambulances, schools, mosques, power generation facilities, and even graveyards.[20] Many of the schools that were targeted by Israel were run by UN bodies and were functioning as shelters for refugees who had been internally displaced.[21] International organizations such as the Red Cross, Human Rights Watch, Amnesty International, and local human rights organizations issued repeated condemnations of Israel's targeting of their institutions as well as its disproportionate use of force and its strategy of collective punishment.[22] The United Nations also accused Israel of carrying out war crimes and grave violations of international law.[23] Whole areas on Gaza's periphery were razed to make room for Israel's ground invasion, and the death toll mounted as Israel's army pressed into densely populated urban centers.[24]

On the same day that Operation Protective Edge was launched, Netanyahu announced that Israel's army did not target civilians. Given Hamas's alleged use of "human shields," whereby Hamas operatives presumably hid among or fired from civilian centers, Netanyahu stressed the movement must be held responsible for civilian deaths and anticipated casualties.[25] These assertions, consistently made by Israeli officials to justify the high civilian death tolls their operations incurred within the Gaza Strip, remain highly contentious and fail to justify Israeli actions.[26] Furthermore, Gaza's high population density and the impermeability of the blockade meant that close to 44 percent of the enclave was subject to "evacuation orders," and at the height of the hostilities almost half a million Gazans—or a quarter of the total population—were displaced and had nowhere to hide from direct crossfire.[27] This entrapment exacerbated the intermingling of the civilian population with the military resistance but did not temper Israel's assault. Israel's narrative of self-defense and its allegations regarding the systematic use of human shields by Hamas blurred the limits of what was an acceptable or legitimate target for Israeli forces.[28]

From the beginning of the offensive, Hamas and other resistance factions sustained their rocket fire into Israel. Hamas boasted of robust local manufacturing capabilities as it showcased missiles that reached significantly further into Israeli cities than before.[29] The movement celebrated its ability to bring the war to Israel, whether in terms of sirens sounding over Israeli cities or through the economic impact on Israel's tourism sector. International organizations condemned Hamas's use of missiles as war crimes given their inability to differentiate between civilians and combatants.[30] But these rockets continued unabated for the duration of Israel's military operation. Casualties on the Israeli side due to rocket fire were limited due to the effectiveness of Israel's missile defense system, known as the Iron Dome.[31]

Alongside Hamas's offensive attacks, the movement's defensive strength was celebrated throughout its publications.[32] Hamas's network of underground tunnels provided ample shelter for Hamas's fighters. Although the majority of these tunnels were used for defensive purposes, a small portion were utilized as gateways for offensives into Israel, whereby resistance factions would ambush targets within Israel's borders.[33] The resistance factions took great pride in the fact that the Israeli army was struggling to advance to any significant measure into the heart of the Gaza Strip. This reinforced the narrative that Hamas produced in Gaza, that it had built a fortress of resistance and was able to secure this strip of land as "liberated" Palestinian territory.[34]

Despite boasting of their wherewithal, Hamas's leaders were overwhelmed by the scale of Israel's attack and by Netanyahu's willingness to expand the offensive despite the possibility of incurring losses.[35] As Musa abu Marzouq noted, "We are not merchants of war. . . . We are saddened by the scale of this destruction wrought by these neo-Nazis. . . . Israelis do all this to force us to accept this reality, raise the white flag and recognize them and what they have usurped. They do this so we can lay our weapons and leave resistance. The Zionist occupation began this battle. We will stay on our land. The future is ours."[36] Reports dispatched from the ground in Gaza conveyed feelings of bewilderment and panic at Israel's ferocious and unrelenting targeting of civilian institutions.[37] Gazans spoke of how despite the destruction wrought on Gaza in previous assaults, Operation Protective Edge appeared intent on maximizing civilian harm and pressuring Gaza's population into submission.[38] This suspicion was magnified given the exceptionally high death toll of children under the age of sixteen, which gave rise to accusations that Israel was systematically targeting Gaza's younger population.[39]

Gazans hypothesized that the brutality of the offensive was a tactic to force them to turn against Hamas. In many instances this worked, particularly when Hamas showed its own merciless face. Under the heavy toll of bombing, Hamas used the chaotic environment of war to settle its own political scores and carry out extrajudicial assassinations of its domestic enemies, including members of Fatah who were held in its jails, as well as suspected collaborators or informants for Israel.[40] More disturbingly, in the early days of Operation Protective Edge, Hamas's Ministry of Interior called on citizens not to respond to evacuation orders by the Israeli army, asserting that these were only issued as a form of psychological warfare to create panic.[41] Many in Gaza criticized Hamas, not least for its role in dragging the coastal enclave into another conflagration. Others were critical of Hamas's governance record and its authoritarian streak.[42] Nonetheless, the sense of duty and support for resistance in the face of Israel's onslaught was a powerful force, one that led to greater solidarity around the notion of "resistance" against Israel's violence.[43] While during previous operations popular support for Gaza brought people to the streets throughout the Arab world, protests were relatively sparse during Protective Edge, as the Middle East was engaged in numerous hot wars. Criticizing the inadequate Arab response, a leader in Gaza noted that "Hamas defends the *umma*'s honor with self-made weapons while all the weapons piling up in the storage warehouses of the Arab armies are rusting, and if they're ever used, they're used against their own people."[44]

As the death toll climbed in the Gaza Strip, so did the suffering of those who survived. Fuel shortages led to prolonged electricity cuts that caused Gaza to grind to a halt. Hospitals buckled under mounting emergency cases and the absence of medical supplies. Sewage systems faltered and spilled out into streets as Gaza's already contaminated water supplies were depleted. The buffer zones around the strip were further tightened inward by the Israeli army, limiting access to agricultural land or fishing zones and strengthening the blockade around the coastal enclave.[45] Upheaval ravaged the tiny strip of land as hundreds of thousands of internally displaced people moved from shelter to shelter, desperate to avoid Israeli bombing and prevented from escaping as refugees from Gaza.[46] Throughout the onslaught, Egyptian president Sisi continued Egypt's crackdown on the tunnels connecting Gaza to the Sinai Peninsula and largely maintained the closure of the Rafah border, even as casualty numbers rose and humanitarian pleas to open the borders gained urgency.[47]

Calls for a ceasefire were relentless, and initially Hamas was the party refusing to yield to an end to hostilities. Netanyahu's formulation of "calm for calm"—suspending Israel's operation in return for the end of rocket fire—was fundamentally at odds with Hamas's disposition. As Meshal noted, before the teenagers were kidnapped there was full calm in the West Bank and relative calm in Gaza. He added that this was unnatural given the persistent occupation and Israel's unyielding stranglehold on the strip. Now that the Palestinians had achieved unity, Meshal questioned, a war was suddenly declared? "Are the Palestinians just meant to surrender and die a slow death?" he asked, noting that Palestinians were being asked to accept their fate of living under occupation in the West Bank and under blockade in the Gaza Strip with no efforts to resist the status quo.[48]

Hamas and other factions insisted that ceasefires would no longer entail a return to calm or to the status quo that had prevailed before this latest flare-up. Instead, they argued that a ceasefire must include the removal of the blockade imposed on the Gaza Strip since 2007, which had not been lifted throughout the ceasefire in place since 2012, despite Hamas's effective policing of the border and Israel's responsibility to do so.[49] Hamas's leaders portrayed the choice between a return to isolation or war as being akin to the choice between a slow death or a quick one. The movement opted for the latter and held its ground. As Meshal said the day after Protective Edge was launched, "[Our people] can no longer accept the blockade in Gaza, under starvation . . . can no longer live in the shadow of settlements, murder, house demolition, violation of villages [in the West Bank]. It is time for the Israeli occupation to end. Our people do not like to escalate and do not seek it. . . . But you have closed all the doors, so blame only yourselves."[50] Unlike previous instances when Hamas and the other resistance factions chose to de-escalate, in this case the movement appeared sufficiently cornered to enter into a dynamic of attrition with Israel. Netanyahu was unrelenting in his response and insisted that if Hamas thought Israel would stop before assurances of quiet and peace were in place, it was mistaken.[51]

Negotiations proceeded with Egyptian, Jordanian, and American mediation against the backdrop of several failed attempts to implement humanitarian truces. Given President Sisi's hostile disposition toward Gaza, Hamas attempted to seek alternative mediators, including Qatar and Turkey.[52] But Israel, Egypt, and the PLO maintained a monopoly on the mediation channels. In the previous wars of 2009 and 2012, ceasefire discussions had circumvented the Palestinian leadership in the West Bank and proceeded indirectly between Hamas and Israel. In 2014, ceasefire talks engaged the PLO and Israel directly under Egyptian mediation. Much to Israel's chagrin, the unity deal that had been signed between Palestinian factions before the outbreak of the war appeared to hold firm.[53] President Abbas reaffirmed the end of the Palestinian division, as he insisted that an attack on a specific faction signaled war against Palestinians in their entirety.[54] Accordingly, ceasefire demands encompassed aspects of the Palestinian struggle that extended beyond lifting the blockade off the Gaza Strip to include issues related to Israel's continued occupation of East Jerusalem and the West Bank.[55]

Israel refused to link Gaza with the broader Palestinian demands and insisted on focusing specifically on disarming Hamas.[56] Hamas refused. Aware of the scale of the catastrophe in Gaza, the Palestinian delegation appeared willing to wait for an "honorable agreement" that would justify, in their perspective, the pain and bloodshed the Palestinians had endured.[57] As Meshal noted, no colonized people ever got rid of their colonizer without paying a staggering price.[58] Palestinian negotiators insisted that the conditions for a ceasefire were not "Hamas conditions"; they were Palestinian conditions. Demands to end the blockade on Gaza could not be separated from the broader national goals of ending the occupation.[59] Senior Fatah negotiators objected to Israel's tactics of addressing ceasefire demands from the perspective of Hamas or Islamic Jihad on one side, or Fatah on the other.[60] Fatah viewed Israel's approach to the negotiations as seeking to entrench the division between Gaza and the West Bank.[61]

Alongside divisive negotiating tactics, Netanyahu escalated militarily to demonstrate most forcefully to Hamas what attrition with Israel entailed. The Israeli air force unleashed pulverizing attacks that led to the complete leveling of Gazan high-rises.[62] Netanyahu summarized quite succinctly Israel's strategy of dealing with Hamas in Gaza: "Our policy toward Hamas is simple: If they fire, they will be hit, and not just hit but hit very hard. And if Hamas does not understand this today, it will understand it tomorrow. And if not tomorrow then the day after tomorrow because in the Middle East, one needs not just military power but stamina and patience."[63] Attrition and deterrence worked from the Palestinian side as well. Noting quite clearly the failure of Israel's military tactics to break the will of resistance, on the forty-fifth day of the war the leader of al-Qassam Brigades warned international flights not to land at Ben Gurion Airport. "The occupiers and all the world must know the truth about what our people are asking for. All we want is for the occupation to go away, from our supplies and the milk of our children, our fuel. But it insists, to hold on, punishing us, strangling us whenever it wants and letting us breathe whenever it wants. This cannot be allowed to go on after today."[64]

On August 26, fifty-one days after Israel's assault began and following endless failed ceasefire attempts, the parties accepted a ceasefire initiative from Cairo. This was an interim agreement that called for an immediate cessation of fire and commencement of reconstruction, with discussions regarding the lifting of the blockade, including Palestinian demands for a seaport and airport in Gaza to ensure access, to begin at a later date.[65] Israel successfully sidestepped all attempts to link this ceasefire to broader Palestinian issues as it claimed that it had dealt Hamas a powerful blow and destroyed its military infrastructure, including its tunnel network. Netanyahu insisted that Hamas achieved none of its ceasefire demands and reiterated that the extreme use of force, particularly leveling tower blocks in the final days of the war, had finally broken Hamas's belief that it could drag Israel into a war of attrition.[66]

There was some veracity to claims that Israel's overwhelming force caused Hamas to pull back.[67] Meshal spoke of the need to act responsibly to protect the people from the "Zionist crimes" that led Hamas to achieve only portions of its demands.[68] Nonetheless, Hamas claimed its own victory. In terms of reconstruction, Hamas's leaders explained that the agreement was to remove the buffer zone around Gaza, to reduce the fishing restrictions, and to open all five crossings with Israel to allow building material into Gaza.[69] Hamas noted that its military infrastructure had been weakened but not destroyed. It had captured Israeli soldiers that could be used for prisoner exchange deals, as it had with Shalit. Most importantly, Hamas held firm and refused Israel's pressure regarding disarmament. The movement viewed this as a temporary ceasefire until real negotiations could commence regarding lifting the blockade.[70] Both Abbas and Meshal continued to stress that Palestinian unity remained a strategic choice.[71]

By the end of Operation Protective Edge, 2,220 Palestinians had been killed, 1,492 of them civilians, 551 of them children, with several whole families obliterated. This was the highest level of civilian casualties Israel had inflicted on the Palestinians in any one year since 1967.[72] From the Israeli side, deaths included sixty-six soldiers and five civilians, as well as one Thai national. Within Gaza, eighteen thousand housing units had been rendered uninhabitable and 108,000 people were left homeless. The only power plant in Gaza had been damaged, seriously crippling the heating, electricity, and water infrastructures in the strip.[73] As the cease-

fire held, negotiations turned to reconstruction, which was estimated to
cost around $7.8 billion. This was to proceed under the auspices of the
Palestinian Authority, which now maintained ostensible control over the
government in the Gaza Strip through the reconciliation agreement.
After the bombs and missiles died down, the standardized approach to
reconstruction discussions restarted in Cairo. As countries from all over
the world and international organizations gathered in Egypt, Hamas was
excluded from participating in the conference or the reconstruction effort. Without its involvement, it is not surprising that destroyed buildings
continue to litter the cities and towns of the Gaza Strip.[74]

Following the end of hostilities, the United Nations established a
commission to investigate the conflagration. While the Palestinian leadership offered full support, the Israeli government boycotted the investigation and prevented the investigators' access into the Gaza Strip.[75]
The UN's investigation accused both Hamas and Israel of carrying out
war crimes. In response, Israel retaliated that the United Nations was
"taken hostage by terrorist organizations" given its anti-Israel bias.[76] A
domestic investigation by Israel's state comptroller, released in 2017,
highlighted troubling findings regarding this operation.[77] The report
noted that in 2013, during the period of calm that Hamas had successfully instituted from Gaza, Prime Minister Netanyahu's government
was warned explicitly and repeatedly that Gaza was on the brink of a
humanitarian catastrophe, and that the situation had to be addressed to
prevent another conflagration between Hamas and Israel. Such warnings went unheeded. Rather than meeting its obligations under the 2012
ceasefire agreement with Hamas, which necessitated easing the crossings into Gaza, Israel's political leaders appeared willing to maintain the
blockade while expecting calm to prevail in return.

This one-sided and unsustainable expectation underscored another
finding made by the Israeli state comptroller's report, which was that Israel had no strategy for dealing with Gaza.[78] Through Protective Edge,
it became evident that Israel was willing to rely on reactive and overwhelming military power as the primary tool for responding to threats

or perceived threats from Gaza.[79] Despite Hamas's increasingly effective role at policing the border, Israel had no political appetite to engage with either the movement or the broader Palestinian predicament. Prime Minister Netanyahu repeatedly asserted Israel's unwillingness to negotiate with any government that included Hamas while also protesting that the Palestinian division meant there was no representative partner with which to negotiate. This paradoxical exercise in futility ensured the absence of any prospects for diplomatic engagement. Israel's reliance on military options produced, at best, sporadic periods of calm and fit well with its approach toward Hamas: isolate and deter, manage rather than resolve. At a cost of several thousand civilian Palestinian lives, Hamas's presence in the West Bank was suppressed and its infrastructure in the Gaza Strip was powerfully bombarded. By the end of Operation Protective Edge, Hamas appeared to have been once again effectively contained and temporarily pacified within the Gaza Strip.

POLITICIDE, CONTAINMENT, AND PACIFICATION

The Government of National Consensus signed before the war held despite Israel's vast military and diplomatic mobilization to ensure it received no legitimacy. But the unity cabinet that was formed remained merely symbolic as the challenge of institutional integration between the West Bank and Gaza persisted. Hamas's attempt to shed its administrative role in Gaza in an effort to avoid compromising its liberation agenda had not overshadowed the fact that it kept its firm hold over the enclave. Even with the agreement to cede the Rafah border crossing to the Palestinian Authority, there was no overlooking the reality that Hamas had developed a structure of rule in Gaza, primarily through al-Qassam, that was separate from the administrative and ministerial institutions of government. Still, Hamas's leaders believed that by relinquishing their legitimate government, including the post of prime minister, the onus would be placed on Abbas to take the next step in healing the division and including Hamas in reformulating the PLO.[80]

President Abbas and the incumbent leadership in the West Bank remained both unwilling and unable to provide Hamas with that official foothold in the Palestinian struggle for liberation. The extent of Israel's refusal to the formation of a unity government marked the challenge that the Palestinian Authority would have to confront were it to integrate Hamas officially into the Palestinian leadership. Taking over the administration of Gaza, particularly after the devastation of 2014, without effective control over the security front was also unappealing.[81] As a result, Hamas was unable to let go of its administrative responsibilities in Gaza, becoming entrenched in the coastal enclave and embroiled in the burdens of government. Simultaneously, Israel's assault had, intentionally or otherwise, offered Hamas a lifeline. Operation Protective Edge pulled the movement away from the brink it had faced in the early days of 2014, as the renegotiated ceasefire meant that border crossings into Gaza were again marginally eased. Hamas's rule and finances stabilized and the initial impetus for the Shati Agreement was removed.

At the time of this writing, in 2017, Israel remains opposed to the reintegration of the Palestinian territories, ostensibly to avoid Hamas's ability to influence the stability of the West Bank and undermine the security coordination that has been instituted between Israel and the Palestinian Authority. Israel has also, however, benefited from Hamas's entrapment in the Gaza Strip, where Hamas has proven extremely adept at managing the various factions that remain committed to resistance against Israel. Since 2007, Hamas has proven both willing and able to enter into and sustain ceasefires with Israel. Equally importantly, Hamas has been successful at stabilizing the coastal enclave. This territory had always presented an exceptional challenge for Israel even though it forms only 1.3 percent of the land of historic Palestine. This is primarily due to its population density, which threatens to offset Israel's Jewish majority if placed under direct Israeli control, a formula that was a key driver in Prime Minister Ariel Sharon's decision to disengage from the strip. Gaza also contains a high proportion of Palestinian refugees who had settled there after fleeing or being driven out of their homes in 1948.

This population mix has meant that Gaza has consistently been a foundation of resistance to Zionism and to Israel's ongoing military rule over Palestinians. Gaza's defiant spirit, as this book has suggested, builds on a decades-old history. It did not begin with Hamas and neither did Israel's lethal disposition toward the small strip of land. Since 1948, Israel has waged more than twelve wars on Gaza, reoccupied the territory, isolated its inhabitants, placed the enclave under siege, and unilaterally disengaged in attempts to rid itself of the challenge it presents.[82] In the 1950s, decades before Hamas's creation, Israel designated Gaza a "*fedayeen*'s nest," a territory that merited constant isolation and military bombardment to break the resistance.[83] In the late 1980s, with the eruption of the First Intifada, Israel began restricting the mobility of Palestinians from Gaza into Israel through the use of a complex permit system. This evolved into the general adoption of closure tactics throughout the 1990s as Gaza was repeatedly placed under blockade. In 1995, an electric fence separating Gaza from the rest of the territories was constructed.[84]

None of these policies, and no combination of them, managed to pacify the Gaza Strip. It is no surprise that Gaza has made its way into Israeli contemporary vernacular, whereby the phrase "Go to Gaza" is now the popular manner of saying "Go to hell."[85] Israel's intermittent closures evolved into a permanent and impermeable blockade after Hamas's takeover of the Gaza Strip in 2007. Hamas's very existence appeared to offer Israel the opportunity to formalize these various means of severing Gaza from the rest of Palestine, both discursively and practically. Under Hamas's rule, Gaza moved from being a "*fedayeen*'s nest" to becoming a "hostile entity" and an "enclave of terrorism." Israeli leaders consistently present Hamas as nothing more than an irrational and bloodthirsty actor seeking Israel's destruction. This framing is part of a longer history of sidestepping the political concerns that animate Palestinian nationalism by labeling movements such as Hamas and the PLO as terrorist organizations. In Hamas's case, its Islamic nature facilitates a greater conflation of its actions with groups such as al-Qaeda and the so-called Islamic State.

Whether inadvertently or cynically, Hamas is often described as the local manifestation of global terror networks.[86] The fact that the word "terrorism" can accommodate both al-Qaeda and Hamas marks the scale of its imprecision and failure to communicate valuable information about political violence. While al-Qaeda is part of a transnational network that wages a global violent struggle against Western hegemony, Hamas adopts armed resistance on a localized front to end an occupation that is deemed illegal by international law. More importantly, unlike networks such as al-Qaeda, Hamas has not rejected democratic politics or implemented a repressive Salafi regime in Gaza. It has also openly clashed with the local manifestations of these transnational networks. Hamas neither espouses an ideology of global terror nor does it seek to create a transnational Islamic caliphate.[87] It is a movement that utilizes Islamic discourse to deal with contemporary ailments and that is geographically tethered to the specific political and social environment of the occupation.[88]

In that sense, Hamas is akin to a religious and armed anticolonial resistance movement.[89] Understanding Hamas's political drivers and motivations, however, would complicate Israel's efforts to present the movement as little more than a terrorist organization committed to its destruction. Such a portrayal has been extremely useful for Israel on several levels. First, it excuses and justifies the forceful marginalization of a democratically elected government and the collective punishment inherent in besieging two million Palestinians. As the preceding chapters have shown, operations carried out by the Israeli army against Gaza are then understood as a legitimate form of self-defense, most often preemptive. For each of the three major operations of the last decade—Cast Lead, Pillar of Defense, and Protective Edge—a clear pattern has emerged whereby Israeli provocations, often after Palestinian unity deals are signed, trigger opportunities for Israel to claim self-defense and launch spectacular attacks on Gaza. By preventing unity and containing Hamas in the Gaza Strip, Israel has effectively cultivated a fig leaf that legitimates its policies toward the strip. Rather than positioning Gaza's marginalization as a result of Hamas, it is perhaps more accurate to state that Hamas has become marginalized as a result of Gaza, as evident in its failure to overcome its entrenchment there.

Second, with Hamas's dismissal as a terrorist organization, the thread linking the early days of Palestinian nationalism, from al-Qassam to the PLO and through to Hamas, gets eclipsed. Central to this continuity from *fedayeen* to "Islamic terrorists" are key Palestinian political demands that remain unmet and unanswered and that form the basis of the Palestinian struggle: achieving self-determination; dealing with the festering injustice of the refugee problem created by Israel's establishment in 1948; and affirming the right to use armed struggle to resist an illegal occupation.[90] In this light, Hamas is the contemporary manifestation of demands that began a century ago. Israeli efforts to continue sidelining these demands, addressing them solely from a military lens, have persisted. From antiguerilla warfare to its own War on Terror, Israel merely employs contemporary language to wage a century-old war.

Israel does not have a Hamas problem; it has a Palestine problem.[91] The fixed fundamentals that Hamas consistently reiterates form the bedrock of Palestinian identity and are a reflection of demands to deal with the tragedy of 1948 as well as the ongoing implications of Israel's occupation following 1967. Many Palestinians reject the rhetoric and action within which Hamas couches its political thought, or even its ideological intransigence. But while Hamas's discourse is exceptional to the movement, much of its politics are at the heart of popular concerns. This is evident in the rallies against Israeli military operations in Gaza. During Operation Protective Edge, backing for Hamas was around 40 percent. But support for the notion of "resistance" writ large claimed a majority of 90 percent or more.[92]

In other words, the political reality that makes Gaza "a hostile entity" extends beyond that strip of land and animates the Palestinian struggle in its entirety. Gaza is one microcosm, one parcel, of the Palestinian experience.[93] Instead of addressing this reality or engaging with Hamas's political drivers, Israel has adopted a military approach that defines Hamas solely as a terrorist organization. This depoliticizes and decontextualizes the movement, giving credence to the persistent "politicide" of Palestinian nationalism, Israel's process of erasing the political ideology animating the Palestinian struggle for self-determination.[94] This approach has allowed successive Israeli governments to avoid taking a position on the demands that have been upheld by Palestinians since before the creation of the State of Israel.

Hamas's ideology was shaped by a desire to sustain the perceived "purity" of the Palestinian struggle that the PLO had begun conceding in 1988. Centrally, this meant the liberation of the entirety of the land of historic Palestine and the reversal of the impact that Zionism has had, and continues to have, on Palestinians. As this book shows, Hamas's cofounders did so by articulating the tenets of Palestinian nationalism in an Islamic framing, imbuing it with religious reasoning. This restricted any ideological maneuverability for the movement's leaders and defined limitations that would make concessions appear blasphemous. In this manner, Hamas protected itself from following the PLO's trajectory and maintained, rhetorically at least, an untarnished narrative of liberation despite immense challenges.

Apart from its Islamic nature, two other factors have undergirded Hamas's ideological strength. The first is the failed precedent of the PLO. Like Hamas, the PLO was ostracized until it accepted formulaic conditions that had been dictated by the United States: the renunciation of armed struggle, and the recognition of Israel. The PLO believed, rightly, that ideological concessions would allow it to negotiate with Israel. It also imagined, mistakenly, that diplomacy would lead to Palestinian statehood. Hamas has learned this lesson and is unlikely to concede on any of its core ideological tenets without guarantees that such compromises would lead to the fulfillment of Palestinian rights. In Hamas's view, the PLO's concessions were its ticket into the corridors of diplomacy at the cost of its legitimacy. Far from securing Palestinian rights, these concessions have weakened the Palestinian struggle and entrenched the Israeli occupation to previously unimaginable levels. The second factor is that Hamas has what it sees as two resounding victories that justify armed struggle. Israel's withdrawals from south Lebanon in 2000 and from the Gaza Strip in 2005 were both unilateral Israeli measures taken after years of armed resistance in each of these locales. Rather than the byproduct of diplomacy or negotiations, these instances of "liberation" are perceived by Hamas as the vindication of resistance.[95]

While remaining ideologically inflexible, Hamas has offered pragmatic concessions when dealing with the three conditions imposed by the international community: renounce violence, recognize Israel, and accept past agreements.[96] As various chapters in this book demonstrate, Hamas has issued repeated offers to end its violence in return for Israeli reciprocity. Throughout the years of the Second Intifada and afterward, Hamas intermittently held fire unilaterally in the face of rapid Israeli militarization. Israel has consistently ignored these overtures. Even after its takeover of the Gaza Strip, Hamas became increasingly effective at policing Gaza's borders, yet calm interludes were systematically ignored by Israel, which maintained its violent chokehold and incursions into the strip. Hamas also made great strides with regard to accepting past agreements, offering to abide by whatever outcome a reformed and representative PLO puts forward. This concession has been made even as successive Israeli governments have themselves failed to respect or uphold past agreements. By 2007, when Hamas accepted the Mecca Agreement, the movement declared its willingness to respect international agreements and defer to the PLO in negotiations with Israel. These political concessions have consistently been deemed insufficient.

The issue that has proven most intractable is Hamas's refusal to recognize Israel. In many ways, this is the backbone of Hamas's ideology. It is both the final trump card before reaching a settlement and the last line that must be defended to safeguard the imagined purity of Palestinian nationalism. For decades, Hamas has explicitly and repeatedly indicated its willingness to accept the creation of a Palestinian state on the 1967 borders, most recently by issuing a revised political manifesto in 2017. Even prior to its election victory in 2006, Hamas consistently explained that its use of armed struggle was limited to forcing Israel to end its occupation rather than the destruction of the state as a whole. Hamas's leaders believe this would offer a peaceful settlement between Israel and the Palestinians and end the bloodshed. Israel is convinced this would be a temporary solution before Hamas rearms and attacks from a strengthened position. While Hamas may indeed continue to harbor ideological aspirations for the liberation of the entirety of Palestine after such a peaceful settlement, the likelihood that the movement would have popular backing for such a step is likely to be nonexistent if a just settlement is offered. Khaled Meshal has even offered written guarantees to international mediators underscoring this, noting that Hamas would abide by the outcome of any referendum to a peace deal delivered to the Palestinian people, including deals that entail mutual recognition, while stressing that Hamas would not accept those outcomes until the deal is implemented.[97]

It is more likely the case that Hamas is simply maintaining this ideological intransigence as a negotiating tactic and a matter of principle, tying into the movement's legitimacy and its effectiveness as an interlocutor.[98] The movement believes that conceding the remaining cards that Hamas still clings to would ensure that Palestinian rights continued to be forfeited, as had happened following the PLO's recognition of Israel. As one leader explained, "Why should we be forced to explicitly recognize Israel if we've already indicated we have a *de facto* acceptance of its presence?"[99] Hamas's implicit acceptance of Israel has gone far beyond what many Israeli political parties, including the dominant ruling Likud party, have offered Palestinians within their charters. With their refusal to recognize the right of Palestinian self-determination, their insistence that the Palestinian people never existed, and the intermittent resurfacing of the "Jordan option," several Israeli political parties have long opposed the notion of a Palestinian state.[100] In 2013, Prime Minister Netanyahu publicly reneged on his highly touted 2009 Bar Ilan speech in which he spoke of the possibility of a demilitarized Palestinian state.[101]

Hamas leaders consistently reaffirmed how their acceptance of the 1967 line is a negotiating tactic made in the full conviction that Israel itself refuses to acknowledge the legitimacy of this border. Israel's refusal to countenance Hamas's repeated offers around the 1967 line reaffirm this conviction. Israel's demand for Hamas's ideological concession prior to any form of diplomatic engagement is likely to remain futile. The PLO's experience shows that Israel has hardly acted as a benevolent occupier. If Hamas were to shift its own policies and accept the Quartet's conditions, it would lose valuable political capital and negotiating clout. Hamas has long called on Palestinian diplomats to hold on to their trump cards rather than negotiate in good faith. Should Israel ever choose to pursue a peace option or itself accept the legitimacy of the 1967 borders, admittedly an unlikely development given the current political climate in Israel, Hamas would present a powerful and effective counterpart. Yet rather than empowering its negotiating partners, Israel has historically pursued a self-fulfilling prophecy that ensures there is "no partner" by weakening its counterparts and undermining their legitimacy.

Israel's refusal to deal with Hamas's diplomatic signals is not solely the result of the movement's use of armed struggle. Hamas's political emergence within the Gaza Strip heightened Israeli worries by rupturing the continued subservience of the Palestinian institutions to the occupation. This compliance had become concretized in the body of the Palestinian Authority following the Oslo Accords. By resuscitating key Palestinian demands that the PLO had conceded, including the goal of liberating historic Palestine, Hamas has attempted to take Palestinian nationalism back to a pre-Oslo period. The Oslo Accords have facilitated the continuation of Israel's occupation and have been followed by a failed peace process that has resumed for two decades at significant cost to Palestinians, while Israel expanded its settlement enterprise. Hamas's efforts to undo the political structures that Oslo created challenged a status quo that has been sustainable, if not beneficial, for Israel and its colonization of Palestinian territories. In essence, Hamas's takeover of Gaza marked the failure of Israel's efforts to centralize Palestinian decision-making with compliant figures like Mahmoud Abbas, who in effect allow Israel to maintain its occupation cost-free.

Hamas's fate is emblematic of Israel's "decision not to decide" on the future of the Palestinian territories and its reliance on military superiority to dismiss the political demands animating the Palestinian national movement.[102] Since the blockade was instituted, Israel's strategy toward the movement has evolved. As a key member of Israel's security establishment noted, "Israel needs Hamas to be weak enough not to attack, but stable enough to deal with the radical terrorist groups in Gaza. This line may be blurry but the logic is clear. The challenge lies with walking this blurry line."[103] Managing Hamas in this manner allows Israel to avoid risking another transmutation of Palestinian nationalism. Defeating Hamas militarily would, obviously, be one way of ridding Israel of its "Hamas problem." But that would simply transport Hamas's ideological drivers to another vehicle that would remain rooted in the key tenants of the Palestinian struggle. Instead, as this book has demonstrated, Israel has worked over the past decade to contain Hamas in the Gaza Strip and to turn it into an administrative authority akin to the Palestinian Authority in the West Bank. This strategy has taken several forms. In the West Bank, extensive security coordination with the Palestinian Authority has effectively, but temporarily, dismantled Hamas's infrastructure.[104] In the Gaza Strip, Hamas is imprisoned through a blockade that structurally severs the movement from the rest of the territories.

Leveraging Hamas's containment over the course of a decade gradually institutionalized a process of pacification that is ongoing but inconclusive. Israel's efforts to definitively achieve "calm for calm" have failed. Palestinians in Gaza view the lifting of the blockade, itself a violent act of war, as a necessary prerequisite for calm. Instead of deterrence, since 2007 Israel's policy toward Hamas has taken the form of what Israel's security establishment refers to as "mowing the lawn."[105] This entails the intermittent use of military power to undercut any growth by the resistance factions in Gaza. Through three major wars and countless incursions that employed its lethal "Dahyieh Doctrine," Israel has used military might to break the spirit of resistance in Gaza, pacify Hamas, and work toward deterrence.[106] The result is that Israel and Hamas are now engaged in the process of maintaining an equilibrium of belligerency. Hamas relies on rocket fire to unsettle the status quo and negotiate enhanced access under the persistent blockade. Israel employs military might to debilitate Hamas.

This modus operandi has enabled both Israel and Hamas to pursue short-term victories at the expense of a sustainable resolution, while they both bide their time. From Israel's perspective, resistance has been sufficiently managed so that Hamas's rule over the Gaza Strip can now be tolerated, even abetted. Throughout 2015 and 2016, Israeli politicians and the security establishment spoke about the need to "stabilize" Gaza under Hamas's rule and as a separate territory from the West Bank.[107] The blockade persists and reconstruction has been left to a minimum.[108] After the end of Protective Edge through 2016, the Rafah border remained largely shut even to humanitarian assistance, apart from seventy-two days of partial opening.[109] Meanwhile, Israel has allowed more supplies to enter through the overland crossings at Erez and Kerem Shalom.[110] These are still controlled to manage quality of life just above the brink of turning Gaza into a humanitarian catastrophe. Loosening access is managed to safeguard the present dynamic, which positions Hamas as Israel's counterpart and as the entity responsible for securing calm on its southern border.[111]

Having failed to off-load its governmental responsibilities, Hamas took its own measures in these two years to enhance its revenues via domestic tax raises and revived diplomatic efforts to salvage regional relations.[112] This included diplomatic engagement with officials such as Tony Blair, the former head of the Quartet, and others, under Qatari mediation.[113] Hamas interpreted this mediation as a sign that the international community has openly conceded the need to engage with the movement.[114] Such diplomacy focused on the need to maintain the ceasefire in Gaza. From Hamas's perspective, a failure to maintain calm and stability threatens to precipitate further Israeli operations at significant cost to both its government and the inhabitants of the strip. The liberation project adopted by the wider movement has inadvertently become weighed down by a calculus that had been less burdensome when Hamas acted solely as a spoiler external to the political establishment rather than as a governing authority. Hamas's popular support is now shaped by the quality of its administration within the Gaza Strip and not by its commitment to resistance.

Often these two areas are in direct conflict with one another, a shift that has not been lost on the Palestinian Authority. Responding to Hamas's consistent condemnation of the Palestinian Authority's security coordination with Israel, Fatah accused Hamas of succumbing, behind closed doors, to calling resistance "acts of aggression"; abiding by ceasefires with Israel; calling rocket fire "treasonous"; and obtaining rewards for good behavior from Israeli generals in an effort to build a so-called Sinai state (or an Islamic emirate) in Gaza.[115] While some of these accusations are self-serving exaggerations, there is also an element of truth behind them. In each of the ceasefire discussions signed with Israel in 2009 and 2012, Hamas had indeed agreed to short-term efforts to restrain the resistance in exchange for stability and the promise of a future easing of the blockade. Hamas views these ceasefires as necessary concessions to sustain its government, give Gazans a break, and avoid further conflagrations with Israel. In the absence of any progress on the political level, these ceasefires are seen as practical short-term compromises that do not undermine Hamas's longer-term liberation project.[116]

Israel's policies toward Hamas have produced a situation whereby Israel is able to exercise effective control over the Palestinian territories without taking responsibility as an occupying force. Whether there is a systematic and explicit Israeli separation policy for the West Bank and Gaza remains unclear, but Israel has nonetheless benefited from and reinforced this division.[117] Within the West Bank, the occupation has been outsourced to a compliant Palestinian Authority. Even as Israel maintains its settlement expansion throughout the territories, the Palestinian Authority is still held accountable for administering and governing the lives of Palestinians under Israel's occupation and for safeguarding Israel's security through extensive security coordination. Within the Gaza Strip, Hamas has become the entity that is in practice held accountable for the well-being of the Palestinians who reside there. Israel continues to act as an "effective and disengaged occupier," ensuring the containment and isolation of the Palestinians in Gaza without having to incur any additional cost for administration.[118]

Instead of Palestinian reconciliation, the outcome is two administrative authorities operating under an unyielding occupation. The crucial difference between Hamas and the Palestinian Authority, however, is that Hamas performs its role of managing resistance in language that remains ideologically pure, leaving room for future escalations. While in the West Bank the Palestinian Authority's interim nature has effectively been made permanent, the situation is likely to be temporary within the Gaza Strip.[119] The Palestinian Authority's permanence has been driven by the illusion of sovereignty and economic development that leaders such as former prime minister Salaam Fayyad have cultivated. There is no such illusion in the Gaza Strip, where there will more likely be an expiration date for Israel's ability to manage what has become one of globe's bleakest humanitarian catastrophes.

Under international law, the blockade amounts to collective punishment and comes at a horrific cost to Gaza's population.[120] Seeing Gaza as an open-air prison does not account for the intermittent bombing campaigns that terrorize and kill its inhabitants, or for the carefully engineered access policy that monitors the quality of life of those incarcerated by the blockade.[121] Rather than the subservience that is inherent in the Palestinian Authority's modus operandi with Israel, Hamas has ensured that the political system it has created in Gaza is rooted in resistance. Hamas believes that the only language of dialogue with Israel is one of violence between occupier and occupied. Therefore, while

Hamas might be contained in the Gaza Strip against its will, and its military struggle may at times remain dormant, it shows no sign of ideological softening beyond what it has already offered. As it endures what it typically refers to as the ebb of armed struggle, the movement continues to build and strengthen its military arsenal while it awaits an opportune moment to relaunch its resistance. This is likely to remain the case until a just political settlement is offered to the Palestinians, even as the process of pacification by force is interspersed with fleeting moments of calm.

ISLAMISM AND THE POLITICS OF RESISTANCE

Hamas's Islamism facilitated the opportunistic dismissal of its political motivations by Israel as well as by regional actors. Throughout 2015 and 2016, Hamas's relationship to the Muslim Brotherhood led countries such as Egypt or factions such as Fatah to call into question its nationalist aims. This was exacerbated by Hamas celebrating the rise of Islamic parties to power throughout the Middle East after the Arab uprisings in 2011. In reality and practice, however, Hamas has limited itself to the political landscape that exists in Israel and the occupied territories. While Hamas often rhetorically falls back on its regional Islamism, it has largely operated within the structures of the nation-state model.[122] That makes Hamas similar to other regional Islamist movements that are shaped by their particular context even while utilizing Islamic political discourse that transcends boundaries.[123]

Nonetheless, like other Islamic parties in the region, Hamas's political aspirations, as they began to manifest themselves in 2005, faced intense local, regional, and international opposition. The political participation of Islamic parties in the Middle East has long been a source of tension. Backed by Western allies, secular and Islamic Arab dictatorships have worked to suppress or co-opt Islamic parties in order to safeguard their authoritarian regimes and limit democratization.[124] Such actions have historically found sympathetic Western backers who worry about the "fundamentalist threat" of an Islamic resurgence.[125] This threat is often portrayed as a monolithic anti-Western and anti-democratic force that has to be suppressed to protect Western democratic and liberal principles as well as regional stability.[126]

Islamic political participation has long raised questions regarding the compatibility of Islam and democracy and the classification of Islamic movements as radical or moderate depending on their use of violence.[127] Hamas's dedication to jihad puts it within the category of radical Islamists that legitimize the use of arms in their revolutionary stance toward the incumbent political order.[128] This distinction between radical and moderate movements, however, is oftentimes arbitrary. Separating radical and moderate Islamists on the basis of whether they have revolutionary (sometimes violent) political goals or gradually transformative social agendas brushes over the fact that a movement, Hamas for instance, may have a wide-reaching social and charitable infrastructure that in many ways underpins its legitimacy as a revolutionary political movement.[129]

Islamist groups fall along a spectrum of moderation to radicalism. This complicates the popular debate regarding Islamism and democracy. While cases can be made for the engagement of moderate Islamist movements in politics, both opponents and supporters of Islamist participation typically view radical parties as being intrinsically at odds with democratic ideals.[130] Proponents of participation uphold the distinction between moderate and radical Islamists by supporting the former (often cited are Jamaat-i-Islami of Pakistan, Ennahda of Tunisia, and the Muslim Brotherhood of Egypt) to become active political parties, and in the process potentially undermine the hold of radical Islamists.[131] This position argues that moderate Islamist parties should be encouraged to compete in democratic elections as a means of forcing compromises and diluting ideology through political alliances and coalitions.[132] This would test whether democratic gain would translate into democratic governance.[133] Such voices cite the need for strong institutional systems that are committed to democratic principles and that can maintain checks and balances to limit the power of any one political party, Islamist or otherwise.[134]

The ostensible moderation of Islamist parties in power is opposed by those who argue that Islamists cannot be allowed to participate in democratic processes in the hope that they will eventually moderate.[135] Opponents of participation have stressed that Islamism is intrinsically incompatible with democratic values. These scholars argue that for nationalist movements to successfully achieve their goals, they cannot be aligned to a particular faith or ethnicity but must rather be secular and equally open to all faiths as a precursor to forming a state for all citizens.[136] Critics state that Islamists believe in the sovereignty of God rather than people; as such, protecting the rights of minorities against discrimination would become redundant when divine legal teachings sanction such discrimination.[137] Further, the implementation of a religious-based political order, even if modernist in outlook, is seen as inherently contradictory to secular democracy.[138] These arguments led to the suppression of Islamist movements to varying degrees within the Arab world in the twentieth century. In instances where political participation was allowed, this was more often than not done in the hope of limiting the influence of Islamic parties. When the Islamic Salvation Front, a Sunni Islamic party in Algeria, actually won the democratic elections in 1991, it was immediately suppressed by the ruling regime, sparking a civil war that lasted close to a decade and resulted in the death of hundreds of thousands of Algerians.[139]

Hamas's engagement in politics offers an interesting and unique contribution to this debate, given its dual nature as a radical Islamist movement that is also engaged in a liberation struggle.[140] As various chapters in this book have shown, Hamas's use of violence dropped significantly while it contemplated engaging with the political system. In the months leading to its participation in the 2006 elections, Hamas appeared committed to the democratic ideals that underpinned its political agenda. The movement's engagement with the political system did not constitute "moderation" in the manner typically understood when speaking of parties transitioning from the battlefield into the political arena. Hamas maintained both its ideological conviction and a readiness to use force to push forward its vision for the Palestinian struggle. However, it did so while engaging fully in the democratic political system that was being constructed in the post-intifada reality.

Although local and international intervention undermined Hamas's democratic experiment, it could still be seen that Hamas was in essence taking part in the politics of resistance, whereby governance, local administration, and political participation did not come at the expense of the struggle for liberation but, rather, complemented it. The goals that had informed the movement's military struggle came to be articulated within the political arena. This further underscores the complexity of Islamist movements by demonstrating how Hamas can exhibit a seemingly moderate stance toward the democratic process domestically while advocating armed struggle against the occupation. Hamas's experience after its takeover of the Gaza Strip provides further insight into its approach to governance. As Hamas centralized its grip on power, concerns were raised regarding its authoritarianism and desire to impose a conservative social order. Such worries are often dismissed by those who state that Islamists are unfairly confronted with a catch-22 scenario when seeking power.[141] In other words, Islamists will be criticized for whatever policies they adopt once in government as a result of a "fundamental fear"—largely on the part of the West— that they are incompatible with democracy.[142] This fear seeks to make Islamism exceptional, as being inherently violent and uniquely incompatible with politics.

Hamas's approach to governance of the Gaza Strip, which is taking place under an exceptional situation given the persistence of Israel's blockade, suggests that the movement is active in the creation of an illiberal democracy, or perhaps a system based on "soft authoritarianism."[143] The movement has repressed political plurality and has maintained a conservative social order while demonstrating an ability to adopt a modernist and pragmatic approach to governance, for instance by

maintaining open channels of communication with human rights organizations.[144] To the ire of Salafi movements, Hamas has avoided implementing *shari'a* law. It has, however, worked to create a virtuous society
that is governed by righteous laws (e.g., sex segregation). This is arguably with the aim of eventually creating a system from which *shari'a* law
could organically develop.[145] Also central to the movement's governance
is the construction of an identity around resistance. The combination
of populist politics and authoritarianism actually mirrors the manner
in which the PLO approached its own institutional building during the
1960s and 1970s.[146]

Understanding Hamas's Islamism and its interplay with the movement's nationalism is imperative for assessing the movement's political
track record. Hamas carries a significant degree of responsibility for
the state of fragmentation within the Palestinian territories today. The
movement's entrenchment in the Gaza Strip and its increasingly authoritarian hold on government are the most obvious sources of concern, particularly for the people under its rule. More broadly, however,
Hamas has made damaging decisions in two intertwined fields that
should be explored separately: the political and the military.

The political damage began with the movement's 2005 decision to
run in the Palestinian legislative elections. The movement's entry into
the political system represented both an embrace of the democratic
mechanisms underpinning modern-day nation-states and a revolution
against the incumbent order within the Palestinian territories. Hamas
was willing to embody the institutions of the state, to lead the civil service, and to use the legislature to govern effectively. It understood the
limits and values of power-sharing and even attempted to form a coalition as its first government. In that sense Hamas accepted, at least
in principle, the democratic process inherent in the political transition
between parties. Concurrently, however, the movement viewed its election victory as a mandate to reconstitute the tenets of the very structure
it was elected into. Although Hamas had been elected into the Palestinian Authority, the body that sits at the very core of the Oslo Accords,

the movement's entire political agenda was based on reformulating the national struggle away from the international agreements that had underpinned the creation of the Palestinian Authority. In other words, Hamas sought to accede to the very institutions it repudiated. In effect, the movement viewed its democratic victory as carte blanche to undo and reassemble the entire systems of "state" and in this manner failed to understand the principles of democratic rule.

Acknowledging this dynamic does not then support the view that Islamic parties are unable to respect the checks and balances inherent in democratic systems that limit the power of any one political party. It is arguably the case that it was Fatah that entrenched its rule and with direct American and Israeli intervention acted as a bulwark against a political transition in its bid to maintain single-party hegemony. The debate around engagement with Hamas as a democratically elected Islamist party in 2006 predates discussions around the success of Islamist parties throughout the region following the Arab uprisings.[147] Many have attempted to understand and influence how these victories can be dealt with. Some scholars have interpreted the early events of the Arab uprisings as emblematic of moderate or reformist streaks of Islam that are open to pluralistic governance and empowerment through democratic processes (e.g., Ennahda in Tunis).[148] Others have put forward the notion of a "modern Islamism."[149] This view argues that rather than focusing on whether Islamism is compatible with democracy, the focus should be on the aspirations of the people in the Muslim world to allow for the emergence of an indigenous form of democracy rather than imposing liberal Western values.

Hamas's rhetoric before and after its election victory certainly suggested a desire for a local form of democratic rule to emerge within the Palestinian struggle. The movement's failure to impose that vision, however, has less to do with the incompatibility of Islam and democracy and more to do with the limits of sovereignty and the relations between state-building and revolutions. For Hamas, respect of past international agreements and the performance of sovereignty that had underpinned

Fatah's rule in the Palestinian Authority were premature developments given the absence of liberation. While Hamas had embraced the democratic process, it had done so less in the spirit of government and more with the desire to lead the Palestinian struggle. In many respects, this development is the belated outcome of the Oslo Accords. Sidelining the Palestinians in a permanent state of restricted autonomy and curtailing their sovereignty did not in fact lead to their pacification, but rather it sparked a search for alternatives that might sustain the national revolution.

This is precisely why Hamas's entry into the political system was threatening to actors invested in maintaining the status quo. Nonetheless, Hamas failed to understand the balance that had to be struck between government and revolution. It had mistakenly assumed that revolution could be launched from within the very systems that had been created to domesticate the national struggle. Transitioning into the political system in many ways mired the movement and compromised its liberation agenda in its efforts to reconstitute the incumbent order. More than half a decade before dictatorships supported by proxy wars would break the Arab uprisings, Hamas's own revolution was crushed. Whether Fatah's belligerency or the international blockade waged against Hamas warranted the movement's reactions and the brutality it showed in its takeover of Gaza in 2007 remains debatable. In facing such opposition, Hamas crossed several red lines and betrayed key tenets it had long upheld regarding the sanctity of Palestinian blood. The violence Hamas unleashed on other Palestinians severely compromised the Palestinian struggle. In effect, Hamas made the choice that forcefully safeguarding its democratic right to govern was a lesser violation than conceding to Fatah's authoritarianism. Palestinians continue to suffer the implications of that decision to this day.

With its takeover of Gaza, Hamas effectively merged revolution and state-building. The movement's approach to governance has been based on an effort to situate the notion of resistance at the heart of the polity within the Gaza Strip. Economically, socially, and militarily, resistance to Israel's continued occupation of Gaza has become central to Hamas's governance of the enclave. Looking at the period between 2007 and 2011, Hamas did indeed settle into a ruling mode. Over the course of these five years, territorial governance overtook reconciliation as the movement's priority. Dismissing concessions that Hamas had previously accepted in the pursuit of unity, the movement chose to maintain its governance over the Gaza Strip rather than prioritize Palestinian unity. Hamas rationalized this move by maintaining that its rule over a "liberated" strip of land was in effect protecting the Palestinians against further concessions by the PLO. This allowed the movement to safeguard its own liberation project, one that remains fundamentally at odds with Fatah's. While that argument may be true, its impact was that territorial governance continued to take precedence over unity.

The second problematic choice Hamas made was in the military arena. Hamas's use of violence, like the PLO before it, has been rooted in arguments of legitimacy, justice, and self-defense. Given Israel's violent occupation of Palestinian land, arms were seen as the only recourse for resistance. Decades of failed diplomacy have done little to undermine this argument. Yet there is no question that Hamas's reliance on jihad has had devastating implications for the Palestinian people. Aside from the moral bankruptcy and the corrosive effect of targeting and killing civilians, dedication to armed resistance against a superb foe like Israel has led to the disintegration of the Palestinian struggle. Strategically, this approach has not only failed; it has also threatened to erode the very social fabric of the Palestinian community under occupation. It has normalized and excused the use of violence as a tactic to achieve political ends and facilitated the dehumanization of opponents. The ease with which Fatah was "othered" as a Zionist outpost and the brutal and fratricidal manner in which the Palestinian factions turned on each other in 2007 is the clearest manifestation of this phenomenon. While social erosion is perhaps a natural outcome of fragmentation under an interminable and relentlessly lethal occupation, the proliferation of violence as a strategy for liberation has also played its part. Hamas, and certainly Fatah, have actively contributed to dividing the national liberation struggle into two competing trajectories and to turning domestic relations into lethal acrimonious battles without foreseeable end.

With the beginning of the Arab uprisings, Hamas's decision to maintain its rule within the Gaza Strip at the cost of reconciliation took an unexpected turn. The closure of the tunnels and the rise of regimes that were hostile to Hamas effectively led to its entrenchment within the Gaza Strip. Efforts to shed its governing responsibilities and transition back into a liberation movement have of course been blocked by both the Palestinian Authority and Israel. For both parties, Hamas's containment in Gaza is a way to isolate and pacify Palestinian resistance. For other Arab regimes, undermining Hamas is important to demonstrate the limits of democratization in the Arab world. The manner in which Hamas and the Muslim Brotherhood have been vilified in Egypt demonstrates the extent of overlap between the interests of Israel and authoritarian rulers in the region. This has historically come at the expense of the Palestinian struggle for self-determination. But it has also allowed the perseverance and stability of oppressive regimes that have long acted against the interests of their people.

In many ways, Hamas's democratic experiment offered a microcosm of the forces that would be unleashed throughout the region half a decade later. Like other Arab uprisings, Hamas's election was a call for change, for a move away from corrupt authoritarian rule that often placed the interests of Western policies in the region above the rights of its people. In Hamas's election, Palestinians sought an alternative. The manner in which that alternative has been demolished and the ensuing fragmentation of the Palestinian polity and territories foreshadowed the darker trends yet to come.[150] Having for the most part averted democratization, Arab states now appear to be offering further avenues for diplomatic openness with Israel despite the absence of any prospects for a just peace on the Palestinian front. While this cooperation is being pursued to maintain the present regional order, Hamas's election and the Arab uprisings that followed should make clear that popular sentiment and outrage is always bubbling beneath the surface.[151] Protests and revolutions have demonstrated their power in making whole regimes collapse. Their temporary pacification should not be taken as a sign of stability or acquiescence.

NEW HAMAS, OLD DYNAMICS

In early 2017, Hamas issued a new "Political Document" after months of speculation that it was looking to revise its problematic charter. The document emerged as the culmination of all the developments that the movement had undergone for the decade of its rule over Gaza. It demonstrated that on the most official level, Hamas accepted the creation of a Palestinian state on the 1967 borders, UN Resolution 194 for the right of return, and the notion of restricting armed struggle to operate within the limits of international law. Although not breaking any new ground in terms of political concessions, the document was a powerful intervention that restated more forcefully than before the position Hamas has adopted since at least 2007, if not since the 1990s. It appeared to define the outer reaches of what the movement might be willing to offer without defaulting on its ideology. In a nod to the Sisi regime in Egypt, the new document officially severed Hamas from its parent organization, the Muslim Brotherhood, making explicit its commitment to Palestinian nationalism, as argued in this book.[152]

Hamas's document was released without a formal renunciation of the movement's charter, alluding to internal power struggles. Elections had been ongoing within the movement for the preceding months. Khaled Meshal had completed his final term as head of Hamas's political bureau and was replaced by Ismail Haniyeh. Yehya Sinwar, a powerful figure within Hamas's military, was elected as the head of Hamas's operations in the Gaza Strip. Sinwar's election indicated both the growing strength of Hamas's military wing and the expanding importance of the "internal leadership" and the Gaza Strip to the movement's decision-making. This publication was in many ways seen as Meshal's last effort to officially document Hamas's political position and to communicate to the international community a starting point for diplomatic engagement before Hamas moves in an unknown direction under new leadership.

Hamas's initiative went largely unnoticed. Netanyahu's spokesman stated in response that "Hamas is attempting to fool the world but it will not succeed."[153] With the inauguration of US president Donald J. Trump into office, tensions that had long been simmering within the region erupted. Empowered by Trump's condemnation of "Islamic extremism," countries such as Saudi Arabia, Egypt, and the United Arab Emirates mobilized to isolate and blockade Qatar, a country they accused of funding terrorism.[154] Similar dynamics had been taking place within the Palestinian territories, where President Abbas had decided to increase pressure on Hamas. In the early months of 2017, Abbas reduced medical shipments into Gaza; cut the salaries paid to Fatah employees based there, severely crippling the local economy; and stopped making payments to Israel for electricity supply into Gaza. This precipitated a major crisis within Gaza as international organizations declared the threat of a "total collapse." Such a catastrophe was avoided by emergency fuel shipments from Egypt, which indicated its willingness to forge a more pragmatic relationship toward Hamas. Having severed its ties to the Muslim Brotherhood, Hamas was more palatable an interlocutor to Sisi, who asked Hamas to strengthen its policing against Sinai militants seeking refuge in Gaza.[155]

These latest developments demonstrate in the clearest manner the success of Israel's divisive tactics toward the Palestinian territories. Abbas's willingness to strengthen the stranglehold on Palestinians in Gaza, effectively accepting the collective punishment of two million Palestinians for his own political interest, has shown the degree to which the Palestinian Authority has become complicit within Israel's regime of occupation. More importantly, subsequent developments after Abbas's decision show that years after the commencement of the blockade in 2007, Hamas, rather than collapsing, appears still able to survive the strongest of chokeholds and to continue consolidating its own power in Gaza. Israel's strategy of conflict management has also proven surprisingly sustainable as the occupation enters its fifth decade and as regional relations shift in Israel's favor. Through the current dynamic, Israel maintains control over the maximum amount of Palestinian land with minimal responsibility for the indigenous population. Despite this violation, the proxy wars that currently dominate the Middle East have meant a greater level of cooperation, intelligence sharing, and general normalization between Sunni Gulf States and Israel as they both contend with the perceived threat from Iran.[156] Years after the *Mavi Marmara* incident, Turkey has also moved to revive diplomatic ties with Israel.[157]

Prospects for Israel's broader integration expanded even further in the fall of 2017 as Saudi Arabia and the United Arab Emirates became more vocal in their desire to formalize relations with Israel. The regional alignment of interests increased the urgency of tackling the question of Palestine to pave the way for these nascent relations to bloom with minimal popular backlash.[158] In October, another unity deal was brokered between Hamas and Fatah, under Egyptian mediation. Although many of the challenges that felled the 2014 Shati deal persisted, including issues related to institutional integration and Hamas's arms, prospects for unity were seen to be more favorable. This was particularly true in light of the rapprochement between the Sisi regime and Hamas. Cautious optimism was primarily due to the determination of regional actors to push through a final settlement for Israel-Palestine, to facilitate their own normalization of ties with Israel. Unity between Hamas and Fatah was seen as a precursor to an agreement signed between Israel and Palestinians, one that many hoped would be proposed by the Trump administration.

As this book went to print, pressure was building on the Palestinian leadership from Saudi Arabia and the United States to accept a rumored deal. Such a deal is anticipated to fall far short of minimum Palestinian demands. Hamas is likely to face similar pressures, namely from Egypt, which controls the Rafah crossing into the Gaza Strip. Such pressure could indeed force the conclusive pacification of Hamas and ensure its acquiescence to the creation of a Palestinian state by name, one that would most likely remain subservient to Israeli hegemony over the entire land of historic Palestine. Yet the lasting success of any Palestinian unity government or even Israeli-Palestinian agreement will ultimately depend on the manner in which core Palestinian grievances are addressed. In that sense, understanding the widespread legitimacy of movements such as Hamas is a necessity, as many of the political motivations that underpin its ideology form core tenets of the Palestinian struggle for self-determination.[159]

Until these fundamental drivers of Palestinian nationalism are addressed, Israel will be forced to continuously manage and advance the structures of control it has developed over both the West Bank and the Gaza Strip to pacify Palestinian resistance. Whether through a formal peace deal or otherwise, the absence of any unrest in the territories should not reflect stability, given that popular grievances will continue to simmer in the absence of a just peace.[160] The "lone knife" attacks that have proliferated since 2015 are one indication of underlying tensions, as are the protests that erupted around Jerusalem's al-Aqsa Mosque in the summer of 2017.[161] The brutality of the 2014 assault on Gaza perhaps ensured a longer period of pacification than previous escalations. But there is little doubt that another conflagration is forthcoming. This will mark the continuation of Israel's strategy of "mowing the lawn" as well as the perseverance of the Palestinian struggle for self-determination. The manner in which the next war unfolds will be event-specific, but the underlying drivers remain unchanged.[162]

As for Hamas, until—and indeed if—it is conclusively pacified through an enforced peace deal, the equilibrium of belligerency between the movement and Israel will continue to mark relations between the two parties. Through Hamas's effective containment in Gaza, Israel can forfeit the viability of any final resolution that would address Palestinian demands while blaming Hamas's terrorism as the underlying cause of unrest. Hamas, for its part, can avoid making additional ideological concessions by arguing, rightfully, that Israel itself has failed to accept either the need to fulfill Palestinian rights or the legitimacy of the 1967 borders. Both Hamas and Israel will continue to focus on short-term survival in a longer-term battle, where political gains can be reaped from intermittent confrontations on the battlefield. This status quo allows Hamas to sustain its power and Israel to maintain its colonization of the West Bank and its stranglehold on the Gaza Strip, where the besieged Palestinians continue to pay the highest price of all.

ACKNOWLEDGMENTS

This is an accidental book. I began this work a decade ago as a part-time project that would allow me to learn more about Israel-Palestine and, through that, my own history. The research was carried out and written over long morning and evening commutes to my day job, on weekends and evenings, in airport lounges, and during business trips and family holidays. Naming all the people who supported this unusual but most rewarding intellectual journey, and who suffered its consequences, would be impossible. To all of them I remain indebted.

In the summer of 2014, as Israel's Operation Protective Edge was starting in Gaza, this undertaking transitioned into a book project. All I remember of that summer is a feeling of absolute helplessness and horror; an inability to make sense of all that death and destruction, or to put an end to it. A coincidental introduction to Kate Wahl at Stanford University Press came at the right time. I decided to leave my job and expand my research into a book manuscript that could help me, and hopefully my readers, get some answers. Three years later, I submitted this manuscript. It is a most unexpected end to a journey that began in what now feels like another lifetime.

The people who guided me along this path are numerous. It all started with George Joffé, at the University of Cambridge, who encouraged my wide-eyed curiosities and patiently shared with me his vast knowledge of Israel-Palestine over many hours in his book-lined living room. In him, I met a mentor, friend, and fellow conversationalist on all things related to the Middle East.

Having grown up in the region, I saw the chance to return for additional fieldwork and spend time there as a researcher and writer to be enriching beyond measure. In Beirut, I want to thank the indefatigable staff at the Institute for Palestine Studies, in particular Jeanette Sarouphim, whose kind patience and command of the archives made the quest for any obscure document a breeze. The staff at al-Zaytouna Centre were always welcoming and professional, and I am grateful to them for taking the time to discuss various aspects of my work. In particular, I want to thank Mohsen Saleh and Wael Sa'ad for their support. In Gaza, I am especially indebted to Wissam Afifeh, whose generosity in opening up al-Resalah's archive to me was a most treasured gift. I also want to thank Ahmad Khalidi and Avi Shlaim for providing documents from their private collections, and Ayala Oppenheimer for assisting me with researching Hebrew-language material.

I have listed in the Bibliography an illustrative sample of interviewees in the Middle East and abroad. Some names have been withheld for a range of reasons. To all those publicly or privately acknowledged, the time you gave is what made this book possible. Whether formal interviews, snippets of informal conversations over coffees and taxi rides, or long tearful chats, from the piers of Gaza to Beirut's alleyways and bookstores, this text was written against the backdrop of a multitude of conversations that have all seeped into its lines.

Very few of those conversations would have happened had it not been for a number of people who worked their magic to make important connections. In particular, I want to thank Paul Aaron, Gilbert Achcar, Hadeel Assali, Hamid Dabashi, Amira Hass, Azmi Kishawi, Oliver McTernan,

Nadim Shehadi, Nathan Stock, Azzam Tamimi, Nathan Thrall, Mandy Turner, and Jose Vericat, as well as all the others along the way whose paths I crossed and who opened up doors in the most unexpected ways.

I am grateful to Lila Abu-Lughod, Rashid Khalidi, and the Middle East Institute at Columbia University for the institutional affiliation that helped me decamp from the region and write in solitude and quiet.

A number of readers looked over the manuscript or portions of it at various stages of writing. They all offered valuable advice, insights, and feedback for which I am most appreciative: Dania Akkad, Alia al-Kadi, Lamis Andoni, Tamara Ben-Halim, Nathan Brown, Sally Davies, Noura Erakat, Fawaz Gerges, Natasha Gill, Hana Habayeb, Ahmad Khalidi, Rashid Khalidi, Zachary Lockman, Beverley Milton-Edwards, Dirk Moses, Tehila Sasson, Yezid Sayigh, Richard Schofield, Avraham Sela, Avi Shlaim, Henry Siegman, Lucy Thirkell Storm, and Julian Weinberg. A special mention goes to Fred Meiton, whose careful reading—and rereading—and patient support I will never be able to repay. Thank you. While this book has benefited immeasurably from these readers' close engagement, all errors remain my own.

Wherever I went on my travels, friends and family added warmth and comfort to my trips. Special thanks go to Yasmeen el-Khoudary, Dima AlMasri, Sonja Najjar, Yousef Shuwayhat, Alaa Tartir, and Natasha Wheatley for their generosity and hospitality.

This book would not have come to fruition without Kate Wahl, whose meticulous editorial interventions and brilliant guidance have made this process an absolute pleasure. I cannot imagine completing this undertaking without her. I also want to thank the rest of the team at SUP, and particularly my editor Jeff Wyneken, for all the care they have taken in shepherding this book through production. Thanks also go to my peer reviewers for their constructive comments and advice, as well as Joel Beinin for his encouragement.

I have not been allowed to spend as much time as I would like to in Gaza. I am deeply aware of my inadequacy in writing about a place whose layered complexity on the ground I have barely begun to peel away. While I claim no authority to speak on Gaza's behalf or on behalf of the Palestinians who live there, I also know that this book is rooted in that land. The entire impetus for this project derived from a desire to challenge a reality in Gaza which is a moral stain on our collective conscience. I hope that this book contributes one small push toward an inevitable and necessary tipping point. The endeavor began as a personal intellectual journey to understand my family history, and the people of Gaza have shown me—up close and at a distance—what it means to be Palestinian.

This book is dedicated to my grandmother, Eva, who taught me to have faith in the mysterious and miraculous ways of the universe. Tata, your humanity knows no bounds; neither does your capacity to forgive. It is because of the values you instilled in me that I have humbly sought answers and tried to humanize, empathize, and understand.

My parents and brothers are my rock. Without ever questioning why I do what I do, they have supported me in every possible way there is to be supported. The love and pride that emanate from them have kept me going, even when I was racked with self-doubt and uncertainty. Thank you for raising me the way you did, for accepting me, and for teaching me to be proud of my identity and my heritage. I would not be the person I am today had you not always been watching over me (maybe a bit too closely at times . . .).

And Seth. Talk about the mysterious and miraculous ways of the universe. I am daily in awe of you, your intellect, warmth, and kindness. Your spirit and gentle smile drew me out of the darkest recesses of this journey. Thank you for helping me find my voice, and for being my partner in this book.

NOTES

PREFACE

1. See, for example, "Sean Hannity Heated Exchange with Yousef Munayyer," *YouTube*, July 29, 2014.

2. There is a debate about whether Golda Meir actually said these words. See Harvey Rachlin, "Misquoting Golda Meir: Did She or Didn't She?," *Haaretz*, June 16, 2015.

3. The viewing spot is known as Kobi Hill. See Robert Mackey, "Israelis Watch Bombs Drop on Gaza from Front-Row Seats," *New York Times*, July 14, 2014. Similar scenes happened in 2009, as depicted in the Israeli documentary *Matador Hamilchama* (The war matador). See "War Matador: Trailer," *YouTube*, December 1, 2011.

4. U.S. Department of State, 2002, as per 22 USCS 2656f.

5. See Teichman, "How to Define Terrorism," 505–17; and Primoratz, "What Is Terrorism?," 129–38.

6. For more on the loaded term and its manipulation, see Freedman, "Terrorism as Strategy," 314–18.

7. On the differences between "civilized violence" and "barbaric violence," see Asad, "Thinking about Terrorism and Just War," 3–24.

8. The role of law in governing liberation struggles is increasingly coming under review, not least because of its historic relation to imperialism and colonialism. See Anghie, *Imperialism, Sovereignty, and the Making of International Law*; and Kennedy, "The International Human Rights Regime," in Dickinson, *Examining Critical Perspectives on Human Rights*.

9. For more on notions of self-defense and preemption, see Gray, *International Law and the Use of Force*. For more on Israel's quest for security and the prolonged occupation see, Moses, "Empire, Resistance, and Security."

10. "Speech for Prime Minister Ismail Haniyeh," *Hamas Info*, March 23, 2014, *Al-Watha'iq al-Arabiyeh* (Arabic Documents) Collection, Institute for Palestine Studies (IPS) Archive, Beirut, Lebanon [hereafter IPS].

11. "Al-Qassam Release," *Al-Qassam*, July 18, 2014, IPS.

12. Asad, "Thinking about Terrorism," 14.

13. All translations are the author's own.

14. This publication is considered a mouthpiece by other scholars. See Nüsse, *Muslim Palestine*, 6. Scholars from within Gaza have also relied on *Filastin al-Muslima* and expressed a view regarding its broad circulation and accurate reflection of Hamas's thinking. Ahmad al-Nuwati, *Hamas Min al-Dakhel. Filastin al-Muslima* [hereafter *FM*] in any case presents itself as the official mouthpiece. See "Goodbye . . . Onto a New Arena of Struggle and Liberation," *FM*, July 19, 2013, 2–3.

15. Discourse analysis allows researchers to critically study various discursive elements by taking into account social, historical, and political considerations with the aim of developing an empirically assessed reality or elucidating a forgotten historiography. See Jørgensen and Phillips,

Discourse Analysis as Theory and Method; Torfing, *New Theories of Discourse*; Der Derian, "Imaging Terror"; and Doty, *Imperial Encounters*. For discourse analysis on Islamic movements, see Khatib, Matar, and Alshaer, *The Hizbullah Phenomenon*.

CHAPTER ONE

1. For a biography of Yassin, see Jawada, *Asma al-Sheikh*; and Adwan, *Al-Sheikh Ahmad Yassin*.

2. Vitullo, "Uprising in Gaza," 46, in Lockman and Beinin, *Intifada*.

3. For more on the First Intifada, see Abu-Amr, "The Palestinian Uprising in the West Bank and Gaza Strip," 384–405; Jarbawi, *Al-Intifada wa al-Qiyada al-Siyasiyya fi al-Diffa al-Gharbiyyeh wa Qita Ghazza*; and Schiff and Ya'ari, *Intifada*.

4. Said, "Intifada and Independence," 20, in Lockman and Beinin, *Intifada*.

5. Abu-Amr, "Palestinian Uprising," 389.

6. As translated in Hroub, *Hamas*, 265.

7. Tamimi, *Hamas*, 55.

8. Unless otherwise indicated, quotes from Hamas's charter are based on the translation in Hroub, *Hamas*, 267–91.

9. Maqdsi, "Charter of the Islamic Resistance Movement (Hamas) of Palestine," 124.

10. Esposito, *The Islamic Threat*, 130–34. For more on the early years of the Muslim Brotherhood, see Mitchell, *The Society of the Muslim Brothers*; Wickham, *The Muslim Brotherhood*; Kandil, *Inside the Brotherhood*; and Lia, *The Society of the Muslim Brothers in Egypt*. For more on al-Banna, see Commins, "Hasan al-Banna (1906–1949)," 125–54, in Rahnema, *Pioneers of Islamic Revival*; and El-Awaisi, "Emergence of a Militant Leader," 46–63.

11. Commins, "Hasan al-Banna," 133–44.

12. El-Awaisi, "The Conceptual Approach of the Egyptian Muslim Brothers towards the Palestine Question, 1928–1949," 227–30; Commins, "Hasan al-Banna," 137–39; and Harris, *Nationalism and Revolution in Egypt*, 164–65.

13. For more on Palestine under the British Mandate, see Segev, *One Palestine, Complete*; and Tessler, *A History of the Israeli-Palestinian Conflict*, 185–269.

14. For more on Zionism, see Brenner, *Zionism*; and Laqueur, *A History of Zionism*.

15. Lia, *Society of the Muslim Brothers*, 162–73; El-Awaisi, "Conceptual Approach of the Egyptian Muslim Brothers," 225–44; Porath, *In Search of Arab Unity 1930–1945*, 152–54; and Jankowski, "Egyptian Responses to the Palestine Problem in the Interwar Period," 1–38. For brotherhood accounts of the centrality of Palestine, see Badr, *Al-Tareeq illa Tahrir Filisteen*; and Ghanem, *Watha'eq Qadiyat Filisteen fi Malafat al-Ikhwan al-Muslimeen 1928–1948*.

16. See Khalidi, *Palestinian Identity*; and Muslih, *The Origins of Palestinian Nationalism*.

17. See Porath, *The Emergence of the Palestinian Arab National Movement*, 80–109; Hirst, *The Gun and the Olive Branch*, 15–108; and Shafir, *Land, Labor and the Origins of the Israeli-Palestinian Conflict, 1882–1914*.

18. Nafi, *Arabism, Islamism and the Palestine Question 1908–1941*, 16; and Piscatori, "Imagining Pan-Islam," 201–19, in Valbjørn and Lawson, *International Relations of the Middle East*. Anti-Zionism was not limited to the Muslim community. Many of the anti-Zionist publications were owned by Christians. Ayalon, *The Press in the Arab Middle East*, 95–101.

19. Nafi, *Arabism, Islamism*, 95. This was a revival of ideas which had been floated in 1922 regarding the prospect of making Palestinian holy places central to the global Muslim community. See Porath, *Emergence of Palestinian Arab National Movement*, 8–13; Kupferschmidt, *The Supreme Muslim Council*; Mattar, *The Mufti of Jerusalem*; and Freas, "Hajj Amin al-Husayni and the Haram al-Sharif," 19–51.

20. For more on factionalism and Palestinian classes, see Khalaf, *Politics in Palestine*; Pappé, *The Rise and Fall of a Palestinian Dynasty*; Seikaly, *Men of Capital*; and Hourani, "Ottoman Reforms and the Politics of the Notables," 83–111, in Hourani, Khoury, and Wilson, *The Modern Middle East*.

21. Sanagan, "Teacher, Preacher, Soldier, Martyr," 317–19. For biographies of al-Qassam, see Lachman, "Arab Rebellion and Terrorism in Palestine 1929–1939," 53–101, in Kedourie and Haim, *Zionism and Arabism in Palestine and Israel*; and Nafi, "Shaykh 'Izz al-Dīn al-Qassām," 185–215.

22. The term "jihad" has a complex genealogy, and its definition as "holy war" is a modern—and somewhat reductive—one. See Kendall and Stein, *Twenty-First Century Jihad*.

23. Al-Qassam's worldview was likely informed by his education at al-Azhar University and his exposure to Islamic reformist thinkers such as Rashid Rida and Jamal al-Din al-Afghani. For more, see Porath, *Emergence of Palestinian Arab National Movement*, 298; Kerr, *Islamic Reform*, 15–16; and Sanagan, "Teacher, Preacher," 326–28. For more on the Islamic reformers, see Rahnema, *Pioneers of Islamic Revival*.

24. As quoted by one of al-Qassam's followers. Johnson, *Islam and the Politics of Meaning in Palestinian Nationalism*, 42.

25. Lachman, "Arab Rebellion and Terrorism in Palestine," 63.

26. Porath, *Emergence of Palestinian Arab National Movement*, 137. Clandestine preparations were made in Haifa by the Young Men's Muslim Association for military operations. Other organizations included the Green Hand in Acre, Safed, and Nazareth; Holy War in Jerusalem; and the Black Hand in northern Palestine. Morris, *Righteous Victims*, 126.

27. Lia, *Society of the Muslim Brothers*, 93–128; and Wickham, *Muslim Brotherhood*, 20–46.

28. Nafi, "Shaykh 'Izz al-Dīn al-Qassām," 211.

29. Johnson, *Islam and the Politics of Meaning*, 53–56; and Porath, *Emergence of Palestinian Arab National Movement*, 183–84. Zuaiter, *Al-Harakah al-wataniyyah al-filastiiniiyyah 1935–1939*, shows how al-Qassam fused Islamist and nationalist elements of the Palestinian movement.

30. For more on the revolt, see Swedenburg, *Memories of Revolt*; and Stein, "The Intifada and the 1936–39 Uprising," 64–85.

31. For more on Arab-Jewish tensions pre-revolt, see Cohen, *Year Zero of the Arab-Israeli Conflict 1929*.

32. See Gershoni, "The Muslim Brothers and the Arab Revolt in Palestine, 1936–1939," 367–97.

33. The brotherhood formed a committee called the General Central Committee to Aid Palestine, headed by al-Banna. Efforts were ineffectual. See Abu-Amr, *Islamic Fundamentalism in the West Bank and Gaza*, 23–53; Lia, *Society of the Muslim Brothers*, 235–47; Mitchell, *Society of the Muslim Brothers*, 15–18; and Mayer, "The Military Force of Islam," 101, in Kedourie and Haim, *Zionism and Arabism in Palestine and Israel*.

34. Al-Husaini, *The Moslem Brethren*, 140; Ramadan, *Al-Ikhwan al-Muslimun wa al-Tanzim al-Sirri*, 71–72; Yasin, *Hamas*, 17; and Lia, *Society of the Muslim Brothers*, 235–47.

35. Lia, *Society of the Muslim Brothers*, 162–73. For a personal view on the Special Section, see Ramadan, *Al-Ikhwan al-Muslimun*, 37–53.

36. Mitchell, *Society of the Muslim Brothers*, 205–8; and Lia, *Society of the Muslim Brothers*, 180–81.

37. See Kelly, "The Revolt of 1936," 28–42; and Khalidi, *The Iron Cage*, 105–40.

38. Lia, *Society of the Muslim Brothers*, 251.

39. For more on supervision from Cairo, see Mayer, "Military Force of Islam," 103–6. For membership base, see Abu-Amr, *Islamic Fundamentalism*, 3.

40. Morris, *Righteous Victims*, 161–81.

41. Tessler, *History of the Israeli-Palestinian Conflict*, 259.

42. For more on the Palestinian rejection, see Khalidi, "Revisiting the UNGA Partition Resolution," 5–21.

43. For more on the 1948 war, see Morris, *Righteous Victims*; Shlaim, *The Iron Wall*; and Khalidi, *All That Remains*.

44. Milton-Edwards, *Islamic Politics in Palestine*, 40–41.

45. Mitchell, *Society of the Muslim Brothers*, 56; and Ramadan, *Al-Ikhwan al-Muslimun*, 74–75. For a personal account from volunteers, see Sabbagh, *Al-Taswib al-Amin li-ma Nasharahu ba'd al-Qadah al-Sabiqin 'an al-tanzim al-khaass lil-Ikhwaan al-Muslimiin*.

46. The brothers' involvement in 1948 remains a contested issue in terms of the number of fighters and the impact on the battlefield. See Abu-Amr, *Islamic Fundamentalism*, 2–3; Sabbagh, *Al-Taswib al-Amin*, 68; Ahmad, *Al-Nuqat fawqa al-huruf*, 187; Abu Bakr, *Hamas*, 11–18; and Ramadan, *Al-Ikhwan al-Muslimun*, 74–75.

47. For more on the refugees, see Morris, *The Birth of the Palestinian Refugee Problem, 1947–1949*.

For contemporary reporting, see Shay Hazkani, "Catastrophic Thinking: Did Ben-Gurion Try to Rewrite History?," *Haaretz*, May 16, 2013.

48. Abu-Amr, *Islamic Fundamentalism*, 4–9; and Milton-Edwards, *Islamic Politics*, 36–73.

49. Milton-Edwards, *Islamic Politics*, 55–64. For more on the brotherhood in Jordan, see Cohen, *Political Parties in the West Bank under the Jordanian Regime, 1949–1967*.

50. During the period 1949–52, the brotherhood had no legal presence in the Gaza Strip, and operated through an organization called Jami'yyat al-Tawhid. Filiu, *Gaza*, 82.

51. For more on Arafat, see Aburish, *Arafat*; Hart, *Arafat*; and Hussein Agha and Ahmad Samih Khalidi, "Yasser Arafat: Why He Still Matters," *The Guardian*, November 13, 2014.

52. Filiu, *Gaza*, 85; and Landau, *Arik*, 20–46. These tactics were also carried out in the West Bank and include the infamous Qibya massacre. See Morris, *Israel's Border Wars, 1949–1956*; and Khalidi and Caplan, "The 1953 Qibya Raid Revisited," 77–98.

53. For more on relations between Gaza, Egypt, and Israel during this time, see Filiu, *Gaza*, 73–106; *Journal of Palestine Studies*, "A Gaza Chronology, 1948–2008," 98–100; and Filiu, "The Twelve Wars on Gaza," 52–60. For more on the administrative reality in Gaza during this time, see Feldman, *Police Encounters*; and Feldman, *Governing Gaza*.

54. For more, see Milton-Edwards, *Islamic Politics*, 42–56; and Zollner, "Prison Talk."

55. Tamimi, *Hamas*, 36.

56. For more on the early phase of Palestinian nationalism, see Baumgarten, "The Three Faces/Phases of Palestinian Nationalism, 1948–2005," 25–37; and Sayigh, *Armed Struggle and the Search for State*, 25–143.

57. For more on Fatah, see Khalidi, *Iron Cage*, 140–82; Abu-Fakhr, "Al-Harakka al-Wataniyya al-Filastiniyyeh al-Mu'sira," 77–81; and Cobban, *The Palestinian Liberation Organisation*, 21–35.

58. Hroub, *Hamas*, 25–36. For a personal account of this resentment, see Gosheh, *The Red Minaret*, 83–115. Fatah is viewed by the Islamic parties as a "secular" nationalist movement, as it does not have an Islamization agenda or seek the creation of an Islamic state. Nonetheless, conferring the label of "secular" on Fatah is contested given that its leaders openly identify as pious Muslims. Similarly, while Hamas is often described as "Islamic," its leaders often protest that this appears to preclude the fact that it is also a nationalist movement. Author interviews, Hamas leaders, Gaza, 2015. For more on Fatah and Islam, see Johnson, *Islam and the Politics of Meaning*, 59–96.

59. See Chamberlin, *The Global Offensive*, 14–43; and Sayigh, *Armed Struggle and the Search for State*, 95–143.

60. For more on the founding of the PLO, see Sayigh, *Armed Struggle and the Search for State*; Shemesh, *The Palestinian Entity 1959–1974*; and Cobban, *Palestinian Liberation Organisation*.

61. For more on the 1967 war, see Segev, *1967*; Louis and Shlaim, *The 1967 Arab-Israeli War*; and Laron, *The Six Day War*. This defeat was arguably set in motion following the 1956 Suez crisis. See Khalidi, "Consequences of the Suez Crisis in the Arab World," 535–51, in Hourani, Khoury, and Wilson, *Modern Middle East*.

62. For more on martyrdom and self-sacrifice within the Palestinian national movement, see Khalili, *Heroes and Martyrs of Palestine*; and Pearlman, *Violence, Nonviolence, and the Palestinian National Movement*.

63. For more on the PLO's revolution, see Chamberlin, *Global Offensive*. For more on Palestinian politics during this time, see Said, *The Politics of Dispossession*; and Jamal, *The Palestinian National Movement*.

64. Sayigh, "Armed Struggle and State Formation," 17–32.

65. Fatah, 1967, in Sayigh, *Armed Struggle and the Search for State*, 212.

66. Ibid. For contemporary studies of Israel as a form of settler-colonialism, see Veracini, *Israel and Settler Society*; Norris, *Land of Progress*; Wolfe, "Settler Colonialism and the Elimination of the Native," 387–409; and Robinson, *Citizen Strangers*. For more on the competing impulses of Zionism's nationalist and colonialist hues, see Penslar, "Is Zionism a Colonial Movement?," 90–111, in Katz, Leff, and Mandel, *Colonialism and the Jews*.

67. Sayigh, *Armed Struggle and the Search for State*, 214.

68. Ibid., 667–70.

69. For more on US-PLO relations before and after the PLO's recalibration toward diplomatic engagement, see Yaqub, *Imperfect Strangers*; and Khalil, "The Radical Crescent."

70. *Journal of Palestine Studies*, "The Palestinian Resistance and Jordan."

71. See Khalidi, *Under Siege*; Brynen, *Sanctuary and Survival*; and Hirst, *Beware of Small States*.

72. Milton-Edwards, *Islamic Politics*, 73–75. For more on the Islamic resurgence, see Piscatori, *Islam in a World of Nation States*, 22–39; and Mitchell, *Society of the Muslim Brothers*, x–xi.

73. See Abu-Amr, *Islamic Fundamentalism*, 11–5; and Milton-Edwards, *Islamic Politics*, 73–144.

74. Abu-Amr, *Islamic Fundamentalism*, 10–22. For more on the Muslim Brotherhood in Gaza in 1967–87, see Khalil, *Harakat al-Ikhwan al-Muslimeen fi al-Qita': Gaza, 1967–1987* (unpublished).

75. The decision to establish the association was based on a successful precedent, the Islamic Society, which had been established in 1967. Tamimi, *Hamas*, 36–38.

76. Milton-Edwards, *Islamic Politics*, 105. For more on Israel's license approval, see Morris, *Righteous Victims*, 563–64; and Tamimi, *Hamas*, 36.

77. In particular, the Islamic movement was seen as a counterforce to communist Palestinian parties. Its clashes with such factions were supported by elements within the PLO. Filiu, "The Origins of Hamas," 63–65.

78. Ibid.; Milton-Edwards, *Islamic Politics*, 103–16; and Morris, *Righteous Victims*, 563. Examples included armed clashes when the Islamic Association attempted to take over the administration of the Palestinian Red Crescent and the Islamic University of Gaza.

79. Between 1967 and 1987, Muslim worshippers in Gaza more than doubled and mosque numbers expanded rapidly. The same occurred in the West Bank, but to a lower degree. See Morris, *Righteous Victims*, 564; and Abu-Amr, *Islamic Fundamentalism*, 15.

80. This was particularly the case given the Islamist clashes with other Palestinian factions rather than the occupation. See Shadid, "The Muslim Brotherhood Movement in the West Bank and Gaza," 658–82.

81. For more on Yassin's "conscious decision" to avoid resistance, see Filiu, "Origins of Hamas" 62–64.

82. Milton-Edwards, *Islamic Politics*, 116–23. For more on Islamic Jihad and other smaller groups, see Shallah, "Israel at a Crossroads," 52–62; Al-Jihad al-Islami, *Masirat al-Jihad al-Islami fi Filastin*; and Hatina, *Islam and Salvation in Palestine*.

83. For more on Islamic Jihad's relations with the Muslim Brotherhood and later Hamas, see Barghouti and Hajjar, "The Islamist Movements in the Occupied Territories," 9–12; and N'eirat, "Hamas wa 'Alaqatuha bi al-Haraka al-Islamiyya wa al-Jihad," 37–53.

84. Abu-Amr, "Hamas," 8–10.

85. Milton-Edwards, *Islamic Politics*, 121–23.

86. For more on Hezbollah, see Saad-Ghorayeb, *Hizbu'llah*; Norton, *Hezbollah*; Jaber, *Hezbollah*; Hamzeh, *In the Path of Hizbullah*; Thanassis, *A Privilege to Die*; and Noe, *Voice of Hezbollah*.

87. For the first phase of expansion between 1967 and 1977, see Gorenberg, *The Accidental Empire*. For later phases, see Gordon, *Israel's Occupation*; Weizman, *Hollow Land*; and Zertal and Eldar, *Lords of the Land*.

88. For more, see Tamimi, *Hamas*, 43–51.

89. Saleh, "Hamas 1987–2005," 56. In 1978, the Palestinian and Jordanian Muslim Brotherhood groups decided to join forces. For more on the relations between the two, see al-Gharaibah, *Jama'at al-Ikhwan al-Muslimin fi al-Urdun, 1946–1996*; and al-Emoush, *Mahatat fi Tarikh al-Ikhwan al-Muslimeen*.

90. Morris, *Righteous Victims*, 569. See also Baumgarten, "Three Faces," 37–38.

91. Tamimi, *Hamas*, 50.

92. Ibid., 43–50.

93. Engagement was made contingent on the PLO's acceptance of UN Resolution 242.

94. For more on the PLO's recalibration, see Muslih, *Toward Coexistence*; Rabie, *U.S.-PLO Dialogue*; Abbas, *Through Secret Channels*; Khalidi, "The Resolutions of the 19th Palestine National Council," 29–42; and Sela, "The PLO at Fifty," 269–333.

95. Tamimi, *Hamas*, 10.

96. For more on Hamas's early years, see Milton-Edwards and Farrell, *Hamas*, 52–68;

Chehab, *Inside Hamas*, 15–39; Ahmad, *From Religious Salvation to Political Transformation*, 13–51; Hroub, *Hamas*, 11–43; Jarbawi, "Hamas," 70–84; Said, *Hamas*; and Tamimi, *Hamas*, 1–52.

97. For more on Hamas's social infrastructure, see Roy, *Hamas and Civil Society in Gaza*; Jamal, *Palestinian National Movement*, 103–20; Mishal and Sela, *The Palestinian Hamas*, 13–27; Robinson, "Hamas as Social Movement," 112–139, in Wiktorowicz, *Islamic Activism*; and Jensen, *The Political Ideology of Hamas*, 47–141.

98. The charter was written and released in Gaza before the official sign-off from Hamas's consultative council. It was also distributed widely in Jordan and Kuwait. Saleh, "Hamas 1987–2005," 59.

99. Hamas's invocation of al-Qassam assumes a dedication to Palestine on al-Qassam's part that might be overstated. While al-Qassam was a central force in the early days of the Palestinian struggle, his "Palestinian-ness"—both his indigeneity and his commitment to Palestinian national-ism in the manner it later evolved—remains questionable. Nationalist parties also celebrate al-Qassam as the forefather of Palestinian nationalism. Sanagan, "Teacher, Preacher," 315–28; and Nafi, *Arabism, Islamism*, 191.

100. Synonymous with "Political Islam," the term "Islamism" is a relatively modern descrip-tion of Islamic parties with a political dimension. Denoeux, "The Forgotten Swamp," 61. Identify-ing Hamas as an Islamic movement rather than a Muslim movement highlights that it does not simply have a predominantly Muslim following but rather that it derives its legitimacy from Islam. For more on Islamism, see Roy, *The Failure of Political Islam*; Eickelman and Piscatori, *Muslim Politics*; and Osman, *Islamism*.

101. Roy, *Failure of Political Islam*, 26.

102. The term "Islamic state" has been put forward by modern Islamic thinkers to reconcile the Islamic polity with the model of sovereign European states. Ayoob, "Political Islam," 2. There is no single model of what an "Islamic state" looks like, as it will depend on the ideology of the Islamic party, the local political context, and legal framings. For more on Islam and states, see Es-posito and Voll, *Islam and Democracy*; and Piscatori, *Islam in a World of Nation States*.

103. The notion of peace inherent in this view is premised on an acceptance of all faiths, including Jews, to flourish freely in Palestine, as long as they do so under Islamic rule. Milton-Edwards, "Political Islam in Palestine in an Environment of Peace?," 220–22; and Sha'er, *Amaliyat al Salam al Filastiniyeh-al Israeliyeh*. On *dhimmis*, the historic status accorded to non-Muslims living under Muslim rule, see Cohen, *Under Crescent and Cross*.

104. For discussions on the anti-Semitic tropes used by Hamas and Hezbollah, see Achcar, *The Arabs and the Holocaust*, 169–281; Nüsse, "The Ideology of Hamas," 97–126, in Nettler, *Studies in Muslim-Jewish Relations*; and Saad-Ghorayeb, *Hizbu'llah*, 168–87. Saleh states that the anti-Semitic tone of the charter caused dissent within the movement and resulted in a drive to revise it after the Second Intifada. Saleh, "Hamas 1987–2005," 60.

105. For more on the *Protocols of the Elders of Zion* and anti-Judaism, see Katz, *From Prejudice to Destruction*; and Nirenberg, *Anti-Judaism*.

106. This differed from the way in which the PLO dealt with Zionism. See Gribetz, "When *The Zionist Idea* Came to Beirut," 243–66.

107. This Islamic endowment is referred to as *waqf*. In its charter, Hamas explains that this history allegedly goes back to the Muslim caliph Umar ibn al-Khatab refusing the division of the conquered lands in Iraq and Syria, choosing to endow them in perpetuity for future generations of Muslims.

108. Arafat's independence speech invoked UN Resolution 181.

109. For more, see Quandt, *Peace Process*, 245–90. Channels of diplomatic engagement with the United States had been ongoing since the 1970s, despite the PLO's designation as a terrorist organization by the United States. For more on the PLO's diplomatic softening, see Khalil, "Pax Americana," 1–42; and Sayigh, "Struggle within, Struggle without," 247–71.

110. For more on the use of violence as strategy, not tactics, see Freedman, "Terrorism as Strategy," 314–39.

111. See Taji-Farouki, "Islamists and the Threat of Jihad."

112. For more on the use of Islam as a popularizing tool, see Milton-Edwards, "The Concept

of Jihad and the Palestinian Islamic Movement," 48–53; and Butko, "Revelation or Revolution," 41–62. Recognizing that Hamas communicates through Islamic rhetoric makes no assessment of the piety of its leaders. For more on Hamas's Islamic reasoning, see Vericat, "The Internal Conversation of Hamas"; and Dunning, "Islam and Resistance," 284–305.

113. See Baumgarten, "Three Faces," 24–48.

114. For more on Hamas and the intifada, see Legrain, "The Islamic Movement and the Intifada," 175–90, in Nassar and Heacock, *Intifada*; and Milton-Edwards and Farrell, *Hamas*, 52–68.

115. Taraki, "The Islamic Resistance Movement in the Palestinian Uprising," 30.

116. Ahmad, *From Religious Salvation to Political Transformation*, 59–73. The united leadership issued thirty-one banners during 1988; Hamas issued thirty-three. In 1990, Arafat offered Hamas seats in the PLO in an effort to integrate the movement into the political establishment. Hamas refused to accept anything below 40 percent representation, a proposal that was rejected by Arafat.

117. Barghouti and Hajjar, "Islamist Movements," 10.

118. Mosques did play an early role in the uprising, acting as a point of communication and coordination. Abu-Amr, "Palestinian Uprising," 384–90.

119. Ibid., 394–95.

120. See King, *A Quiet Revolution*; and Pearlman, *Violence, Nonviolence*.

121. For more on this, see Rabinovich, *Yitzhak Rabin*, 155–58.

122. Morris, *Righteous Victims*, 580–94.

123. Milton-Edwards, *Islamic Politics*, 155–57.

124. Hamas was more prominent in its attacks than Islamic Jihad in 1988 and 1989, mostly due to its size. Morris, *Righteous Victims*, 577–79.

125. For more on this period, see Tamimi, *Hamas*, 52–71.

126. Ibid. For more on Hamas's structure, see al-Nuwati, *Hamas Min al-Dakhel*; and Sharbel, *Meshal*. For more on the Islamic movement in Israel, see Dakoor, "Al-Harakka al-Islamiyya fi al-Dakhel al-Filastini," 83–90.

127. Tamimi, *Hamas*, 52–71. For more on the history of the consultative council and *shura* in al-Banna's thinking, see Moussalli, *Moderate and Radical Islamic Fundamentalism*, 107–32.

128. For more on the state of the territories at the beginning of the 1990s, see Kuttab, "Current Developments and the Peace Process," 100–107.

129. For more insight into the Palestinian reaction to the Gulf War, see Husseini, "Palestinian Politics after the Gulf War," 99–108; and Piscatori "Religion and Realpolitik," 17–39.

130. Saleh, "Hamas 1987–2005," 64–65. For more on Hamas and Jordan, see Abu Rumman, *Jordanian Policy and the Hamas Challenge*.

131. For more on the genealogy of the name, see Ramadan, *Al-Ikhwan al-Muslimun*, 46–47.

132. In December 1992, Hamas captured Sergeant-Major Nissim Toledano and asked for the release of Sheikh Yassin from prison in return, the first ransom of its kind. See Milton-Edwards, *Islamic Politics*, 157–58. The West Bank became a prominent center for Hamas activities under the leadership of Imad Aqel, a senior military leader around Hebron who was assassinated by Israel in 1993. Mishal and Sela, *Palestinian Hamas*, 65–67. For more on Aqel, see Dawar, *Imad Akel*.

133. Hamas Political Office, "Bayan Regarding Israel's Request to Jordan," April 16, 1994, IPS. Hamas also targeted Palestinians accused of being collaborators. The success of Israel's targeting of Hamas's leaders was seen as the result of successful infiltration into Hamas. See Abu-Bakr, *Hamas*, 42–50.

134. For more on the deportation, see Ramadan, *'Ala masharef al-watan*; Tamimi, *Hamas*, 66–68; and Milton-Edwards, "Political Islam in Palestine," 203–5.

135. For more on the role of Islam in shaping such a worldview, see Kandil, *Inside the Brotherhood*. For more on the anticipated failure of secularism, see Zahhar and Hijazi, "Hamas," 81–88.

CHAPTER TWO

1. The term "peace process" is fraught. It is arguably the case that the architecture of the process was designed to prevent rather than achieve peace. See Khalidi, *Brokers of Deceit*; and Christison, *Perceptions of Palestine*.

2. The origin of suicide bombing arguably goes back to the Tamil Tigers, but Hamas ap-

pears to have adopted this tactic from Hezbollah during the Marj al-Zuhur deportation. Ayyash had recommended its use before then. See Reuter, *My Life Is a Weapon*, 100. For more on "suicide bombing contagion," see Bloom, *Dying to Kill*, 122–25.

3. Ali and Post, "The History and Evolution of Martyrdom in the Service of Defensive Jihad," 625–37; and Milton-Edwards, "Concept of Jihad," 48–53. For martyrdom in Christianity/Judaism, see Hatina, *Martyrdom in Modern Islam*, 19–36.

4. Volunteers do not fit a single profile. See Bloom, "Female Suicide Bombers," 94–102; Carr, *The Infernal Machine*, 256–67; and Hafez, *Manufacturing Human Bombs*, 44–50. Major operations tend to be carried out by well-educated mentally stable bombers. Benmelech and Berrebi, "Human Capital and the Productivity of Suicide Bombers," 223–24; Mesquita, "The Quality of Terror," 515–30; Gambetta and Hertog, *Engineers of Jihad*; and Krueger and Malecková, "Education, Poverty and Terrorism," 119–44. For more on volunteers, the Islamist appeal, and the glorification of terrorism, see Post, Sprinzak, and Denny, "The Terrorists in Their Own Words," 171–84; Reuter, *My Life Is a Weapon*, 52–115; and Zuhur, "A Hundred Osamas," 23–32.

5. Suicide operations are not inherent to a particular religion; they are the product of political, social, and economic contexts within which bombers find themselves. See Pape, "The Strategic Logic of Suicide Terrorism," 343–61; Reuter, *My Life Is a Weapon*, 19–32; and Asad, *On Suicide Bombing*. Desperation rather than Islam is often seen as the driver. Gambetta and Hertog, *Engineers of Jihad*, 34–85; Andoni, "Searching for Answers," 33–45; Hage, " 'Comes a Time We Are All Enthusiasm'," 65–89; and Sarraj, "On Violence and Resistance."

6. For more on the Oslo Accords and the subsequent decade of the peace process, see Eisenberg and Caplan, *Negotiating Arab-Israeli Peace*, 165–253; Abu-Amr, "The View from Palestine," 75–83; Kimmerling and Migdal, *The Palestinian People*, 315–98; and Shlaim, "The Oslo Accord," 24–40.

7. For more on the charter of the Palestinian Authority and self-administration, see Aruri and Carroll, "A New Palestinian Charter," 5–17.

8. Alpher, "Israel's Security Concerns in the Peace Process," 229–41. For more on the mechanisms of security coordination, see Cohen, "Society-Military Relations in a State-in-the-Making," 463–85; and Usher, "The Politics of Internal Security," 21–34.

9. A Palestinian police force was also established for civil order. Milton-Edwards, "Palestinian State-Building," 95–119. See also Brynjar, *A Police Force without a State*.

10. Hamas often used the Palestinian Authority and PLO interchangeably. Given that both institutions are dominated by the same Fatah leaders, they are often referred to collectively as "*al-sulta*," or "the authority."

11. For more on the impact of Arafat's return and this agreement on Gaza, see Roy, " 'The Seeds of Chaos, and of Night.' ," 85–98.

12. This hope was misplaced. Rashid Khalidi, "Beyond Abbas and Oslo," *New Yorker*, October 12, 2015.

13. This was formed in 1991 and called the Ten Resistance Organizations. Despite its charter excoriating the Communists and leftist groups, Hamas had no issues tactically lauding them when they confronted the hegemony of the PLO. See Yasin, *Hamas*, 71. For the impact of the Oslo Accords on Hamas, see Milton-Edwards, "Political Islam in Palestine," 206–10; and Kristianasen, "Challenge and Counterchallenge," 19–36.

14. In late 1993, polls indicated 73 percent favored negotiations and 60 percent supported the PLO. Only 17 percent supported Hamas. Milton-Edwards, *Islamic Politics*, 163.

15. Milton-Edwards and Farrell, *Hamas*, 123. Some Israeli analysts viewed this as an excuse. Author interview, Yoram Schweitzer, 2015.

16. In 1994 and 1995, the Palestinian Authority launched twelve arrest campaigns against Hamas with more than one thousand arrests. It also launched a system of highly controversial midnight trials and detention. See Hroub, "Harakat Hamas Bayn al-Sulta al-Filastiniyyeh wa Israel," 24–37.

17. Israel accused Hamas in Jordan of inciting the internal leadership. Hamas denied these accusations. "Bayan Regarding Israel's Request," April 16, 1994, IPS.

18. Targeted assassinations have changed how states deal with threats or perceived threats through notions of preemption and self-defense. Israel's use of targeted assassinations pioneered

this practice and transformed policies of "extrajudicial assassinations" to the more acceptable "targeted killings." For more, see Cassese, "Expert Opinion on Whether Israel's Targeted Killings of Palestinian Terrorists Is Consonant with International Humanitarian Law"; Melzer, *Targeted Killing in International Law*; Weizman, *Hollow Land*, 237–59; and Vlasic, "Assassination and Targeted Killing," 259–333.

19. Revenge animated many of Hamas's and Israel's attacks. See Brym and Araj, "Suicide Bombing as Strategy and Interaction," 1969–86; Araj, "From Religion to Revenge," 375, in LeVine and Shafir, *Struggle and Survival in Palestine/Israel*; and Jaeger and Paserman, "Israel, the Palestinian Factions and the Cycle of Violence," 45–49.

20. Abu-Amr, "View from Palestine," 79–80.

21. Hamas ultimately allowed members to run as independents. See el-Mabhouh, *Opposition in the Political Thought of Hamas Movement, 1994–2006*; and Baconi, "The Demise of Oslo and Hamas's Political Engagement," 503–20. For more on Hamas's thinking at the time, see Ashhab, *Hamas*; Ashhab, *Imarat Hamas*; and Badwan, *Pages from the History of the Palestinian Struggle*.

22. Andoni, "The Palestinian Elections," 5–16; and Khalidi, "The Palestinians' First Excursion into Democracy," 20–28.

23. See Kydd and Walter, "Sabotaging the Peace," 263–96; Karmon, "Hamas' Terrorism Strategy," 66–79; Berrebi and Klor, "On Terrorism and Electoral Outcomes," 899–925; and Stedman, "Spoiler Problems in Peace Processes," 7–16. Polls indicated support for suicide bombing was very low. In November 1998, 75 percent opposed suicide bombing; in 1999, support for suicide bombing was under 20 percent and support for Hamas below 12 percent. Bloom, *Dying to Kill*, 25.

24. For more insight into Meshal's life, see McGeough, *Kill Khalid*.

25. Jordan: "Press Release for Abdelraouf al-Rawabdeh," *Al-Ahram*, Cairo, February 10, 2000, IPS. Hamas: "Statement from Ibrahim Gosheh," *Al-Hayat*, March 30, 2000, IPS. For more on Hamas's regional relations during the 1990s, see Muslih, "The Foreign Policy of Hamas."

26. Between 1997 and 1999, five suicide attacks took place, none claimed by Hamas, compared to eleven claimed by Hamas or Hamas affiliates in the two years prior. Esposito, "The Al Aqsa Intifada," 104. For more on the shift toward social services, see Roy, "The Transformation of Islamic NGOs in Palestine," 24–26; and Roy, *Hamas and Civil Society in Gaza*, 70–97.

27. For more on Barak's tenure, see Ben-Ami, *Scars of War, Wounds of Peace*, 240–85.

28. Roy, "De-development Revisited," 64–82.

29. Maha Abdel Hadi, "After Entry into Final Status Negotiations," *FM*, March 22, 2000, 17.

30. "Dr Abdel Aziz Rantissi Talks to *FM*," *FM*, April 18, 2000, 17.

31. "The Zionists Are Our Enemies," *FM*, January 27, 2000, 20.

32. See Nizar Ramadan, "Hamas Cell in Taiba," *FM*, April 18, 2000, 14. Hamas's resources are often limited following increased security coordination between Israel and the Palestinian Authority. Karmon, "Hamas' Terrorism Strategy," 66–79; and Schweitzer, "Palestinian Istishhadia," 667–89.

33. The separation of Hamas's military and political wings is the subject of much debate. Most academic studies maintain that a distinction can be upheld in terms of finances, particularly for the social services.

34. Mo'men Bseiso, "Palestinian Figures Answer the Question," *FM*, May 17, 2000, 15.

35. For more on Hezbollah's resistance in south Lebanon, see Saad-Ghorayeb, *Hizbu'llah*, 112–34; and Norton, "Hizballah and the Israeli Withdrawal from Southern Lebanon," 22–35.

36. "The Arab Reality Supports Lebanon," *FM*, March 22, 2000, 3. For Hamas's memo on Lebanon, see "Lebanon Today, Palestine Tomorrow," *FM*, June 16, 2000, 45.

37. "Why Did the Syrian Track Mobilise?," *FM*, February 17, 2000, 3.

38. For more on Camp David, see Shlaim, *Iron Wall*, 674–710; Eisenberg and Caplan, *Negotiating Arab-Israeli Peace*, 222–52; and Robert Malley and Hussein Agha, "Camp David: The Tragedy of Errors," *New York Review of Books*, August 9, 2001. For Hamas's take, see "Camp David's Ominous Summit," *FM*, August 21, 2000, 19. For more on Hamas, see Hroub, "Khiyarat Hamas fi Thill al-Taswiyya al-Muqbilah," 31–43.

39. For more on Clinton's efforts, see Indyk, *Innocent Abroad*; Miller, *The Much Too Promised*

Land; Ross, *The Missing Peace*; and Ahmad Samih Khalidi, "Fantasies of a Middle East Envoy," *Cairo Review of Books* no. 16, 2016.

40. "Press release for Hamas's Spiritual Leader," *Al-Hayat*, July 18, 2000, IPS.

41. Malley and Agha, "Camp David."

42. "On the Doors of Jerusalem," *FM*, August 21, 2000, 25.

43. Arafat had cautioned Sharon against the visit, but Palestinian security forces and Israel's internal security said it would pass smoothly. Morris, *Righteous Victims*, 660. Hamas released a cautionary memo. "Hamas's Memo," *Palestine-Info*, September 27, 2000, IPS.

44. For more on the Second Intifada, see Shlaim, *Iron Wall*, 710–51; Rabinovich, *The Lingering Conflict*, 128–63; and Meital, *Peace in Tatters*. See Abu Amer's analysis of the Second Intifada as a turning point that leads to Israel's disengagement from Gaza. Abu Amer, *The Expulsion of the Occupation from the Gaza Strip*.

45. Roy, "Palestinian Society and Economy," 5–20.

46. Esposito, "Al Aqsa Intifada," 85. For more on Israel's early militarization, see Bregman, *Cursed Victory*, 217–68; and Byman, *A High Price*, 124–28.

47. Tamimi, *Hamas*, 199–200.

48. Arafat maintained ambiguity regarding his support of armed operations. Many in Israel and the United States suggested Arafat was the chief architect of the uprising. The Mitchell Report and Israel's Or Commission both concluded that Arafat did not mastermind the eruption of the intifada. Zoughbie, *Indecision Points*, 11. For more, see International Crisis Group, "Who Governs the West Bank?"

49. See Usher, "Fatah's Tanzim," 6–15.

50. Marwan Barghouti, Tanzim's leader, was seen as Arafat's right-hand man. For contemporary reporting on this, see Amos Harel and Avi Issacharoff, "Grilling of Top Palestinian Militant," *Haaretz*, April 20, 2012.

51. For more on Israel's insufficiently discriminate and politically flawed use of targeted assassinations and their role in escalating the violence of the Second Intifada, see Honig, "Explaining Israel's Misuse of Strategic Assassinations," 563–77; and Korn, "Israeli Press and the War against Terrorism," 209–34.

52. "Al-Aqsa Intifada," *FM*, November 23, 2000, 3. See also "Intifada of Arabs and Muslims," *FM*, November 23, 2000, 23–27.

53. For example, "Hamas Statement," *Palestine-Info*, October 3, 2000, IPS.

54. Analysis based on figures in Esposito, "Al Aqsa Intifada," 103–21.

55. "Al-Qassam Martyrs," *FM*, January 13, 2001, 12.

56. "Martyrs Create Earthquakes," *FM*, June 14, 2001, 9.

57. Badr al-Din Mohammad, "Sheikh Ahmad Yassin Talks to *FM*," *FM*, November 23, 2000, 16.

58. "Izz al-Din al-Qassam Statement," *Al-Qassam Bayan*, October 5, 2000, IPS.

59. Resisting the occupation is a valuable currency to develop political legitimacy, resulting in competitive bidding between factions. See Bloom, "Palestinian Suicide Bombing," 65–69; Bloom and Horgan, "Missing Their Mark," 579–614; Hoffman, *Inside Terrorism*, 147; and Hroub, "Hamas after Shaykh Yasin and Rantisi," 26.

60. Badr al-Din Mohammad, "Sheikh Ahmad Yassin talks to *FM*," *FM*, November 23, 2000, 16.

61. Ibrahim Gosheh, "Hamas between Two Intifadas," *FM*, December 19, 2000, 29.

62. Majed abu Deyak, "Al-Intifada, and Fatah," *FM*, December 19, 2000, 15.

63. Cardici, *Hamas*, 149.

64. Majed abu Deyak, "Al-Aqsa Intifada," *FM*, November 23, 2000, 9.

65. Maha Abdel Hadi, "Stones Crush Seven Lean Years," *FM*, November 23, 2000, 10.

66. Ibrahim Gosheh, "Hamas between Two Intifadas," *FM*, December 19, 2000, 28.

67. Badr al-Din Mohammad, "Differences with the PA," *FM*, February 21, 2001, 20.

68. For examples of earlier ceasefires, see "Bayan Clarifying Statements of the Head of the Political Office," April 21, 1994, IPS; and "Press Release for Sheikh Ahmad Yassin," *Al-Hayat*, July 24, 2000, IPS.

69. "Press Release for al Rantissi," *Al-Hayat*, January 15, 2001, IPS. For more on Hamas's strategy for the intifada, see "Press Release for Khaled Meshal," *Al-Hayat*, November 15, 2000, IPS.

70. "Dr Abd al-Aziz al-Rantissi," *FM*, April 18, 2000, 19; and "Meshal's Speech," *Palestine-Info*, April 24–25, 2001, IPS.

71. For example, "Intifada of Arabs and Muslims," *FM*, November 23, 2000, 23–27.

72. For example, Ra'afat Murra, "Arabic Islamic Conference," *FM*, March 17, 2001, 34–36.

73. "Victory Waves on the Horizon," *FM*, December 19, 2000, 3.

74. Kimmerling, *Politicide*; Ben-Ami, *Scars of War*, 285–312. For more on Ariel Sharon, see Landau, *Arik*.

75. Abu-Amr and Abdel Shafi, "Interviews from Gaza," 115–21; and Hass, "Israel's Closure Policy," 5–20.

76. For more on the Sabra and Shatila massacre, see al-Hout, *Sabra and Shatila*; Schiff and Ya'ari, *Israel's Lebanon War*; Sayigh, "Seven Day Horror"; and Seth Anziska, "A Preventable Massacre," *New York Times*, September 16, 2012.

77. For Hamas's reaction, see "The Zionists Have Had Their Say," *FM*, March 17, 2001, 3.

78. Esposito, "Al Aqsa Intifada," 87–88.

79. "Al-Qassam Succeed," *FM*, April 12, 2001, 12. This was similar to Hezbollah's own "Balance of Terror" in 1996. See Gambill, "The Balance of Terror," 51–66. For insight into the impact this had on Israelis, see Ari Shavit, "Letter from Jerusalem: No Man's Land—The Idea of a City Disappears," *New Yorker*, December 9, 2002, 56–60.

80. Hamas and Israel became engaged in a "violent dialogue." Ayyash, "Hamas and the Israeli State," 103–23. For more on Hamas's discourse, see Baconi, "Politicizing Resistance," 311–55.

81. Esposito, "Al Aqsa Intifada," 86.

82. "Determination of the Resistance," *FM*, June 14, 2001, 3.

83. For more on this period, see Bregman, *Cursed Victory*, 268–89; and Zoughbie, *Indecision Points*, 9–33.

84. "Security Coordination," *FM*, May 17, 2001, 18.

85. "Hamas Issues a Political Statement," *FM*, July 19, 2001, 18–19.

86. Ibid., 18.

87. "Determination of the Resistance," *FM*, June 14, 2001, 3.

88. For more on such justifications, see Ahmad, "Palestinian Resistance and 'Suicide Bombing,'" 87–103, in Bjorgo, *Root Causes of Terrorism*; and Bloom, *Dying to Kill*, 47.

89. Studies support the claim that movements such as Hamas effectively use suicide bombing strategically to force governments into territorial concessions. See Pape, "The Strategic Logic of Suicide Terrorism," 342–52; and Pape, *Dying to Win*, 44–45. For more on Hamas's approach to this "controlled violence," see Mishal and Sela, *Palestinian Hamas*, 49–83.

90. For example, see "Press Release for Dr Rantissi," *Al-Hayat*, June 4, 2001, IPS.

91. "Martyrs Create Earthquakes," *FM*, June, 14, 2001, 9.

92. "Al-Qassam Succeed," *FM*, April 12, 2001, 12.

93. "Press Release for al-Qassam," *Al-Safir*, June 4, 2001, IPS.

94. "Zionist Plans," *FM*, May 17, 2001, 30–31.

95. "Press Release for Sheikh Ahmad Yassin," *Al-Ahram*, August 20, 2001, IPS.

96. As hope for the success of peace negotiations plummets, public polls indicate rising support for suicide bombing. Bloom, "Palestinian Suicide Bombing," 65–69. Hamas quoted a Birzeit University poll which stated that support for the peace process had dropped to 17 percent and for suicide bombing had increased to 53 percent. "Al-Aqsa Intifada Proceeds," *FM*, March 17, 2001, 15. Polls taken in the summer of 2001 by the Palestinian Center for Policy and Survey Research (PCPSR) show that 92 percent supported armed confrontations against the Israeli army in occupied territories; 58 percent supported armed attacks against Israeli civilians inside Israel; and 70 percent believed that armed confrontation had achieved Palestinian rights in ways that negotiations could not. See Public Opinion Poll Two, July 2001.

97. See cover page, *FM*, May 17, 2001; and Badr al-Din Mohammad, "Ismail Haniyeh Speaks," *FM*, April 12, 2001, 11.

98. Mahmoud al-Ali, "Analysis of the Performance of Resistance," *FM*, October 17, 2002, 23–25.

99. Esposito, "Al Aqsa Intifada," 87–88. For more on Israel's counterterrorism processes during this time, see Pedahzur, *The Israeli Secret Services and the Struggle against Terrorism*, 111–28.

100. Zoughbie, *Indecision Points*, 17.

101. Esposito, "Al Aqsa Intifada," 88.

102. For Hamas's condemnation, see Majed abu Deyak, "After the Return of Security Coordination," *FM*, July 19, 2001, 12–13.

103. "Joint Release by al-Qassam and al-Aqsa," *Al-Nahar*, June 5, 2001, IPS. Yassin indicated no prior awareness of this ceasefire offer in an interview that afternoon. "Phone Interview with Yassin," *Al-Hayat*, June 5, 2001, IPS.

104. "Press Release for Ibrahim Gosheh," *Al-Hayat*, January 10, 2001, IPS.

105. The majority of Hamas's suicide bombings were in Israel proper. See Esposito, "Al Aqsa Intifada," 103–8.

106. For a record of Israel's assassinations, see Esposito, "Al Aqsa Intifada," 111–21.

107. The leaders were Jamal Mansour and Jamal Salim. Tamimi, *Hamas*, 201.

108. "Press Release for Dr Rantissi," *Al-Hayat*, August 1, 2001, IPS. Israel had attacked Hamas politicians before, but this did indicate a shift toward higher-profile members.

109. Tamimi, *Hamas*, 201.

110. See the movement's publications; for example, "The Blood of Martyrs," *FM*, August 17, 2001, 3. Hamas had already publicized the release of another ten bombers; see "A New Tenner," *FM*, August 17, 2001, 12–14.

111. For more on al-Qaeda and 9/11, see Wright, *The Looming Tower*.

112. For more on the Bush doctrine, see Bacevich, *America's War for the Greater Middle East*.

113. See Seitz, "Hamas Stands Down?," 4–7.

114. Congressional hearings in the United States to freeze Hamas's financial assets globally as part of the War on Terror demonstrated the conflation of al-Qaeda with Hamas. See U.S. Congress, House, Committee on Financial Services, "The Hamas Asset Freeze and Other Government Efforts to Stop Terrorist Funding," 108th Congress, September 24, 2003 (Washington: U.S. Government Printing Office, 2003).

115. For more on Israel's war against Arafat, see Tyler, *Fortress Israel*, 434–54.

116. Zoughbie, *Indecision Points*, 22–23.

117. Hamas military leader Mahmoud abu Hanud was assassinated on November 23, 2001.

118. Fatah and the Palestinian Authority were fracturing along generational and geographic lines. See Usher, "Facing Defeat," 21–40.

119. For Hamas's commentary, see Nizar Ramadan, "Campaign Launched by the PA," *FM*, January 18, 2002, 16–17.

120. Ibrahim Gosheh, "Glance on the Palestinian Situation," *FM*, May 17, 2001, 26.

121. "Press Release for Dr Rantissi," *Al-Safir*, December 3, 2001, IPS.

122. Esposito, "Al Aqsa Intifada," 89.

123. "Press Release for al-Qassam," *Al-Safir*, December 10, 2001, IPS. Minor operations persisted. "Al-Qassam Hit the Depth of the Zionist Entity," *FM*, February 13, 2002, 9–11.

124. "Press Release for al-Qassam," *Al-Safir*, December 10, 2001, IPS.

125. The impact security coordination had on Hamas's decision to halt fire can be seen in its publications; for example, "Fighters Who Have Tasted the Bitterness," *FM*, January 18, 2002, 12–13.

126. Earlier that year, Meshal had clearly indicated Hamas's view that it was going against the tide by stopping these operations. See "Press Release for Meshal," *Al-Hayat*, London, June 2, 2001, IPS. Hamas's operations were seen as retaliations against Israeli offensives and were generally popular, unlike Arafat's crackdown on the movement. Polls by the PCPSR after 9/11 showed that 92 percent of Palestinians supported armed attacks against soldiers and settlers; 58 percent supported attacks against civilians inside Israel; 98 percent viewed Israel's violence against Palestinians as acts of terror; and 87 percent did not see Palestinian violence against Israel in the same way. Public Opinion Poll Three, December 19–24, 2001.

127. "Press Release for al-Qassam," *Al-Safir*, December 10, 2001, IPS.

128. "Press Release for Hassan Youssef," *Al-Quds al-Arabi*, January 3, 2002, IPS.

129. "Press Release for al-Zahhar," *Al-Ahram*, January 2, 2002, IPS.

130. See commentary, "Hamas Stops the Spark of Civil War," *FM*, January 18, 2002, 3.

131. See James Bennet, "Seized Arms Would Have Vastly Extended Arafat Arsenal," *New York Times*, January 12, 2002.

132. "Pushing the Boat Out," *The Economist*, January 8, 2002.

133. Esposito, "Al Aqsa Intifada," 90. For more on reactions inside the administration, see Rice, *No Higher Honor*, 135–38; and Abrams, *Tested by Zion*, 20–27.

134. Esposito, "Al Aqsa Intifada," 90–91; and "Toppling Arafat?," *The Economist*, January 25, 2002.

135. See, for example, coverage in Ibrahim Said, "Zionist Campaign," *FM*, April 16, 2003, 16–18.

136. During that year its use of suicide operations peaked relative to subsequent years in the intifada, both in terms of the absolute number of operations it carried out and its contribution to operations executed by other factions. Figures for this analysis are obtained from Esposito, "Al Aqsa Intifada." For other reviews of Hamas's military performance, see al-Achcar and Bseiso, *Al-Amaliyat al-Askariyya li al-Muqawama al-Filastiniyyeh, 29/09/2000–31/12/2004*.

137. "Khaled Meshal: We Will Continue," *FM*, March 17, 2002, 34–35.

138. Ibid.

139. See, for instance, "Press Release from al-Qassam," *Al-Safir*, January 16, 2002, IPS.

140. Esposito, "Al Aqsa Intifada," 109–11.

141. For example, "Advancement of Operations," *FM*, March 17, 2002, 3.

142. See Badr al-Din Mohammad, "Qassams Hit the Depth of the Zionist Entity," *FM*, February 13, 2002, 10.

143. See Thomas L. Friedman, "An Intriguing Signal from the Saudi Crown Prince," *New York Times*, February 17, 2002.

144. "Yasser Arafat's Speech," *Al-Wafa*, February 20, 2002, IPS.

145. "Press Release for Hassan Youssef," *Al-Hayat*, March 21, 2002, IPS; and "Meshal Calls on Arab Leaders," *FM*, April 1, 2002, 6.

146. Private correspondence between Khaled Meshal and international mediators held with Professor Avi Shlaim at Oxford University.

147. "Press Release from Hamas," *Al-Hayat*, March 29, 2002, IPS.

148. Suzanne Goldenberg and Graham Usher, "Suicide Bombing Kills 16 Israelis in Hotel," *The Guardian*, March 28, 2002.

149. For more, see Hamzeh and May, *Operation Defensive Shield*; and Weizman, *Hollow Land*, 185–221.

150. The operations were heavily animated by Israel's incursions into refugee camps. See "Press Release from al-Qassam," *Al-Nahar*, April 11, 2002, IPS.

151. "Resistance Shakes the IDF's Base," *FM*, April 1, 2002, 11. Hamas also maintained its rocket fire. See Badr al-Din Mohammad, "Hamas's Rockets Terrify Zionists," *FM*, April 1, 2002, 18–19.

152. "Press Release for al-Rantissi," *Al-Nahar*, May 13, 2002, IPS.

153. "Press Release for Yassin," *Al-Nahar*, May 12, 2002, IPS.

154. This damaging back-and-forth by the Bush administration was the result of a domestic tug-of-war between the White House, seen as "pro-Israel," and the State Department, seen as "pro-Palestinian." For more insight into this, see Abrams, *Tested by Zion*, 19–98.

155. This effectively entailed regime change in Palestine. See Zoughbie, *Indecision Points*, 33–55.

156. "Yasser Arafat's Speech," *Al-Wafa*, May 15, 2002, IPS.

157. "Americanized Reform," *FM*, June 29, 2002, 3.

158. For example, "Press Conference with Musa abu Marzouq," *Palestine-Info*, May 2002, IPS. Targeted assassinations were ongoing, resulting in the killing of Muhammad al-Taher, Hamas's bomb-maker in Nablus, on June 30. See "Statement from al-Qassam," *Al-Safir*, July 7, 2002, IPS.

159. Cardici, *Hamas*, 154. For more on the Cairo Dialogues, see Kumaraswamy, "The Cairo Dialogue and the Palestinian Power Struggle," 43–59. For Hamas's perspective on the ceasefire talks, see "Press Release for Ismail Haniyeh," *Al-Safir*, July 25, 2002, IPS. For articles on Salah Shehadeh, see Badr al-Din Mohammad, "Al-Sheikh *al-Mujahid*," *FM*, March 22, 2000, 21–23.

160. "Press Release for Arafat," *Al-Wafa*, July 23, 2002, IPS.

161. "Press Release for Sheikh Ahmad Yassin," *Al-Hayat*, July 25, 2002. For al-Qassam's response, see "Press Release from al-Qassam," *Al-Safir*, July 25, 2002, IPS.

162. For Hamas's take, see Badr al-Din Mohammad, "Yassin Speaks to *FM*," *FM*, September 1, 2002, 20–23. For pressure on Arafat, see *Journal of Palestine Studies*, "Washington Watch," 90–98.

163. Clandestine and indirect American attempts were reportedly taking place during this time to seek a ceasefire. Although reportedly promising, these were upended when Israel, in full knowledge of these discussions, arrested a Hamas official in Ramallah on September 9, undermining the exchange. Roy, *Hamas and Civil Society in Gaza*, 196–97.

164. For more on tension within Fatah, see Usher, "Letter from the Occupied Territories," 42–56.

165. "Slumbering *Fitna*," *FM*, November 23, 2002, 3.

166. This was from its attack in the Ariel settlement on October 27 to its Haifa bombing on March 5, 2003. Nonsuicide operations persisted, although they were relatively restrained.

167. "Hamas in Its Fifteenth Year," *FM*, January 18, 2003, 3.

168. "Press Release for Sheikh Ahmad Yassin," *Al-Nahar*, January 24, 2003, IPS.

169. "Press Release for Ismail Haniyeh," *Al-Nahar*, January 21, 2003, IPS.

170. Fatah's request: "Press Conference for Abu Mazen," *Al-Hayat*, February 24, 2003, IPS. Hamas's take: "Press Release for Sheikh Ahmad Yassin," *Al-Nahar*, January 24, 2003, IPS.

171. "Press Release for Ismail Haniyeh," *Al-Nahar*, January 21, 2003, IPS. See also "Press Release for Abdel Aziz Rantissi," *Al-Nahar*, February 15, 2003, IPS.

172. "To the Trenches," *The Economist*, February 1, 2003. For more on the Cairo Proposal and Dialogues, see Ra'fat Murra, "Palestinian Dialogue in Cairo," *FM*, February 21, 2003, 18–19.

173. "Press Release from the PLO," *Al-Wafa*, May 3, 2003, IPS.

174. See "Israel's Roadmap Reservations," *Haaretz*, May 27, 2003.

175. See Bregman, *Cursed Victory*, 268–89. Sharon's acceptance of the roadmap was met with intense opposition and seen as a shift in his long-held rejection of Palestinian statehood. See Landau, *Arik*, 440–61.

176. "Press Release for al-Aqsa Leader," *Al-Hayat*, May 30, 2003, IPS.

177. Example Badr al-Din Mohammad, "Dialogue with Hamas and Fatah," *FM*, February 21, 2003, 20–21. Hamas referred to the roadmap as a "*fitna* project," one aimed at precipitating a civil war. "Warrior's Rest," *FM*, August 22, 2003, 3.

178. "Press Conference for Abbas," *Al-Nahar*, June 10, 2003, IPS. Ceasefire discussions were effective because Abbas had asked Marwan Barghouti to intervene from his jail cell with Hamas.

179. "The Major Sins in Abbas's Speech," *FM*, July 19, 2003, 3.

180. For more on Hamas's view on the American invasion of Iraq, see "Baghdad Fell," *FM*, May 24, 2003, 3.

181. For more on this, see *Majallat al-Dirasat al-Filastiniyyeh*, "Kharitat al-Tariq," 16–20.

182. "Press Release for Sheikh Ahmad Yassin," *Al-Safir*, May 29, 2003, IPS.

183. Cardici, *Hamas*, 155–59.

184. "Press Conference for Abbas," *Al-Nahar*, June 10, 2003, IPS.

185. "Press Release from al-Qassam," *Al-Safir*, June 11, 2003, IPS; and "Press Release for Rantissi," *Al-Nahar*, June 15, 2003, IPS.

186. "Hamas and Islamic Jihad Announcement," *Al-Nahar*, June 30, 2003. Hamas indicated at that time a sense that there was popular support for a ceasefire.

187. "Press Release for Abbas," *Al-Hayat*, July 22, 2003, IPS. Bush supported Sharon's policies. "Sharon Gets His Way, Again," *The Economist*, August 2, 2003.

188. "The Enemy Exceeded the Limits," *FM*, September 19, 2003, 20–21.

189. "Press Release from Fatah," *Al-Wafa*, July 3, 2003, IPS.

190. "Warrior's Rest," *FM*, August 22, 2003, 3.

191. "Roadmap Which Lost the Way," *FM*, June 27, 2003, 3.

192. "Press Release for Ismail Haniyeh," *Al-Hayat*, August 12, 2003, IPS. Islamic Jihad also refused disarming. See "Joint *Bayan*," *Al-Safir*, July 14, 2003, IPS.

193. "Press Release for Abbas," *Al-Hayat*, July 22, 2003, IPS.

194. See, for instance, "Joint Statement," *Al-Safir*, July 14, 2003, IPS.

195. "Press Release for Ahmad Yassin," *Yedioth Ahronoth*, July 10, 2003, IPS.

196. Amos Harel, "The Mohammed Sidr Operation," *Haaretz*, August 15, 2003.

197. Islamic Jihad initially claimed the attack as retaliation. But later reports obtained by Israel confirmed the attacker was a member of Hamas and that this attack was "an isolated incident." Cardici, *Hamas*, 155–59.

198. Ibid.

199. "Abu Shanab's Assassination," *FM*, September 19, 2003, 3. See also "Why Did Sharon Want to Destroy the *Hudna*?," *FM*, September 19, 2003, 18–19. For more on Abu Shanab's assassination, see "Why Abu Shanab?," *FM*, September 19, 2003, 12.

200. "PA Release," *Al-Wafa*, Ramallah, August 21, 2003, IPS.

201. "Press Release from Fatah," *Al-Wafa*, September 6, 2003, IPS.

202. For Hamas's retrospective on the ceasefire and its collapse, see "Abu Marzouq Speaks to *FM*," *FM*, September 19, 2003, 20.

203. Author interview, Yoram Schweitzer, 2015.

204. Hamas's focus on the occupied territories rather than Israel was conveyed to British and American interlocutors in private meetings. See Perry, *Talking to Terrorists*, 130.

205. "Resistance Factions Cannot Negotiate," *FM*, January 17, 2004, 3.

CHAPTER THREE

1. Quotes in this paragraph are obtained from "Address to the Fourth Herzliya Conference," *Israel's Ministry of Foreign Affairs*, December 18, 2003.

2. Weizman, *Hollow Land*, 161–85. For more on the wall, see Dolphin, *The West Bank Wall*; and Sorkin, *Against the Wall*.

3. Members of the Bush administration accepted this unilateral grab, despite alleged pushback. See Abrams, *Tested by Zion*, 78–79.

4. "The Legal Consequences of the Construction of a Wall in the Occupied Palestinian Territory," *International Court of Justice*, July 9, 2004.

5. Avi Shlaim, "How Israel Brought Gaza to the Brink of a Humanitarian Catastrophe," *The Guardian*, January 7, 2009.

6. Figures according to B'Tselem, Israeli Information Center for Human Rights in the Occupied Territories.

7. Roy, "Praying with Their Eyes Closed," 66.

8. Sharon's disengagement plan entailed an ideological shift within Likud to accept the partition of the land of Eretz Yisrael as a prerequisite to maintaining Israel's Jewish majority. See Rynhold and Waxman, "Ideological Change and Israel's Disengagement from Gaza," 11–37.

9. See Pelham, "Gaza's Tunnel Phenomenon," 7; Roy, "Reconceptualizing the Israeli-Palestinian Conflict, 73–75; and Ghanem, "Unilateral Withdrawal," 35–41.

10. This was a continuation of Sharon's policies from the beginning of the Second Intifada. See Kimmerling, *Politicide*, 155–81.

11. Ari Shavit, "Top PM Aide: Gaza Plan Aims to Freeze the Peace Process," *Haaretz*, October 6, 2004.

12. See "Joint Press Conference between Bush and Sharon," *U.S. Department of State*, April 14, 2004, IPS.

13. Maha Abdel Hadi, "Plan to Withdraw," *FM*, March 25, 2004, 12–13.

14. Ra'fat Murra, "Osama Hamdan Talks to *FM*," *FM*, March 25, 2004, 16.

15. For example, Ibrahim al-Sa'id, "Snowball," *FM*, March 25, 2004, 14.

16. "Press Release for Rantissi," *Al-Noor*, March 1, 2004, IPS.

17. Esposito, "Al Aqsa Intifada," 94.

18. The attack was carried out by Reem al-Riyashi. This was celebrated in Hamas's publica-

tions as a sign of progressive values—that Hamas allowed women fighters on the frontline. See "Press Release for Yassin," *Al-Intiqad*, January 23, 2004, IPS. For more on female suicide bombers, see Bloom, "Female Suicide Bombers," 94–102.

19. See "Al-Qassam Intensified Fire," *FM*, March 25, 2004, 19.

20. See Yassir Ali, "Milestones in the Intifada's Progress," *FM*, October 17, 2002, 20–22.

21. Esposito, "Al Aqsa Intifada," 94–95. For Hamas's take, see "Hamas's Future," *FM*, May 19, 2004, 41.

22. "Guardian of Palestinian National Unity," *FM*, April 9, 2004, 9.

23. "Press Conference for Meshal," *Al-Hayat*, March 23, 2004, IPS.

24. A poll after Yassin's assassination indicated that for the first time Hamas was the most popular movement among Palestinians. Hroub, "Hamas after Shaykh Yasin and Rantisi," 21.

25. See "Press Release from PA," *Al-Wafa*, March 22, 2004, IPS; and "Press Release from the Arab League," *Arab League*, March 22, 2004, IPS.

26. For example, "Guardian of Palestinian National Unity," *FM*, April 9, 2004, 9.

27. "Press Release for George Bush," *U.S. Department of State*, March 23, 2004, IPS.

28. For instance, "Press Release from the Former European Envoy," *Al-Hayat*, March 23, 2004, IPS. For more on Israel's decision, see Tyler, *Fortress Israel*, 454–63.

29. "Press Release for Zahhar," *Al-Noor*, April 1, 2004, IPS.

30. "Guardian of Palestinian National Unity," *FM*, April 9, 2004, 9.

31. This sentiment was seen throughout Hamas's publications and was even commented on by academics such as Ziad abu Amr. For instance, see Yasser abu Hein, "Expert on Islamic Movements," *FM*, April 5, 2005, 36–38.

32. "Press Release for Rantissi," *Al-Quds*, March 24, 2004, IPS.

33. "Press Release for Meshal," *Assafir*, March 28, 2004, IPS. See also "Implications of Yassin's Assassination," *FM*, April 9, 2004, 18.

34. "Press Release for Meshal," *Assafir*, March 28, 2004, IPS.

35. Author interviews with Hamas's leaders elucidated that its strategy was based on both fixed principles (*thawabet*) and variables (*motaghayerat*). The movement's pragmatic nature is seen in its ability to adapt the variables, for instance in restraining armed struggle or accepting engagement in the political establishment, as long as its fixed principles are left unharmed. For more, see Haniyeh's explanation in "Press Release for Ismail Haniyeh," *Palestine-info*, June 10, 2004, IPS.

36. See, for instance, Ala'a Hassan, "Hamas and the Pillars of Resistance," *FM*, January 2, 2004, 26–27.

37. "Speech for Khaled Meshal," *Al-Quds*, March 24, 2004, IPS; and "Press Conference for al-Zahhar," *Al-Noor*, April 2004, IPS.

38. "Press Release for Rantissi," *Assafir*, March 28, 2004, IPS. Groups such as al-Qaeda also promised revenge, raising fears that Hamas would be tempted to attack abroad. The movement's leaders stressed that their operations were limited to Israel and promised never to attack abroad or to target American (versus Israeli) interests. See "Press Conference for Meshal," *Al-Hayat*, April 22, 2004, IPS.

39. During March–April, Israel carried out thirty assassination operations, five of which targeted Hamas members. The share of Hamas combatants out of the total combatants killed by Israel was roughly a third. Fatah combatants were about half. Hamas's view of itself as the principal recipient of Israel's offensive lay in the fact that a higher proportion of its top leadership was targeted, compared to other factions.

40. See, for example, this from a later date: Mohammad Nazzal, "Martyrdom of Hamas's Leadership," *FM*, April 5, 2005, 18–19.

41. Saleh, "Hamas 1987–2005," 80.

42. Publications outlined that Hamas had shifted to local fundraising, raising insufficient funds for major operations. Mohammad Badr al-Din, "Months after the Assassinations," *FM*, July 7, 2004, 18.

43. Hroub, "Hamas after Shaykh Yasin and Rantisi," 21.

44. For Hamas's take on these rumors, see "Press Conference for Mahmoud al-Zahhar," *Al-Noor*, April 2004, IPS.

45. "Press Release for Rantissi," *Al-Sharq al-Awsat*, March 31, 2004, IPS.

46. For example, Yasser al-Za'atrah, "Abd al-Aziz al-Rantissi," *FM*, May 19, 2004, 4–5.

47. "Military Wings Promise a Thunderous Response," *FM*, May 19, 2004, 26–27.

48. This was expressed in reflections posted at a later date. See "Palestinian Resistance Overcomes," *FM*, October 1, 2004, 28.

49. "Press Conference for Meshal," *Al-Hayat*, April 22, 2004, IPS.

50. See "Hamas's Future," *FM*, May 19, 2004, 41.

51. For more, see Halevi, "Self-Government, Democracy and Mismanagement under the Palestinian Authority," 35–48.

52. Maha Abdel Hadi, "Reading the Domestic Political Environment," *FM*, May 19, 2004, 46–48. For more on Hamas's gradual politicization, see Berti, *Armed Political Organizations*, 79–130; Gunning, "Peace with Hamas?," 233–55.

53. "Press Release for Yasser Arafat," *Al-Ayyam*, April 5, 2004, IPS.

54. Alliances also took on an internal/external dimension. Hamas's external bureau negotiated with figures from Fatah's external leadership. Many Fatah members abroad continued to advocate resistance and reject Oslo, and were close to Hamas's vision. See "Bayan Issued by the Palestinian Resistance," *Palestine-info*, June 21, 2004, IPS. For more on domestic, versus US-led, reform, see Ghanem and Khayed, "In the Shadow of the al-Aqsa Intifada," 31–50.

55. Drafts of agreements between the national and Islamic factions were published in early April. "Draft Agreement," *Al-Quds*, April 4, 2004, IPS.

56. "Hamas's Future," *FM*, May 19, 2004, 40.

57. Esposito, "Al Aqsa Intifada," 95. The Israeli incursion was condemned by the UN Security Council, with an American abstention, as well as by international human rights organizations. See Human Rights Watch, "Razing Rafah."

58. For some examples of international responses, see "World's Response to Israeli Carnage in Rafah," *Al-Jazeera*, May 30, 2004.

59. To strengthen Sharon's domestic hand, Bush sent Sharon a letter affirming that future borders for Israel would have to take into account the realities on the ground created through Israel's settlement enterprise. See "Letter from President Bush to Prime Minister Sharon," *White House*, April 14, 2004. For more, see Abrams, *Tested by Zion*, 107–9.

60. See, for example, "Leaving Gaza, Maybe, and to an Uncertain Future," *The Economist*, October 16, 2004. And at a later date: "Can the Dangerous Vacuum in Gaza Be Peacefully Filled," *The Economist*, May 22, 2005.

61. "Press Conference for Ismail Haniyeh," *Palestine-info*, June 10, 2004, IPS.

62. See "Press Conference with Mahmoud Zahhar," *Al-Quds*, August 11, 2004, IPS. A memo entitled "Document on the Approach to the Anticipated Withdrawal from the Gaza Strip" had been circulated among Hamas's leadership. Roy, *Hamas and Civil Society in Gaza*, 200.

63. "Interview with Khaled Meshal," *Palestine-info*, July 28, 2004, IPS.

64. This plan was put forward following a major workshop in Gaza which included members of the National and Islamic Factions (NIF), professional businesspersons, union representatives, and public figures. "Palestinian Security Plan," *Al-Ahram*, March 13, 2004, IPS.

65. "Interview with Khaled Meshal," *Palestine-info*, July 28, 2004, IPS.

66. "Press Conference for Meshal," *Al-Hayat*, April 22, 2004, IPS.

67. Ra'fat Murra, "Osama Hamdan Talks to *FM*," *FM*, March 25, 2004, 17. See also "Khaled Meshal," *FM*, September 7, 2005, 9.

68. See, for instance, reflections on this at a later date: Maha Abdel Hadi, "Hamas Politically and Militarily," *FM*, April 5, 2005, 24–25.

69. "Press Release for Nazzal," *Palestine-info*, August 16, 2004, IPS.

70. "Press Release for Ismail Haniyeh," *Palestine-info*, June 10, 2004, IPS.

71. "Position of Palestinian Factions," *FM*, February 26, 2004, 32.

72. "Discussion with Zahhar," *Palestine-info*, June 15, 2004.

73. See, for instance, "Press Release for Nazzal," *Al-Hayat*, September 18, 2004, IPS.

74. "Discussion with Zahhar," *Palestine-info*, June 15, 2004, IPS.

75. Ibid.

76. Author interview, Wassim Afifeh, 2015.

77. See Mohammad Nazzal, "For a Deeper Understanding," *FM*, October 1, 2004, 2–3.

78. Hamas reported on Israelis discovering at least twelve tunnels between Egypt and Gaza in late 2004 and early 2005 that were used for smuggling rockets. Hamas estimated on average it was firing thirty rockets a day into Israel in early 2005. "Press Conference with Mahmoud Zahhar," *Al-Quds*, August 11, 2004, IPS.

79. These included "Operation Active Shield" and "Operation to Widen the North Gaza Buffer Zone" as well as "Operation Full Court Press," which targeted al-Aqsa Brigades specifically.

80. Esposito, "Al Aqsa Intifada," 96–97.

81. "After One Old Man Has Gone," *The Economist*, November 13, 2004.

82. For more, see Ghanem, *Palestinian Politics after Arafat*; Legrain, "The Successions of Yasir Arafat," 5–20; and Agha and Khalidi, "Yasser Arafat," *The Guardian*, November 13, 2014.

83. See, for example, Maha Abdel Hadi, "PA's Political Orientation," *FM*, December 3, 2004, 26–27.

84. "Press Release for Haniyeh," *Al-Quds*, November 25, 2004, IPS.

85. "Press Release for the Head of the PNC," *Al-Quds*, November 21, 2004, IPS.

86. "Israel's Position Following Arafat's Death," *Tawasul*, November 10, 2004, IPS.

87. For more on Hamas's platform, see its online platform at http://islah.ps/new2/?news=128.

88. For more on the candidates, see "Stages of Municipal Elections," *FM*, March 10, 2005, 23.

89. Ibid.

90. For example, see Samira al-Halaiga et al., "Municipalities Which Hamas Won," *FM*, March 10, 2005, 26–27.

91. Saleh, "Hamas 1987–2005," 85.

92. Muhammad al-Halaiga, "Hebron Municipal Elections," *FM*, January 11, 2005, 28–31.

93. "First Phase of Municipal Elections," *FM*, March 10, 2005, 22.

94. Yasser abu Hein, "Palestinian Presidential Elections," *FM*, January 11, 2005, 30–31.

95. Author interview, Ahmad Yousef, 2015.

96. These allegations built on the fact that other popular candidates were convinced not to run, including Marwan Barghouti, a popular Palestinian leader.

97. Usher, "Letter from the Occupied Territories," 42–56. Abbas's trip to Gaza soon after reinforced Hamas's conviction that it had become a force that could no longer be ignored. See Hamas's take: Ra'fat Murra, "Deployment of Palestinian Security," *FM*, February 8, 2005, 20.

98. "Doc. 2: Nazzal's Speech, January 7, 2005," al-Watha'iq al-Filastiniyyah [hereafter *WF*], 19–22.

99. "Bayan from Mahmoud Abbas," *Wafa*, November 17, 2004, IPS.

100. See, for example, "Unified Palestinian Leadership," *FM*, December 3, 2004, 22–23.

101. "Press Release for Zahhar," *Dar al-Hayat*, December 5, 2004, IPS.

102. "Peace in Our Time?," *The Economist*, February 12, 2005.

103. "Palestinian Factions Refuse," *FM*, February 8, 2005, 22.

104. See, for instance, "Interview with Jibril Rajoub," *Al-Quds*, November 21, 2004, IPS.

105. "Khaled Meshal Talks to *Filastin al-Muslima*," *FM*, March 10, 2005, 41.

106. For instance, Beit Lahiya in Gaza. Ibrahim al-Sa'id, "Panic in the Zionist Entity," *FM*, March 10, 2005, 30–31.

107. "Khaled Meshal Talks to *Filastin al-Muslima*," *FM*, March 10, 2005, 41.

108. Ibid., 42.

109. Ibid., 43.

110. Maha Abdel Hadi, "Hamas Politically and Militarily," *FM*, April 5, 2005, 24.

111. "Musa abu Marzouq," *FM*, October 1, 2004, 54.

112. "Press Release for Rantissi," *Al-Noor*, March 1, 2004, IPS.

113. Maha Abdel Hadi, "Between Dialogue, *Tahdi'ah*," *FM*, May 6, 2005, 36–37.

114. Ra'fat Murra, "Deployment of Palestinian Security," *FM*, February 8, 2005, 20.

115. See, for instance, Dahlan's comments on Israeli television in which he insisted the Pal-

estinian Authority's forces would prevent any factions from taking advantage of the withdrawal to threaten Israel's security. "Doc. 36: Dahlan's Declaration, April 18, 2005," *WF*, 82.

116. Maha Abdel Hadi, "Between Dialogue, *Tahdi'ah*," *FM*, May 6, 2005, 36–37.

117. "Khaled Meshal Talks to *FM*," *FM*, March 10, 2005, 40.

118. Ibid.

119. "Doc. 29: Closing Statement, March 17, 2005," *WF*, 69. See text of the Palestinian Cairo Declaration, July 4, 2007, https://web.archive.org/web/20070704163620/http://www.pal estine-pmc.com/details.asp?cat=2&id=849.

120. Ibid. Abbas's advisors noted an understanding that it would be difficult to implement this agreement, but still it offered a way to contain Hamas in the political establishment. Author interview, Rafiq Husseini, 2015.

121. Samira al-Halaiga, "Hamas's Political Leader," *FM*, June 3, 2005, 42–43.

122. For Hamas's coverage, see Maha Abdel Hadi, "Between Dialogue, *Tahdi'ah*," *FM*, May 6, 2005, 36–37.

123. Arguments were put forward that the Palestinian political establishment could be changed from the inside out. Author interview, Bassem Naim, 2015.

124. Cardici, *Hamas*, 175–78.

125. For a comparison between Hamas's 1996 and 2005 decision, see El-Mabhouh, *Opposition in the Political Thought of Hamas*, 106–47; and Baconi, "Demise of Oslo," 503–20.

126. Zahhar elaborated in an interview ahead of the 2006 legislative elections that Hamas had needed to wait until the failure of the Oslo Accords would be demonstrated before running. See Badr al-Din Mohammad, "Hamas's Political Vision," *FM*, December 5, 2005, 39.

127. "Doc. 28: Hamas Release, March 12, 2005," *WF*, 68–69.

128. "Hamas's Participation," *FM*, May 6, 2005, 3.

129. Ibid.

130. Cover page, *FM*, March 10, 2005. See also "Khaled Meshal Talks to *FM*," *FM*, March 10, 2005, 40–43.

131. Mohammad Nazzal, "Martyrdom of Hamas's Leaders," *FM*, April 5, 2005, 18–19.

132. See Raed N'eirat, "The Palestinian Political Map," *FM*, January 5, 2006, 14–15.

133. Ibid. See also Maha Abdel Hadi, "Between Dialogue, *Tahdif'ah*," *FM*, May 6, 2005, 36–37. For more on how the legislature was built post-Oslo, see Brown, *Palestinian Politics after the Oslo Accords*, 94–138; and Abu-Amr, "The Palestinian Legislative Council," 90–97.

134. Author interviews with Change and Reform Parliamentarians indicated that several ran in the hope Hamas would achieve cleaner governance, 2015.

135. Badr al-Din Mohammad, "Hamas's Political Vision," *FM*, December 5, 2005, 39.

136. "Doc. 21: Text of Khaled Meshal's Speech, February 23, 2005," *WF*, 52.

137. "Meshal's Interview," *Al-Hayat*, December 17, 2005, IPS.

138. Samir al-Halaiga, "Sheikh Hassan Youssef," *FM*, January 11, 2005, 22.

139. Ibrahim al-Sa'id, "Panic in the Zionist Entity," *FM*, March 10, 2005, 30–31.

140. Saleh, "Hamas 1987–2005," 85.

141. For more on these elections, see Tamimi, *Hamas*, 211–17; and Milton-Edwards and Far-rell, *Hamas*, 243–44. For Hamas's coverage, see Yasser abu Hein, "Second Round," *FM*, May 6, 2005, 24–25.

142. "Municipal Elections," *FM*, February 8, 2015, 15.

143. Author interview, Ahmad Yousef, 2015.

144. Graham Usher, "Year of Elections: Fact and Fiction," *Middle East Report* no. 238 (2006): 2–11; and John B. Judis, "Clueless in Gaza: New Evidence That Bush Undermined a Two-State Solution," *New Republic*, February 19, 2013.

145. Hamas candidates believed that the United States was hoping their democratic engage-ment would enable Israel to contain the movement. Author interview, Bassem Naim, 2015. See also Zoughbie, *Indecision Points*, 89.

146. "A Dangerous Double Delay," *The Economist*, June 11, 2005.

147. "Attack of PA Forces," *FM*, August 9, 2005, 12–13.

148. "Doc. 88: Press Release from Hamas, November 23, 2005," *WF*, 173–74. Hamas sus-

pected Abbas had been given instructions by the Bush administration to delay elections. "Abu Mazen to Palestinians," *FM*, July 7, 2005, 3.

149. For Hamas's take regarding disarmament, see "Hamas Responds," *FM*, June 3, 2005, 13.

150. See "Doc. 49: Interview with Osama Hamdan, July 20, 2005," *WF*, 106.

151. Maha Abdel Hadi, "Palestinian *Tahdi'ah*," *FM*, July 7, 2005, 24–25.

152. Israel's focus on Tulkarem was because this was the home of many Islamic Jihad fighters.

153. Hamas's sequence of events is highlighted in "The Authority Inflames *Fitna*," *FM*, August 9, 2005, 16.

154. "Practices of the 'Eradicating Current,'" *FM*, October 31, 2005, 28–30.

155. "Abbas's PA Removes the Mask," *FM*, August 9, 2005, 3.

156. "Attack of PA Forces," *FM*, August 9, 2005, 12–13.

157. "PA Characters Enflaming *Fitna*," *FM*, August 9, 2005, 16.

158. "PA Opens Fire," *FM*, August 9, 2005, 10–11.

159. "Military Wings Call for the Resignation," *FM*, August 9, 2005, 15–16.

160. "Al-Qassam Celebrates," *FM*, August 9, 2005, 19. Hamas's leaders reaffirmed these red lines and their dedication to Palestinian unity. See "PA Characters Enflaming *Fitna*," *FM*, August 9, 2005, 16.

161. "Al-Qassam Celebrates," *FM*, August 9, 2005, 19.

162. See Meshal's take on it at a later date: "Meshal's Interview," *Al-Ghad*, August 15, 2005, IPS.

163. "No Command and Less Control," *The Economist*, September 17, 2005.

164. For coverage, see "Defeat in Gaza," *FM*, September 7, 2005, 3.

165. "Khaled Meshal," *FM*, September 7, 2005, 9.

166. Dajani, "Lessons from the Gaza Disengagement," 13–17. Certain figures within the Palestinian Authority, albeit less so Abbas, were also opposed to a bilateral coordinated disengagement as they feared that might implicitly legitimize the occupation.

167. "Doc. 53: Hamas's Political Statement, August 13, 2005," *WF*, 112–13.

168. "Political Communiqué for Hamas," *FM*, September 7, 2005, 10. The desire for Palestinians to run their own affairs was made clear early on with Hamas's resolute rejection of proposals that Arab forces, rather than the Palestinian Authority's forces, would safeguard security in Gaza after the withdrawal. "No to the Arab Security," *FM*, July 7, 2004, IPS, 3.

169. "Political Communiqué for Hamas," *FM*, September 7, 2005, 10.

170. See Makovsky, *Engagement through Disengagement*. For a contemporary discussion, see Avishay Ben Sasson-Gordis, "The Strategic Balance of Israel's Gaza Withdrawal (2005–2016)," Molad: Center for Renewal of Israeli Democracy, August 22, 2016.

171. The head of the Quartet charged with these discussions, James Wolfensohn, offers a full account of the marginalization of his efforts in his memoirs. See Wolfensohn, *A Global Life*, 399–441.

172. Pelham, "Gaza's Tunnel Phenomenon," 8.

173. Author interviews with Israeli security analysts noted that before Hamas's victory, Israeli policy toward Gaza had already taken the form of tightly controlling borders to pressure Hamas, 2015. See also Roy, *Failing Peace*, 311–22; Roy, "Praying with Their Eyes Closed," 64–75; and Tawil-Souri, "Digital Occupation," 27–43. The agreement was portrayed by international mediators as a way to provide Palestinians with control over Gaza's borders for the first time since 1967. Hamas accused the Palestinian Authority of accepting this agreement to protect post-Oslo vested interests. "The Rafah Agreement," *FM*, December 5, 2005, 3.

174. See Gisha, "Disengaged Occupiers."

175. Zoughbie, *Indecision Points*, 91.

176. See "Resistance Leaders," *FM*, September 7, 2005, 40–41. Publications noted the challenges for maintaining resistance from the West Bank lay in the difficulty of smuggling weapons there. See Samir Khweireh, "Resistance Moves to Activate West Bank," *FM*, October 8, 2005, 34–35.

177. For Hamas's refusal to disarm, see Yasser abu Hein, "Hamas Leader Sheikh Said Sayyam," *FM*, September 7, 2005, 36.

178. "Meshal's Interview," *Al-Ghad*, August 15, 2005, IPS.

179. "Doc. 70: Interview with Meshal, September 26, 2005," *WF*, 137–38.

180. Saleh, "Hamas 1987–2005," 85. Hamas's support base had a greater proportion of women than men and a broader segment of low-income voters. For polls, see Hilal, "Hamas's Rise as Charted in the Polls, 1994–2005," 6–19.

181. Badr al-Din Mohammad, "Hamas's Political Vision," *FM*, December 5, 2005, 39.

182. "The *Hudna* Has Ended," *FM*, February 13, 2006, 21. Hamas's restraint was most evident following Israel's ostensibly accidental assassination of Fawzi abu al-Karei, a top Qassam leader who, by chance, happened to be in the same car as al-Aqsa leader Hassan al-Mahdoun, Israel's primary target. "Wrong Guy to Kill," *The Economist*, November 5, 2005.

183. Arnon Regular, "Hamas's Zahar," *Haaretz*, October 26, 2005.

184. "The Hamas Conundrum," *The Economist*, November 12, 2005. This comment was made within the larger context of Hamas discussing the possibility of negotiating directly with Israel if the latter withdrew from the West Bank. The spokesman (Mahmoud Ghazzal) denied making these statements upon receiving criticism from his constituency. See Abu-Bakr, *Hamas*, 91.

185. "*Tahdi'ah* Has Outlived Its Use," *FM*, January 5, 2006, 3.

186. See, for instance, Osama Abd al-Hakim, "Why Did the US Oppose?," *FM*, February 13, 2006, 36–37.

187. See Nizar Ramadan, "Hamas between Arrests," *FM*, December 5, 2005, 28.

188. Ibid., 28–29.

189. "Doc. 113: Meshal's Speech, December 30, 2005," *WF*, 222–27.

190. See "Doc. 13: Interview with Mahmoud al-Ramhi, January 19, 2006," *WF*, 43–44. For more on Hamas's manifesto, see Raed N'eirat, "The Palestinian Political Map," *FM*, January 5, 2006, 15.

191. "Doc. 13: Interview with Mahmoud al-Ramhi, January 19, 2006," *WF*, 43–44.

192. Close to nine thousand prisoners, many of them political, were detained indefinitely by Israel at that point.

193. "Key Points of the Electoral Programs," *FM*, January 5, 2006, 12. In its manifesto, Hamas spoke of ensuring conservative social values and reforming the judicial system so that it is based on the legal body of *shari'a* law. See "Hamas's Electoral Manifesto," *FM*, February 13, 2006, 28–29.

194. Hamas published thought-pieces from academics who elaborated on this approach. See Raed N'eirat, "The Palestinian Political Map," *FM*, January 5, 2006, 14–15.

195. Zoughbie, *Indecision Points*, 91. At this point the United States was convinced that Fatah would win the elections. See Judis, "Clueless in Gaza."

196. Osama Abd al-Hakim, "Why Did the US Oppose?," *FM*, February 13, 2006, 36–37.

197. The United States issued no similar reservations about Fatah's participation in the elections, despite the fact that al-Aqsa Brigades is a Fatah-affiliated militia, one that was active during the Second Intifada. This was ostensibly because its arms could be integrated into the Palestinian security forces, as Fatah monopolized the Palestinian Authority. The United States also allowed Hezbollah to participate in the Lebanese elections in the 1990s, adopting similar positions of strengthening the incumbent to undermine Hezbollah's political rise. See Pelletiere, "Hamas and Hizbollah," 20.

198. "Doc. 10: Press Release for Hamas, January 12, 2006," *WF*, 41.

199. "Doc. 13: Interview with Mahmoud al-Ramhi, January 19, 2006," *WF*, 46–47. By comparison, Islamic Jihad boycotted these elections because they saw them as being a product of the Oslo Accords. See "Doc. 16: Islamic Jihad Bayan, January 23, 2006," *WF*, 50–51.

200. The list was split across generational lines. For Hamas's take, see "Fatah's Institutional Crisis," *FM*, January 5, 2006, 24–25. For Fatah's campaign, see "Doc. 3: Sha'ath Meets Fatah's Candidates, January 2, 2006," *WF*, 32.

201. See Mo'men Bseiso, "Abu Mazen's Reform," *FM*, January 5, 2006, 40–41.

202. "Highest Election Count," *FM*, January 5, 2006, 16.

203. Mo'men Bseiso, "Palestinian Election Campaigns," *FM*, February 13, 2006, 26–27.

204. Claims were that under Abbas's tenure more than 80 percent of all security incidents involved the official security forces. Mo'men Bseiso, "Abu Mazen's Reform," *FM*, January 5, 2006, 40–41.

205. Ibrahim abu al-Haija', "The Main Questions," *FM,* January 5, 2006, 38–39.

206. Fatah launched its election from Yasser Arafat's shrine. "Doc. 6: Fatah Launches Its Campaign, January 3, 2006," *WF,* 36–37.

207. "Doc. 4: Hamas's Bayan, January 3, 2006," *WF,* 33–34.

208. Ibid.

209. Ibid. Hamas's focus on women and Christians was aimed at alleviating concerns directed from Fatah members. Hamas protested the imposition of "Western feminism," however, and argued that it had achieved equality within the movement. The veil was seen as a natural reflection of the conservative society in which Hamas exists. Author interview, Change and Reform Parliamentarian, 2015. For more on Hamas's take on the veil, see Samir Khweireh, "Priorities Are Now to End Corruption," *FM,* May 8, 2006, 47. For more on Western feminism versus indigenous female empowerment, see Massad, *Islam in Liberalism,* 110–213; and Ababneh, "The Palestinian Women's Movement versus Hamas," 35–53.

210. "Fatah's Electoral Manifesto," *FM,* February 13, 2006, 30.

211. The popular vote was closer, with Hamas winning by only a slim margin. For Hamas's reactions, see "Hamas in Front of the PA's Difficult Test," *FM,* February 13, 2006, 3. Some members claimed this victory was unsurprising given internal polls within the movement. Author interview, Ahmad Yousef, 2015.

212. Ra'fat Murra, "After the Elections," *FM,* February 13, 2006, 45.

213. "Doc. 37: Interview with Abu Marzouq, February 2, 2006," *WF,* 88.

214. "Hamas in Front of the PA's Difficult Test," *FM,* February 13, 2006, 3.

CHAPTER FOUR

Chapter title: Quote by Benjamin Netanyahu referring to American and Israeli efforts to deal with Hamas after its election victory. Wiki-leaks cable, E.O. 12958: DECL: 04/17/2017, Ref TEL AVIV 1086.

1. Abrams, *Tested by Zion,* 163.

2. Zoughbie, *Indecision Points,* 104–12. For insight into the American administration's thinking, see Abrams, *Tested by Zion,* 163–77; and Rice, *No Higher Honor,* 413–20.

3. Zoughbie, *Indecision Points,* 104–12; and Roy, *Hamas and Civil Society,* 39–50. For investigative reporting on this, see John B. Judis, "Clueless in Gaza: New Evidence That Bush Undermined a Two-State Solution," *New Republic,* February 19, 2013; David Rose, "The Gaza Bombshell," *Vanity Fair,* April 2008; and Alastair Crooke, "Elliott Abram's Uncivil War," *Conflicts Forum,* January 7, 2007.

4. Rice, *No Higher Honor,* 417–18.

5. Author interviews with Change and Reform ministers suggested that many understood their victory to have been in large measure propelled by the inefficiency and corruption of Fatah and left-wing factions. For more on the elections and the postvictory reality for dealing with Hamas, see Usher, "The Democratic Resistance," 20–36; International Crisis Group, "Enter Hamas"; and Zweiri, "The Hamas Victory," 675–87.

6. Abbas believed that rather than isolation Hamas should be left to fail on its own accord. Author interview, Rafiq Husseini, 2015.

7. Zoughbie, *Indecision Points,* 104–12. See also Perry, *Talking to Terrorists,* 135.

8. Zoughbie, *Indecision Points,* 104. For more on this, see Milton-Edwards and Farrell, *Hamas,* 282–86.

9. Steven Erlanger, "US and Israelis Are Said to Talk of Hamas Ouster," *New York Times,* February 14, 2006; and "A Tricky Jigsaw," *The Economist,* February 25, 2006. For Hamas's reporting, see Osama Abdel Hakim, "The Future of American-Palestinian Relations," *FM,* March 6, 2006, 42–43.

10. Zoughbie, *Indecision Points,* 100.

11. Erlanger, "US and Israelis Are Said to Talk of Hamas Ouster."

12. Quartet Statement, January 26, 2006. For more, see Elgindy, "The Middle East Quartet," 2–34. These were referred to as the "Abrams conditions" among Palestinian leaders. Author interview, Rafiq Husseini, 2015.

13. See Ibrahim al-Said, "The Occupation Puts a Plan," *FM*, March 6, 2006, 26–27.

14. Erlanger, "US and Israelis Are Said to Talk of Hamas Ouster."

15. Author interview, Taher al-Nounou, 2015. For more on Hamas's early reaction, see Rabbani, "Khaled Meshal Yashrah Mawqef Hamas min al-Qadayya al-Rahina," 58–81; and Shobaki, *Political Change from Perspective of Islamist Movements*.

16. This was in reference to Algeria's civil war after the electoral success of the Islamic Salvation Front.

17. Author interview, Bassem Naim, 2015.

18. "Reactions to Hamas's Victory," *FM*, February 13, 2006, 46.

19. "Doc. 41: Meshal's Speech, February 7, 2006," *WF*, 98.

20. "Doc. 44: Interview with Osama Hamdan, February 13, 2006," *WF*, 109.

21. Zoughbie, *Indecision Points*, 100–101. This underscored concerns by Egypt and other officials in the United States that Hamas would seek funding from Iran if Western funds were cut off. Milton-Edwards and Farrell, *Hamas*, 266. For more on Hamas's relations with Russia, see Abi 'Isa, *The Russian Stance towards Hams: 2006–2010*.

22. Hamas referred to the French Republic and the US Congress as potential benchmarks. "Why Did the Palestinian Factions Refuse?," *FM*, April 12, 2006, 39.

23. "Doc. 47: Interview with Said Sayyam, February 16, 2006," *WF*, 114–17.

24. "Hamas Prepares for Office," *The Economist*, February 1, 2006.

25. Author interview, Rafiq Husseini, 2015.

26. "Doc. 62: Interview with Yasser Abed Rabbo, March 11, 2006," *WF*, 151.

27. For an example of Hamas's coverage, see "The Godfather," *FM*, September 6, 2004, 32–34.

28. "Doc. 24: Release for Dahlan, January 27, 2006," *WF*, 58.

29. Author interview, Issam Da'lis, 2015.

30. "A High Wire Act," *The Economist*, June 3, 2006. For more on these measures, see Itani, *Conflict of Authorities between Fatah and Hamas in Managing the Palestinian Authority, 2006–2007*; and Usher, "Year of Elections," 2–11. For Hamas's reporting, see Ibrahim Hamami, "One Year of Abbas's Presidency," *FM*, January 5, 2006, 36–38.

31. "Conspiracy to Defeat Hamas," *FM*, March 6, 2006, 3.

32. "Doc. 47: Interview with Said Sayyam, February 16, 2006," *WF*, 116.

33. Maha Abdel Hadi, "Hamas's Government Launches," *FM*, April 12, 2006, 36–37.

34. Hamas's leaders believed Abbas hardened his stance because of American pressure. Author interview, Ahmad Yousef, 2015.

35. As recounted in "Doc. 123: Interview with Nabil Sha'ath, April 24, 2006," *WF*, 279–283.

36. "Doc. 58: Interview with Abbas, March 2–3, 2006," *WF*, 138–39.

37. "Doc. 123: Interview with Nabil Sha'ath, April 24, 2006," *WF*, 280.

38. For Hamas's take on PLO reform, see "Doc. 124: Interview with Musa abu Marzouq, April 25, 2006," *WF*, 283–91. See also Kjorlien, "Hamas," 4–7.

39. Author interview, Bassem Naim, 2015.

40. Maha Abdel Hadi, "Hamas's Government Launches," *FM*, April 12, 2006, 36–37.

41. Ibid.

42. This generated several accusations of unilateralism. "Doc. 102: Interview with Marwan Barghouti, April 15, 2006," *WF*, 228–29.

43. Author interviews confirmed that there was little institutional separation.

44. "Doc. 77: Haniyeh's Speech, March 28, 2006," *WF*, 174–84.

45. "Doc 69: The Political Program, March 20, 2006," *WF*, 160.

46. Ibid, 161.

47. "Doc. 77: Haniyeh's Speech, March 28, 2006," *WF*, 174–84.

48. "Doc. 71: Text of Letter, March 23, 2006," *WF*, 164–65.

49. Ibid.

50. "Doc. 58: Interview with Abbas, March 2–3, 2006," *WF*, 134–35.

51. "Doc. 41: Meshal's Speech, February 7, 2006," *WF*, 96–97.

52. Ibid.

53. See, for example, "Doc. 30: Letter from Hamas, January 30, 2006," *WF*, 63.

54. "Doc. 37: Interview with Abu Marzouq, February 2, 2006," *WF*, 88.

55. "Doc. 41: Meshal's Speech, February 7, 2006," *WF*, 96–97.

56. Repeated in several interviews between the author and Hamas leaders and Change and Reform parliamentarians in Gaza and the West Bank.

57. Publications discussed how foreign aid was never aimed at producing a functioning economy but was rather a cover to sustain the diplomatic process. Nasser Atyani, "International Aid," *FM*, March 6, 2006, 30. See Sayigh, "Inducing a Failed State in Palestine," 7–40; Turner and Shweiki, *Decolonizing Palestinian Political Economy*; and Hever, *The Political Economy of Israel's Occupation*.

58. "The New Government's Proposed Economic Agenda," *FM*, March 6, 2006, 34.

59. "Doc. 13: Interview with Mahmoud al-Ramhi, January 19, 2006," *WF*, 43–44.

60. "Doc. 44: Interview with Osama Hamdan, February 13, 2006," *WF*, 106.

61. Author interview, Osama Hamdan, 2011.

62. Milton-Edwards and Farrell, *Hamas*, 270–71.

63. Zoughbie, *Indecision Points*, 106–8.

64. Conal Urquhart, "Gaza on Brink of Implosion as Aid Cut-Off Starts to Bite," *The Guardian*, April 16, 2006.

65. "Doc. 94: Press Release for Hamas, April 10, 2006," *WF*, 219.

66. For more on Hamas's response to international efforts to isolate it, see Cardici, *Hamas*, 199–226.

67. "Doc. 88: Text of Letter, April 4, 2006," *WF*, 206–8.

68. Maha Abdel Hadi, "The Political and Economic Siege," *FM*, May 8, 2006, 34.

69. "Doc. 44: Interview with Osama Hamdan, February 13, 2006," *WF*, 111.

70. "Doc. 53: Interview with Meshal, February 22, 2006," *WF*, 122–26. For more on efforts to circumvent the "iron-wall," see Ibrahim al-Sa'id, "Occupation Implements an 'Iron Wall,'" *FM*, March 6, 2006, 27.

71. Author interview, Issam Da'lis, 2015.

72. The presidents of Egypt and Turkey refused to meet Hamas's leaders, sending delegates instead. Hamas viewed this as being the result of behind-the-scenes pressure. "Doc. 67: Interview with Mohammad Nazzal, March 16, 2006," *WF*, 156. Soon after Hamas's cabinet was formed, Jordan accused Hamas of smuggling weapons through its territories, a version of events that Hamas entirely denied. See "Doc. 150: Hamas Release, May 15, 2006," *WF*, 385.

73. "Doc. 188: Interview with Meshal, June 13, 2006," *WF*, 479.

74. Ibid., 478.

75. See "Doc 69: The Political Program, March 20, 2006," *WF*, 160.

76. "Doc. 53: Interview with Meshal, February 22, 2006," *WF*, 122–26.

77. "Shut Your Eyes and Think of Palestine," *The Economist*, May 6, 2006.

78. Author interview, Hamas leaders, Gaza, 2015.

79. For more on Israel's refusal to engage with Hamas's political efforts, see Eldar, *Lehakir et Hamas*. For English reviews of Eldar's book, see Jose Vericat, "Representing Hamas (Part 1)," *Jadaliyya*, June 10, 2014; and Jose Vericat, "Representing Hamas (Part 2)," *Jadaliyya*, June 13, 2014.

80. See, for example, Abrams's reasoning on the Bush letter to Sharon, in Abrams, *Tested by Zion*, 107–9.

81. For more, see Shenhav, *Beyond the Two State*; Azoulay and Ophir, *The One-State Condition*; and Gordon, *Israel's Occupation*.

82. "Doc. 188: Interview with Meshal, June 13, 2006," *WF*, 479.

83. "Doc. 53: Interview with Meshal, February 22, 2006," *WF*, 122–26.

84. Ibid., 125.

85. For Islamic Jihad's reasoning, see "Doc. 120: Interview with Ramadan al Shalah, April 22, 2006," *WF*, 271.

86. Adnan abu Amer, "A New Zionist Hypothesis," *FM*, November 6, 2006, 16–17.

87. "Isolated, in Its Violent Corner," *The Economist*, April 22, 2006.

88. Author interviews, Hamas leaders, Gaza, 2015. The movement was open about receiv-

ing Iranian funding but stressed that it made "Palestinian decisions." "Doc. 61: TV Interview with Khaled Meshal, March 6, 2006," *WF*, 150.

89. Ibid.

90. "Hamas and the Arabs," *The Economist*, May 20, 2006.

91. Milton-Edwards and Farrell, *Hamas*, 284–85.

92. Instead of working with Zahhar as foreign minister, Abbas appointed Farouk Kaddoumi in Tunisia as the PLO representative in international affairs. This led to significant turf wars between Kaddoumi and Zahhar.

93. See, for example, "Doc. 124: Interview with Abu Marzouq, April 25, 2006," *WF*, 283–91.

94. "Doc. 121: Press Release for Hamas, April 24, 2006," *WF*, 273–75.

95. "Doc. 239: Interview with Nazzal, September 16, 2006," *WF*, 606.

96. Author interview, Issam Da'lis, 2015.

97. Meshal's speech demonstrated the fault line between Hamas's movement and government. Hamas's cabinet issued a statement noting that it was not responsible for Meshal's rhetoric and directed Palestinians to abide by the statements of the cabinet's official spokesperson. Haniyeh did, however, stress that he backed the crux of Meshal's sentiments and condemned Fatah's refusal to relinquish power. "Doc. 121: Press Release for Hamas, April 24, 2006," *WF*, 273–75.

98. "Doc. 115: Meshal's Speech," *WF*, April 21, 2006, 261.

99. Ibid.

100. Ibrahim abu al Haija', "Policies, Decisions," *FM*, June 5, 2006: 23.

101. Saad and Ibhais, *Security Developments in the Palestinian Authority, 2006–2007*; and Saleh, *Conflict of Wills between Fatah and Hamas and Other Relevant Parties 2006–2007*.

102. "How Was It Formed?," *FM*, February 5, 2007, 18. For more on the Executive Force, see Milton-Edwards, "Order without Law?," 663–76.

103. Author interviews, Hamas leaders, Gaza, 2015.

104. "Doc. 253: Haniyeh's Speech, October 2, 2006," *WF*, 629–30.

105. Hamas claimed the Death Squads had been formed by Dahlan to assassinate its members and create chaos. "Doc. 239: Interview with Nazzal, September 16, 2006," *WF*, 607. In contrast, Hamas's publications stressed that relief was noticeable in Gaza after the establishment of the executive force. "Support Unit," *FM*, June 5, 2006, 15.

106. Author interviews with Change and Reform elected ministers gave examples of armed forces attacking their workplaces and offices. Hamas's publications suggested these forces were colluding with Israel.

107. "A High Wire Act," *The Economist*, June 3, 2006.

108. "Seeking a Bypass as the Money Runs Out," *The Economist*, May 13, 2006.

109. "Hamas and the Arabs," *The Economist*, May 20, 2006.

110. Maha Abdel Hadi, "Economic and Political Siege," *FM*, May 8, 2006, 34–36.

111. "Doc. 188: Interview with Meshal, June 13, 2006," *WF*, 469–82. For Hamas's coverage of this situation see Samir Khweireh, "Crisis of Money," *FM*, June 5, 2006, 16–18.

112. "Doc. 188: Interview with Meshal, June 13, 2006," *WF*, 469–82.

113. This reportedly included $100 million from Iran, $50 million from Qatar, $92 million from Saudi Arabia, $20 million from the United Arab Emirates, $20 million from Bahrain, and $4.5 million from Syria.

114. "The Rafah Border," *FM*, June 5, 2006, 3. Publications reported that Olmert's policies depended heavily on Arab support from Cairo, Amman, and Rabat, which were working to remind their people of the consequences of an Islamist ascendance to power. Ibrahim al-Sa'id, "Efforts to Defeat Haniyeh's Government," *FM*, June 5, 2006, 24–25.

115. "Doc. 132: Interview with Government Spokesman, May 1, 2006," *WF*, 305–306.

116. "Doc. 167: Abbas's Speech, May 26, 2006," *WF*, 432.

117. A follow-up was issued by prisoners from six other detention centers stating that they opposed the prisoners' document and deferred to Hamas's leadership. See "Doc. 169: Clarification Letter, May 26, 2006," *WF*, 436–37.

118. "Doc. 182: Letter from Haniyeh, June 9, 2006," *WF*, 461–64.

119. "Doc. 176: Interview with Khaled Meshal, June 1, 2006," *WF*, 446.

120. "Abbas's Gamble," *The Economist*, June 7, 2006.

121. For Hamas's reporting, see Maha Abdel Hadi, "Palestinian-Palestinian Dialogue," *FM*, July 6, 2006, 30–31.

122. Within Hamas, hardliners were allegedly uncomfortable with Haniyeh's rising influence. Author interview, Rafiq Husseini, 2015.

123. Zoughbie, *Indecision Points*, 111. For Hamas's reaction, see "Doc. 196: Hamas Release, June 17, 2006," *WF*, 503–4.

124. Hamas's external leadership had at various times asserted control over the military wing given that it provides it with funding and resources. Author interviews, Hamas leaders, 2015. Hamas's leadership denied that the external office was involved in planning this directly. See Milton-Edwards and Farrell, *Hamas*, 273–74; and al-Nuwati, *Hamas min al-Dhakel*, 157–59.

125. Tamimi, *Hamas*, 239. See also "Doc. 199: Resistance Is the Strategic Choice, June 20, 2006," *WF*, 506–8.

126. "Doc. 205: Modified National Dialogue Statement, June 28, 2006," *WF*, 514–17.

127. Hamas's leadership claimed the United States informed it behind the scenes that this agreement was unacceptable. Hamas's leadership suggested that the ball would be in Abbas's court to push back on American pressure. "Doc. 236: Interview with Osama Hamdan, September 5, 2006," *WF*, 599.

128. For more on the Shalit operation and eventual swap, see Saleh, *Shalit*; Baskin, *The Negotiator*; and Ronen Bergman, "The Human Swap," *New York Times Magazine*, November 13, 2011, 34–39.

129. "Doc. 204: Hamas Release, June 28, 2006," *WF*, 513–14.

130. "Resistance in Palestine and Lebanon," *FM*, September 8, 2006, 3.

131. See Brown, "The Road out of Gaza," 5–7.

132. Zoughbie, *Indecision Points*, 112; and "A Deadly Cycle," *The Economist*, July 8, 2006. For Hamas's take, see "The Occupation Continues," *FM*, September 8, 2006, 34. "Assassination of the PA," *FM*, September 8, 2006, 4.

133. Norton, *Hezbollah*, 135–43; Byman, *High Price*, 251–67; Tyler, *Fortress Israel*, 463–77. For more on this solidarity, see Khalili, " 'Standing with My Brother,' " 276–303.

134. Cover page, *FM*, August 8, 2006.

135. For more, see Harel and Issacharoff, *34 Days*; Hirst, *Beware of Small States*; and Hovespian, *The War on Lebanon*.

136. Khalidi, "Al-Tahuwwlat al-Istratigiyyeh al-Askariyyeh wa al-Amniyyeh al-Israeliyyeh," 4; and Khalidi, "The Dahiya Doctrine, Proportionality, and War Crimes," 5–13.

137. Zoughbie, *Indecision Points*, 113. See also Sobelman, "Learning to Deter."

138. "From 'Scattered Hope,' " *FM*, August 8, 2006, 3.

139. "Assassination of the PA," *FM*, September 8, 2006, 4.

140. "Reactions to the Kidnapping," *FM*, September 8, 2006, 38–39. For more, see Abdaljawwad, *The Fake Democracy and the Usurped Immunity.*

141. "Gangster Ways," *FM*, September 8, 2006: 36–37.

142. See Giyath Nasser, "Comprehensive Discussion with Musa abu Marzouq," *FM*, September 6, 2006, 43.

143. Ibrahim abu al-Haija, "Arresting Democracy," *FM*, September 8, 2006, 40–41.

144. "Doc. 199: Resistance Is the Strategic Choice, June 20, 2006," *WF*, 506–8.

145. Shalit's captors broke off dialogue after Israel bombed the Islamic University and government buildings in Gaza.

146. "Resistance in Palestine and Lebanon," *FM*, September 8, 2006, 3.

147. Giyath Nasser, "Comprehensive Discussion with Musa abu Marzouq," *FM*, September 6, 2006, 43.

148. "Doc. 239: Interview with Nazzal, September 16, 2006," *WF*, 603–8.

149. Ibid.

150. "Doc. 243: Text of the Political Program, September 20, 2006," *WF*, 614–15.

151. For insight into how these agreements constituted a "New Hamas," see Hroub, "A 'New Hamas' through Its 'New Documents,' " 6–27.

152. Zoughbie, *Indecision Points*, 117.

153. "Joint Press Conference by FM Livni and Spanish FM Moratinos after Meeting," *Israeli Ministry of Foreign Affairs*, September 11, 2006.

154. "Doc. 245: Mahmoud Abbas's Speech, September 21, 2006," *WF*, 617–620.

155. "Doc. 274: Interview with Abbas, November 7, 2006," *WF*, 672–81.

156. Abbas later explained his position. "Doc. 301: Abbas's Speech, December 16, 2006," *WF*, 744.

157. "Doc. 247: Hamas Release, September 24, 2006," *WF*, 621.

158. "Their Slogan Is 'Israel First,'" *FM*, November 6, 2006, 3.

159. Author interviews, Hamas leaders, 2015.

160. "The Palestinian Test Case—Moderates and Rejectionists," *The Economist*, October 21, 2006.

161. For Fatah's accusations, see "Doc. 252: Bayan for Fatah, October 1, 2006," *WF*, 628. For Hamas's accusations, see "Doc. 253: Ismail Haniyeh's Speech, October 2, 2006," *WF*, 629–30.

162. "An Arab and Islamic Tour," *FM*, January 8, 2007, 24–25.

163. Haniyeh was reportedly carrying $32 million in his briefcase. "Assassination Attempt," *FM*, January 8, 2007, 30.

164. "Doc. 302: Dahlan: Assassinating Haniyeh, December 16, 2006," *WF*, 755–56. Some Hamas ministers insist that Abbas had no knowledge of this attempt, which was entirely planned by Dahlan. Author interview, Bassem Naim, 2015. Hamas's publications reported on assassination attempts on Sayyam and Zahhar as efforts to stage a confrontation. "Abbas Prepares," *FM*, January 8, 2007, 26–27.

165. "Doc. 262: Qatar's Initiative, October 9, 2006," *WF*, 646.

166. "Doc. 4: Interview with Egyptian President, January 5, 2007," *WF*, 36–38.

167. "Doc. 309: Text of Hudna, December 19, 2006," *WF*, 766–67.

168. "Doc. 301: Mahmoud Abbas's Speech, December 16, 2006," *WF*, 745–56.

169. Giyath Nasser, "The Hamas Leader," *FM*, January 8, 2007, 22.

170. "There Is an Internal and an External Project," *FM*, January 8, 2007, 31.

171. Ibid. For more on Hamas's time in office, see Saleh, *Critical Assessment of the Experience of Hamas and Its Government*; and Abdel Maqsoud, *Hamas*.

172. The ten opposition factions met in Damascus and rejected the early elections. "Doc. 306: Bayan from the Opposition Factions, December 17, 2006," *WF*, 763–65. For Hamas's reporting, see "Abbas's Invitation," *FM*, January 8, 2007, 32–33.

173. Abbas himself admitted that his call for presidential and legislative elections paved the way for more unrest. "Doc. 10: Abbas's Speech, January 11, 2007," *WF*, 50–54.

174. "Doc. 263: Interview with Said Sayyam, October 11, 2006," *WF*, 647.

175. Papers leaked to al-Jazeera demonstrate the extent of cooperation between Israel, members of Fatah, and the United States in dealing with the security situation presented by Hamas. See "Quadrapartite Meeting of Gaza Security Committee," March 11, 2007, Confidential Memorandum, accessed at al-Jazeera Palestine Papers (www.ajtransparency.com/en/projects/thepalestine papers/20121823365500785.html); and "2nd Quadrilateral Security Meeting," April 3, 2007, Confidential Memorandum, accessed at al-Jazeera Palestine Papers (www.ajtransparency.com/en/projects/thepalestinepapers/20121822533171669.html).

176. Ibrahim abu al-Haija', "The Game of Mobilizing," *FM*, November 6, 2006, 34–35.

177. "Security Tension," *FM*, January 8, 2007, 3.

178. Author interviews, Hamas leaders, 2011 and 2015.

179. See "Doc. 3: Hamas Bayan, January 5, 2007," *WF*, 34–35.

180. "Doc. 7: Bayan from PLO, January 9, 2007," *WF*, 40–43.

181. Hamas issued leaflets describing the chronology of events. "Doc. 8: Hamas Bayan, January 10, 2007," *WF*, 43–47.

182. "Doc. 3: Hamas Bayan, January 5, 2007," *WF*, 35.

183. Ibrahim abu al-Haija', "Mobilizing the Illusions of Peace," *FM*, February 5, 2007, 40–41.

184. "Doc. 268: Interview with Mushir al-Masri, October 21, 2006," *WF*, 656–58. For more on Hamas's political performance, see Shikaki, "With Hamas in Power."

185. Ibrahim abu al-Haija', "The Game of Mobilizing," *FM*, November 6, 2006, 34–35.

For more on this, see Alastair Crooke, "Permanent Temporariness," *London Review of Books*, April 1, 2011.

186. "The Israeli Role," *FM*, November 6, 2006, 32–33.

187. Maha Abdel Hadi, "The Goal Is to Support Abbas," *FM*, November 6, 2006, 36–37.

188. "Olmert-Abu Mazen," *FM*, January 8, 2007, 21.

189. See Ibrahim al-Said, "American-Zionist Agreement," *FM*, February 5, 2007, 38–39. The movement latched on to statements by Olmert that he would support Abbas and moderates against Hamas and radicals. It was seen as treasonous for Abbas to seek support from Israelis over Palestinians. See "Doc. 311: Olmert's Statements, December 19, 2006," *WF*, 769–70.

190. Maha Abdel Hadi, "The Revolutionaries," *FM*, February 5, 2007, 42.

191. Zoughbie, *Indecision Points*, 126. The contradictory nature of Rice's statements, claiming for example that lawlessness in Gaza was the result of Hamas's inability to govern rather than the direct result of US efforts to arm militias, came under much criticism. Crooke, "Elliott Abram's Uncivil War."

192. Zoughbie, *Indecision Points*, 103.

193. "Hamas Carries on with the Dance," *The Economist*, November 18, 2006.

194. "Military Solutions in the Air," *The Economist*, November 4, 2006.

195. According to Hamas's sources, see "Fattening the Presidential Guards," *FM*, February 5, 2007, 17.

196. "The Gazafication of the West Bank," *The Economist*, February 3, 2007.

197. "Doc. 39: Hamas Release, February 3, 2007," *WF*, 103–5.

198. Giyath Nasser, "Hamas Participation," *FM*, January 8, 2007, 23.

199. Ibid.

200. Maha Abdel Hadi, "Revolutionaries," *FM*, February 5, 2007, 42–43.

201. "Doc. 9: Interview with Khaled Meshal, January 10, 2007," *WF*, 47.

202. "The Israeli Palestinian Truce," *The Economist*, November 29, 2006.

203. "Doc. 11: Hamas Bayan, January 13, 2007," *WF*, 55.

204. "Doc. 9: Interview with Khaled Meshal, January 10, 2007," *WF*, 49–50.

205. Author interviews, Hamas leaders, 2015.

206. "Doc. 17: Joint Bayan, January 21, 2007," *WF*, 65; and Ra'fat Murra, "Abbas and Meshal," *FM*, February 5, 2007, 36–37.

207. "Doc. 28: Hamas Bayan, January 29, 2007," *WF*, 82.

208. For more on the Mecca Agreement, see International Crisis Group, "After Gaza"; and *Journal of Palestine Studies*, "PA President Mahmud Abbas and Hamas Political Leader Khalid Meshal, Mecca Accord, Mecca, 7 February 2007," 189.

209. For Hamas's reporting, see Ra'fat Murra, "Mecca Agreement," *FM*, March 1, 2007, 25.

210. "Doc. 49: Abbas's Speech, February 7, 2007," *WF*, 117–18.

211. "Doc. 50: Khaled Mishal's Opening, February 7, 2007," *WF*, 120.

212. Ibid.

213. "Doc. 52: Text of Mecca Agreement, February 8, 2007," *WF*, 122.

214. "Mecca Agreement," *FM*, February 5, 2007, 3.

215. This was a clear sign of Hamas's pragmatism, its ability to make concessions while couching them in language of ideological purity. For more, see Wagemakers, "Legitimizing Pragmatism," 357–77.

216. Ibrahim abu al-Haija ', "A Year Since," *FM*, February 5, 2007, 17.

217. "Doc. 99: Interview with Abu Marzouq, March 29, 2007," *WF*, 204–8.

218. "Doc. 55: Formation of a National Unity Government, February 8, 2007," *WF*, 126–27.

219. Author interviews, Hamas leaders, 2015. Interviews revealed that they viewed this as the first of many times that Hamas entirely gave up on its government in an effort to form a unity cabinet. This was presented as a clear indication that the onus fell on Abbas to follow through and ensure a deal would be produced.

220. "Doc. 126: Interview with Ramadan Shalah, May 14, 2007," *WF*, 286.

221. Norway was the first country to restore diplomatic relations. "The Squeeze Continues," *The Economist*, March 24, 2007.

222. "Doc. 116: Interview with Khaled Meshal, April 30, 2007," *WF*, 256–62.

223. Zoughbie, *Indecision Points*, 120–21. For insight into the UN's role, see Serry, *The Endless Quest for Israeli-Palestinian Peace.*

224. Zoughbie, *Indecision Points*, 120–21.

225. "Doc. 81: Program of the National Unity Government, March 16, 2007," *WF*, 169–73.

226. "Saudi Arabia's Moment," *The Economist*, March 22, 2007.

227. Ibid. See also International Crisis Group, "After Mecca."

228. See Maha Abdel Hadi, "After the Mecca Agreement," *FM*, March 15, 2007, 26.

229. "Doc. 127: Mahmoud Abbas's Speech, May 15, 2007," *WF*, 294.

230. "Doc. 105: Interview with Ali Sartawi, April 13, 2007," *WF*, 224–27.

231. For Hamas's reporting, see Mohammad Rajeh, "Palestinian Unity Government," *FM*, May 4, 2007, 22–23.

232. "Doc. 106: The Security Plan, April 14, 2007," *WF*, 227–33.

233. "Doc. 108: Hani Qawasmeh's Resignation, April 17, 2007," *WF*, 233–35. Following skirmishes at the Rafah border on May 6, 2007, Rashid abu Shbak allegedly ordered Fatah's forces on to the streets in Gaza without agreement from either Hamas or the minister. This resulted in violence which left forty dead and forced the minister to quit; he was replaced by Haniyeh. "Gunning in Gaza," *The Economist*, May 19, 2007.

234. In a later speech, Abbas bemoaned taking money through the president's office rather than the cabinet, as that exacerbated division. He saw no other way to get finances to the Palestinians. "Doc. 151: Abbas's Speech, June 5, 2007," *WF*, 328. On security coordination, see "Doc. 93: Hamas Decree, March 25, 2007," *WF*, 191–92.

235. Kidnappings included the abduction of Alan Johnson, a BBC reporter, on March 12, 2007.

236. Hamas reported it intercepted intelligence from Rashid abu Shbak being shared with "outside forces" regarding the resistance operations, an accusation that he was collaborating with Israelis to attack the Executive Force. "Doc. 134: Press Release, May 18, 2007," *WF*, 304–35.

237. "Hamas in the Eye of the Storm," *FM*, June 5, 2007, 3.

238. "Doc. 160: Release from Hamas, June 11, 2007," *WF*, 342–44.

239. "Doc. 158: Fatah Bayan, June 8, 2007," *WF*, 338–39.

240. "Doc. 160: Hamas Bayan, June 11, 2007," *WF*, June 11, 2007, 344.

241. Dayton underscored that the US investment in their training had been worthwhile. See Milton-Edwards and Farrell, *Hamas*, 280–81.

242. Hamas pleaded innocence too far. Replying to accusations that it had killed a member of Fatah by throwing him off a building, Hamas responded he "fell of his own accord trying to escape from the bathroom window after taking care of his needs." "Doc. 161: Letter from Hamas, June 13, 2007," *WF*, 345.

243. "Doc. 135: Press Release from Hamas, May 18, 2007," *WF*, 305–6.

244. Leaders stressed that Hamas did not realize the events would escalate as they had, and that the decision to mobilize was made solely to inflict a powerful hit and deter further lawlessness. Author interview, Ahmad Yousef, 2015. See "War between Brothers," *The Economist*, June 16, 2007.

245. "Full Chronology," *FM*, July 4, 2007, 26–28.

246. For an example of Dayton's assurances, see "Doc. 143: Press Release for Dayton, May 24, 2007" *WF*, 314–15.

247. See, for instance, "Remarks with Israeli Foreign Minister Tzipi Livni after Their Meeting," *U.S. Department of State*, February 8, 2006.

248. Author interviews, Gaza, 2015. See also International Crisis Group, "After Gaza."

249. See, for example, Rose, "The Gaza Bombshell"; and Judis, "Clueless in Gaza."

250. "Doc. 181: Report from Fatah, June 20, 2007," *WF*, 380–87. The order for confrontation with Hamas came not from Fatah's Central Committee but rather from Dahlan, whose appointment and stockpiling of arms the report criticized. Furthermore, the report noted that many officials within the security forces were not motivated to fight "Dahlan's war" against Hamas. The report criticized the vacuum at the top of the security forces and suggested there was never a transition from revolution to authority within Fatah.

251. Zoughbie, *Indecision Points*, 127. These clashes were used as proof of a historic animosity between factions. See Schanzer, *Hamas vs. Fatah*. This view, however, is reductionist and overlooks the impact of active foreign intervention. For more on the division, see al-Dabak, *Al-Inqisamat al-Filastiniyyah*.

252. See "WikiLeaks: Possibility of Israeli-Palestinian Co-operation over Gaza," *The Telegraph*, December 20, 2010; and Barak Ravid, "Fatah Asked Israel to Help Attack Hamas during Gaza Coup, WikiLeaks Cable Shows," *Haaretz*, December 20, 2010.

CHAPTER FIVE

1. Hamas politicians reiterated in interviews with the author that there had always been a level of political and social division between Gaza and the West Bank, as a result of the geographic separation. But this was the first time there was an institutional rupture within the Palestinian leadership body purportedly leading these territories.

2. See Nathan Thrall, "Our Man in Palestine," *New York Review of Books*, October 14, 2010.

3. "Doc. 184: Speech for Mahmoud Abbas, June 20, 2007," *WF*, 391.

4. Meshal attributed Hamas's military effectiveness to the experience its fighters had gained in their resistance against Israel. "Doc. 237: Meshal Interview, July 28, 2007," *WF*, 553–559.

5. "Doc. 225: Abbas's Speech, July 18, 2007," *WF*, 488–93.

6. "Meshal: The Problem Is Not with Fatah," *FM*, July 4, 2007, 29.

7. Ibid.

8. See "Doc. 187: Press Conference Hosted by Hamas, June 22, 2007," *WF*, 405–12.

9. Author interviews, Hamas leaders, 2015.

10. "Doc. 191: Haniyeh—Closing the Door, June 24, 2007," *WF*, 416–19.

11. Giyath Nasser, "Musa abu Marzouq," *FM*, July 4, 2007, 42.

12. "Abu-Mazen," *FM*, July 4, 2007, 3.

13. "Meshal: The Problem Is Not with Fatah," *FM*, July 4, 2007, 29.

14. "Doc. 162: Letter from Hamas, June 14, 2007," *WF*, 347–49.

15. See Hamas, *The White Book*.

16. Maha Abdel Hadi, "The Duo," *FM*, July 4, 2007, 34–36.

17. Zoughbie, *Indecision Points*, 127.

18. Tax returns on goods entering Gaza are collected by Israel and sent to the Palestinian Authority in Ramallah for distribution, in accordance with the Oslo Accords.

19. *Journal of Palestine Studies*, "Gaza Chronology," 120. These policies depoliticized Gaza, separating it from the rest of the Palestinian conflict and presenting it solely as a humanitarian problem. For more on viewing Gaza through the lens of humanitarianism, see Feldman, "Gaza's Humanitarianism Problem," 22–37.

20. See Roy, *The Gaza Strip*; Roy, *Failing Peace*, 79–123; and Avi Shlaim, "How Israel Brought Gaza to the Brink of a Humanitarian Catastrophe," *The Guardian*, January 7, 2009.

21. For the blockade's immediate impact, see OCHA, "Gaza Strip."

22. Roy, "Praying with Their Eyes Closed," 64–74.

23. Levy, *The Punishment of Gaza*, viii. For more on Israel as the disengaged occupier and its legal status, see Gisha, "Disengaged Occupiers," 194–98; and Darcy and Reynolds, "An Enduring Occupation," 211–43.

24. Hamas's coverage: "Abu-Mazen," *FM*, July 4, 2007, 3.

25. This order trickled down to various bodies. See, for example, "Doc. 169: Decision of Head of Police, June 15, 2007," *WF*, 359–60.

26. "Doc. 193: Abbas's Speech, June 25, 2007," *WF*, 422–24.

27. "Doc. 171: Presidential Decree, June 16, 2007," *WF*, 361. Hamas published two comprehensive reports between 2007 and 2009 documenting this security crackdown. See Hamas, *The Black Book: Facts*; and Hamas, *The Black Book: Violations*.

28. "Abbas an Agent," *FM*, August 2, 2007, 23.

29. "Doc. 238: Joint Release, July 28, 2007," *WF*, 559–60.

30. "Abbas an Agent," *FM*, August 2, 2007, 23.

31. See International Crisis Group, "The Israeli-Palestinian Conflict"; and Kurz, "The Post-Annapolis Dynamic."

32. For Hamas's coverage, see "International Peace Conference," *FM*, August 2, 2007, 3.

33. "Doc. 213: Hamas Release, July 4, 2007," *WF*, 466. Interviewees in Gaza questioned how Abbas could accept policies that impose collective punishment on his people, regardless of what his political motivations were. Author interview, Palestinian analyst, 2015.

34. "Abbas and Complete Fusion," *FM*, September 14, 2007, 3.

35. "Members from PA's Security," *FM*, July 4, 2007, 38–39.

36. Giyath Nasser, "Musa abu Marzouq," *FM*, July 4, 2007, 40.

37. For more on Hamas's consolidation of power in Gaza, see Milton-Edwards, "The Ascendance of Political Islam," 1585–99.

38. "Martyrs or Traitors," *The Economist*, June 23, 2007.

39. Author interviews, human rights activists, Gaza, 2015.

40. Ibrahim Mansour, "Program for Administration," *FM*, August 2, 2007, 29.

41. "Doc. 271: Hamas Document, September 2, 2007," *WF*, 632–33.

42. "Doc. 277: Letter from the Palestinian Centre, September 13, 2007," *WF*, 644–49. Both the Palestinian Authority and Hamas carried out a range of abuses following the separation. See Human Rights Watch, "Internal Fight."

43. This included a range of activities that were seen as being incompatible with Gaza's "conservative society." Author interview, Issam Da'lis, 2015.

44. Studies confirm that crime dropped. See Milton-Edwards, "Order without Law?" For more on Hamas's approach to security and policing, see Berti and Gutierrez, "Rebel-to-Political and Back?," 1059–76; and Sayigh, " 'We Serve the People.' "

45. Ibrahim Mansour, "Program for Administration," *FM*, August 2, 2007, 28–29. See International Crisis Group, "Inside Gaza."

46. This was reiterated by Hamas's politicians and confirmed by analysts. Author interviews, Bassem Naim; Adnan abu Amer; Raji Sourani, 2015.

47. Author interviews with Israeli analysts and Hamas leaders, 2015.

48. The journalist had been held captive for sixteen weeks. Hamas's role in his release was used as a sign of its ability to maintain security, law, and order. "Doc. 214: Article Written by Meshal, July 5, 2007," *WF*, 468–69. For more on mediation by Ghazi Hamad, a senior leader within Hamas, see Ibrahim Awni, "Ghazi Hamad," *FM*, August 2, 2007, 32–33. See also Macintyre, *Gaza*.

49. Author interview, Adnan abu Amer, 2015. The justice system continued to follow the Palestinian Basic Law with minor provisions to "police" criminal behavior. Author interview, Issam Da'lis, 2015. See also Hovdenak, "The Public Services under Hamas in Gaza."

50. "Doc. 231: Interview with Haniyeh, July 21, 2007," *WF*, 505–8.

51. Eitidal al-Qunaita, "Gaza after a Month," *FM*, August 2, 2007, 24–27.

52. Author interviews, Bassem Naim; Issam Da'lis, 2015. Ziad al-Zaza described this as, "Acts like a liberation movement, governs like a state." Author interview, Ziad al-Zaza, 2015.

53. Eitidal al-Qunaita, "Gaza after a Month," *FM*, August 2, 2007, 25.

54. Conal Urquhart, "Israel Declares Gaza Strip Hostile Territory," *The Guardian*, September 20, 2007.

55. International Crisis Group, "After Gaza," 24.

56. Author interviews, Change and Reform elected officials, Gaza, 2015. Human rights activists in Gaza condemned Hamas's justice system, saying it lacked impartiality and was frequently abused by the movement. Author interview, human rights activists, Gaza, 2015. This was supported by international organizations. Human Rights Watch, "Abusive System."

57. Author interview, Bassem Naim, 2015.

58. Ibrahim Mansour, "Program for Administration," *FM*, August 2, 2007, 28.

59. "Doc. 220: Zahhar Stressing That Hamas Will No Longer Agree to the Previous State of Affairs in Gaza, July 12, 2007," *WF*, 477–78.

60. Ibid., 477.

61. Author interview, Ziad al-Zaza, 2015.

62. Ibid. Most of the population of the Gaza Strip is below the age of fifteen. It has high literacy rates, and school completion and university graduates match those in the West Bank. For

more, see Saleh, *Gaza Strip*. For more on Hamas's approach to development, see Burton, "Hamas and Its Vision of Development," 525–40.

63. Author interviews, Change and Reform elected officials, Gaza, 2015.

64. Brown, "Road out of Gaza," 4. Health and education civil servants left in the summer of 2008, creating a severe crisis for Hamas. While the movement sought replacement, it also forced many civil servants to return by taking harsh measures, for instance shutting down their private clinics. Author interview, Mostafa Ibrahim, 2015.

65. Author interview, Ziad al-Zaza, 2015.

66. Abumdallal and Abu Hatab, *The Tunnel Economy in the Gaza Strip*, 7–12.

67. Pelham, "Gaza's Tunnel Phenomenon," 6–31; and Pelham, "The Role of the Tunnel Economy," 200–219, in Turner and Shweiki, *Decolonizing Palestinian Political Economy*.

68. Nicolas Pelham, "Gaza: A Way Out?," *New York Review of Books*, October 26, 2012.

69. "The PA's Security," *FM*, August 2, 2007, 40–41.

70. "Abbas's Forces," *FM*, September 14, 2007, 34–35. Hamas's accusations of Fatah's intolerance of its religiosity were not new, dating to the early 1990s. Even in prisons, Hamas accused Fatah prisoners of refusing to share cells with religious members. See "Establishing Hamas," *FM*, December 17, 2007, 20.

71. "Abbas and Fayyad's Gift," *FM*, October 4, 2007, 40–41. This was seen as a way to destroy Hamas's popularity in the West Bank by targeting its social infrastructure and media outlets.

72. Author interviews, Change and Reform ministers, 2015.

73. Ibrahim Mansour, "The Future of the Relationship," *FM*, September 14, 2007, 37.

74. Milton-Edwards, "Law without Order?," 10.

75. "Abu Mazen's Permanently Failed Bets," *FM*, October 4, 2007, 3.

76. Ibrahim Mansour, "The Future of the Relationship," *FM*, September 14, 2007, 36.

77. International Crisis Group, "After Gaza," 14–16. In numerous interviews, the author was told that Abbas's personal feelings and dislike of Hamas consistently undermined prospects for reconciliation. Author interview, Omar Shaban, 2015.

78. Hamas claimed to uphold the slogan "*la ghaleb wala maghloub*"—no winner, no loser—as the basis for discussion.

79. Zoughbie, *Indecision Points*, 132–33.

80. For more on Annapolis, see Heller, "Israelis and Palestinians after Annapolis."

81. "Hamas Facing an Eradication War," *FM*, January 10, 2008, 20.

82. Although Israel had not launched official operations for fifteen months, air strikes, assassinations, bulldozing, and cross-border fire had persisted. *Journal of Palestine Studies*, "Israeli Military Operations against Gaza, 2000–2008," 137.

83. Brown, "Road out of Gaza," 3.

84. For Hamas's coverage, see Ibtisam Saymeh, "Zionist Massacre," *FM*, February 12, 2008, 35.

85. Brown, "Road out of Gaza."

86. Pelham, "Gaza's Tunnel Phenomenon," 8.

87. Mohammad Yahya, "Blockade till Death," *FM*, January 10, 2008, 46.

88. "Why Do the Egyptian Authorities Work against Palestinians?," *FM*, September 4, 2008, 3.

89. For more, see Sabry, *Sinai*, 85–109.

90. *Journal of Palestine Studies*, "Gaza Chronology," 120. For more on the situation in Gaza one year after the blockade, see Brown, "Road out of Gaza."

91. "The Shifting Balance of Power," *The Economist*, February 2, 2008.

92. Pelham, "Gaza's Tunnel Phenomenon," 9.

93. See front page of *FM*, February 12, 2008.

94. "National Palestinian Conference," *FM*, February 12, 2008, 30.

95. "*Al-Mujahid* Khaled Meshal," *FM*, February 12, 2008, 31.

96. Ibid.

97. "Closing Statement," *FM*, February 12, 2008, 33.

98. "War Is Coming, Maybe," *FM*, March 6, 2008, 3.

99. "Zionist Entity," *FM*, August 2, 2007, 30–31.

100. "Zionist Testimonials," *FM*, November 5, 2007, 3.

101. For instance, Hamas celebrated that Israel refers to all missiles into its territories as Qassam missiles, even though many are fired by other factions. See Atef al-Golani, "Hamas Broke the Impossible," *FM*, December 17, 2007, 12.

102. "Zionist Authorities," *FM*, January 10, 2008, 38–39.

103. Ibid., 14.

104. "Doc. 276: Interview with Osama Hamdan, September 12, 2007," *WF*, 641–44.

105. For more on this "violent dialogue," see Ayyash, "Hamas and the Israeli State," 103–23.

106. Cover of *FM*, June 26, 2008, with the caption, "*Al-Muqawama's* Rockets on Asqalan [Ashkelon] Bring Back the Balance of Terror Theory."

107. Author interviews, Hamas leaders, Gaza, 2015.

108. Sabry, *Sinai*, 51–85.

109. "Discussion with Abu Ubaida," *FM*, December 17, 2007, 30–31.

110. "War Might Be Coming," *FM*, March 8, 2008, 3. Such actions were seen as proof that "hardliners" within Hamas seeking to consolidate power in Gaza were winning over "moderates" seeking unity and reconciliation. See Brown, "Road out of Gaza," 5–7.

111. For more on rocket fire in 2007–8 and the impact it had on Israel, see Byman, *High Price*, 182–89.

112. *Journal of Palestine Studies*, "Israeli Military Operations against Gaza," 137.

113. Ibid., 138.

114. "The Five Day War," *FM*, March 30, 2008, 3.

115. Ibid.

116. For instance, "When the Murderer Confesses," *FM*, May 5, 2008, 3.

117. "Hamas's Battle for Hearts and Minds," *The Economist*, March 29, 2008.

118. "When the Killer Admits," *FM*, May 5, 2008, 3.

119. Ra'fat Murra, "What after the Hamas-Carter Meetings?," *FM*, May 5, 2008, 33.

120. "*Tahdi'ah*," *FM*, June 26, 2008, 38–39.

121. "Two Track Tango," *The Economist*, May 24, 2008.

122. "The Bloody Conundrum of Gaza," *The Economist*, March 8, 2008.

123. "The Zionist View," *FM*, July 8, 2008, 16–17.

124. "Israel's Tottering Prime Minister," *The Economist*, May 31, 2008.

125. "Illusionary Negotiations," *FM*, June 26, 2008, 3. These meetings were seen as promising; see Bernard Avishai, "A Plan for Peace That Still Could Be," *New York Times*, February 7, 2011.

126. See, for instance, Inbar, "Gaza."

127. "The Wandering Palestinian," *The Economist*, May 10, 2008. Hamas showed strong performances among student elections in Birzeit, Hebron University and Polytechnic. Nowaf al-Amer, "Student Union Elections," *FM*, June 26, 2008, 36–37.

128. "*Tahdi'ah*," *FM*, June 26, 2008, 38–39. See also "The Swap," *FM*, August 4, 2008, 3.

129. For more on the truce, see *Journal of Palestine Studies*, "Prelude to Operation Cast Lead," 162–64.

130. "Can a Ceasefire Hold?," *The Economist*, June 21, 2008; and International Crisis Group, "Radical Islam in Gaza," 1–47.

131. The committee charged with coordinating resistance activities was representative of the factions on the ground. Author interview, Ahmad Yousef, 2015.

132. "Leader of IDF," *FM*, November 8, 2008, 20–21.

133. Abdallah Hamdan, "Large Popular Relief," *FM*, July 8, 2008, 18.

134. Adnan abu Amer, "*Tahdi'ah* . . . Warriors Break," *FM*, August 4, 2008, 38–39.

135. For a detailed account, see *Journal of Palestine Studies*, "Prelude to Operation Cast Lead," 164–66. See also Jimmy Carter, "An Unnecessary War," *Washington Post*, January 8, 2009; and Aleem Maqbool, "Truce Barely Eases Gaza Embargo," *BBC*, August 19, 2008.

136. "WikiLeaks: Israel Aimed to Keep Gaza Economy on Brink of Collapse," *Haaretz*, January 5, 2011. Reports received by NGOs through legal means show drafts of Israeli policies to count the minimal sustenance needed to maintain Gaza's population just above malnutrition, a point defined as a "Red Line." Israel's government stressed these reports were never used as a basis

for implementing civilian policy in the Gaza Strip. "Food Consumption in the Gaza Strip—Red Lines," *COGAT*, translated by Gisha, September 2012.

137. Sumaira, "Political Performance of Hamas and Other Resistance Factions during the Assault," 75–97, in al-Kayyali, *The Israeli Aggression on Gaza Strip*; and Hattit, "Military Performance of Hamas and Other Resistance Factions during the Assault," 97–125, in al-Kayyali, *Israeli Aggression on Gaza Strip*.

138. "*Tahdi'ah*," *FM*, July 8, 2008, 3.

139. Hamas reported on Israelis viewing the ceasefire as a victory for Hamas "*Tahdi'ah*," *FM*, July 8, 2008, 19.

140. Maha Abdel Hadi, "Internal Palestinian Dialogue," *FM*, July 8, 2008, 24–25.

141. "Report on Terroristic Procedures," *FM*, October 10, 2008, 28–29.

142. "Abbas-Fayyad-Dayton Forces," *FM*, November 27, 2008, 24–26.

143. For more on how many of Hamas's suspicions were later validated, see "From the Treasures of the WikiLeaks," *FM*, March 2, 2011, 20.

144. Ali Badwan, "Behind the Scenes," *FM*, August 4, 2008, 34–35.

145. "Arab Forces," *FM*, October 10, 2008, 3.

146. For more on reconciliation talks, see Hilal, "Al-Istiqtab fi al-Haqel al-Siyyassi al-Filastini," 24–39. For Hamas's coverage, see Ali Badwan, "Egyptian Proposal," *FM*, October 10, 2008, 48–49.

147. "Resistance Is the Most Important Element," *FM*, November 27, 2008, 3.

148. Ra'fat Murra, "Notes on the Egyptian Document," *FM*, November 8, 2008, 31. Hamas believed Abbas was pushing for reconciliation before the end of his presidential term in January 2009, as that would allow him to extend his term until legislative and presidential elections could be held. Hamas opposed this move. See "January 9, 2009," *FM*, November 8, 2008, 39–41.

149. "The Return of Blood and Anger," *The Economist*, November 15, 2008.

150. For more on Hamas's decision, see Mohammad, *The Palestinian Struggle at a Crossroads*.

151. Pelham, "Gaza's Tunnel Phenomenon," 10.

152. Ibid., 6–31; and Sabry, *Sinai*, 85–109.

153. "Latest Cairo Dialogue," *FM*, November 27, 2008, 28.

154. *Journal of Palestine Studies*, "Prelude to Operation Cast Lead," 165. For an account of the rockets, see "Summary of Rocket Fire and Mortar Shelling in 2008," Intelligence and Terrorism Information Center at the Israel Intelligence and Commemoration Center, 2009, 6.

155. "The Return of Blood and Anger," *The Economist*, November 15, 2008.

156. To see Hamas's effectiveness in halting fire, see Nancy Kanwisher, Johannes Haushofer, and Anat Biletzki, "Reigniting Violence: How Do Ceasefires End?," *Huffington Post*, February 6, 2009. For accounts by Israeli security members, see Henry Siegman, "Israel's Lies," *London Review of Books*, January 29, 2009.

157. The prisoners released a decree calling on Hamas to end this ceasefire on December 22. Sumaira, "Political Performance," 79. For Abbas's take, see Masri, "Political Performance of the Palestinian Authority and Fatah during the Assault," 133, in al-Kayyali, *Israeli Aggression on Gaza Strip*.

158. The private correspondence demonstrating this exchange is kept in the private library of Professor Avi Shlaim, University of Oxford.

159. Sumaira, "Political Performance," 78.

160. Roy, *Hamas and Civil Society*, 229. See also Barak Ravid, "Disinformation, Secrecy and Lies: How the Gaza Offensive Came About," *Haaretz*, December 31, 2008.

161. "Israel's Livni Vows to End Hamas Control of Gaza," *Al-Arabiya*, December 25, 2008.

162. Given that the police force was a civilian force, this was seen as a violation of international law. See UN Human Rights Council, "Report of the United Nations Fact-Finding Mission on Gaza Conflict," A/HRC/12/48, September 25, 2009, 17–19.

163. *Journal of Palestine Studies*, "The Israeli Arsenal Deployed against Gaza during Operation Cast Lead," 175–91.

164. *Journal of Palestine Studies*, "Day-by-Day Casualties, Israeli Sorties, and Palestinian Missiles Fired," 202. The total number of rockets launched from Gaza was estimated to be around six hundred. See also Hattit, "Military Performance," 99–100.

165. For accounts from the ground, see Chomsky and Pappé, *Gaza in Crisis*; and Gilbert and Fosse, *Eyes in Gaza*.

166. See Bahgat, "The Gaza War and the Changing Strategic Landscape in the Middle East," 65. To show how Israel learned from its 2006 war in Lebanon and applied that knowledge in Cast Lead, see Lambeth, "Israel's War in Gaza," 81–118; and Cordesman, " 'The Gaza War.' "

167. Norton, "The Gaza War."

168. Uri Blau, "IDF Sources, Conditions Not Yet Optimal for Gaza Pullout," *Haaretz*, January 8, 2009.

169. For a record of these operations, see *Journal of Palestine Studies*, "Israeli Military Operations against Gaza," 122–38. The figure is quoted in Ilan Pappé, "Dummy or Real," *London Review of Books*, January 14, 2009.

170. Roy, *Hamas and Civil Society*, 228. Hamas reported on Israeli figures such as Yossi Beilin who warned their government that military options were futile given the degree of Hamas's ground support. See "Zionist Opinions," *FM*, January 6, 2009, 44–45.

171. Shlaim, "How Israel Brought Gaza to the Brink."

172. Anshel Pfeffer, "Israel Claims Success in the PR War," *Jewish Chronicle*, December 31, 2008.

173. "The Struggle for Gaza—Where Will It End?," *The Economist*, January 10, 2009.

174. Idriss, "Arab Positions towards the Aggression," 153–99, in al-Kayyali, *Israeli Aggression on Gaza Strip*.

175. Sumaira, "Political Performance," 83.

176. "Gaza Offensive," *FM*, February 3, 2009, 40–41.

177. "Egypt to Keep Gaza Border Closed: Mubarak," *Al-Arabiya*, December 30, 2008.

178. Masri, "Political Performance," 132.

179. Idriss, "Arab Positions," 171.

180. For more on reactions from Muslim countries, see El-Din, "Islamic Positions towards the Aggression" 199–227, in al-Kayyali, *Israeli Aggression on Gaza Strip*.

181. "The Struggle for Gaza—Where Will It End?," *The Economist*, January 10, 2009.

182. For more insight into these discussions, see Rice, *No Higher Honor*, 724–28.

183. For more on Israel's approach toward the rocket threats, see Rubin, "The Missile Threat from Gaza," 27–59.

184. For more, see Eisenberg and Caplan, *Negotiating Arab-Israeli Peace*, 1–35. For more on Israel's policies toward Gaza and the ceasefires with Hamas, see Brom, "The Real Choice"; and Cohen, "The Futility of Operation Cast Lead."

185. For different assessments of Israel's operations, particularly relative to the 2006 war with Hezbollah, see Byman, *High Price*, 190–205; and Cohen and White, "Hamas in Combat."

186. "Hamas Communiqué," *FM*, February 3, 2009, 34–35.

187. Author interview, Hamas leader, 2015.

188. "Hamas Communiqué," *FM*, February 3, 2009, 34. Reflecting on their performance, they conceded the limited capabilities of the rockets which were manufactured locally. "Resistance in Gaza," *FM*, February 3, 2009, 42–43.

189. Cover page, *FM*, February 3, 2009.

190. Ali Badwan, "Victory of Resilience," *FM*, February 3, 2009, 39–40.

191. For more on this, see Rabbani, "Israel's Assault on Gaza," 43–44.

192. Idriss, "Arab Positions," 190–91.

193. "Hamas Communiqué," *FM*, February 3, 2009, 34.

194. "Gaza Offensive," *FM*, February 3, 2009, 40–41.

195. "Opinion Polls," *FM*, March 3, 2009, 18–19.

196. Hamas's popularity rose from the low figure of 28 percent to 33 percent after the war, while Fatah's dropped from 42 percent to 40 percent. Palestinian Center for Policy and Survey Research, Poll 31, 5–7, March 2009.

197. "Gaza Offensive," *FM*, February 3, 2009, 40–41.

198. "Hamas Communiqué," *FM*, February 3, 2009, 35.

199. Ibid.

200. Ra'fat Murra, "Meetings and Letters," *FM*, March 30, 2009, 44. The most prominent example was a meeting between Khaled Meshal and a European parliamentary delegation in Damascus, which included fifteen parliamentarians from Britain, Ireland, Scotland, Greece, and Italy. For Hamas's coverage, see "*Al-Mujahid* Meshal," *FM*, March 30, 2009, 45. Publications also referred to a letter signed by American ex-officials calling for engagement with Hamas, sent to President Obama.

201. "The Future of the PA," *FM*, February 3, 2009, 48. For more on this, see Ghanem, "The Fallout from Israel's War on Gaza."

202. "The Future of the PA," *FM*, February 3, 2009, 49. For more, see Norton, "Gaza War"; and Blecher, "Operation Cast Lead in the West Bank," 65.

203. "The Future of the PA," *FM*, February 3, 2009, 48.

204. Ibid.

205. "Preparation for the Phase of Netanyahu," *FM*, March 3, 2009, 3.

206. Sumaira, "Political Performance," 87.

207. Olmert unsuccessfully attempted to complete such an agreement before he left office, creating a great deal of strain between Egypt and Israel. "A Long Bumpy Road," *The Economist*, January 31, 2009.

208. "Ismail Radwan," *FM*, March 3, 2009, 39.

209. Attempts by donor agencies to circumvent Hamas politicizes their operations. See Qarmout and Beland, "The Politics of International Aid to the Gaza Strip," 32–47.

210. Al-Nimel, "The Political Economy of Gaza's Reconstruction," 299, in al-Kayyali, *Israeli Aggression on Gaza Strip*. Reconstruction mechanisms were seen as being corrupt and served vested interests of politicians in the West Bank. Author interview, Omar Shaban, 2015.

211. For Hamas's reporting, see Ali Badwan, "Cairo Dialogues," *FM*, March 30, 2009, 30–32.

212. Ali Badwan, "On the Way," *FM*, July 1, 2009, 41.

213. "The American Administration," *FM*, May 5, 2009, 15. Hamas initially noted a "shift in discourse, albeit limited," by Obama's administration regarding its marginalization. Ali Badwan, "On the Way," *FM*, July 1, 2009, 40–41.

214. Ali Badwan, "The Third Round," *FM*, May 5, 2009, 30.

215. "Not Nearly Back to Normal," *The Economist*, May 2, 2009.

216. "Not Quite as Gloomy as They Look," *The Economist*, August 1, 2009. Hamas claimed it was experiencing a resurgence of support in the West Bank driven by sympathy, given Fayyad's crackdown. See "Hamas Progressing," *FM*, May 5, 2009, 15.

217. Termed "Fayyadism," these policies were criticized for focusing on economic growth under occupation at the expense of liberation. For more on the political economy of Palestinian institutions, see Khan, Giacaman, and Amundsen, *State Formation in Palestine*; Turner and Shweiki, *Decolonizing Palestinian Political Economy*; and Khalidi and Samour, "Neoliberalism as Liberation." For Hamas's criticisms, see "Salam Fayyad," *FM*, October 2, 2009, 3.

218. "The Campaign against Hamas," *FM*, July 1, 2009, 38–39.

219. Author interviews, human rights activists, Gaza, 2015. See also Roy, *Hamas and Civil Society*, 191–226.

220. In the summer of 2009, a radical movement called Ansar Jund Allah under the leadership of Abdel Latif Mousa declared an emirate in Rafah, in south Gaza. Hamas had been in dialogue with members of this movement to subdue their activities. Once the emirate was declared, however, Hamas transitioned "from dialogue to confrontation." See cover of *FM*, September 2, 2009.

221. "Obama's Speech in Cairo," *New York Times*, June 4, 2009.

222. "Full Text of Netanyahu's Foreign Policy Speech at Bar Ilan," *Haaretz*, June 14, 2009.

223. "Israel FM Rejects Annapolis Deal," *BBC*, April 1, 2009.

224. Nabil Shabib, "Western Openness," *FM*, June 2, 2009, 39. See also "The Two State Solution," *FM*, May 5, 2009, 3.

225. "Provocation Ruins," *FM*, August 26, 2009, 3.

226. "The PA and the Occupation," *FM*, September 2, 2009, 34–35.

227. "Report of the United Nations Fact-Finding Mission on the Gaza Conflict," 13–36. While the investigation found clear evidence of Israeli soldiers using Palestinians as human shields, no evidence was found that Hamas did the same during this operation. For its part, Hamas was condemned for launching military attacks within or close to densely populated civilian areas. See Human Rights Watch, "Turning a Blind Eye." For more on this, see Shalom, "Unjust and Illegal," 123–49, in Faruqi, *From Camp David to Cast Lead.*

228. "Stranded between America and the Street," *The Economist*, October 10, 2009.

229. Fadi al Hosni, "Hamas Survived," *FM*, November 5, 2009, 19. Hamas's leaders indicated willingness to cooperate with the investigation and deal with accusations directed at the movement.

230. "Is Israel Too Strong for Barak Obama?," *The Economist*, November 7, 2009.

231. Richard Goldstone, "Reconsidering the Goldstone Report on Israel and War Crimes," *Washington Post*, April 1, 2011.

232. "Goldstone U.N Report Retraction Spurned by Co-authors," *CNN*, April 14, 2011.

233. "Hamas Preparing to Launch," *FM*, December 5, 2009, 13.

234. "Al Aqsa, Goldstone and the Female Prisoners," *FM*, November 5, 2009, 3.

235. "The 22nd Anniversary," *FM*, January 2, 2010, 21.

236. Mustafa al-Suwwaf, "Hamas and Its Principles," *FM*, January 2, 2010, 46–47. At this point, analysts noted, having gained experience in governance the movement had internally reconciled that it was truly a nationalist party, and that its religious ideology informed its nationalism. Author interview, Adnan abu Amer, 2015.

237. Wisam Afifeh, "Hamas . . . Has It Succeeded?," *FM*, January 2, 2010, 49.

238. Author interview, Bassem Naim, 2015.

239. Pelham, "Gaza's Tunnel Phenomenon," 13–16.

240. Author interview, Mostafa Ibrahim, 2015.

241. For example, "Abbas-Fayyad Military Courts," *FM*, July 1, 2010, 22–23.

242. Robert Boot, "Israeli Attack on Gaza Flotilla Sparks International Outrage," *The Guardian*, May 31, 2010. For Hamas's coverage, see "Hamas and the Freedom Fleet," *FM*, July 1, 2010, 35.

243. "Widespread Palestinian Rejection," *FM*, September 2, 2010, 27. The factions included the Popular Front for the Liberation of Palestine, Islamic Jihad, PFLP-General Comman, Fatah, the Democratic Front for the Liberation of Palestine, and a number of smaller groups.

244. For Hamas's reporting, see Ra'fat Murra, "A Reading of the Direct Negotiations," *FM*, September 2, 2010, 24.

245. Ghassan Dowar, "Expectations for the Continuation," *FM*, October 6, 2010, 24–25.

246. "Apologies," *FM*, October 6, 2010, 3.

247. Ibid. For more reporting, see "More than a Thousand Arrests," *FM*, October 6, 2010, 28–29.

248. Publications reported on Israeli media channels which feared the extent of Hamas's capabilities after all the efforts invested in destroying the movement in the West Bank. See "Zionist Reactions," *FM*, October 6, 2010, 30–31.

249. "They Attacked the Resistance," *FM*, October 6, 2010, 26.

250. "Palestinian *thawabet*," *FM*, November 3, 2010, 3.

251. "Meshal Calls for the Lifting Off," *FM*, January 4, 2011, 11.

252. Ala' Salem, "The Last Round," *FM*, December 3, 2010, 29.

253. Nawaf Amer, "The PA's Invitation," *FM*, March 2, 2011, 34–35.

254. Author interview, Omar Shaban, 2015.

CHAPTER SIX

1. For more on the Arab uprisings, see Filiu, *The Arab Revolutions*; Ramadan, *Islam and the Arab Awakening*; and Lynch, *The New Arab Wars*.

2. Given America's alliance with dictatorships such as Egypt and Saudi Arabia, the Bush administration's "Freedom Agenda" and its focus on Saddam Hussein were seen as hypocritical. It was in keeping with the understanding that America's interests in the region are driven by three policies: safeguarding the flow of oil, limiting the spread of the Iranian revolution, and maintaining Israel's

security, rather than the oft-repeated rhetoric that the United States acted in support of human rights and democracy. Lynch, *New Arab Wars*, 47–75. See also Bacevich, *America's War*; Mann, *Rise of the Vulcans*; and Crist, *The Twilight War*.

3. For more on Hamas's take on the revolutions, see Meshaal, "Hamas's Political Thought and Stances in Light of the Arab Uprisings."

4. Author interviews, Issam Da'lis, 2015.

5. "Hamas Salutes the Blessed Intifada," *FM*, January 31, 2011, 16.

6. "Meshal Reveals Important Initiatives," *FM*, March 2, 2011, 13.

7. "Arab Revolutions," *FM*, March 2, 2011, 3.

8. For more on this period, see Sabry, *Sinai*, 125–61. Armed deployment in the Sinai was a breach of the 1979 Egyptian-Israeli Camp David peace treaty. Hamas's publications hypothesized that peace deals such as Camp David and the Oslo Accords, which it claimed were held in place by authoritarian elites against popular will, could now be revisited. "Palestine and the Arab Mobilization," *FM*, May 4, 2011, 3.

9. "The Fall of Mubarak's Regime," *FM*, March 2, 2011, 28.

10. Ibid. See also Hidayah Mohammad, "Palestinian Politicians," *FM*, March 2, 2011, 41.

11. For instance, see Mohamad Amin, "Egypt's Foreign Policy," *FM*, April 1, 2011, 38–39.

12. Meshal allegedly spoke repeatedly with Assad behind the scenes to soften his repression of protestors. Hamas leaders ultimately felt that support for the Palestinian people from the Assad regime could not come at the expense of Syrian blood. Author interview, Change and Reform Parliamentarian, West Bank, 2015.

13. "The Palestine Papers," *Al-Jazeera*, www.aljazeera.com/palestinepapers/.

14. David Poort, "PA's Foreknowledge of the Gaza War?," *Al-Jazeera*, January 27, 2011.

15. Jonathan Freedland, "Palestine Papers: Now We Know: Israel Had a Peace Partner," *The Guardian*, January 23, 2011.

16. Hidayah Mohammad, "Palestinian Politicians," *FM*, March 2, 2011, 40.

17. "The *Jazeera* Documents," *FM*, March 2, 2011, 42–43.

18. "Palestinian State," *FM*, January 31, 2011, 3. For more on the performance of sovereignty through the statehood bid, see Darryl Li, "Preening Like a State," *Middle East Research and Information Project*, April 3, 2014.

19. For Hamas's coverage, see "Fatah Is Divided," *FM*, January 31, 2011, 16.

20. "Terrorism," *FM*, January 31, 2011, 2.

21. Harriet Sherwood and Hazem Balousha, "Gaza and West Bank Protests Demand End to Palestinian Divisions," *The Guardian*, March 15, 2011. Hamas leaders stressed to the author that there would be no "Arab Spring" in Gaza because Hamas did not oppress Gaza's inhabitants, claiming more free press than most places in the region. Human rights activists did indeed confirm that Hamas was open to criticism and that there was relative freedom of speech (as long as it was not political); however, there was no denying Hamas's strong security hold, Islamization agenda, and policing of "indecent behavior." Author interviews, Hamas ministers and human rights activists, Gaza, 2015. For more on human rights in the Palestinian territories, see Allen, *The Rise and Fall of Human Rights*.

22. Author interview, Issam Da'lis, 2015.

23. Nawaf Amer, "The PA's Invitation," *FM*, March 2, 2011, 34–35. Opposition to the elections was forthcoming from other factions too.

24. Performance was quite poor in Hamas's government given inexperience and the fact that major segments of the civil service were replacements. Author interview, Mostafa Ibrahim, 2015.

25. For more reporting on these reforms, see Amina Ziyara, "Ministerial Amendments," *FM*, April 1, 2011, 24–25.

26. Ibid.

27. Ala' Salem, "Palestinian Reconciliation," *FM*, March 2, 2011, 46–47.

28. "In the Shadow of Ending Division," *FM*, April 1, 2011, 22–23.

29. "Palestinian Reconciliation" *FM*, April 1, 2011, 3.

30. For more on Hamas "settling in" in Gaza, see Brown, "Gaza Five Years On." For Hamas's perspective, see "Talk of Getting the Palestinian House in Order," *FM*, April 1, 2011, 20–21.

31. Pelham, "Gaza's Tunnel Phenomenon," 19–21.

32. "Meshal: Palestinian Reconciliation," *FM*, January 31, 2011, 12.

33. Ala' Salem, "Member of Hamas's Political Office," *FM*, May 4, 2011, 41.

34. "Hamas Leader," *FM*, May 4, 2011, 36.

35. Haniyeh announced that an agreement had been reached for Egypt and Qatar to jointly deal with Gaza's reconstruction as a top priority, with a commitment from the Islamic Development Bank to extend $137 million over four months. "Reconstruction in Gaza," *FM*, May 31, 2011, 15. Hamas also reported that Saudi Arabia pledged $71 million to construct housing projects for refugees in Rafah in August. See "Saudi Arabia Pledges," *FM*, September 13, 2011, 9.

36. Nicolas Pelham, "Gaza: A Way Out?," *New York Review of Books*, October 26, 2012.

37. Pelham, "Gaza's Tunnel Phenomenon," 15–16.

38. Ibid., 16–25.

39. Accusations began surfacing that Hamas showed favoritism toward its constituency. Author interviews, human rights activists, Gaza, 2015.

40. Sabry, *Sinai*, 125–61.

41. Ra'ed abu Jarad, "Vittorio Arigoni," *FM*, May 4, 2011, 18–19.

42. Ibid. See also "Jail for Four Killers," *FM*, October 8, 2012, 7.

43. International Crisis Group, "Gaza: The Next Israeli-Palestinian War?," 1–3.

44. For resistance factions describing their right to armed struggle, see Ala' Bayan, "Stressing Their Right to Resist," *FM*, May 4, 2011, 48–49.

45. For more on the agreement, see Rabbani, "Between Hamas and the PA." For more, see Adnan abu Amer, "Reconciliation Agreement," *FM*, May 31, 2011, 44–45. This was seen as the first real effort by the factions, and by Hamas, to achieve reconciliation. Author interview, Khalil Shikaki, 2015.

46. For Hamas's reporting, see Ala' Salem, "Palestinian Reconciliation," *FM*, May 31, 2011, 40–41.

47. For Hamas's reporting, see "Joy Overwhelms," *FM*, May 31, 2011, 38–39.

48. Maha Abdel Hadi, "Hamas-Fatah Agreement," *FM*, May 31, 2011, 50–51.

49. "Meshal Briefs on Reconciliation," *FM*, May 31, 2011, 14.

50. "Hamas's First Priorities," *FM*, May 31, 2011, 15.

51. Analysts in Hamas's publications noted that duplication in legislation was present in all areas ranging from foreign affairs to internal judicial, constitutional, and security-related amendments. Aziz Kayed, "Reconciliation," *FM*, July 5, 2011, 28–29.

52. Brown, "Gaza Five Years On," 17–18.

53. "Arrests in the West Bank," *FM*, July 5, 2011, 36–37.

54. For Hamas's take on the obstacles to reconciliation, see "Minister Hassan Youssef," *FM*, September 13, 2011, 17.

55. Author interview, Change and Reform Parliamentarian, Gaza, 2015.

56. "Delaying the Reconciliation," *FM*, September 13, 2011, 2.

57. For more, see Hijazi, "Harakat Hamas bayn Khayarai al-Sharaka wa al-Tafarod."

58. "Hamas Delegation," *FM*, September 13, 2011, 12.

59. For the impact of this regional shift on Israel, see Jones and Milton-Edwards, "Missing the 'Devils' We Knew?" For more on these regional changes, see Shadi Hamid, "The Rise of the Islamists: How Islamists Will Change Politics, and Vice Versa," *Foreign Affairs* 90, no. 3 (May/June 2011): 40–47.

60. For more on this, see Gold, "Sinai Security," 3–6.

61. See Adnan abu Amer, "Hurricane of Protests," *FM*, September 13, 201, 18–19. For more on protests in Israel, see Asher Schechter, "A Short Guide to Israel's Social Protest," *Haaretz*, July 11, 2012.

62. "The Occupation Lost Twice," *FM*, September 13, 2011, 3.

63. See, for example, Ibrahim al-Sa'id, "How Did the Arab Revolutions Shape Israel's Reaction?," *FM*, September 12, 2011, 24–25.

64. Cover of *FM*, October 5, 2011.

65. "Turkish Egyptian Israeli Relations," *FM*, October 5, 2011, 35.

66. "Palestinian Leader Mahmoud Abbas Makes UN Statehood Bid," *BBC*, September 23, 2011.

67. Ala' Salem, "The State of Palestinians," *FM*, August 5, 2011, 40–41.

68. "Hamas Supports Any Effort," *FM*, September 13, 2011, 12.

69. "The State of Palestine . . . ?," *FM*, October 5, 2011, 3.

70. For Hamas's reporting on the complex negotiations over the five-year period, including with Turkish, Qatari, and German mediators, see "Loyalty of the Free," *FM*, November 4, 2011, 51–52. A few years after Shalit's release, Hamas broadcast a video to show the humane treatment of prisoners of war in its custody. See Jack Khoury, "Barbeque and TV," *Haaretz*, January 3, 2016.

71. Hamas noted that those freed were responsible for killing 569 "Zionists" and wounding thousands. "October 18," *FM*, November 4, 2011, 8–9. Hamas publications also reported on Israeli reactions. See Adnan abu Amer, "Prisoner Exchange," *FM*, November 4, 2011, 10–11.

72. "Meshal: Huge Accomplishment," *FM*, November 4, 2011, 22.

73. Ala' Salem, "Prisoner Exchange," *FM*, November 4, 2012, 6–7.

74. Ibid., 6.

75. "October 18," *FM*, November 4, 2011, 9.

76. "Let's Raise Our Hats," *FM*, January 4, 2012, 3.

77. Ibid. On its twenty-fourth anniversary, al-Qassam issued a report celebrating the scale of their operations since their establishment. "Al-Qassam," *FM*, January 4, 2012, 14.

78. Ayman Hamad, "Palestinian Political Maturity," *FM*, January 4, 2012, 18–19.

79. "Huge Accomplishment," *FM*, November 4, 2011, 22.

80. Ala' Salem, "Prisoner Exchange," *FM*, November 4, 2012, 6–7.

81. For Hamas's reporting, see "Palestinian Reconciliation," *FM*, December 4, 2011, 3.

82. Avi Issacharoff, "Abbas: Israel to Blame for Failed Peace Talks in Jordan," *Haaretz*, January 29, 2012. For Hamas's take, see "Amman Negotiations," *FM*, February 7, 2012, 3.

83. Lynch, *New Arab Wars*, 1–47.

84. Ibid., 44. For more on ISIS, see Cockburn, *The Rise of Islamic State*; Gerges, *ISIS*; and McCants, *Apocalypse*.

85. For more on the early impact of the Arab Spring on Hamas, see Kurz, Berti, and Konrad, "The Institutional Transformations of Hamas and Hizbollah," 92–97.

86. See "Haniyeh Leaves Gaza," *FM*, January 4, 2012, 15.

87. Hamas's ability to maintain a "neutral position" was undermined when the Assad regime asked for either firm support or exile. Author interview, Hamas leader, 2015.

88. Author interview, Adnan abu Amer, 2015. Leaks reflect this tension. See Jack Khoury, "Senior Hamas Official Slams Iran in Leaked Recording: Tehran Hasn't Helped Us Since 2009," *Haaretz*, January 31, 2016.

89. For more on the brotherhood's performance, see Wickham, *The Muslim Brotherhood*, 247–89; and Milton-Edwards, *The Muslim Brotherhood*. For the impact on Hamas, see International Crisis Group, "Light at the End of Their Tunnels?"

90. Pelham, "Gaza: A Way Out?"

91. For more on the Doha Declaration, see Pelham, "Hamas's Leadership Struggle and the Prospects for Palestinian Reconciliation," *Norwegian Centre for Conflict Resolution (NOREF)*, February 2012; Brown, "Is Hamas Mellowing?"; Hani-al Masri, "Putting Doha in Context," *Bitter-Lemons*, February 13, 2012; and Zvika Krieger, "Welcome to 'Fortress Gaza,' Home of the Newly Radicalized Hamas," *The Atlantic*, September 25, 2012.

92. For Hamas's reporting, see Ala' Salem, "The Doha Declaration," *FM*, March 8, 2012, 34–35.

93. "Palestinian Rivals Agree to Form Unity Government," *Reuters*, February 6, 2012.

94. See "Doha Declaration," *FM*, March 8, 2012, 3. Even publications such as *Filastin al-Muslima* suggested that it would have been helpful to communicate this declaration to the people before Meshal and Abbas signed it. Objections came from other factions who were not included in these discussions. Leading Hamas members in Gaza were unaware of the agreement and expressed surprise before rejecting its clauses.

95. Author interview, Adnan abu Amer, 2015.

96. Ibid.

97. For analysis in Hamas's publications, see Abdel Karim Samouni, "Palestinian Leaders," *FM*, March 8, 2012, 36–37.

98. "Solid Foundation," *FM*, March 8, 2012, 38–39.

99. Pelham, "Gaza's Tunnel Phenomenon," 24. For Hamas's reporting, see Ayman Hamad, "Who Is Behind the Fuel Crisis?," *FM*, June 11, 2012, 17–18. For more on Gaza's electricity crisis, see Tareq Baconi, "Gas Politics in Gaza," *Foreign Affairs*, October 15, 2015.

100. The attack killed the leader of the Palestinian Resistance Committees (PRC), who was targeted for assassination and who was presumably responsible for the attacks against Israel in 2011. The PRC denies these claims. For Hamas's reporting, see "26 Martyrs," *FM*, April 3, 2012, 28–29.

101. Author interviews with Hamas leaders in Gaza revealed the ease of obtaining weapons through the tunnels during this time. Increased militant activity in the Sinai was also evident and could be attributed directly to Egyptian policies for dealing with the peninsula. Sabry, *Sinai*, 125–61. For Hamas's coverage, see "Sinai's Nomads," *FM*, April 3, 2012, 9.

102. Filiu, "Twelve Wars on Gaza," 57.

103. "Meshal Talks with Erdogan," *FM*, April 3, 2012, 11.

104. "Gaza . . . Not an Experimental Field," *FM*, April 3, 2012, 3.

105. "Palestinians Undermine Israeli Goals," *FM*, April 3, 2012, 38–39.

106. Abdel Karim Yehya, "Resistance Broke the Occupation's Will," *FM*, April 3 2012, 30.

107. Ibid.

108. Publications claimed al-Qassam fired eighty-six rockets in self-defense and deterrence, "without broadcasting its arsenal," as it suspected this was Israel's goal from the attack. "Attack on Gaza," *FM*, July 18, 2012, 20–21.

109. Abdel Karim Yehya, "Resistance Broke the Occupation's Will," *FM*, April 3 2012, 30.

110. Ibid.

111. Author interviews with Hamas leaders in Gaza revealed that Hamas was active in managing coordination between the various factions and that this all happened in agreement.

112. "Palestinian Reconciliation," *FM*, June 11, 2012, 3.

113. Blame was also directed at American and Israeli opposition to reconciliation, which translated into financial pressure on Abbas. Ala' Salem, "Reconciliation," *FM*, July 18, 2012, 28–29.

114. Ayman Ahmad, "Hamas Minister," *FM*, July 18, 2012, 30–31.

115. "Hamas . . . A Revolution," *FM*, February 7, 2012, 40–41.

116. The prospect for Israel to push the Gaza Strip toward Egypt gathered pace during this time. Author interview, Israeli security analysts, 2015.

117. See "Khaled Meshal Visits," *FM*, August 7, 2012, 18. Other signs of confidence included offers by Hamas's government to donate funds to Palestinian refugee camps in Lebanon. "Haniyeh Supports Development," *FM*, June 11, 2012, 7. A delegation under Meshal's leadership also traveled to Saudi Arabia to offer condolences following the death of Prince Nayef bin Abdul Aziz, the crown prince of Saudi Arabia. See "Delegation from Hamas," *FM*, July 18, 2012, 12.

118. Missiles fell on Eilat again in April 2012. This time Israel noted that they were from Sinai, not Gaza. For Hamas's reporting, see "Rockets Fall," *FM*, May 9, 2012, 15.

119. Sabry, *Sinai*, 125–79. For Hamas's reporting, see "Zionist Entity," *FM*, May 9, 2012, 6.

120. For Hamas's reporting, see "Sinai's Crime," *FM*, September 10, 2012, 32.

121. Hamas's publications hypothesized the tunnel closure was the result of an Israeli-Egyptian conspiracy to turn the tide against both Hamas and the Muslim Brotherhood. It likened this to explosions of the synagogues in Iraq in the 1940s and 1950s to force Iraqi Jews to flee to Israel. "The Palestinians and the Sinai," *FM*, September 10, 2012, 40–41. There is much debate around the perpetrators of these explosions. See Tom Segev, "Now It Can Be Told," *Haaretz*, April 6, 2006.

122. Abdel Karim Yehya, "Who Killed the Egyptian Soldiers?!," *FM*, September 10, 2012, 36–37.

123. "Resistance Factions," *FM*, September 10, 2012, 10. For more on Hamas's engagement

with other Islamist groups in Gaza and the Sinai, see Milton-Edwards, "Islamist versus Islamist," 259–76.

124. Abdel Karim Yehya, "Who Killed the Egyptian Soldiers?!," *FM*, September 10, 2012, 36–37.

125. For Hamas's coverage, see "Sinai and Lifting the Blockade," *FM*, September 10, 2012, 3.

126. "Meshal Explores," *FM*, August 7, 2012, 8.

127. Ayman Hamad, "Leader in Hamas," *FM*, September 10, 2012, 46.

128. "Escalation in Gaza," *FM*, October 8, 2012, 28–29.

129. Daniel Byman, "Israel's Gamble in Gaza," *Foreign Affairs*, November 15, 2012.

130. See, for instance, Aluf Benn, "Israel Killed Its Subcontractor in Gaza," *Haaretz*, November 14, 2012.

131. For more, see Mouin Rabbani, "Israel Mows the Lawn," *London Review of Books*, July 31, 2014.

132. For more on Hamas's development of its "national liberation army," see Ayman Hamad, "Al-Qassam Leader," *FM*, March 5, 2013, 28–29.

133. Ibid.

134. Islamic Jihad developed stronger military capabilities after increased Iranian funding and expanded its support and cooperation with Hamas. Author interviews, Hamas's leaders, Gaza, 2015.

135. Ra'ed Yahya, "Joint Resistance," *FM*, November 5, 2012, 22–23.

136. Author interview, Hamas leader, 2015.

137. For more on the ceasefire, see Thanassis Cambanis, "Where Hamas Goes from Here," *Foreign Affairs*, November 25, 2012; and Nathan Thrall, "Hamas's Chances," *London Review of Books*, August 1, 2014.

138. For examples of how Hamas's publications celebrated this resistance, see Ra'fat Murra, "Zionist Fears," *FM*, January 7, 2013, 26–27.

139. Author interview, Hamas leader, 2015.

140. These remarks were stated by Abbas two years later with regard to this ceasefire. See "Mahmoud Abbas's Speech," *Wafa News Agency*, June 21, 2014, IPS.

141. "Victory in Gaza," *FM*, January 7, 2013, 20–21.

142. Omar Fayed, "Between Two Offensives," *FM*, January 7, 2013, 30–31.

143. Ra'fat Murra, "Words That Are 65 Years Old," *FM*, February 4, 2013, 26.

144. "After an Absence of 45 Years," *FM*, January 7, 2013, 14.

145. At this point reconciliation was also the desire of the Morsi government, further affirming to Hamas that nationalism trumped pan-Islamism for the ascendant Muslim Brotherhood movement. Author interview, Adnan abu Amer, 2015.

146. "Minister Ibrahim Dahbour," *FM*, May 5, 2013, 17. Repeated author interviews with Hamas leaders suggested that part of the reason Abbas avoided reconciliation and sustained Gaza's isolation was because he personally held deep grudges toward Hamas and resented the Gaza Strip. The sense that Abbas had "turned his back on Gaza" was quite prevalent. For instance, author interview, Omar Shaban, 2015.

147. An agreement to oversee the transfer of goods was signed between Egypt and Qatar on January 17. The Qatar Development Committee opened an office in Gaza to oversee the construction. The emir of Qatar had first visited Gaza to lay the cornerstone for these projects in October 2012. See Pelham, "Gaza: A Way Out?"

148. For Hamas's coverage, see Abdel Karim al-Samouni, "Qatari Reconstruction," *FM*, March 5, 2013, 14–16.

149. Ra'fat Murra, "Hamas Completes Its Elections," *FM*, May 5, 2013, 23–24.

150. Author interview, Adnan abu Amer, 2015. For more on Meshal's thinking for Hamas, see Meshaal, *The Political Thought of the Islamic Resistance Movement Hamas*.

151. See, for instance, "Hamas," *FM*, May 7, 2013, 3.

152. Ra'fat Murra, "Hamas Completes Its Elections," *FM*, May 5, 2013, 24.

153. "Press Release for Osama Hamdan," *Palestine-Info*, July 22, 2013, IPS.

154. Anne Gearan and William Booths, "Kerry Announces $4 Billion Economic Development Proposal for West Bank," *Washington Post*, May 26, 2013.

155. "Press Release for Salah Bardawil," *Al-Quds*, July 2, 2013, IPS.

156. "Communiqué from Hamas's Government," *Hamas-Info*, July 31, 2013, IPS.

157. For more, see Sabry, *Sinai*, 179–203; Laub, "Egypt's Sinai Peninsula and Security"; Berti and Gold, "Hamas, the Islamic State, and the Gaza-Sinai Crucible"; Pelham, "Sinai"; and Saleh, *Egypt and the Gaza Strip*.

158. Shadi Hamid, "In Egypt, One Coup Leads to Another," *Washington Post*, July 12, 2013.

159. Peter Hessler, "Egypt's Failed Revolution," *New Yorker*, January 2, 2017.

160. For more, see Ben Shitrit and Jaraba, "Hamas in the Post Morsi Period," 2013.

161. "Press Release from PLC," *Palestine News*, July 8, 2013, IPS.

162. "Press Release for Hamas's Leader," *Hamas-Info*, July 26, 2013, IPS.

163. "Bayan Issued from the PLO," *Fateh Media*, July 3, 2013, IPS.

164. "Press Release for Fatah's Spokesman," *Fateh Media*, July 15, 2013, IPS.

165. "Press Release for Palestinian Ambassador," *Al-Wafa*, August 25, 2013, IPS.

166. "Press Release for Fatah Spokesman," *Fateh Media*, July 7, 2013, IPS.

167. "Bayan Issued from Hamas," *Hamas-Info*, July 3, 2013, IPS.

168. "Press Release for Hamas's Spokesman," *Al-Sabeel*, July 7, 2013, IPS.

169. See "Hamas Bayan," *Palestine-Info*, July 24, 2013, IPS. Hamas's government reaffirmed its commitment to journalistic rights but reiterated security as its priority. "Bayan from Hamas's Government," *Palestine-Info*, July 26, 2013, IPS. In fact, the rights of journalists within both Gaza and the West Bank had been severely criticized. See Human Rights Watch, "No News Is Good News."

170. "Press Release for Egyptian Ambassador," *Al-Ayyam*, July 23, 2013, IPS.

171. "Press Release for Osama Hamdan," *Al-Resalah*, July 29, 2013, IPS.

172. "TV Interview with President Assad," *Al-Mayadeen*, October 21, 2013, IPS. For more on the Muslim Brotherhood and Syria, see Lefevre, *Ashes of Hama*.

173. "Press Release for Hamdan," *Al-Resalah*, July 29, 2013, IPS.

174. "Speech in Beirut for Hassan Nassrallah," *Moqawama*, August 2, 2013, IPS. Hezbollah secretary general Hassan Nassrallah noted that Palestine continued to be the rallying call that united all Arabs and Muslims, and declared that Meshal and Nassrallah had met in Beirut in 2011 to put a reconciliation framework in place for Syria, which was initially accepted by Bashar al-Assad before he stepped back from it. See also "Speech for Hassan Nassrallah," *Al-Manar*, November 14, 2013, IPS. For more, see Giorgio Cafiero and Peter Certo, "Hamas and Hezbollah Agree to Disagree on Syria," *Atlantic Council*, January 30, 2014.

175. "Press Release for Izzat Risheq," *Hamas-Info*, October 6, 2013, IPS.

176. Author interview, Adnan abu Amer, 2015.

177. "Press Release for Musa abu Marzouq," *Al-Quds*, August 4, 2013, IPS.

178. See, for example, "Press Release for Fatah's Spokesman," *Al-Wafa*, September 8, 2013, IPS.

179. "Press Release for Musa abu Marzouq," *Hamas-Info*, August 18, 2013, IPS. For more on Tamarod, see Asmaa al-Ghoul, "Tamarod Protest Fails in Gaza," *Al-Monitor*, November 12, 2013. For more on accusations that Fatah was working to unseat Hamas, see Adnan abu Amer, "Seized Documents Suggest Fatah Plot to Frame Hamas in Egypt," *Al-Monitor*, August 6, 2013.

180. "Press Release for Salah Bardawil," *Hamas-Info*, August 26, 2013, IPS.

181. For Hamas's take, see "Interview with Izzat Risheq," *Rayya*, September 29, 2013, IPS.

182. "Speech for Ismail Haniyeh," *Hamas-Info*, October 19, 2013, IPS.

183. "Press Release for Spokesman of Egyptian Military Forces," *Egypt State Information Service*, September 15, 2013, IPS.

184. "Report Released from the Office for the Coordination of Humanitarian Affairs [OCHA]," *OCHA*, September 23, 2013, IPS. For Hamas's take, see "Bayan from Ismail Haniyeh," *Palestine-Info*, September 17, 2013, IPS.

185. "Press Release for Ahmad Assaf," *Al-Wafa*, September 16, 2013, IPS.

186. "Speech for Ismail Haniyeh," *Hamas-Info*, October 19, 2013, IPS.

187. "Radio Interview with Hamdan," *Hamas-Info*, November 18, 2013, IPS.

188. "UNRWA Release," *UNRWA* (UN Relief and Works Agency for Palestine Refugees in the Near East), September 11, 2013, IPS.

189. "Press Release for Quartet," *Quartet Representative*, December 16, 2013, IPS.

190. "Press Release about Haniyeh's Phone Discussions," *Palestine-Info*, December 12, 2013, IPS.

191. "Press Release about Meshal's Phone Discussion," *Hamas-Info*, December 15, 2013, IPS.

192. "Letter from Permanent Representative for Palestine at the UN," *Al-Wafa*, December 25, 2013, IPS.

193. "Press Release for Islamic Jihad's Saraya al-Quds," *Saraya al-Quds*, January 19, 2013, IPS.

194. "Press Release for Islamic Jihad's Spokesman," *Ma'an News*, January 22, 2013, IPS.

195. Fatah accused Hamas of indirect negotiations with Israel with mediators in Switzerland, whereby the two parties agreed on Hamas's continued rule over the Gaza Strip in return for security on the resistance front. This was a continuation of the 2012 ceasefire agreement. See "Press Release for Fatah's Spokesman," *Fateh Media*, February 19, 2014, IPS.

196. "Press Release for Egypt's Minister of Interior," *Al-Masr al-Youm*, January 2, 2014, IPS.

197. Ibid.

198. "Press Release from Hamas," *Hamas-Info*, January 2, 2014, IPS.

199. In 2013, Hamas had initially experimented with allowing Salafis to operate in Gaza as long as they didn't fire rockets at Israel. That worked for awhile until ISIS began gaining ground in Iraq, prompting Salafis to become more confident in Gaza. Hamas shifted to dealing with them through the lens of security. Author interview, Adnan abu Amer, 2015. For more, see Brenner, *Gaza under Hamas*, 65–117.

200. "Press Release for Ahmad Assaf," *Fateh Media*, December 25, 2013, IPS.

201. "Hamas Bayan," *Hamas-Info*, March 2, 2014, IPS. For more on this, see Yasmine Saleh, "Court Bans Activities of Islamist Hamas in Egypt," *Reuters*, March 4, 2014.

202. "Hamas Condemns Egypt's Decision," *Hamas-Info*, March 4, 2014, IPS.

203. "Press Release for Hamas's Spokesman," *Hamas-Info*, December 29, 2013, IPS.

204. "Press Release for Mahmoud Zahhar," *Fars News*, March 10, 2014, IPS.

205. "Speech for Ismail Haniyeh," *Palestine-Info*, January 2, 2014, IPS.

206. "Press Release for Ismail Haniyeh," *Palestine-Info*, January 16, 2014, IPS.

207. "Haniyeh's Speech," *Palestine-Info*, February 9, 2014, IPS.

208. "Interview with Salah Bardawil," *Palestine-Info*, March 25, 2014, IPS.

209. Peter Beaumont, "Israel Risks Becoming Apartheid State If Peace Talks Fail, Says John Kerry," *The Guardian*, April 28, 2014.

210. "Closing Statement for the PLO's Twenty-Six Session," *Al-Wafa*, April 27, 2014, IPS.

211. Abbas was hoping that Hamas would say no to its offer, thereby strengthening the Palestinian Authority's hand. Author interview, Fatah advisor, 2015.

212. See Ehud Yaari and Neri Zilber, "The Hamas-Fatah Reconciliation Agreement: Too Early to Judge," *Washington Institute for Near East Peace*, April 24, 2014.

213. "Obama: US Will Persist with Middle East Peace Effort," *BBC*, April 25, 2014.

214. "Press Release for Hamadan," *Hamas-Info*, April 27, 2014, IPS.

215. Ibid.

216. The military wing within Hamas was opposed to this deal. Author interview, Palestinian analyst, 2015. Israeli security analysts noted a complete collapse of Hamas's central authority because of this deal. Author interview, Israeli security analysts, 2015.

217. "Press Release for Musa abu Marzouq," *Palestine-Info*, April 28, 2014, IPS.

218. "Press Release for Musa abu Marzouq," *Palestine-Info*, May 5, 2014, IPS.

219. "Press Release for Sami abu Zuhri," *Palestine-Info*, April 27, 2014, IPS.

220. "Press Release for Musa abu Marzouq," *Palestine-Info*, April 28, 2014, IPS.

221. "Press Release for Musa abu Marzouq," *Palestine-Info*, May 3, 2014, IPS.

222. Author interview, Adnan abu Amer, Gaza, 2015.

223. "Joint Press Conference," *Hamas-Info*, May 27, 2014, IPS.

224. "President Abbas's Speech," *Al-Wafa*, May 31, 2014, IPS.

225. Lesley Wroughton and Patricia Zengerle, "Obama Administration to Work with Palestinian Unity Government," *Reuters*, June 2, 2014.

226. "Decree from President Abbas to the Election Committee," *Al-Wafa*, June 4, 2014, IPS.

227. "Press Release for Unity Government Spokesman," *Fateh Media*, June 9, 2014, IPS.

228. Author interview, Omar Shaban, 2015.

CONCLUSION

1. "Gaza Could Become Uninhabitable in Less Than Five Years due to Ongoing 'De-development'—UN report," *UN News Center*, September 1, 2015.

2. Tareq Baconi, "How Israel's 10–Year Blockade Brought Gaza to the Brink of Collapse," *The Nation*, July 7, 2017.

3. "Gaza Ten Years Later," *UN Country Team*, July 2017. For more on the impact of the blockade, see Shaban, "The Implications of Siege and the Palestinian Division on the Situation in the Gaza Strip since 2007."

4. See, for instance, "Press Release for Fatah Spokesman," *Al-Wafa*, June 10, 2014, IPS.

5. Author interview, Omar Shaban, 2015.

6. "Bayan from Palestinian Leadership," *Al-Wafa*, June 16, 2014, IPS.

7. Hamas's leadership denied any involvement but praised the operation. See "TV Statement for Khaled Meshal," *Hamas-Info*, June 23, 2014, IPS.

8. See Nathan Thrall, "Hamas's Chances," *London Review of Books*, August 1, 2014; and Blumenthal, *The 51 Day War*, 9–11.

9. Thrall, "Hamas's Chances."

10. "Statement by Palestinian Prime Minister," *Al-Wafa*, July 7, 2014, IPS. The PLO hoped that Palestine's new status as nonobserver member state at the United Nations would provide it some protection.

11. The Palestinian Authority issued a release discussing how this violence was systematically supported across all levels of government within Israel. See "Bayan from Palestinian Foreign Ministry," *Al-Wafa*, July 7, 2014, IPS. For more on "Israeli terrorists," see Sara Yael Hirschorn, "Israeli Terrorists, Born in the U.S.," *New York Times*, September 4, 2015.

12. "Netanyahu's Speech at a Quartet Meeting," *Israel's Prime Minister's Office*, June 17, 2014, IPS. See also Isabel Kershner, "New Light on Hamas's Role in Killings of Teenagers That Fueled Gaza War," *New York Times*, September 4, 2014.

13. The majority of the rockets fired in June were by Salafi jihadist actors in Gaza. See Benedetta Berti, "Hamas and Israel at the Brink," *Cairo Review of Global Affairs*, July 9, 2014. For al-Qassam's statement, see "Press Release from al-Qassam," *Al-Qassam*, July 8, 2014, IPS.

14. "Press Conference for Abu Ubaida," *Palestine-Info*, July 3, 2014, IPS. Reactions from Gaza showed the failure of Israel's efforts to separate Gaza from the West Bank from a security perspective, given that factions in Gaza often respond to Israeli violations in East Jerusalem and the West Bank with rocket fire. See Brom, "Operation Protective Edge," 95, in Kurz and Brom, *The Lessons of Operation Protective Edge*.

15. "Press Release for Fawzi Barhoum," *Palestine-Info*, July 7, 2014, IPS. For more on the dynamic between Israel and the Palestinians in the lead-up to and after the war, see Mustafa and Abu Saif, *Post Israel 2014 War against Gaza*.

16. Thrall, "Hamas's Chances."

17. The Israeli army found thirty-two tunnels, fourteen of which extended into Israel. "Report of the Independent Commission of Inquiry Established Pursuant to Human Rights Council Resolution S-21/1," *UN General Assembly Human Rights Council*, June 24, 2015, 5–8.

18. For more on the so-called terror tunnels, see Dershowitz, *Terror Tunnels*.

19. "2014 Gaza Conflict," *Israel Ministry of Foreign Affairs*, 2015, 3.

20. During this operation, the UN Office for the Coordination of Humanitarian Affairs (OCHA) focused specifically on Israel's targeting of residential buildings and urban neighborhoods because the scale of those attacks was a disturbing new development. Israel's attacks on UN shelters, medical facilities, ambulances, and other critical forms of infrastructure were deemed a pattern that had already been systematically used by Israel and investigated by OCHA in past operations. Most of the attacks on residential blocks in this operation were carried out in the evenings or at dawn when residents were at home and families gathered for Ramadan meals. The systematic

nature of these attacks raised concerns that they reflected a broader policy and constituted tacit agreement at the highest level of government to increase civilian deaths. "Report of the Independent Commission of Inquiry," 7–11. There was also mounting evidence during the war that Israel targeted health professionals and infrastructure deliberately and systematically. See "New Evidence of Deliberate Attacks on Medics by Israeli Army," *Amnesty International*, August 7, 2014; "Statement by UN Division Monitoring Palestinian Rights," *UN Multi Media*, July 11, 2014, IPS; and "Press Release for Mezan Center for Human Rights in Gaza," *Mezan*, July 12, 2014, IPS.

21. These were bombarded despite their coordinates having been repeatedly communicated to the Israeli army. See, for instance, the United Nations Relief and Works Agency for Palestine Refugees in the Near East (UNRWA) condemning an Israeli attack on a school housing one thousand refugees: "UNRWA Statement Regarding the Emergency Situation," *UNRWA*, July 22, 2014, IPS.

22. For a sample, see "Press Release from UN Condemning Israel's Disproportionate Use of Force," *United Nations*, July 11, 2014, IPS; "Press Release for Mezan Center for Human Rights in Gaza Regarding Israel's Targeting of Palestinian Disability Centers," *Mezan*, July 12, 2014, IPS; "Press Release for Palestinian Network of Healthcare Professionals Condemning Israel's Targeting of Its Professionals," *Al-Wafa*, July 12, 2014, IPS; and "Report by Human Rights Watch," *Human Rights Watch*, July 10, 2014, IPS.

23. See "Report of the Independent Commission of Inquiry," 18–20. See also Amnesty International, " 'Strangling Necks,' " 10.

24. The UN commission carried out an in-depth investigation in three large areas that were leveled to the ground: Shuja'iya (on July 19, 20, and 30); Khuza'a (from July 20 to August 1); and Rafah (from August 1 to 3). It concluded that Israel's military used heavy explosive weapons in densely populated areas and adopted destruction as a tactic of war. It deemed the warnings used to alert civilians ineffective. It concluded that Israel adopted a policy known as the "Hannibal Directive" in which it carried out all measures to prevent the capture of its own soldiers, including permitting its army to fire at civilians, who all became legitimate targets. See "Report of the Independent Commission of Inquiry," 11–16. These policies are reflected in soldier testimonials from the Israeli army. See Breaking the Silence, "This Is How We Fought in Gaza."

25. "Israel's Announcement of the Launch," *Minister of Foreign Affairs*, July 8, 2014, IPS; and "Prime Minister's Declaration," *Prime Minister's Office*, July 8, 2014, IPS. Israel had itself used human shields nearly a decade prior during its operations in the West Bank as well as during the Second Intifada. See Human Rights Watch, "In a Dark Hour"; and B'tselem, "Human Shield." This policy continued in more recent wars. See "Soldiers' Punishment for Using Boy as 'Human Shield' Inadequate," *Human Rights Watch*, November 26, 2010. In 2014, reports emerged of Israelis intentionally targeting civilians in urban centers; see "Gaza: Israeli Soldiers Shoot and Kill Fleeing Civilians," *Human Rights Watch*, August 4, 2014. While evidence that Hamas deliberately uses human shields is scant, the movement has come under condemnation for carrying out military operations from close to civilian areas and for hiding and storing weapons in civilian centers. See "UNRWA Condemns Placement of Rockets, for a Second Time, in One of Its Schools," *UNRWA*, July 22, 2014. For these instances that have been recorded, see "Report of the Independent Commission of Inquiry," 15. Human rights activists in Gaza denied Hamas was using human shields. Author interview, Raji Sourani, 2015. Hamas also denied that it was using human shields, noting that previous UN investigation committees found assertions that Hamas fired rockets from within schools to be untrue. For Hamas's reporting on this, see "Press Release for Osama Hamdan," *Hamas-Info*, July 19, 2014, IPS. Author interviews also stressed that Hamas did not intentionally put civilians in harm's way, but recognized that due to the heavy population density in Gaza, al-Qassam inadvertently operated close to civilian areas. Author interview, Hamas leaders, 2015.

26. The United Nations reported on its inability to verify these claims after Operation Protective Edge. "Report of the Independent Commission of Inquiry," 3–4. In the three instances during this war where Hamas had verifiably fired from close to civilian populations, the United Nations asserted that Israel was still legally obliged to abide by the rules of warfare as stipulated by international law to attempt to reduce civilian casualties. Ibid., 16. For Israel's assessment of its military conduct during these operations, see "IDF Conduct of Operations," *Ministry of Foreign Affairs*, 38.

27. Author interview, Raji Sourani, 2015. See also "Report of the Independent Commission of Inquiry," 6–7; and "Fragmented Lives," *OCHA*, March 2015.

28. This is a manifestation of a shift in Israel's military strategy from fighting armies to fighting non-state actors in civilian areas, which produced policies of heavy bombardment in densely populated centers. It can be traced to Israel's 1982 invasion of Beirut through the 2006 war in Lebanon and the successive wars in Gaza since. See Gal and Hammerman, *From Beirut to Jenin*. For criticisms of Israel's claim to self-defense and unintentionality in targeting civilians, see Nadia abu El-Haj, "Nothing Unintentional," *London Review of Books*, July 29, 2014; and Noura Erekat, "No, Israel Does Not Have the Right to Self-Defense in International Law against Occupied Palestinian Territory," *Jadaliyya*, July 11, 2014. For debates supporting the legality of Israel's assault, see Yishai Schwartz, "Israel's Deadly Invasion of Gaza Is Justified," *New Republic*, July 21, 2014.

29. "Press Release from al-Qassam," *Palestine-Info*, July 12, 2014, IPS. Al-Qassam claimed it had fired 571 rockets into Israel as well as exploded booby-trapped tunnels in operations that startled the Israeli army.

30. "Report of the Independent Commission of Inquiry," 18–20. See also "Human Rights Watch Report Says Rocket Fire from Gaza Indiscriminate," *Human Rights Watch*, July 10, 2014, IPS. For more on the limitations of international humanitarian law in regulating the present situation in Gaza, see Paul W. Kahn, "What Gaza and Ukraine Have in Common," *Al-Jazeera America*, July 19, 2014.

31. Landau and Bermant, "Iron Dome Protection," 37–43, in Kurz and Brom, *Lessons of Operation Protective Edge*.

32. See, for example, "Al-Qassam Bayan," *Al-Qassam*, July 13, 2014, IPS.

33. Author interviews, Hamas leaders, 2015. See also Khalidi, "Al-Tahuwwlat al-Istratigiyyeh."

34. Author interviews, Hamas leaders, Gaza, 2015.

35. This was also noted on the Israeli side. See Kurz and Brom, *Lessons of Operation Protective Edge*.

36. "Press Release for Musa abu Marzouq," *Hamas-Info*, July 13, 2014, IPS.

37. See Omer, *Shell-Shocked*.

38. Hamas's Ministry of Interior noted that more than 90 percent of those killed were civilians. "Press Release from Ministry of Interior in Gaza," *Ministry of Interior*, July 10, 2014, IPS. International sources show that about 70 percent of those killed were civilians.

39. See "A War Waged on Gaza's Children," *Defence for Children International*, 2015.

40. These assassinations are typically preceded by torture and interrogation sessions by Hamas's members to extract "confessions" from prisoners, who do not have access to a credible judicial process. Author interviews, human rights activists, Gaza, 2015. See also Amnesty International, "'Strangling Necks'"; and "Report of the Independent Commission of Inquiry," 16.

41. "Press Release by Ministry of Interior," *Ministry of Interior*, July 10, 2014, IPS. There is no indication that these attempts by Hamas increased the civilian death toll, and it is unclear if they were part of a cynical intention to increase the rate of casualties or to deter Israel from carrying out its attacks. Author discussions in Gaza suggested that most of these messages were in any case ignored by residents of apartment blocks who indeed did seek shelter. Furthermore, Israel's evacuation alerts—known as "knocking on the roof"—were themselves heavily criticized. See "Press Release for PCHR in Gaza," *Palestinian Center for Human Rights*, July 10, 2014, IPS; and "Fragmented Lives," *OCHA*, March 2015, 10.

42. Author interviews, human rights activists, Gaza, 2015.

43. See, for instance, Yousef Alhelou, "In Gaza, Palestinians Celebrate Resistance and Credit It with 'Victory,'" *Mondoweiss*, August 28, 2014.

44. "Press Release for Izzat Risheq," *Palestine-Info*, July 12, 2014, IPS.

45. For more on the impact of this development, see Internal Displacement Monitoring Center, "Under Fire."

46. "UNRWA Statement Regarding the Emergency Situation," *UNRWA*, July 26, 2014, IPS.

47. For Egypt's declarations, see "Press Release for Egyptian Foreign Ministry," *Ministry of Foreign Affairs*, July 12, 2014, IPS. For calls from Hamas, see "Press Release for Ministry of Interior," *Ministry of Interior*, July 20, 2014, IPS.

48. "Khaled Meshal's Address," *Al-Aqsa TV*, July 9, 2014, IPS.

49. "Bayan from Resistance Factions," *Palestinian Resistance Factions*, July 9, 2014, IPS.

50. "Khaled Meshal's Address," *Al-Aqsa TV*, July 9, 2014, IPS. Behind the scenes, Hamas's leaders reportedly sought to deescalate, but publicly they had to cater to the military wing and those advocating for war. See Berti, "Hamas and Israel at the Brink." Other leaders concurred with Meshal. See "Press Release for Osama Hamdan," *Palestine-Info*, July 22, 2014, IPS; and "Press Release for Abu Zuhri," *Hamas-Info*, July 18, 2014, IPS.

51. "Press Conference for Benjamin Netanyahu," *Prime Minister's Office*, July 18, 2014, IPS. Hamas's willingness to escalate, unlike previous conflicts, was seen as a testament to its desperation. See Golov, "Rethinking the Deterrence of Hamas," 87–91, in Kurz and Brom, *Lessons of Operation Protective Edge*. However, it was also due to the recognition that even with calm Israel failed to ease access, as 2012 had shown. Thrall, "Hamas's Chances."

52. "Press Release for Hamdan Regarding Turkish-Qatari Efforts to End War," *Hamas-Info*, July 19, 2014, IPS.

53. See, for example, "Press Release from Ismail Haniyeh," *Palestine-Info*, July 8, 2014, IPS.

54. "Address by President Abbas," *Al-Ayyam*, July 9, 2014, IPS.

55. "Bayan from Palestinian Leadership," *Al-Wafa*, July 23, 2014, IPS. Hamas lauded Abbas's speech. "Press Release for Hamas Leader," *Al-Quds*, July 24, 2014, IPS.

56. See, for instance, "Press Release for Benjamin Netanyahu," *Prime Minister's Office*, August 4, 2014, IPS. For more on why the demand to disarm Hamas was a "red herring," see Daniel Levy, "Gaza Demilitarization Won't Solve Israeli-Palestinian Conflict," *Al-Monitor*, August 14, 2014.

57. See, for example, "Press Release for Izzat Rishaq," *Hamas-Info*, August 5, 2014, IPS.

58. "Press Release for Khaled Meshal," *Hamas-Info*, August 11, 2014, IPS.

59. "Press Release for Palestinian Prime Minister," *Aswat*, August 13, 2014, IPS.

60. "Press Release for Head of Palestinian Delegation," *Al-Wafa*, August 13, 2014, IPS. Hamas and Islamic Jihad demonstrated effective tactical coordination in managing the armed struggle during this period. Author interview, Adnan abu Amer, 2015.

61. There was tremendous tension behind the scenes, particularly between Abbas and Hamas's leadership, during these ceasefire discussions. Abbas continued to harbor deep suspicions of Hamas and to face intense pressure from Israel to dismantle the unity deal. Abbas was allegedly approached by Israeli Shin Bet officers during these discussions and told of a plot by Hamas to assassinate him in the West Bank. Discussions between the factions were mediated in Qatar. Private minutes of those meetings were given to the author by Ahmad Khalidi.

62. Amnesty International reported on these attacks as war crimes. "Israel's Destruction of Multistory Buildings: Extensive, Wanton and Unjustified," *Amnesty International*, December 9, 2014.

63. "PM Benjamin Netanyahu's Statement," *Prime Minister's Office*, August 20, 2014. For more on this, see Dekel, "Operation Protective Edge," 13–20, in Kurz and Brom, *Lessons from Operation Protective Edge*.

64. "Al-Qassam Bayan Warning International Flights," *Al-Qassam*, August 20, 2014, IPS.

65. Author interviews in Israel over the summer of 2015, one year after the war ended, revealed a great deal of suspicion and skepticism within Israeli security circles regarding Hamas's motivations for seeking a seaport.

66. "Benjamin Netanyahu Statement," *Prime Minister's Office*, August 27, 2014, IPS. Israel's conduct in the war was heavily criticized by the security establishment. See Shlomi Eldar, "The One Thing Israel Could Do to Avoid Another War," *Al-Monitor*, May 11, 2016.

67. Author interview, Adnan abu Amer, 2015. Author discussions with residents in Gaza in the summer of 2015 revealed that these attacks created immense terror and were seen as a turning point internally, as the fear became crippling and Gazans wanted the assault to end.

68. "Press Conference for Khaled Meshal," *Al-Qassam*, August 28, 2014, IPS.

69. "Press Conference for Musa abu Marzouq," *Al-Qassam*, August 27, 2014, IPS.

70. "Press Release for Musa abu Marzouq," *Al-Qassam*, August 27, 2014, IPS.

71. "Interview with Khaled Meshal," *Hamas-Info*, September 3, 2014, IPS.

72. Amnesty International, " 'Strangling Necks,' " 5.

73. Ibid., 10.

74. The reconstruction mechanism has been heavily criticized. See Nuriya Oswald, "Gaza Reconstruction Mechanism: Profiting Israel, Entrenching the Blockade," *Jadaliyya*, July 7, 2015.

75. Israel has also failed to carry out its own investigations. See Gili Cohen, "Three Years Later, Gaza War Crime Probes by Israeli Army Still Languishing," *Haaretz*, June 23, 2017.

76. See Jodi Rudoren and Somini Sengupta, "U.N. Report on Gaza Finds Evidence of War Crimes by Israel and by Palestinian Militants," *New York Times*, June 22, 2015.

77. John Reed, "Israel State Comptroller Criticises Netanyahu for Gaza War Conduct," *Financial Times*, February 28, 2017.

78. For more on debates within Israel about Gaza, see David Shulman, "Gaza: The Murderous Melodrama," *New York Review of Books*, November 20, 2014; and Giora Eiland, "The Situation in Gaza Is Much Worse Than Prior to the War in 2014," *Fathom*, 2017.

79. Hamas is seen as "a tactical not a strategic threat." Author interview, Israeli security analyst, 2015.

80. Author interview, Omar Shaban, 2015.

81. Hamas leaders noted that Abbas was uninterested in taking over any kind of responsibility for the Gaza Strip. Author interview, Ahmad Yousef, 2015.

82. For more on Israel's historic policies toward Gaza, see Filiu, *Gaza*, 57–125; and Khalidi, "Al-Tahuwwlat al-Istratigiyyeh."

83. Filiu, "Twelve Wars on Gaza," 53.

84. For a useful timeline of contemporary enclosures, see "A Guide to the Gaza Strip," *Al-Jazeera*, June 26, 2017.

85. Hass, *Drinking the Sea at Gaza*, 10.

86. Israeli politicians, including Benjamin Netanyahu, frequently invoke the claim that Hamas and Islamic State or al-Qaeda are one and the same. For instance, see "Binyamin Netanyahu: ISIS and Hamas 'Branches of the Same Poisonous Tree,'" *The Guardian*, September 29, 2014.

87. For more on the various strands of political Islam and the transnational terror networks, see Devji, *Landscapes of Jihad*; Kepel, *Jihad*, 23–43; and Wiktorowicz, "The New Global Threat," 18–38.

88. The fact that such parties receive international funding should not be confused with their specificity to a particular context. While funding has enabled them to survive, their origins and raison d'être are context-specific. For more on this, see Khashan, "The New World Order and the Tempo of Militant Islam," 1–21. For critics who argue Hamas is a transnational terror group because of global funding, see Levitt, *Hamas*.

89. For more on this, see Al-Azm, "Al-Dawla al-Eilmaniya wa al-Mas'ala al-Diniyyeh," 13.

90. For more on the right to armed struggle, see Falk, "International Law and the al-Aqsa Intifada."

91. See Noura Erekat, "The Real Reason Israel Attacks Gaza," *The Nation*, July 20, 2016.

92. Palestinian Center for Public Opinion, Poll 191.

93. For a useful resource, see "Gaza in Context," www.gazaincontext.com.

94. At least since the eruption of the Second Intifada, successive Israeli leaders have chosen not to engage with Palestinian political demands and have dealt with Palestinians primarily through the prism of Israel's security. For more on this, see Cypel, *Walled*.

95. In taking this line, Hamas has failed to account for Israel's withdrawal from other occupied territories through negotiated settlements, as was the case following the 1979 peace treaty signed with Egypt.

96. For more on Hamas's pragmatism, see Roy, "Hamas and the Transformation(s) of Political Islam in Palestine," 13–20.

97. This included commitments to abide by the Arab Peace Initiative if accepted by the Palestinian people in a public referendum. Private correspondence between Meshal and international mediators, in the possession of Avi Shlaim, University of Oxford.

98. For more on this and for how Meshal offered such a vision directly to Yuval Diskin and Ehud Olmert, see Shlomi Eldar, "Straight Talk Needed Regarding Israel and Hamas," *Al-Monitor*, February 1, 2013.

99. Author interview, Bassem Naim, 2015.

100. Anziska, "Neither Two States nor One." The Jordan option is based on the notion that Jordan could act as a replacement state for the Palestinians, either by relocating Palestinians to Jordan or through a confederate model.

101. See, for example, Harriet Sherwood," Binyamin Netanyahu Rejects Calls for Palestinian State within 1967," *The Guardian*, January 20, 2013.

102. Raz, *The Bride and the Dowry*, 44. See also Anziska and Baconi, "The Consequences of Conflict Management in Israel/Palestine."

103. Yaakov Amidror, "Hamas's Irrational Rationale," *Israel Hayom*, July 21, 2017.

104. Mouin Rabbani, "Fatah: From Liberation Movement to West Bank Government," *Al-Jazeera*, December 6, 2016.

105. Efraim Inbar and Eitan Shamir, "Mowing the Grass in Gaza," *Jerusalem Post*, July 22, 2014. See also Mouin Rabbani, "Israel Mows the Lawn," *London Review of Books*, July 31, 2014.

106. Khalidi, "Dahiya Doctrine."

107. Author interviews, Israeli security analysts, 2015. See also Kurz and Brom, *Lessons from Operation Protective Edge*.

108. OCHA, "Gaza One Year On."

109. "The Gaza Strip: The Humanitarian Impact of the Blockade," *OCHA*, November 14, 2016.

110. OCHA, "Gaza One Year On."

111. See, for instance, Ahmad abu Amer, "Will Opening of Israeli Crossing Help Gaza's Economy?," *Al-Monitor*, May 18, 2016.

112. Author interviews, Hamas leaders, 2015. For more on Hamas's current financial state of affairs, see Adnan abu Amer, "Hamas Scrambles to Make Up Budget Shortfalls," *Al-Monitor*, April 11, 2016.

113. See David Hearst, "Blair Met Khaled Meshaal to Negotiate End of Gaza Siege," *Middle East Eye*, June 21, 2015.

114. Author interview, Adnan abu Amer, 2015.

115. See, for instance, "Fatah Bayan," *Fateh Media*, June 18, 2014, IPS.

116. Author interview, Adnan abu Amer, 2015.

117. Some Israeli analysts noted that Israel has not developed such a policy, mostly because it has no strategy toward Gaza, but has nonetheless actively reinforced the division for its benefit. Others stressed that it is a policy within Israel to deal with each of the entities, the Palestinian Authority and Hamas's government, separately. Author interviews, Israeli security analysts, 2015. See also Ilana Feldman, "Isolating Gaza," *Stanford University Press Blog*, July 28, 2014; and Gisha, "What Is the 'Separation Policy'?"

118. Gisha, "Disengaged Occupiers."

119. For more on the American and EU policies to maintain the current state of affairs, see Alastair Crooke, "Permanent Temporariness," *London Review of Books*, April 1, 2011.

120. "UN Chief Ban Ki-Moon Calls for Israel to End 'Collective Punishment' Blockade of Gaza," *Haaretz*, June 29, 2016.

121. Gaza has been described as a laboratory for Israel to test a military arsenal used in the global fight against terror by allies such as the United States. For more on Gaza as a site of experimentation for tactics that can be employed for the pacification of an unruly population, see Weizman, *The Least of All Possible Evils*; Khalili, *Time in the Shadows*; and Tawil-Souri, "Digital Occupation," 27–43. See also Tawil-Souri and Matar, *Gaza as Metaphor*.

122. For more on Islamic movements and the nation-state model, see Piscatori, *Islam in a World of Nation States*; Zubaida, *Islam, the People and the State*; and Esposito and Voll, *Islam and Democracy*.

123. Ayoob, "Political Islam," 2.

124. For more on sclerotic Arab regimes, see Owen, *The Rise and Fall of Arab Presidents for Life*.

125. This was exemplified by the Iranian revolution, as Islam was increasingly seen as a threat to American security and the "clash of civilizations" theory emerged as a framing device with the end of the Cold War. See Khashan, "New World Order," 5–9; Tehranian, "Militant

Religious Movements," 3213–24; Bernard Lewis, "The Roots of Muslim Rage," *The Atlantic*, September 1, 1990; and Samuel Huntington, "The Clash of Civilizations?," *Foreign Affairs*, Summer 1993. For more on the relationship between Islam and the West, see Halliday, *Islam and the Myth of Confrontation*, 107–33; Saikal, *Islam and the West*; Gerges, *America and Political Islam*; Said, *Covering Islam*, 3–36; Esposito, *Islamic Threat*, 5–23; Crooke, *Resistance*; and Mamdani, *Good Muslim, Bad Muslim*.

126. For more on Islam and liberalism, see Hamid, *Temptations of Power*; Massad, *Islam in Liberalism*; Roy, *Secularism Confronts Islam*; Burgat, *Face to Face with Political Islam*; and Dalacoura, *Islam, Liberalism and Human Rights*.

127. For more on Islam and democracy, see Mandaville, *Islam and Politics*; Salamé, *Democracy without Democrats?*; Mernissi, *Islam and Democracy*; and Hamid, *Islamic Exceptionalism*.

128. Denoeux, "Forgotten Swamp," 72. Radical Islamism is a wide categorization. For instance, Hamas is a Sunni group guided by the teachings of forefathers such as Sayyid Qutb, whereas Shia Islamist groups are guided by Ayatollah Khomeini. For more on Qutb, see Qutb, *Milestones*; and Tripp, "Sayyid Qutb," 154–84, in Rahnema, *Pioneers of Islamic Revival*.

129. Denoeux, "Forgotten Swamp," 72–78.

130. Ahmad and Zartman, "Political Islam?," 75.

131. Ibid., 68–74.

132. Scholars such as Mumtaz Ahmad refer to the "habituation" process of democracy: once a decision is made, Islamist movements will learn to live with it. Ibid., 72.

133. Graham E. Fuller, "The Future of Political Islam." *Foreign Affairs* 81, no. 2 (2002), 52.

134. Ahmad and Zartman, "Political Islam," 76.

135. Ibid.

136. Al-Azm, "Al-Dawla al-Eilmaniya wa al-Mas'ala al-Diniyyeh," 14. It should be noted here that many scholars who question Islam's compatibility with democracy have no similar concerns about the compatibility of Israel's explicit Jewish character with its democratic nature, despite the fact that its democratic credentials are strongly contested by religious preference. See Gorenberg, *The Unmaking of Israel*; and Yiftachel, *Ethnocracy*.

137. Denoeux, "Forgotten Swamp," 72. For more on the tension between obtaining authority for governance from God or the people, see Gunning, *Hamas in Politics*, 55–94.

138. Ahmad and Zartman, "Political Islam," 81.

139. For more on the significance of Algeria, see Malley, *The Call from Algeria*; McDougall, *A History of Algeria*; and Byrne, *Mecca of the Revolution*.

140. For more on this, see Brown and Hamzawy, *Between Religion and Politics*, 161–81.

141. Mumtaz Ahmad rightly counters fears that rising Islamist movements in the Middle East *might* be authoritarian by suggesting that the regimes they are seeking to replace are known and active despotic regimes. In doing so, he undermines this irrational fear of an emerging authoritarianism. Ahmad and Zartman, "Political Islam," 73.

142. To use the phrase from Sayyid, *A Fundamental Fear*.

143. See Brown, "Gaza Five Years On."

144. Author interviews, human rights activists, Gaza, 2015.

145. For more on the history of *shari'a* law and how it has developed to work within the nation-state model, see Zubaida, *Law and Power in the Islamic World*.

146. Sayigh, *Armed Struggle and the Search for State*, 670–74.

147. For an example of such discussions, see Milton-Edwards, "Revolt and Revolution, the Place of Islamism," 219–36; and Esposito, Sonn, and Voll, *Islam and Democracy after the Arab Spring*.

148. Kurzman, "Liberal Islam," 11–19.

149. Fuller, "Future of Political Islam," 50–56.

150. See Ahmad Samih Khalidi, "Revolutionary Change in the Arab World: What Prospects for Palestinians?," *Open Democracy*, October 21, 2011.

151. See Chalcraft, *Popular Politics in the Making of the Modern Middle East*; and Achcar, *Morbid Symptoms*.

152. For more on Hamas's Islamism and the influence of the experiences of regional Islamic parties, see Adnan abu Amer, "Will Hamas Abandon Political Islam?," *Al-Monitor*, June 3, 2016.

153. Nidal al-Mughrabi and Tom Finn, "Hamas Softens Stance on Israel, Drops Muslim Brotherhood Link," *Reuters*, May 1, 2017.

154. For more on this and its impact on Hamas, see Gregg Carlstrom, "The Qatar Crisis Is Pushing Hamas Back to Iran," *The Atlantic*, June 14, 2017; and David Hearst, "Why Hamas Was Not on the Saudi List of Demands for Qatar," *Middle East Eye*, June 27, 2017.

155. For more on relations between Hamas and Egypt, see Omar Shaban, "Egypt and Hamas—Cooperation in the Works?," *Middle East Institute*, June 16, 2016.

156. See Daniel Levy, "Netanyahu's New and Dishonest Vision of Peace: Without the Palestinians," *Haaretz*, August 1, 2016.

157. For more on this, see Mitchell, "Israel-Turkey."

158. See Marwan Beshara, "Sadat to Salman: Israel at the Expense of Palestine," *Al-Jazeera*, November 23, 2017.

159. This is why many international actors have long advocated engagement with Hamas. For more on engagement with Hamas, see Milton-Edwards and Crooke, "Elusive Ingredient," 39–52; Siegman, "US Hamas Policy Blocks Middle East Peace"; and Daniel Byman, "How to Handle Hamas: The Perils of Ignoring Gaza's Leadership," *Foreign Affairs* (2010): 45–63.

160. International Crisis Group, "No Exit?"

161. See Bashir Abu-Manneh, "Explaining the New Violence in Palestine," *Jacobin*, March 17, 2016.

162. For reflections on the Gaza wars and the Palestinian struggle for self-determination, see Siegman, "Gaza and the Palestinian Struggle for Statehood."

BIBLIOGRAPHY

ARCHIVAL SOURCES
Al-Resalah Office, Gaza City, Gaza.
Al-Resalah, 2006–14.

Institute for Palestine Studies, Beirut, Lebanon.
Al-Watha'iq al-Arabiyeh (Arabic Documents) Collection. [IPS]
Filastin al-Muslima, 2000–2013. [*FM*]

UNPUBLISHED PRIMARY DOCUMENTS
Private Papers of Ahmad Khalidi, London, UK.
Private Papers of Avi Shlaim, Oxford, UK.
Khalil, Nihad al-Sheikh. *Harakat al-Ikhwan al-Muslimeen fi al-Qita': Gaza, 1967–1987*, Gaza.

PUBLISHED PRIMARY DOCUMENTS
Al-Zaytouna Centre, Beirut, Lebanon.
Saleh, Mohsen M., and Wael Sa'ad, eds. *Mukhtarat min al-Watha'iq al-Filastiniyyah li Sanat 2005* [Palestinian documents for the year 2005]. Beirut: Al-Zaytouna Centre, 2006. [*WF*]
———. *Al-Watha'iq al-Filastiniyyah li Sanat 2006*. Beirut: Al-Zaytouna Centre, 2008.
———. *Al-Watha'iq al-Filastiniyyah li Sanat 2007*. Beirut: Al-Zaytouna Centre, 2009.
———. *Al-Watha'iq al-Filastiniyyah li Sanat 2009*. Beirut: Al-Zaytouna Centre, 2011.
———. *Al-Watha'iq al-Filastiniyyah li Sanat 2010*. Beirut: Al-Zaytouna Centre, 2015.
Saleh, Mohsen M., Wael Sa'ad, and Abdul-Hameed F. al-Kayyali, eds. *Al-Watha'iq al-Filastiniyyah li Sanat 2008*. Beirut: Al-Zaytouna Centre, 2011.

Hamas Media Office, Gaza.
Hamas. *The White Book: The Decisive Operation in Gaza—Necessity not Choice*. Hamas Media Office, 2007.
Hamas. *The Black Book: Facts Database and Documentation for the Actions of the "Dayton" Government and Its Security Forces in the West Bank, June 14, 2007—June 15, 2008*. Hamas Media Office, 2008.
Hamas. *The Black Book: Violations of the Oslo Team and Their Security Forces, June 16, 2008—December 31, 2009*. Hamas Media Office, 2010.
U.S. Congress. House. Committee on Financial Services. "The Hamas Asset Freeze and Other Government Efforts to Stop Terrorist Funding." 108th Congress, September 24, 2003. Washington: U.S. Government Printing Office, 2003.

ARABIC PERIODICALS AND WEBSITES
Al-Ahram (Cairo)
Al-Ghad (Amman)

Al-Hayat (Beirut, London)
Al-Hiwar (London)
Al-Intiqad (Beirut)
Al-Nahar (Beirut)
Al-Noor (Beirut, London)
Al-Resalah (Gaza)
Al-Quds (Damascus, Gaza)
Al-Quds al Arabi (London)
Al-Safir (Beirut)
Al-Sharq al Awsat (electronic)
Al-Wafa (electronic)
Arab Net (electronic)
Assafir (Gaza)
Hamas websites
Masr al-Youm (Cairo)
Qassam websites

ENGLISH PERIODICALS AND WEBSITES

+972
Al-Monitor
BBC
Cairo Review of Books
Foreign Affairs
Haaretz
Israel Prime Minister Office (PMO)
Jacobin
Jadaliyya
London Review of Books
Middle East Research and Information Project (MERIP)
New York Review of Books
New Yorker
The Atlantic
The Economist
The Guardian
The Nation
The New York Times
U.S. Department of State
Vanity Fair
Yediot Aharonot

INTERVIEWEES

The following is a partial list, as some names have been removed for anonymity at the request of interviewees.

Gaza

Adnan abu Amer, Dean of the Faculty of Arts and Head of the Press and Information Section at Al Ummah University Open Education, June 2015.

Wissam Afifah, Editor in Chief of *Al-Resalah*, June 2015.

Taher al-Nounou, Previous Spokesman for the Hamas Government, June 2015.

Ziad al-Zaza, Deputy Prime Minister, June 2015.

Issam Da'lis, Hamas Political Member, Financial Advisor, June 2015.

Haider Eid, Associate Professor of Postcolonial and Postmodern Literature at Gaza's al-Aqsa University, June 2015.

Mostafa Ibrahim, Member of the Independent Commission for Human Rights, June 2015.
Sobhia Joma'a, Member of the Independent Commission for Human Rights, June 2015.
Nihad al-Sheikh Khalil, Lecturer of Modern and Contemporary History at the Islamic University of Gaza, June 2015.
Bassem Naim, Head of the Council on International Relations, Ex-Minister of Health, July 2015.
Omar Shaban, Founder of Pal-Think, June 2015.
Raji Sourani, Founder and Director of the Palestinian Center for Human Rights, July 2015.
Ahmad Yousef, Senior Advisor to Ismail Haniyeh, June 2015.

West Bank and Jerusalem
Samira Halaiga, Change and Reform Parliamentarian, Hebron, June 2015.
Rafiq Husseini, Former Chief of Staff for President Mahmoud Abbas, Jerusalem, June 2015.
Khalil Shikaki, Director of the Palestinian Center for Policy and Survey Research, Ramallah, June 2015.
Mohammad Totah, Change and Reform Parliamentarian, Ramallah, June 2015.

Israel
Yoram Schweitzer, Head of the Institute for National Security Studies, Program on Terrorism, Tel Aviv, July 2015.
Gabi Siboni, Director of the Military and Strategic Affairs Program, Institute for National and Security Studies, July 2015.

Lebanon
Ali Baraka, Political Official of Hamas, Beirut, August 2011.
Osama Hamdan, Head of International Affairs for Hamas, Beirut, August 2011.
Ra'fat Murra, Hamas Representative in Lebanon, Beirut, August 2011.
Mohsen M. Saleh, Director of al-Zaytouna Centre, Beirut, August 2011.

United Kingdom
Majed al-Zir, Director of the Palestine Return Center, London, June 2011.
Azzam Tamimi, Chairman of al-Hiwar TV, London, June 2011.

SECONDARY LITERATURE
Books and Articles in Arabic
All translations in this book—whether quotations or the titles of the archival works—are by the author, unless otherwise indicated. All book titles are transliterated unless the titles are provided in English, in which case the English title is used instead.

Abdaljawwad, Naser A. *The Fake Democracy and the Usurped Immunity: Sighings of a West Bank Deputy in the Palestinian Council.* Beirut: Al-Zaytouna Centre, 2013.
Abdel Maqsoud, Salah. *Hamas: Min al-Mu'aradah ila al-Sultah: Qira'a fi Ab'ad al-Tajribah Wa Afaquha.* Al-Jiza: Markaz al-Ilam al-Arabi, 2009.
Abi 'Isa, Wisam. *The Russian Stance towards Hamas: 2006–2010.* Beirut: Al-Zaytouna Centre, 2011.
Abu Amer, Adnan. *The Expulsion of the Occupation from the Gaza Strip: The Beginning of the Defeat of the Zionist Project.* Beirut: Baheth Center, 2007.
Abu Bakr, Bakr. *Hamas: Suyuf wa Manabir.* Filastin: Bakr abu Bakr, 2008.
Abu-Fakhr, Sager. "Al-Harakka al-Wataniyya al-Filastiniyyeh al-Mu'sira." *Majallat al-Dirasat al-Filastiniyyeh* 22, no. 87 (2011): 77–92.
Adwan, Atef. *Al-Sheikh Ahmad Yassin: Hayatuhu wa Jihaduhu.* Gaza: Al-Jama'a al-Islamiyyeh, 1991.
Ahmad, Adil Kamal. *Al-Nuqat fawqa al-huruf: Al-Ikhwan al-Muslimun wa-al-nizam al-Khass.* Cairo: Al-Zahra lil 'lam al-Arabi, 1987.
Al-Achcar, Ismail Abdel Latif, and Mo'men Mohammad Ghazi Bseiso. *Al-Amaliyat al-Askariyya li al-Muqawama al-Filastiniyyeh, 29/09/2000–31/12/2004.* Gaza: Al-Arabi Center for Research and Studies, 2005.

Al-Azm, Sadiq Jalal. "Al-Dawla al-Eilmaniya wa al-Mas'ala al-Diniyyeh: Turkiyya Namouthajan."
   Majallat al-Dirasat al-Filastiniyya 21, no. 82 (2010): 13–23.
Al-Dabak, Imad. *Al-Inqisamat al-Filastiniyyah: Asbabuha wa Nata'juha* [Palestinian divisions: causes
   and implications]. Amman: Al Ahlia, 2014.
Al-Emoush, Bassam. *Mahatat fi Tarikh al-Ikhwan al-Muslimeen.* Amman: Academics for Publishing
   and Distribution, 2008.
Al-Gharaibah, Ibrahim. *Jama'at al-Ikhwan al-Muslimin fi al-Urdun, 1946–1996.* Amman: Al-Urdun
   Al-Jadeed Research Center and Dar Sindbad Publications, 1997.
Al-Jihad al-Islami. *Masirat al-Jihad al-Islami fi Filastin.* Beirut: Beit al-Maqdis, 1989.
Al-Kayyali, Abdul-Hameed, ed. *The Israeli Aggression on Gaza Strip: Cast Lead Operation.* Beirut: Al-
   Zaytouna Centre, 2009.
Al-Nuwati, Mohib Salman Ahmad. *Hamas min al-Dakhel.* Gaza: Dar al-Shuruq, 2002.
Ashhab, Naim. *Hamas: Min al-Rafd ila al-Saltah.* Ramallah: Dar al-Tanwir, 2006.
———. *Imarat Hamas.* Ramallah: Dar al-Tanwir, 2006.
Badr, Badr Mohammad. *Al-Tareeq illa Tahrir Filisteen.* Cairo: Dar al-Bayan, 2011.
Badwan, Ali. *Pages from the History of the Palestinian Struggle.* Damascus: Dar Safahat, 2008.
Dakoor, Jamil. "Al-Harakka al-Islamiyya fi al-Dakhel al-Filastini: Hiwar ma' al-Sheikh Raed
   Salah." *Majallat al-Dirasat al-Filastiniyyeh* 36, no. 2 (2007): 83–90.
Dawar, Ghassan. *Imad Akel: The Legend of Jihad and Resistance.* London: Filastin al-Muslima, 1994.
El-Mabhouh, Wael Abed Elhamid. *Opposition in the Political Thought of Hamas Movement, 1994–2006.*
   Beirut: Al-Zaytouna Centre, 2012.
Ghanem, Ibrahim Al-Bayoumi. *Watha'eq Qadiyat Filisteen fi Malafat al-Ikhwan al-Muslimeen* 1928–
   1948. Cairo: Shorouk International, 2011.
Gosheh, Ibrahim. *The Red Minaret: Memoirs of Ibrahim Ghusheh.* Beirut: Al-Zaytouna Centre, 2008.
Hijazi, Mohammad. "Harakat Hamas bayn Khayarai al-Sharaka wa al-Tafarod." *Majallat al-
   Dirasat al-Filastiniyyeh* 22, no. 87 (2011): 59–66.
Hilal, Jamil. "Al-Istiqtab fi al-Haqel al-Siyyassi al-Filastini." *Majallat al-Dirasat al-Filastiniyyeh* 21,
   no. 83 (2010): 24–39.
Hroub, Khaled. "Harakat Hamas Bayn al-Sulta al-Filastiniyyeh wa Israel: Min Muthalath al-
   Quwwa ila al-Mitraqa wa al-Sindan." *Majallat al-Dirasat al-Filastiniyyeh* 5 no. 18 (1994): 24–37.
———. "Khiyarat Hamas fi Thill al-Taswiyya al-Muqbilah." *Majallat al-Dirasat al-Filastiniyyeh* 11,
   no. 42 (2000): 31–43.
Itani, Mariam. *Conflict of Authorities between Fatah and Hamas in Managing the Palestinian Authority, 2006–
   2007.* Beirut: Al-Zaytouna Centre, 2008.
Jarbawi, Ali. *Al-Intifada wa al-Qiyada al-Siyasiyya fi al-Diffa al-Gharbiyyeh wa Qita Ghazza.* Beirut: Dar
   al-Tal'a, 1989.
———. "Hamas: Madkhal Al-Ikhwan al-Muslimun illa al-Sharia al-Siyasiyya." *Majallat al-Dirasat
   al-Filastiniyyeh* 4, no. 13 (1993): 70–84.
Jawada, Ahmad. *Asma al-Sheikh: Ahmad Yassin.* Jerusalem: Zahrat al-Mada'in, 2004.
Khalidi, Ahmad Samih. "Al-Tahuwwlat al-Istratigiyyeh al-Askariyyeh wa al-Amniyyeh al-Israeli-
   yyeh." Paper presented at the Institute for Palestine Studies Conference, Ramallah, 2015.
Majallat al-Dirasat al-Filastiniyyeh. "Kharitat al-Tariq: Ismail abu Shanab (Roadmap)." *Majallat al-
   Dirasat al-Filastiniyyeh* 14, no. 55 (2003): 16–20.
Meshaal, Khaled. "Hamas's Political Thought and Stances in Light of the Arab Uprisings." Paper
   presented at conference convened by Al-Zaytouna Centre, Beirut, November 28–29, 2012.
———. *The Political Thought of the Islamic Resistance Movement Hamas.* Translated by Daud Abdullah,
   Maha Salah, and Zulaikha Abdullah. London: Memo Publishers, 2013.
Mohammad, Abd al Alim. *The Palestinian Struggle at a Crossroads.* Cairo: Mahrosa, 2010.
Mustafa, Mohanad, and Atef abu Saif. *Post Israel 2014 War against Gaza: Israeli Perspective.* Ramallah:
   Madar, The Palestinian Forum for Israeli Studies, 2014.
Ne'irat, Raed. "Hamas wa 'Alaqatuha bi al-Haraka al-Islamiyya wa al-Jihad." In *Harakat Hamas.*
   Dubai: Al Mesbar Studies and Research Center, 2008.
Qutb, Sayyid. *Milestones.* Beirut: Holy Koran Publishing House, 1980.
Rabbani, Mouin. "Khaled Meshal Yashrah Mawqef Hamas min al-Qadayya al-Rahina" [Khaled

Meshal explains Hamas's position regarding current affairs]. *Majallat al-Dirasat al-Filastiniyyeh* 19, no. 76 (2008): 58–81.

Ramadan, Abd al-Azim Muhammad Ibrahim. *Al-Ikhwan al-Muslimun wa al-Tanzim al-Sirri*. Cairo: Maktabat Ruz al-Yusuf, 1982.

Ramadan, Nizar Abdel Aziz. *'Ala masharef al-watan: Al-Mub'adoun al-Filastinyoun fi Marj al-Zuhur*. Beirut: Dar al-Rashad al-Islamiyya, 1993.

Sa'ad, Wael, and Hasan Ibhais. *Security Developments in the Palestinian Authority, 2006–2007*. Beirut: Al-Zaytouna Centre, 2008.

Sabbagh, Mahmud. *Al-Taswib al-Amin li-ma Nasharahu ba'd al-Qadah al-Sabiqin 'an al-tanziim al-khaass lil-Ikhwaan al-Muslimiin*. Cairo: Maktabat al-Turath al-Islami, 1998.

Said, Samir. *Hamas: Jihad—Victory or Martyrdom*. Al-Mansoura: Dar al-Wafa, 2002.

Saleh, Mohsen, ed. *Critical Assessment of the Experience of Hamas and Its Government, 2006–2007*. Beirut: Al-Zaytouna Centre, 2007.

———. *Conflict of Wills between Fatah and Hamas and Other Relevant Parties 2006–2007*. Beirut: Al-Zaytouna Centre, 2008.

———. *Shalit: From the "Dispelled Illusion" Operation till "Devotion of the Free" Deal*. Beirut: Al-Zaytouna Centre, 2012.

———. *Gaza Strip: Development and Construction in the Face of Siege and Destruction*. Beirut: Al-Zaytouna Centre, 2014.

———. *Egypt and the Gaza Strip: From the Revolution of 25 January 2011 to Summer 2014*. Beirut: Al-Zaytouna Centre, 2015.

———. *Islamic Resistance Movement (Hamas): Studies of Thought and Experience*. Beirut: Al-Zaytouna Centre, 2015.

Saleh, Mohsen. "Hamas 1987–2005: Rasid al-Tajrubba." In *Harakat Hamas*. Dubai: Al Mesbar Studies and Research Center, 2008.

———. *The Suffering of Jerusalem and the Holy Sites under Israeli Occupation*. Beirut: Al-Zaytouna Centre, 2011.

Sha'er, Naser al Din. *Amaliyat al Salam al Filastiniyeh al Israeliyeh: Wijhet Nathar Islamiyeh*. Nablus: Center for Palestinian Research and Studies, 1999.

Sharbel, Ghassan. *Meshal: Harakat Hamas wa Tahrir Filastin*. Beirut: Al-Nahhar, 2006.

Shobaki, Bilal. *Political Change from Perspective of Islamist Movements: The Model of Hamas*. Ramallah: Muwatin, 2008.

Yasin, Abd al-Qadir. *Hamas: Harakat al-Muqawamah al-Islamiyah fi Filastin*. Cairo: Sina lil Nashr, 1990.

Zuaiter, Akram. *Al-Harakah al-wataniyyah al-filastiiniiyyah 1935–1939: Yawmiyaat Akram Zuaiter*. Beirut: Mu'assasat al-Diraasaat al-Filastiiniiyah, 1980.

Books and Articles in English

Ababneh, Sarah. "The Palestinian Women's Movement versus Hamas: Attempting to Understand Women's Empowerment outside of a Feminist Framework." *Journal of International Women's Studies* 15, no. 1 (2014): 35–53.

Abbas, Mahmoud. *Through Secret Channels*. Reading: Garnet Publishing, 1995.

Abrams, Elliott. *Tested by Zion: The Bush Administration and the Israeli-Palestinian Conflict*. Cambridge: Cambridge University Press, 2013.

Abu-Amr, Ziad. "The Palestinian Uprising in the West Bank and Gaza Strip." *Arab Studies Quarterly* 10, no. 4 (1988): 384–405.

———. "Hamas: A Historical and Political Background." *Journal of Palestine Studies* 22, no. 4 (1993): 5–19.

———. *Islamic Fundamentalism in the West Bank and Gaza: Muslim Brotherhood and Islamic Jihad*. Bloomington: Indiana University Press, 1994.

———. "The View from Palestine: In the Wake of the Agreement." *Journal of Palestine Studies* 23, no. 2 (1994): 75–83.

———. "The Palestinian Legislative Council: A Critical Assessment." *Journal of Palestine Studies* 26, no. 4 (1997): 90–97.

Abu-Amr, Ziad, and Haider Abdel Shafi. "Interviews from Gaza: Palestinian Options under Siege." *Middle East Policy* 9, no. 4 (2002): 115–21.

Abu Rumman, Mohammad. *Jordanian Policy and the Hamas Challenge: Exploring Grey Areas and Bridging the Gap in Mutual Interests.* Edited by Mona abu Rayyan. Translated by Issam Khoury. Amman: Friedrich Ebert-Stiftung, 2009.

Abumdallal, Sameer, and Ghassan AbuHatab. *The Tunnel Economy in the Gaza Strip: A Catholic Marriage.* Ramallah: Birzeit University, 2014.

Aburish, Said K. *Arafat: From Defender to Dictator.* London: Bloomsbury, 1999.

Achcar, Gilbert. *The Arabs and the Holocaust: The Arab-Israeli War of Narratives.* Translated by G. M. Goshgarian. London: Saqi Books, 2010.

———. *Morbid Symptoms: Relapse in the Arab Uprisings.* Stanford: Stanford University Press, 2016.

Ahmad, Hisham H. *From Religious Salvation to Political Transformation: The Rise of Hamas in Palestinian Society.* Jerusalem: Palestinian Academic Society for the Study of International Affairs, 1994.

Ahmad, Mumtaz, and I. William Zartman. "Political Islam: Can It Become a Loyal Opposition?" Middle East Policy 5, no. 1 (1997): 68–84.

Al-Hout, Bayan Nuwayhed. *Sabra and Shatila: September 1982.* London: Pluto Press, 2004.

Al-Husaini, Ishak Musa. *The Moslem Brethren: The Greatest of Modern Islamic Movements.* Translated by John F. Brown. Beirut: Khayat's College Book Cooperative, 1956.

Ali, Farhana, and Jerrold Post. "The History and Evolution of Martyrdom in the Service of Defensive Jihad: An Analysis of Suicide Bombers in Current Conflicts." *Social Research* 75, no. 2 (2008): 615–54.

Allen, Lori. *The Rise and Fall of Human Rights: Cynicism and Politics in Occupied Palestine.* Stanford: Stanford University Press, 2013.

Alpher, Joseph. "Israel's Security Concerns in the Peace Process." *International Affairs* 70, no. 2 (1994): 229–41.

Amnesty International. " 'Strangling Necks': Abductions, Torture and Summary Killings of Palestinians by Hamas Forces during the 2014 Gaza/Israel Conflict." May 2015.

Andoni, Lamis. "The Palestinian Elections: Moving toward Democracy or One-Party Rule?" *Journal of Palestine Studies* 25, no. 3 (1996): 5–16.

———. "Searching for Answers: Gaza's Suicide Bombers." *Journal of Palestine Studies* 26, no. 4 (1997): 33–45.

Anghie, Antony. *Imperialism, Sovereignty, and the Making of International Law.* Cambridge: Cambridge University Press, 2004.

Anziska, Seth. "Neither Two States nor One: The Palestinian Question in the Age of Trump." *Journal of Palestine Studies* 46, no. 3 (2017): 57–74.

Anziska, Seth, and Tareq Baconi. "The Consequences of Conflict Management in Israel/Palestine." Norwegian Peacebuilding Resource Center, January 12, 2016.

Aruri, Naseer H., and John J. Carroll. "A New Palestinian Charter." *Journal of Palestine Studies* 23, no. 3 (1994): 5–17.

Asad, Talal. *On Suicide Bombing.* New York: Columbia University Press, 2007.

———. "Thinking about Terrorism and Just War." *Cambridge Review of International Affairs* 23, no. 1 (2010): 3–24.

Ayalon, Ami. *The Press in the Arab Middle East: A History.* Oxford: Oxford University Press, 1995.

Ayoob, Mohammed. "Political Islam: Image and Reality." *World Policy Journal* 21, no. 3 (2004): 1–14.

Ayyash, Mark Muhannad. "Hamas and the Israeli State: A 'Violent Dialogue.' " *European Journal of International Relations* 16, no. 1 (2010): 103–23.

Azoulay, Ariella, and Adi Ophir. *The One-State Condition: Occupation and Democracy in Israel/Palestine.* Translated by Tal Haran. Stanford: Stanford University Press, 2013.

Bacevich, Andrew J. *America's War for the Greater Middle East: A Military History.* New York: Random House, 2016.

Baconi, Tareq. "The Demise of Oslo and Hamas's Political Engagement." *Conflict, Security and Development* 15, no. 5 (2015): 503–20.

———. "Politicizing Resistance: The Transformative Impact of the Second Intifada on Hamas's Resistance Strategy, 2000–2006." *Humanity* 8, no. 2 (2017): 311–35.

Bahgat, Gawdat. "The Gaza War and the Changing Strategic Landscape in the Middle East: An Assessment." *Mediterranean Quarterly* 20, no. 3 (2009): 63–76.

Barghouti, Iyad, and Lisa Hajjar. "The Islamist Movements in the Occupied Territories: An Interview with Iyad Barghouti." *Middle East Report* no. 183 (1993): 9–12.

Baskin, Gershon. *The Negotiator: Freeing Gilad Schalit from Hamas.* London: Toby Press, 2013.

Baumgarten, Helga. "The Three Faces/Phases of Palestinian Nationalism, 1948–2005." *Journal of Palestine Studies* 34, no. 4 (2005): 25–48.

Ben-Ami, Shlomo. *Scars of War, Wounds of Peace: The Israeli-Arab Tragedy.* Oxford: Oxford University Press, 2006.

Ben Shitrit, Lihi, and Mahmoud Jaraba. "Hamas in the Post Morsi Period." Washington: Carnegie Endowment for International Peace, August 1, 2013.

Benmelech, Efraim, and Claude Berrebi. "Human Capital and the Productivity of Suicide Bombers." *Journal of Economic Perspectives* 21, no. 3 (2007): 223–38.

Berrebi, Claude, and Esteban F. Klor. "On Terrorism and Electoral Outcomes: Theory and Evidence from the Israeli-Palestinian Conflict." *Journal of Conflict Resolution* 50, no. 6 (2006): 899–925.

Berti, Benedetta. *Armed Political Organizations: From Conflict to Integration.* Baltimore: Johns Hopkins University Press, 2013.

Berti, Benedetta, and Zack Gold. "Hamas, the Islamic State, and the Gaza-Sinai Crucible." Washington: Carnegie Endowment for International Peace, January 12, 2016.

Berti, Benedetta, and Beatriz Gutierrez. "Rebel-to-Political and Back? Hamas as a Security Provider in Gaza between Rebellion, Politics and Governance." *Democratization* 23, no. 6 (2016): 1059–76.

Bjorgo, Tore, ed. *Root Causes of Terrorism: Myths, Reality, and Ways Forward.* London: Routledge, 2005.

Blecher, Robert. "Operation Cast Lead in the West Bank." *Journal of Palestine Studies* 38, no. 3 (2009): 64–71.

Bloom, Mia. "Palestinian Suicide Bombing: Public Support, Market Share, and Outbidding." *Political Science Quarterly* 119, no. 1 (2004): 61–88.

———. *Dying to Kill: The Allure of Suicide Terror.* New York: Columbia University Press, 2005.

———. "Female Suicide Bombers: A Global Trend." *Daedalus* 136, no. 1 (2007): 94–102.

Bloom, Mia, and John Horgan. "Missing Their Mark: The IRA's Proxy Bomb Campaign." *Social Research* 75, no. 2 (2008): 579–614.

Blumenthal, Max. *The 51 Day War: Ruin and Resistance in Gaza.* New York: Nation Books, 2015.

Breaking the Silence. "This Is How We Fought in Gaza: Soldier's Testimonies and Photographs from Operation Protective Edge." 2014.

Bregman, Ahron. *Cursed Victory: A History of Israel and the Occupied Territories.* London: Pegasus Books, 2014.

Brenner, Björn. *Gaza under Hamas: From Islamic Democracy to Islamist Governance.* London: I.B. Tauris, 2017.

Brenner, Michael. *Zionism: A Brief History.* Translated by Shelley L. Frisch. Princeton: Markus Wiener, 2011.

Brom, Shlomo. "The Real Choice: Ceasefire or Reoccupation of Gaza." Tel Aviv: Institute for National Security Studies, March 14, 2008.

Brown, Nathan J. *Palestinian Politics after the Oslo Accords: Resuming Arab Palestine.* Berkeley: University of California Press, 2003.

———. "The Road out of Gaza." Washington: Carnegie Endowment for International Peace, February 2008.

———. "Gaza Five Years On: Hamas Settles In." Washington: Carnegie Endowment for International Peace, 2012.

———. "Is Hamas Mellowing?" Washington: Carnegie Endowment for International Peace, 2012.

Brown, Nathan J., and Amer Hamzawy. *Between Religion and Politics.* Washington: Carnegie Endowment for International Peace, 2010.

Brym, Robert J., and Bader Araj. "Suicide Bombing as Strategy and Interaction: The Case of the Second Intifada." *Social Forces* 84, no. 4 (2006): 1969–86.

Brynen, Rex. *Sanctuary and Survival: The PLO in Lebanon.* Boulder: Westview Press, 1990.

Brynjar, Lia. *A Police Force without a State: A History of the Palestinian Security Forces in the West Bank and Gaza.* Reading: Ithaca Press, 2006.

B'tselem. "Human Shield: Use of Palestinian Civilians as Human Shields in Violation of High Court of Justice Order." B'tselem, November 2002.

Burgat, Francois. *Face to Face with Political Islam.* London: I.B. Tauris, 2003.

Burton, Guy. "Hamas and Its Vision of Development." *Third World Quarterly* 33, no. 3 (2012): 525–40.

Butko, Thomas J. "Revelation or Revolution: A Gramscian Approach to the Rise of Political Islam." *British Journal of Middle Eastern Studies* 31, no. 1 (2004): 41–62.

Byman, Daniel. *A High Price: The Triumphs and Failures of Israeli Counterterrorism.* Oxford: Oxford University Press, 2011.

Byrne, Jeffrey James. *Mecca of the Revolution: Algeria, Decolonization, and the Third World Order.* New York: Oxford University Press, 2016.

Cambanis, Thanassis. *A Privilege to Die: Inside Hezbollah's Legions and Their Endless War against Israel.* New York: Simon & Schuster, 2010.

Cardici, Paola. *Hamas: From Resistance to Government.* Translated by Andrea Teti. New York: Seven Stories Press, 2012.

Carr, Matthew. *The Infernal Machine: A History of Terrorism.* New York: New Press, 2006.

Cassese, Antonio. "Expert Opinion on Whether Israel's Targeted Killings of Palestinian Terrorists Is Consonant with International Humanitarian Law." In *Supreme Court of Israel: The Public Committee against Torture et al. v The Government of Israel et al.* HCJ 769/02.

Chalcraft, John T. *Popular Politics in the Making of the Modern Middle East.* Cambridge: Cambridge University Press, 2016.

Chamberlin, Paul Thomas. *The Global Offensive: The United States, the Palestine Liberation Organization, and the Making of the Post-Cold War Order.* Oxford: Oxford University Press, 2012.

Chehab, Zaki. *Inside Hamas: The Untold Story of Militants, Martyrs and Spies.* London: I.B. Tauris, 2007.

Chomsky, Noam, and Ilan Pappé. *Gaza in Crisis: Reflections on Israel's War against the Palestinian.* Chicago: Haymarket Books, 2010.

Christison, Kathleen. *Perceptions of Palestine: Their Influence on US-Middle East Policy.* Berkeley: University of California Press, 2001.

Cobban, Helena. *The Palestinian Liberation Organisation: People, Power and Politics.* Cambridge: Cambridge University Press, 1984.

Cockburn, Patrick. *The Rise of Islamic State: ISIS and the New Sunni Revolution.* London: Verso, 2015.

Cohen, Amnon. *Political Parties in the West Bank under the Jordanian Regime, 1949–1967.* London: Cornell University Press, 1982.

Cohen, Hillel. "Society-Military Relations in a State-in-the-Making: Palestinian Security Agencies and the 'Treason Discourse' in the Second Intifada." *Armed Forces and Society* 38, no. 3 (2012): 463–85.

———. *Year Zero of the Arab-Israeli Conflict 1929.* Translated by Haim Watzman. Lebanon, N.H.: Brandeis University Press, 2015.

Cohen, Mark R. *Under Crescent and Cross: The Jews in the Middle Ages.* Princeton: Princeton University Press, 1994.

Cohen, Stuart A. "The Futility of Operation Cast Lead." Perspectives Paper no. 68. Begin-Sadat Center for Strategic Studies (February 2009).

Cohen, Yoram, and Jeffrey White. "Hamas in Combat: The Military Performance of the Palestinian Islamic Resistance Movement." Policy Focus, no. 97. Washington: Washington Institute for New East Peace, 2009.

Cordesman, Anthony H. " 'The Gaza War': A Strategic Analysis." Washington: Center for Strategic and International Studies, February 2, 2009.

Crist, David. *The Twilight War: The Secret History of America's Thirty Year Conflict with Iran.* New York: Penguin, 2012.

Crooke, Alastair. *Resistance: The Essence of the Islamist Revolution.* London: Pluto Press, 2009.

Cypel, Sylvain. *Walled: Israeli Society at an Impasse.* New York: Other Press, 2006.

Dajani, Mohammed. "Lessons from the Gaza Disengagement." *Palestine-Israel Journal of Politics, Economics, and Culture* 13, no. 2 (2006): 13–17.

Dalacoura, Katerina. *Islam, Liberalism and Human Rights.* London: I.B. Tauris, 1998.

Darcy, Shane, and John Reynolds. "An Enduring Occupation: The Status of the Gaza Strip from the Perspective of International Humanitarian Law." *Journal of Conflict and Security Law* 15, no. 2 (2010): 211–43.

Denoeux, Guilain. "The Forgotten Swamp: Navigating Political Islam." *Middle East Policy* 9, no. 2 (2002): 56–81.

Der Derian, James. "Imaging Terror: Logos, Pathos and Ethos." *Third World Quarterly* 26, no. 1 (2005): 23–37.

Dershowitz, Alan. *Terror Tunnels: The Case for Israel's Just War against Hamas.* New York: Rosetta Books, 2014.

Devji, Faisal. *Landscapes of Jihad: Militancy, Morality, Modernity.* London: Hurst, 2005.

Dickinson, Rob, et al., eds. *Examining Critical Perspectives on Human Rights.* Cambridge: Cambridge University Press, 2012.

Dolphin, Ray. *The West Bank Wall: Unmaking Palestine.* London: Pluto Press, 2006.

Doty, Roxanne Lynn. *Imperial Encounters: The Politics of Representation in North-South Relations.* Minneapolis: University of Minnesota Press, 1996.

Dunning, Tristan. "Islam and Resistance: Hamas Ideology and Islamic Values in Palestine." *Critical Studies on Terrorism* 8, no. 2 (2015): 284–305.

Eickelman, Dale F., and James Piscatori. *Muslim Politics.* Princeton: Princeton University Press, 1996.

Eisenberg, Laura Zittrain, and Neil Caplan. *Negotiating Arab-Israeli Peace: Patterns, Problems, Possibilities.* Bloomington: Indiana University Press, 2010.

El-Awaisi, Abd al-Fattah M. "The Conceptual Approach of the Egyptian Muslim Brothers towards the Palestine Question 1928–1949." *Journal of Islamic Studies* 2, no. 2 (1991): 225–44.

——— . "Emergence of a Militant Leader: A Study of the Life of Hasan Al-Banna: 1906–1928." *Journal of South Asian and Middle Eastern Studies* 22, no. 1 (1998): 46–63.

Eldar, Shlomi. *Lehakir et Hamas* [To know Hamas]. Jerusalem: Keter, 2012. (Hebrew).

Elgindy, Khaled. "The Middle East Quartet: A Post-Mortem." Analysis Paper, no. 25. Washington: Brookings Institution, February 2012.

Esposito, John L. *The Islamic Threat: Myth or Reality?* Oxford: Oxford University Press, 1999.

Esposito, John L., Tamara Sonn, and John O. Voll. *Islam and Democracy after the Arab Spring.* Oxford: Oxford University Press, 2016.

Esposito, John L., and John O. Voll. *Islam and Democracy.* Oxford: Oxford University Press, 1996.

Esposito, Michele K. "The Al Aqsa Intifada: Military Operations, Suicide Attacks, Assassinations and Losses in the First Four Years." *Journal of Palestine Studies* 34, no. 2 (2005): 85–122.

Falk, Richard. "International Law and the al-Aqsa Intifada." *Middle East Report* no. 217 (2000).

Faruqi, Daanish, ed. *From Camp David to Cast Lead.* London: Lexington Books, 2011.

Feldman, Ilana. *Governing Gaza: Bureaucracy, Authority and the Work of Rule, 1917–1967.* Durham: Duke University Press, 2008.

——— . "Gaza's Humanitarianism Problem." *Journal of Palestine Studies* 38, no. 3 (2009): 22–37.

——— . *Police Encounters: Security and Surveillance in Gaza under Egyptian Rule.* Stanford: Stanford University Press, 2015.

Filiu, Jean-Pierre. *The Arab Revolutions: Ten Lessons from the Democratic Uprising.* London: Hurst, 2011.

——— . "The Origins of Hamas: Militant Legacy or Israeli Tool?" *Journal of Palestine Studies* 41, no. 3 (2012): 54–70.

——— . *Gaza: A History.* Translated by John King. Oxford: Oxford University Press, 2014.

——— . "The Twelve Wars on Gaza." *Journal of Palestine Studies* 44, no. 1 (2014): 52–60.

Freas, Erik. "Hajj Amin al-Husayni and the Haram al-Sharif: A Pan-Islamic or Palestinian Nationalist Cause?" *British Journal of Middle Eastern Studies* 39, no. 1 (2012): 19–51.

Freedman, Lawrence. "Terrorism as Strategy." *Government and Opposition* 42, no. 3 (2007): 314–39.

Gal, Irit, and Ilana Hammerman. *From Beirut to Jenin: The Lebanon War 1982–2002.* Tel Aviv: Am Oved, 2002. (Hebrew).

Gambetta, Diego, and Steffen Hertog. *Engineers of Jihad: The Curious Connection between Violent Extremism and Education.* Princeton: Princeton University Press, 2016.

Gambill, Gary C. "The Balance of Terror: War by Other Means in the Contemporary Middle East." *Journal of Palestine Studies* 28, no. 1 (1998): 51–66.

Gerges, Fawaz A. *America and Political Islam: Clash of Cultures or Clash of Interests?* Cambridge: Cambridge University Press, 1999.

———. *ISIS: A History.* Princeton: Princeton University Press, 2016.

Gershoni, Israel. "The Muslim Brothers and the Arab Revolt in Palestine, 1936–1939." *Middle Eastern Studies* 22, no. 3 (1986): 367–97.

Ghanem, As'ad. "Unilateral Withdrawal: A New Phase in Israel's Approach to the Palestinian Question." *Palestine-Israel Journal of Politics, Economics, and Culture* 13, no. 2 (2006): 35–41.

———. "The Fallout from Israel's War on Gaza: A Turning Point in the Israeli-Palestinian Conflict?" *Holy Land Studies* 8, no. 2 (2009): 195–210.

———. *Palestinian Politics after Arafat: A Failed National Movement.* Bloomington: Indiana University Press, 2010.

Ghanem, As'ad, and Aziz Khayed. "In the Shadow of the al-Aqsa Intifada: The Palestinians and Political Reform." *Civil Wars* 6, no. 3 (2003): 31–50.

Gilbert, Mads, and Erik Fosse. *Eyes in Gaza.* Translated by Guy Puzey and Frank Stewart. London: Quartet, 2010.

Gisha. "Disengaged Occupiers: The Legal Status of Gaza." Tel Aviv: Gisha: Legal Center for Freedom of Movement, January 2007.

———. "What Is the 'Separation Policy'?" Tel Aviv: Gisha: Legal Center for Freedom of Movement, May 2012.

Gold, Zack. "Sinai Security: Opportunities for Unlikely Cooperation among Egypt, Israel, and Hamas." Analysis Paper, no. 30. Washington: Brookings Institution, 2013.

Gordon, Neve. *Israel's Occupation.* Berkeley: University of California Press, 2008.

Gorenberg, Gershom. *The Accidental Empire: Israel and the Birth of the Settlements, 1967–1977.* New York: Henry Holt, 2006.

———. *The Unmaking of Israel.* New York: Harper Perennial, 2011.

Gray, Christine. *International Law and the Use of Force.* Oxford: Oxford University Press, 2004.

Gribetz, Jonathan Marc. "When *The Zionist Idea* Came to Beirut: Judaism, Christianity, and the Palestine Liberation Organization's Translation of Zionism." *International Journal of Middle East Studies* 48, no. 2 (2016): 243–66.

Gunning, Jeroen. "Peace with Hamas? The Transforming Potential of Political Participation." *International Affairs* 80, no. 2 (2004): 233–55.

———. *Hamas in Politics: Democracy, Religion, Violence.* London: Hurst, 2007.

Hafez, Mohammed. *Manufacturing Human Bombs: The Making of Palestinian Suicide Bombers.* Washington: United States Institute of Peace Press, 2006.

Hage, Ghassan. " 'Comes a Time We Are All Enthusiasm': Understanding Palestinian Suicide Bombers in Times of Exighophobia." *Public Culture* 15, no. 1 (2003): 65–89.

Halevi, Ilan. "Self-Government, Democracy and Mismanagement under the Palestinian Authority." *Journal of Palestine Studies* 27, no. 3 (1998): 35–48.

Halliday, Fred. *Islam and the Myth of Confrontation.* New York: I.B. Tauris, 2003.

Hamid, Shadi. *Temptations of Power: Islamists and Illiberal Democracy in a New Middle East.* Oxford: Oxford University Press, 2014.

———. *Islamic Exceptionalism: How the Struggle over Islam Is Reshaping the World.* New York: St. Martin's Press, 2016.

Hamzeh, A Nizar. *In the Path of Hizbullah.* Syracuse: Syracuse University Press, 2004.

Hamzeh, Muna, and Todd May, eds. *Operation Defensive Shield: Witnesses to Israeli War Crimes.* Chicago: University of Chicago Press, 2003.

Harel, Amos, and Avi Issacharoff. *34 Days: Israel, Hezbollah, and the War in Lebanon.* New York: Basingstoke, 2008.

Harris, Christina Phelps. *Nationalism and Revolution in Egypt: The Role of the Muslim Brotherhood.* The Hague: Mouton, 1964.

Hart, Alan. *Arafat: A Political Biography.* Bloomington: Indiana University Press, 1989.

Hass, Amira. *Drinking the Sea at Gaza: Days and Nights in a Land under Siege.* Translated by Elana Wesley and Maxine Kaufman-Lacusta. New York: Henry Holt, 1999.

———. "Israel's Closure Policy: An Ineffective Strategy of Containment and Repression." *Journal of Palestine Studies* 31, no. 3 (2002): 5–20.

Hatina, Meir. *Islam and Salvation in Palestine: The Islamic Jihad Movement.* Tel Aviv: Tel Aviv University, 2001.

———. *Martyrdom in Modern Islam: Piety, Power and Politics.* Cambridge: Cambridge University Press, 2014.

Heller, Mark. "Israelis and Palestinians after Annapolis." INSS Insight, no. 37. Tel Aviv: Institute for National Security Studies, November 27, 2007.

Hever, Shir. *The Political Economy of Israel's Occupation: Repression beyond Exploitation.* London: Pluto Press, 2010.

Hilal, Jamil. "Hamas's Rise as Charted in the Polls, 1994–2005." *Journal of Palestine Studies* 35, no. 3 (2006): 6–19.

Hirst, David. *The Gun and the Olive Branch: The Roots of Violence in the Middle East.* London: Faber and Faber, 1977.

———. *Beware of Small States: Lebanon, Battleground of the Middle East.* London: Faber, 2010.

Hoffman, Bruce. *Inside Terrorism.* New York: Columbia University Press, 2006.

Honig, Or. "Explaining Israel's Misuse of Strategic Assassinations." *Studies in Conflict and Terrorism* 30, no. 6 (2007): 563–77.

Hourani, Albert, Philip S. Khoury, and Mary C. Wilson, eds. *The Modern Middle East.* London: I.B. Tauris, 1993.

Hovdenak, Are. "The Public Services under Hamas in Gaza: Islamic Revolution or Crisis Management? PRIO Report, no. 3-2010. Oslo: Peace Research Institute Oslo, 2010.

Hovespian, Nubar, ed. *The War on Lebanon: A Reader.* Moreton-in-March: Arris, 2008.

Hroub, Khaled. *Hamas: Political Thought and Practice.* Washington: Institute for Palestine Studies, 2000.

———. "Hamas after Shaykh Yasin and Rantisi." *Journal of Palestine Studies* 33, no. 4 (2004): 21–38.

———. "A 'New Hamas' through Its 'New Documents.' " *Journal of Palestine Studies* 35, no. 4 (2006): 6–27.

Human Rights Watch. "In a Dark Hour: The Use of Civilians during IDF Arrest Operations." *Human Rights Watch* 14, no. 2 (2002).

———. "Razing Rafah: Mass Home Demolitions in the Gaza Strip." *Human Rights Watch* (2004).

———. "Internal Fight: Palestinian Abuses in Gaza and the West Bank." *Human Rights Watch* (2008).

———. "Turning a Blind Eye: Impunity for Laws-of-War Violations during the Gaza War." *Human Rights Watch* (2010).

———. "No News Is Good News: Abuses against Journalists by Palestinian Security Forces." *Human Rights Watch* (2011).

———. "Abusive System: Failures of Criminal Justice in Gaza." *Human Rights Watch* (2012).

Husseini, Faisal. "Palestinian Politics after the Gulf War: An Interview with Faisal Husseini." *Journal of Palestine Studies* 20, no. 4 (1991): 99–108.

Inbar, Efraim. "Gaza: Risks and Opportunities." *Perspectives Paper*, no. 38. The Begin-Sadat Center for Strategic Studies (February 2008).

Indyk, Martin. *Innocent Abroad: An Intimate Account of American Peace Diplomacy in the Middle East.* New York: Simon & Schuster, 2009.

Internal Displacement Monitoring Center. "Under Fire: Israel's Enforcement of Access Restricted Areas in the Gaza Strip." January 2014.

International Crisis Group. "Who Governs the West Bank? Palestinian Administration under Israeli Occupation." *Middle East Report* no. 32 (September 28, 2004).

———. "Enter Hamas: The Challenges of Political Integration." *Middle East Report* no. 49 (January 18, 2006).

———. "After Mecca: Engaging Hamas." *Middle East Report* no. 62 (February 28, 2007).

———. "After Gaza." *Middle East Report* no. 68 (August 2, 2007).

————. "The Israeli-Palestinian Conflict: Annapolis and After." *Middle East Report* no. 22 (November 20, 2007).

————. "Inside Gaza: The Challenge of Clans and Families." *Middle East Report* no. 71 (December 20, 2007).

————. "Gaza: The Next Israeli-Palestinian War?" *Middle East Report* no. 30 (March 24, 2011).

————. "Radical Islam in Gaza." *Middle East Report* no. 104 (March 29, 2011).

————. "Light at the End of Their Tunnels? Hamas and the Arab Uprisings." *Middle East Report* no. 129 (August 14, 2012).

————. "No Exit? Gaza and Israel between Wars." *Middle East Report* no. 162 (August 26, 2015).

Jaber, Hala. *Hezbollah: Born with a Vengeance.* New York: Columbia University Press, 1997.

Jaeger, David A., and M. Daniele Paserman. "Israel, the Palestinian Factions and the Cycle of Violence." *American Economic Review* 96, no. 2 (2006): 45–49.

Jamal, Amal. *The Palestinian National Movement: Politics of Contention, 1967–2005.* Bloomington: Indiana University Press, 2005.

Jankowski, James. "Egyptian Responses to the Palestine Problem in the Interwar Period." *International Journal of Middle East Studies* 12, no. 1 (1980): 1–38.

Jensen, Michael Irving. *The Political Ideology of Hamas: A Grassroots Perspective.* Translated by Sally Laird. London: I.B. Tauris, 2009.

Johnson, Nels. *Islam and the Politics of Meaning in Palestinian Nationalism.* London: Kegan Paul International, 1982.

Jones, Clive, and Beverley Milton-Edwards. "Missing the 'Devils' We Knew? Israel and Political Islam amid the Arab Awakening." *International Affairs* 89, no. 2 (2013): 399–415.

Jørgensen, Marianne, and Louise J. Phillips. *Discourse Analysis as Theory and Method.* London: Sage Publications, 2002.

Journal of Palestine Studies. "The Palestinian Resistance and Jordan." *Journal of Palestine Studies* 1, no. 1 (1971): 162–70.

————. "Washington Watch: The Bush Administration's Media Campaign to Pressure Arafat," *Journal of Palestine Studies* 31, no. 3 (2002): 90–98.

————. "PA President Mahmud Abbas and Hamas Political Leader Khalid Meshal, Mecca Accord, Mecca, 7 February 2007." *Journal of Palestine Studies* 36, no. 3 (2007): 189.

————. "A Gaza Chronology, 1948–2008." *Journal of Palestine Studies* 38, no. 3 (2009): 98–121.

————. "Israeli Military Operations against Gaza, 2000–2008." *Journal of Palestine Studies* 38, no. 3 (2009): 122–38.

————. "Prelude to Operation Cast Lead: Israel's Unilateral Disengagement to the Eve of War." *Journal of Palestine Studies* 38, no. 3 (2009): 139–68.

————. "The Israeli Arsenal Deployed against Gaza during Operation Cast Lead." *Journal of Palestine Studies* 38, no. 3 (2009): 175–91.

————. "Day-by-Day Casualties, Israeli Sorties, and Palestinian Missiles Fired." *Journal of Palestine Studies* 38, no. 3 (2009): 201–6.

Kandil, Hazem. *Inside the Brotherhood.* London: Polity Press, 2015.

Karmon, Ely. "Hamas' Terrorism Strategy: Operational Limitations and Political Constraints." *Middle East Review of International Affairs* 4, no. 1 (2000): 66–79.

Katz, Ethan B., Lisa Moses Leff, and Maud S. Mandel, eds. *Colonialism and the Jews.* Bloomington: Indiana University Press, 2017.

Katz, Jacob. *From Prejudice to Destruction: Anti-Semitism, 1700–1933.* Cambridge: Harvard University Press, 1982.

Kedourie, Elie, and Sylvia G. Haim, eds. *Zionism and Arabism in Palestine and Israel.* London: Frank Cass, 1982.

Kelly, Matthew Kraig. "The Revolt of 1936: A Revision." *Journal of Palestine Studies* 44, no. 2 (2014): 28–42.

Kendall, Elisabeth, and Ewan Stein. *Twenty-First Century Jihad: Law, Society and Military Action.* London: I.B. Taurus, 2015.

Kepel, Gilles. *Jihad: The Trail of Political Islam.* Translated by Anthony E. Roberts. London: I.B. Tauris, 2008.

Kerr, Malcolm H. *Islamic Reform: The Political and Legal Theories of Muhammad Abduh and Rashid Rida.* Los Angeles: University of California Press, 1966.

Khalaf, Issa. *Politics in Palestine: Arab Factionalism and Social Disintegration, 1939–1948.* Albany: State University of New York Press, 1991.

Khalidi, Ahmad S. "The Palestinians' First Excursion into Democracy." *Journal of Palestine Studies* 25, no. 4 (1996): 20–28.

Khalidi, Raja, and Sobhi Samour. "Neoliberalism as Liberation: The Statehood Program and the Remaking of the Palestinian National Movement." *Journal of Palestine Studies* 40, no. 2 (2011): 6–25.

Khalidi, Rashid. *Under Siege: PLO Decision Making During the 1982 War.* New York: Columbia University Press, 1986.

———. "The Resolutions of the 19th Palestine National Council." *Journal of Palestine Studies* 19, no. 2 (1990): 29–42.

———. *The Iron Cage: The Story of the Palestinian Struggle for Statehood.* Boston: Beacon Press, 2006.

———. *Palestinian Identity: The Construction of Modern National Consciousness.* New York: Columbia University Press, 2009.

———. *Brokers of Deceit: How the U.S. Has Undermined Peace in the Middle East.* Boston: Beacon Press, 2013.

———. "The Dahiya Doctrine, Proportionality, and War Crimes." *Journal of Palestine Studies* 44, no. 1 (2014): 5–13.

Khalidi, Walid. "Revisiting the UNGA Partition Resolution." *Journal of Palestine Studies* 27, no. 1 (1997): 5–21.

———, ed. *All That Remains: The Palestinian Villages Occupied and Depopulated by Israel in 1948.* Washington: Institute for Palestine Studies, 2015.

Khalidi, Walid, and Neil Caplan. "The 1953 Qibya Raid Revisited: Excerpts from Moshe Sharett's Diaries." *Journal of Palestine Studies* 31, no. 4 (2002): 77–98.

Khalil, Osama. "Pax Americana: The United States, the Palestinians, and the Peace Process, 1948–2008." *New Centennial Review* 8, no. 2 (2008): 1–42.

———. "The Radical Crescent: The United States, the Palestine Liberation Organisation, and the Lebanese Civil War, 1973–1978." *Diplomacy and Statecraft* 27, no. 3 (2016): 496–522.

Khalili, Laleh. *Heroes and Martyrs of Palestine: The Politics of National Commemoration.* Cambridge: Cambridge University Press, 2007.

———. " 'Standing with My Brother': Hizbullah, Palestinians and the Limits of Solidarity." *Society for Comparative Studies in Society and History* 49, no. 2 (2007): 276–303.

———. *Time in the Shadows: Confinement in Counterinsurgencies.* Stanford: Stanford University Press, 2013.

Khan, Mushtaq Husain, George Giacaman, and Inge Amundsen, eds. *State Formation in Palestine: Viability and Governance during a Social Transformation.* London: Routledge Curzon, 2004.

Khashan, Hilal. "The New World Order and the Tempo of Militant Islam." *British Journal of Middle Eastern Studies* 24, no. 1 (1997): 5–24.

Khatib, Lina, Dina Matar, and Atef Alshaer. *The Hizbullah Phenomenon: Politics and Communication.* Oxford: Oxford University Press, 2014.

Kimmerling, Baruch. *Politicide: Ariel Sharon's War against the Palestinians.* London: Verso, 2003.

Kimmerling, Baruch, and Joel S. Migdal. *The Palestinian People: A History.* Cambridge: Harvard University Press, 2003.

King, Mary Elizabeth. *A Quiet Revolution: The First Palestinian Intifada and Nonviolent Resistance.* New York: Nation Books, 2007.

Kjorlien, Michele L. "Hamas: In Theory and Practice." *Arab Studies Journal* 2 (1993): 4–7.

Korn, Alina. "Israeli Press and the War against Terrorism: The Construction of the 'Liquidation Policy.' " *Crime, Law and Social Change* 41, no. 3 (2004): 209–34.

Kristianasen, Wendy. "Challenge and Counterchallenge: Hamas's Response to Oslo." *Journal of Palestine Studies* 28, no. 3 (1999): 19–36.

Krueger, Alan B., and Jitka Malecková. "Education, Poverty and Terrorism: Is There a Casual Connection?" *Journal of Economic Perspectives* 17, no. 4 (2003): 119–44.

Kumaraswamy, P. R. "The Cairo Dialogue and the Palestinian Power Struggle." *International Studies* 42, no. 1 (2005): 43–59.

Kupferschmidt, Uri M. *The Supreme Muslim Council: Islam under the British Mandate for Palestine.* Leiden: E. J. Brill, 1987.

Kurz, Anat. "The Post Annapolis Dynamic: The Hamas Factor." INSS Insight, no. 38. Tel Aviv: Institute for National Security Studies, December 3, 2007.

Kurz, Anat, Benedetta Berti, and Marcel Konrad. "The Institutional Transformations of Hamas and Hizbollah." *Strategic Assessment* 15, no. 3 (2012): 87–98.

Kurz, Anat, and Shlomo Brom, eds. *The Lessons of Operation Protective Edge.* Tel Aviv: Institute for National Security Studies, 2014.

Kurzman, Charles. "Liberal Islam: Prospects and Challenges." *Middle East Review of International Affairs* 3, no. 3 (1999): 11–19.

Kuttab, Daoud. "Current Developments and the Peace Process." *Journal of Palestine Studies* 22, no. 1 (1992): 100–107.

Kydd, Andrew, and Barbara F. Walter. "Sabotaging the Peace: The Politics of Extremist Violence." *International Organization* 56, no. 2 (2002): 263–96.

Lambeth, Benjamin S. "Israel's War in Gaza: A Paradigm of Effective Military Learning and Adaptation." *International Security* 37, no. 2 (2012): 81–118.

Landau, David. *Arik: The Life of Ariel Sharon.* New York: Alfred A. Knopf, 2014.

Laqueur, Walter. *A History of Zionism: From the French Revolution to the Establishment of the State of Israel.* London: Tauris Parke, 2003.

Laron, Guy. *The Six Day War: The Breaking of the Middle East.* New Haven: Yale University Press, 2017.

Laub, Zachary. "Egypt's Sinai Peninsula and Security." New York: Council on Foreign Relations, December 12, 2013.

Lefevre, Raphael. *Ashes of Hama: The Muslim Brotherhood in Syria.* Oxford: Oxford University Press, 2013.

Legrain, Jean Francois. "The Successions of Yasir Arafat." *Journal of Palestine Studies* 28, no. 4 (1999): 5–20.

LeVine, Mark, and Gershon Shafir, eds. *Struggle and Survival in Palestine/Israel.* Berkeley: University of California Press, 2012.

Levitt, Matthew. *Hamas: Politics, Charity and Terrorism in Service of Jihad.* New Haven: Yale University Press, 2006.

Levy, Gideon. *The Punishment of Gaza.* London: Verso, 2010.

Lia, Brynjar. *The Society of the Muslim Brothers in Egypt: The Rise of an Islamic Movement 1928–1942.* Reading: Ithaca Press, 1998.

Lockman, Zachary, and Joel Beinin, eds. *Intifada: The Palestinian Uprising against Israeli Occupation.* Washington: Middle East Research and Information Project, 1989.

Louis, Wm. Roger, and Avi Shlaim, eds. *The 1967 Arab-Israeli War: Origins and Consequences.* Cambridge: Cambridge University Press, 2012.

Lynch, Marc. *The New Arab Wars: Uprisings and Anarchy in the Middle East.* New York: Public Affairs, 2016.

Macintyre, Donald. *Gaza: Preparing for Dawn.* London: Oneworld, 2017.

Makovsky, David. *Engagement through Disengagement: Gaza and the Potential for Renewed Israeli-Palestinian Peacemaking.* Washington: Washington Institute for Near East Policy, 2005.

Malley, Robert. *The Call from Algeria: Third Worldism, Revolution, and the Turn to Islam.* London: University of California Press, 1996.

Mamdani, Mahmood. *Good Muslim, Bad Muslim: America, the Cold War, and the Roots of Terror.* New York: Pantheon Books, 2004.

Mandaville, Peter. *Islam and Politics.* London: Routledge, 2014.

Mann, James. *Rise of the Vulcans: The History of Bush's War Cabinet.* New York: Penguin, 2004.

Maqdsi, Muhammad. "Charter of the Islamic Resistance Movement (Hamas) of Palestine." *Journal of Palestine Studies* 22, no. 4 (1993): 122–34.

Massad, Joseph A. *Islam in Liberalism.* Chicago: University of Chicago Press, 2015.

Mattar, Philip. *The Mufti of Jerusalem: Al-Hajj Amīn al-Husaynī and the Palestinian National Movement.* New York: Columbia University Press, 1988.

McCants, William. *Apocalypse: The History, Strategy and Doomsday Vision of the Islamic State.* New York: St. Martin's Press, 2015.

McDougall, James. *A History of Algeria.* Cambridge: Cambridge University Press, 2017.

McGeough, Paul. *Kill Khalid: The Failed Mossad Assassination of Khalid Mishal and the Rise of Hamas.* New York: New Press, 2009.

Meital, Yoram. *Peace in Tatters: Israel, Palestine, and the Middle East.* Boulder: Lynne Rienner Publishers, 2006.

Melzer, Nils. *Targeted Killing in International Law.* Oxford: Oxford University Press, 2008.

Mernissi, Fatima. *Islam and Democracy: Fear of the Modern World.* Translated by Mary Jo Lakeland. New York: Basic Books, 1992.

Mesquita, Ethan Bueno de. "The Quality of Terror." *American Journal of Political Science* 49, no. 3 (2005): 515–30.

Miller, Aaron David. *The Much Too Promised Land: America's Elusive Search for Arab-Israeli Peace.* New York: Bantam Books, 2008.

Milton-Edwards, Beverley. "The Concept of Jihad and the Palestinian Islamic Movement: A Comparison of Ideas and Techniques." *British Journal of Middle Eastern Studies* 19, no. 1 (1992): 48–53.

———. *Islamic Politics in Palestine.* London: I.B. Tauris, 1996.

———. "Political Islam in Palestine in an Environment of Peace?" *Third World Quarterly* 17, no. 2 (1996): 119–225.

———. "Palestinian State-Building: Police and Citizens as Test of Democracy." *British Journal of Middle Eastern Studies* 25, no. 1 (1998): 95–119.

———. "Order without Law? Anatomy of Hamas Security: The Executive Force (Tanfithya)." *International Peacekeeping* 15, no. 5 (2008): 663–76.

———. "The Ascendance of Political Islam: Hamas and Consolidation in the Gaza Strip." *Third World Quarterly* 29, no. 8 (2008): 1585–99.

———. "Revolt and Revolution, the Place of Islamism." *Critical Studies on Terrorism* 5, no. 2 (2012): 219–36.

———. "Islamist versus Islamist: Rising Challenge in Gaza." *Terrorism and Political Violence* 26, no. 2 (2014): 259–76.

———. *The Muslim Brotherhood: The Arab Spring and Its Future Face.* London: Routledge, 2016.

Milton-Edwards, Beverley, and Alastair Crooke. "Elusive Ingredient: Hamas and the Peace Process." *Journal of Palestine Studies* 33, no. 4 (2004): 39–52.

Milton-Edwards, Beverley, and Stephen Farrell. *Hamas: The Islamic Resistance Movement.* Cambridge: Polity Press, 2010.

Mishal, Shaul, and Avraham Sela. *The Palestinian Hamas: Vision, Violence and Coexistence.* New York: Columbia University Press, 2000.

Mitchell, Gabriel. "Israel-Turkey: Where to from Now?" Washington: Middle East Institute, July 11, 2016.

Mitchell, Richard P. *The Society of the Muslim Brothers.* Oxford: Oxford University Press, 1993.

Morris, Benny. *Israel's Border Wars, 1949–1956: Arab Infiltration, Israeli Retaliation and the Countdown to the Suez War.* Oxford: Clarendon Press, 1993.

———. *Righteous Victims: A History of the Zionist-Arab Conflict, 1881–2001.* New York: Vintage Books, 2001.

———. *The Birth of the Palestinian Refugee Problem, 1947–1949.* Cambridge: Cambridge University Press, 2004.

Moses, A. Dirk. "Empire, Resistance, and Security: International Law and the Transformative Occupation of Palestine." *Humanity Journal* 8, no. 2 (2017).

Moussalli, Ahmad S. *Moderate and Radical Islamic Fundamentalism: The Quest for Modernity, Legitimacy and the Islamic State.* Gainesville: University Press of Florida, 1999.

Muslih, Muhammad Y. *The Origins of Palestinian Nationalism.* New York: Columbia University Press, 1988.

——. *Toward Coexistence: An Analysis of the Resolutions of the Palestine National Council.* Washington: Institute for Palestine Studies, 1990.

——. "The Foreign Policy of Hamas." New York: Council on Foreign Relations, 1999.

Nafi, Basheer M. "Shaykh 'Izz al-Dīn al-Qassām: A Reformist and a Rebel Leader." *Journal of Islamic Studies* 8, no. 2 (1997): 185–215.

——. *Arabism, Islamism and the Palestine Question 1908–1941: A Political History.* Reading: Ithaca Press, 1998.

Nassar, Jamal R., and Roger Heacock, eds. *Intifada: Palestine at the Crossroads.* New York: Praegar, 1990.

Nettler, Ronald L., ed. *Studies in Muslim-Jewish Relations.* Chur: Harwood Academic Publishers, 1993.

Nirenberg, David. *Anti-Judaism: The History of a Way of Thinking.* New York: W. W. Norton, 2013.

Noe, Nicholas, ed. *Voice of Hezbollah: The Statements of Sayyed Hassan Nasrallah.* Translated by Ellen Khouri. London: Verso, 2007.

Norris, Jacob. *Land of Progress: Palestine in the Age of Colonial Development, 1905–1948.* Oxford: Oxford University Press, 2013.

Norton, Augustus Richard. "Hizballah and the Israeli Withdrawal from Southern Lebanon." *Journal of Palestine Studies* 30, no. 1 (2000): 22–35.

——. *Hezbollah: A Short History.* Princeton: Princeton University Press, 2007.

——. "The Gaza War: Antecedents and Consequences." Madrid: Elcano Royal Institute, February 3, 2009.

Nüsse, Andrea. *Muslim Palestine: The Ideology of Hamas.* Amsterdam: Harwood Academic, 1998.

OCHA. "Gaza Strip: Humanitarian Fact Sheet." East Jerusalem: United Nations Office for the Coordination of Humanitarian Affairs (OCHA), Occupied Palestinian Territory, 2008.

——. "Fragmented Lives: Humanitarian Overview, 2014." East Jerusalem: United Nations Office for the Coordination of Humanitarian Affairs (OCHA), Occupied Palestinian Territory, March 2015.

——. "Gaza One Year On: The Crisis Never Ended." East Jerusalem: United Nations Office for the Coordination of Humanitarian Affairs (OCHA), Occupied Palestinian Territory, July 7, 2015.

Omer, Mohammed. *Shell-Shocked: On the Ground under Israel's Gaza Assault.* Chicago: Haymarket Books, 2015.

Osman, Tarek. *Islamism: What It Means for the Middle East and the World.* New Haven: Yale University Press, 2016.

Owen, Roger. *The Rise and Fall of Arab Presidents for Life.* Cambridge: Harvard University Press, 2012.

Pape, Robert A. "The Strategic Logic of Suicide Terrorism." *American Political Science Review* 97, no. 3 (2003): 343–61.

——. *Dying to Win: The Strategic Logic of Suicide Terrorism.* New York: Random House, 2005.

Pappé, Ilan. *The Rise and Fall of a Palestinian Dynasty: The Husaynis 1700–1948.* London: Saqi Books, 2010.

Pearlman, Wendy. *Violence, Nonviolence, and the Palestinian National Movement.* Cambridge: Cambridge University Press, 2011.

Pedahzur, Ami. *The Israeli Secret Services and the Struggle against Terrorism.* New York: Columbia University Press, 2009.

Pelham, Nicolas. "Gaza's Tunnel Phenomenon: The Unintended Dynamics of Israel's Siege." *Journal of Palestine Studies* 41, no. 4 (2012): 6–31.

——. "Sinai: The Buffer Erodes." London: Royal Institute of International Affairs, 2012.

Pelletiere, Stephen C. "Hamas and Hizbollah: The Radical Challenge to Israel in the Occupied Territories." Strategic Studies Institute, 1994.

Penslar, Derek. *Israel in History: The Jewish State in Comparative Perspective.* London: Routledge, 2006.

Perry, Mark. *Talking to Terrorists: Why America Must Engage with Its Enemies.* New York: Basic Books, 2010.

Piscatori, James P. *Islam in a World of Nation States.* Cambridge: Cambridge University Press, 1986.

——. "Religion and Realpolitik: Islamic Responses to the Gulf War." *Bulletin of the American Academy of Arts and Sciences* 45, no. 1 (1991): 17–39.

Porath, Yehoshua. *In Search of Arab Unity 1930–1945.* London: Frank Cass, 1986.

——. *The Emergence of the Palestinian Arab National Movement: From Riots to Rebellion 1929–1939.* London: Frank Cass, 1977.

Post, Jerrold, Ehud Sprinzak, and Laurita M. Denny. "The Terrorists in Their Own Words: Interviews with 35 Incarcerated Middle Eastern Terrorists." *Terrorism and Political Violence* 15, no. 1 (2003): 171–84.

Primoratz, Igor. "What Is Terrorism?" *Journal of Applied Philosophy* 7, no. 2 (1990): 129–38.

Qarmout, Tamer, and Daniel Beland. "The Politics of International Aid to the Gaza Strip." *Journal of Palestine Studies* 41, no. 4 (2012): 32–47.

Quandt, William B. *Peace Process: American Diplomacy and the Arab Israeli Conflict since 1967.* Berkeley: University of California Press, 2001.

Rabbani, Mouin. "Israel's Assault on Gaza: A Transformational Moment? An Interview with Azmi Bishara." *Journal of Palestine Studies* 38, no. 3 (2009): 38–53.

——. "Between Hamas and the PA: An Interview with Islamic Jihad's Khalil al-Batsh." *Journal of Palestine Studies* 42, no. 2 (2013): 61–70.

Rabie, Mohamed. *U.S.-PLO Dialogue: Secret Diplomacy and Conflict Resolution.* Gainesville: University Press of Florida, 1995.

Rabinovich, Itamar. *The Lingering Conflict: Israel, the Arabs and the Middle East, 1948–2011.* Washington: Brookings Institution, 2011.

——. *Yitzhak Rabin: Soldier, Leader, Statesman.* New Haven: Yale University Press, 2017.

Rahnema, Ali, ed. *Pioneers of Islamic Revival.* London: Zed Books, 2005.

Ramadan, Tariq. *Islam and the Arab Awakening.* Oxford: Oxford University Press, 2012.

Raz, Avi. *The Bride and the Dowry: Israel, Jordan and the Palestinians in the Aftermath of the June 1967 War.* New Haven: Yale University Press, 2012.

Reuter, Christoph. *My Life Is a Weapon: A Modern History of Suicide Bombing.* Princeton: Princeton University Press, 2004.

Rice, Condoleezza. *No Higher Honor: A Memoir of My Years in Washington.* New York: Crown Publishers, 2011.

Robinson, Shira. *Citizen Strangers: Palestinians and the Birth of Israel's Liberal Settler State.* Stanford: Stanford University Press, 2013.

Ross, Dennis. *The Missing Peace: The Inside Story of the Fight for the Middle East.* New York: Farrar, Straus and Giroux, 2004.

Roy, Olivier. *The Failure of Political Islam.* Translated by Carol Volk. Cambridge: Harvard University Press, 1994.

——. *Secularism Confronts Islam.* Translated by George Holoch. New York: Columbia University Press, 2007.

Roy, Sara. "'The Seeds of Chaos, and of Night': The Gaza Strip after the Agreement." *Journal of Palestine Studies* 23, no. 3 (1994): 85–98.

——. *The Gaza Strip: The Political Economy of De-development.* Washington: Institute for Palestine Studies, 1995.

——. "De-development Revisited: Palestinian Economy and Society since Oslo." *Journal of Palestine Studies* 28, no. 3 (1999): 64–82.

——. "The Transformation of Islamic NGOs in Palestine." *Middle East Report* no. 214 (2000): 24–26.

——. "Palestinian Society and Economy: The Continued Denial of Possibility." *Journal of Palestine Studies* 30, no. 4 (2001): 5–20.

——. "Hamas and the Transformation(s) of Political Islam in Palestine." *Current History* 102, no. 660 (2003): 13–20.

——. "Praying with Their Eyes Closed: Reflections on the Disengagement from Gaza." *Journal of Palestine Studies* 34, no. 4 (2005): 64–74.

——. *Failing Peace: Gaza and the Palestinian-Israeli Conflict.* London: Pluto Press, 2007.

————. *Hamas and Civil Society in Gaza: Engaging the Islamist Social Sector.* Princeton: Princeton University Press, 2011.

————. "Reconceptualizing the Israeli-Palestinian Conflict: Key Paradigm Shifts." *Journal of Palestine Studies* 41, no. 3 (2012): 71–91.

Rubin, Uzi. "The Missile Threat from Gaza: From Nuisance to Strategic Threat." Mideast Security and Policy Studies, no. 91. Ramat Gan: Begin-Sadat Center for Strategic Studies, December, 2011.

Rynhold, Jonathan, and Dov Waxman. "Ideological Change and Israel's Disengagement from Gaza." *Political Science Quarterly* 123, no. 1 (2008): 11–37.

Saad-Ghorayeb, Amal. *Hizbu'llah: Politics and Religion.* London: Pluto Press, 2002.

Sabry, Mohannad. *Sinai: Egypt's Linchpin, Gaza's Lifeline, Israel's Nightmare.* Cairo: American University in Cairo Press, 2015.

Said, Edward W. *The Politics of Dispossession: The Struggle for Palestinian Self-Determination, 1969–1994.* New York: Pantheon Books, 1994.

————. *Covering Islam: How the Media and the Experts Determine How We See the Rest of the World.* New York: Vintage Books, 1997.

Saikal, Amin. *Islam and the West: Conflict or Cooperation?* London: Palgrave Macmillan, 2003.

Salamé, Ghassan, ed. *Democracy without Democrats? The Renewal of Politics in the Muslim World.* New York: I.B. Tauris, 1994.

Sanagan, Mark. "Teacher, Preacher, Soldier, Martyr: Rethinking Izz al-Din al-Qassam." *Welt des Islams* 53, nos. 3–4 (2013): 315–52.

Sarraj, Iyad. "On Violence and Resistance." *Palestinian Israeli Journal* 10, no. 1 (2003).

Sayigh, Rosemary. "Seven Day Horror." Bethlehem: BADIL Resource Center for Palestinian Residency & Refugee Rights, 2001.

Sayigh, Yezid. "Struggle within, Struggle without: The Transformation of PLO Politics since 1982." *International Affairs* 65, no. 2 (1989): 247–71.

————. "Armed Struggle and State Formation." *Journal of Palestine Studies* 26, no. 4 (1997): 17–32.

————. *Armed Struggle and the Search for State: The Palestinian National Movement, 1949–1993.* Oxford: Oxford University Press, 1997.

————. "Inducing a Failed State in Palestine." *Survival* 49, no. 3 (2007): 7–40.

————. " 'We Serve the People': Hamas Policing in Gaza." No. 5. Waltham: Brandeis University, Crown Center for Middle East Studies, 2011.

Sayyid, Bobby. *A Fundamental Fear: Eurocentrism and the Emergence of Islamism.* New York: Zed Books, 2003.

Schanzer, Jonathan. *Hamas vs. Fatah: The Struggle for Palestine.* New York: Palgrave Macmillan, 2010.

Schiff, Ze'ev, and Ehud Ya'ari. *Israel's Lebanon War.* Translated by Ina Friedman. New York: Simon & Schuster, 1984.

————. *Intifada: The Palestinian Uprising: Israel's Third Front.* New York: Simon & Schuster, 1990.

Schweitzer, Yoram. "Palestinian Istishhadia: A Developing Instrument." *Studies in Conflict and Terrorism* 30, no. 8 (2007): 667–89.

Segev, Tom. *One Palestine, Complete: Jews and Arabs under the British Mandate.* Translated by Haim Watzman. London: Abacus, 2001.

————. *1967: Israel, the War, and the Year That Transformed the Middle East.* Translated by Jessica Cohen. New York: Metropolitan Books, 2007.

Seikaly, Sherene. *Men of Capital: Scarcity and Economy in Mandate Palestine.* Stanford: Stanford University Press, 2016.

Seitz, Charmaine. "Hamas Stands Down?" *Middle East Report* no. 221 (2001): 4–7.

Sela, Avraham. "The PLO at Fifty: A Historical Perspective." *Contemporary Review of the Middle East* 1, no. 3 (2014): 269–333.

Serry, Robert. *The Endless Quest for Israeli-Palestinian Peace: A Reflection from No Man's Land.* Gewerbestrasse: Palgrave Macmillan, 2017.

Shaban, Omar. "The Implications of Siege and the Palestinian Division on the Situation in the Gaza Strip since 2007." *Palestine-Israel Journal* 22, no. 2 (2017): 70–77.

Shadid, Mohammad K. "The Muslim Brotherhood Movement in the West Bank and Gaza." *Third World Quarterly* 10, no. 2 (1988): 658–82.

Shafir, Gershon. *Land, Labor and the Origins of the Israeli-Palestinian Conflict, 1882–1914.* Berkeley: University of California Press, 1996.

Shallah, Ramadan. "Israel at a Crossroads: Unable to Vanquish Resistance or Negotiate Peace: An Interview with Ramadan Shallah." *Journal of Palestine Studies* 44, no. 2 (2015): 52–62.

Shemesh, Moshe. *The Palestinian Entity 1959–1974: Arab Politics and the PLO.* London: Frank Cass, 1988.

Shenhav, Yehouda. *Beyond the Two State: A Jewish Political Essay.* Cambridge: Polity Press, 2012.

Shikaki, Khalil. "With Hamas in Power: Impact of Palestinian Domestic Developments on Options for the Peace Process." Waltham: Brandeis University, Crown Center for Middle East Studies, February 2007.

Shlaim, Avi. "The Oslo Accord." *Journal of Palestine Studies* 23, no. 3 (1994): 24–40.

———. *The Iron Wall: Israel and the Arab World.* London: W. W. Norton, 2014.

Siegman, Henry. "US Hamas Policy Blocks Middle East Peace." Oslo: Norwegian Peacebuilding Resource Centre (NOREF), September 2010.

———. "Gaza and the Palestinian Struggle for Statehood." Oslo: Norwegian Peacebuilding Resource Center (NOREF), August 2014.

Sobelman, Daniel. "Learning to Deter: Deterrence Failure and Success in the Israel-Hezbollah Conflict, 2006–16." *International Security* 41, no. 3 (2016): 151–96.

Sorkin, Michael, ed. *Against the Wall: Israel's Barrier to Peace.* New York: New Press, 2005.

Stedman, Stephen. "Spoiler Problems in Peace Processes." *International Security* 22, no. 2 (1997): 5–53.

Stein, Kenneth W. "The Intifada and the 1936–39 Uprising: A Comparison." *Journal of Palestine Studies* 19, no. 4 (1990): 64–85.

Swedenburg, Ted. *Memories of Revolt: The 1936–1939 Rebellion and the Palestinian National Past.* Minneapolis: University of Minnesota Press, 1995.

Taji-Farouki, Suha. "Islamists and the Threat of Jihad: Hizb al-Tahrir and al-Muhajiroun on Israel and the Jews." *Middle Eastern Studies* 36, no. 4 (2000): 21–46.

Tamimi, Azzam. *Hamas: Unwritten Chapters.* London: Hurst, 2007.

Taraki, Lisa. "The Islamic Resistance Movement in the Palestinian Uprising." *Middle East Report*, no. 156 (1989): 30–32.

Tawil-Souri, Helga. "Digital Occupation: Gaza's High-Tech Enclosure." *Journal of Palestine Studies* 41, no. 2 (2012): 27–43.

Tawil-Souri, Helga, and Dina Mattar, eds. *Gaza as Metaphor.* London: Hurst, 2016.

Tehranian, Majid. "Militant Religious Movements: Rise and Impact." *Economic and Political Weekly* 32, no. 50 (1997): 3213–24.

Teichman, Jenny. "How to Define Terrorism." *Philosophy* 64, no. 250 (1989): 505–17.

Tessler, Mark. *A History of the Israeli-Palestinian Conflict.* Bloomington: Indiana University Press, 2009.

Torfing, Jacob. *New Theories of Discourse: Laclau, Mouffe and Žižek.* Oxford: Blackwell, 1999.

Turner, Mandy, and Omar Shweiki, eds. *Decolonizing Palestinian Political Economy: De-development and Beyond.* London: Palgrave Macmillan, 2014.

Tyler, Patrick. *Fortress Israel: The Inside Story of the Military Elite Who Run the Country—and Why They Can't Make Peace.* New York: Farrar, Straus and Giroux, 2012.

Usher, Graham. "The Politics of Internal Security: The PA's New Intelligence Services." *Journal of Palestine Studies* 25, no. 3 (1996): 21–34.

———. "Fatah's Tanzim: Origins and Politics." *Middle East Report* no. 217 (2000): 6–15.

———. "Facing Defeat: The Intifada Two Years On." *Journal of Palestine Studies* 32, no. 2 (2003): 21–40.

———. "Letter from the Occupied Territories: The Palestinians after Arafat." *Journal of Palestine Studies* 34, no. 3 (2005): 42–56.

———. "The Democratic Resistance: Hamas, Fatah, and the Palestinian Elections." *Journal of Palestine Studies* 35, no. 3 (2006): 20–36.

———. "Year of Elections: Fact and Faction." *Middle East Report* no. 238 (2006): 2–11.

Valbjørn, Morten, and Fred H. Lawson, eds. *The International Relations of the Middle East*, vol. 3. Los Angeles: Sage Reference, 2015.

Veracini, Lorenzo. *Israel and Settler Society.* London: Pluto Press, 2006.

Vericat, Jose. "The Internal Conversation of Hamas: Salafism and the Rise of the 'Ulama.'" Doctoral dissertation, University of Oxford, 2016.

Vlasic, Mark V. "Assassination and Targeted Killing: A Historical and Post-Bin Laden Legal Analysis." *Georgetown Journal of International Law* 43 (2012): 259–333.

Wagemakers, Joas. "Legitimizing Pragmatism: Hamas' Framing Efforts from Militancy to Moderation and Back?" *Terrorism and Political Violence* 17, no. 3 (2005): 358–78.

Weizman, Eyal. *Hollow Land: Israel's Architecture of Occupation.* London: Verso, 2007.

———. *The Least of All Possible Evils: Humanitarian Violence from Arendt to Gaza.* London: Verso, 2011.

Wickham, Carrie Rosefsky. *The Muslim Brotherhood: Evolution of an Islamist Movement.* Princeton: Princeton University Press, 2013.

Wiktorowicz, Quintan. "The New Global Threat: Transnational Salafis and Jihad." *Middle East Policy* 8, no. 4 (2001): 18–38.

———, ed. *Islamic Activism: A Social Movement Theory Approach.* Bloomington: Indiana University Press, 2003.

Wolfe, Patrick. "Settler Colonialism and the Elimination of the Native." *Journal of Genocide Research* 8, no. 4 (2006): 387–409.

Wolfensohn, James D. *A Global Life: My Journey among Rich and Poor, from Sydney to Wall Street to the World Bank.* New York: Public Affairs, 2010.

Wright, Lawrence. *The Looming Tower: Al-Qaeda and the Road to 9/11.* New York: Alfred A. Knopf, 2006.

Yaqub, Salim. *Imperfect Strangers: Americans, Arabs, and U.S.-Middle East Relations in the 1970s.* Ithaca: Cornell University Press, 2016.

Yiftachel, Oren. *Ethnocracy: Land and Identity Politics in Israel/Palestine.* Philadelphia: University of Pennsylvania Press, 2006.

Zahhar, Mahmud, and Hussein Hijazi. "Hamas: Waiting for Secular Nationalism to Self-Destruct. An Interview with Mahmud Zahhar." *Journal of Palestine Studies* 24, no. 3 (1995): 81–88.

Zertal, Idith, and Akiva Eldar. *Lords of the Land: The War over Israel's Settlements in the Occupied Territories, 1967–2007.* Translated by Vivian Eden. New York: Nation Books, 2009.

Zollner, Barbara. "Prison Talk: The Muslim Brotherhood's Internal Struggle during Gamal Abdel Nasser's Persecution, 1954 to 1971." *International Journal of Middle East Studies* 39, no. 3 (2007): 411–33.

Zoughbie, Daniel E. *Indecision Points: George W. Bush and the Israeli-Palestinian Conflict.* Cambridge: MIT Press, 2014.

Zubaida, Sami. *Islam, the People and the State: Political Ideas and Movements in the Middle East.* London: I.B. Tauris, 2009.

———. *Law and Power in the Islamic World.* London: I.B. Tauris, 2005.

Zuhur, Sherifa. "A Hundred Osamas: Islamist Threats and the Future of Counterinsurgency." Strategic Studies Institute, 2005.

Zweiri, Mahjoob. "The Hamas Victory: Shifting Sands or Major Earthquake?" *Third World Quarterly* 27, no. 4 (2006): 675–87.

INDEX

1967 borders: establishment of, 14–15, 18; Government of National Consensus (2014) and, 208; Hamas's acceptance of, 46, 82, 93, 102, 107–108, 113, 229–231, 245; Hamas's resistance to occupation beyond, 40, 104, 108; Israel's demographics and, 41, 66, 267n8; Israel's failure to accept, 107–109, 119, 231, 249; in the Prisoners' Document (2006), 115–116; in unity negotiations, 114, 119, 153. *See also* two-state solution

Abbas, Mahmoud: Annapolis agreement (2007) and, 143–147; Cairo Initiative (2008) and, 152–154, 286n148; call for new elections (2007), 121–122; disengagement (2005), 81, 85–92; Doha Declaration (2012) and, 187–189, 292n94; elected president of Palestinian Authority (2005), 78; emergency West Bank government (2007), 133–138; Gaza Reconstruction Committee (2009) and, 162–163; on Gaza smuggling, 114; Goldstone Report (2009) and, 164–165; Government of National Consensus (2014) and, 207–209, 223–224; on Hamas in Palestinian Authority, 93–95, 98, 100–104, 109–112, 212–213, 223–226; interim unity government (2011-2012) and, 176–177, 179–182, 187–189; Israel (2005) negotiations, 79–81, 86, 95; Israel (2010) negotiations, 168–169; Mecca Agreement (2007) and, 125–132, 280n219; National Reconciliation Document (2006), 118–122; Operation Cast Lead (2008) and, 154, 158, 161; in *The Palestine Papers*, 174–175; personal dislike of Hamas, 143, 284n77, 294n146; on PLO restructuring and Cairo Declaration,

79–83; as prime minister of Palestinian Authority (2003), 57, 68, 78; resignation of, 61, 68; on Roadmap for Peace (2002), 57–61, 78–79; speech at the UN (2006), 119–120; statehood application to UN (2011), 175, 182–183, 184, 197; on UN reports of war crimes, 165, 289n227, 297–298n20; on overturning Hamas's election victory, 122–125, 279n173, 279n175, 280n189

Abu Marzouq, Musa: in external leadership, 19, 27, 72; on Hamas government, 105; on interim government (2014), 207; on Israeli military offensive (2014), 216;; on political resistance, 80, 96

Abu Shanab, Ismail, 58–59, 60

Abu Shbak, Rashid, 281n233, 281n236

al-Ahdath, 20

Algeria, 238

al-Jazeera, 174, 186, 279n175

al-Qaeda: Hamas government control of, 47, 139; Israeli claims of arms from, 192; Palestinian factions compared to, 47–48, 61, 97, 225–226, 264n114, 301n86; Rantissi assassination and, 268n38

Annapolis Peace Conference (2007), 143–144

Ansar Jund Allah, 288

Aqaba summit (2003), 59

Aqel, Imad, 259n132

al-Aqsa Intifada. *See* Second Intifada

al-Aqsa Martyrs Brigades: ceasefire offer of (2001), 45–46; Fatah and, 38, 273; female suicide bomber, 66; on Roadmap for Peace (2002), 58, 79

al-Aqsa Mosque, 36–37, 248, 262n43

Arab League, 157, 180

Arab Peace Initiative (API; 2002), 52, 137

Arab Revolt (1936), 7–8

255n46; predictions of an uninhabitable Gaza, 211; Relief and Works Agency, 141, 298n21; Resolution 194 (1948), 10; on Shati Agreement, 206; war crimes investigations by, 164–166, 215, 222, 289n227, 289n229, 297–299nn20–26. *See also* right of return

United Nations Relief and Works Agency (UNRWA), 141, 298n21

United States: Abbas and, 78, 86, 110, 121–122, 132, 137, 174; alleged coup backed by (2006), 122–125, 279n175, 280n189, 280n191; Annapolis Peace Conference (2007), 143–144; Arab uprisings and, 173; arming Fatah, 98, 124, 147, 273n197, 279n175; blockade and, 69, 98–99, 106, 135–137, 264n114; ceasefire negotiations (2012), 194–195; in dividing Fatah and Hamas, 110, 113, 121–125, 168–170; on Hamas's victory, 97–98; Hezbollah and, 273n197; Iraq invasion by, 52, 56–57, 266n163; on Operation Cast Lead(2008), 161; Kerry Initiative (2013), 198–199; Middle East agenda of, 289–290n2; Palestinian security forces assistance, 124, 280n189; PLO and, 16, 20, 23–24; on the Prisoners' Document (2006), 278n127; on right to self-determination, 54; Roadmap for Peace (2002), 54–60, 86; September 11, 2001 attacks, 47–54; on settlements in occupied lands, 43, 108–109, 143, 163–164, 269n59; on two-state solution, 97, 108, 143, 163–164, 206; on Palestinian unity negotiations (2017), 247; War on Terror, 33, 50, 90, 258n109, 264n114, 302n121. *See also under names of presidents*

unity negotiations: 1967 borders in, 114, 119, 153; in 2008, 286n148; in 2009, 162, 164, 166; Government of National Consensus (2014), 207–209, 223–224; Hamas-Fatah reconciliation, 142–143; interim unity government formation (2011-2012), 176–177, 179–181, 187–189; Israel on Government of National Consensus (2014), 212, 219–220, 224, 226–227, 232; National Reconciliation Document (2006), 114–120; right of return in, 114, 128; Shati Agreement (2014), 205–209; unity agreement (2017), 247–248

UN Resolution 194. *See* right of return

waqf, 258n107
wall of separation, 63–64, 90

war crimes investigations, 164–166, 215, 222, 289n227, 289n229, 297–299nn20–26
War of Independence (1948; al-Nakba), 10
War on the Mosques, 152
Weisglass, Dov, 65, 106
West Bank: in 1948, 10; al-Qassam attack on settlers in (2010), 168–169; Arab Peace Initiative (2002) and, 52; blockade of Gaza and, 136–138; crackdown on protest in 161, 123–125, 163–164, 167, 175; current separation policy for, 224, 232–235, 249; disarmament of, 137–138, 140, 142, 144, 145; disengagement and, 64–66, 88–91; elections in (2004-2005), 76; elections in (2011), 175–176; financial support to, 135, 136–138, 198; in the First Intifada, 25–28; Government of National Consensus (2014), 207–209, 223–224; Hamas's attacks on settlers in (2010), 168–169; Israeli annexation of, 14, 18, 66; Israeli attacks (2001) on, 42–43, 45–47; Israeli attacks (2002) on, 48–50, 53–54; Israeli attacks (2005) on, 86–87; Israeli division of, 27, 31; Israeli reoccupation of (2002), 54; as Judea and Samaria, 64; kidnap of settlers' children in, 212–214, 218; Palestinian conflict in, 123–125; peace talks (2005), 83, 85; in proposed state of Palestine, 23, 40, 82; release of prisoners in, 180–181; relocation of settlers from, 88–90; Shati Agreement (2014), 205–209; wall around, 63–64, 90. *See also* division of Gaza from West Bank; Fatah; Palestinian Authority; settlements; unity negotiations

Yassin, Sheikh Ahmad: arrest of, 48; assassination of, 67–70, 75; First Intifada and, 25; Hamas formation, 1–3, 4, 20–21; imprisonment of, 26, 34, 259n132; Islamic Association, 17–18; on Roadmap for Peace (2002), 60; Second Intifada and, 38–39; on suicide bombings, 53, 56; transition to armed struggle, 20, 36
Yemen, 186

al-Zahhar, Mahmoud: assassination attempts on, 71; ceasefire offer by, 155; on Hamas charter, 91; in Hamas government, 103, 107, 141, 188, 277n92; on Palestinian elections, 74–75, 84, 271n126; on Sinai, 193
al-Zaytouna Centre (Beirut), xxiii
Ze'evi, Rehavam, 48